Gender and power in Britain, 1640–1990

Gender and Power in Britain, 1640-1990 accomplishes that often called for but rarely executed synthesis of social and political narratives about the past. Kent depicts the transformation of political power at every level of British society over a wide expanse of time in relation to overlapping and ever shifting social divides of class, race, religion, and region, as well as gender.

Gender and Power in Britain, 1640-1990 will be an indispensable text for general surveys as well as women's history courses. In its combination of accessible prose, conceptual sophistication, chronological sweep, thematic scope, and engagement with the latest scholarship, Kent's book is without effective rival.

Susan Thorne, Duke University

Gender and Power in Britain, 1640–1990 is an original and exciting history of Britain from the early modern period to the present, focusing on the interaction of gender and power in political, social, cultural, and economic life. Using a chronological framework, the book examines:

- the roles, responsibilities, and identities of men and women
- how power relationships were established within these various gender systems
- how women and men reacted to the institutions, laws, customs, beliefs, and practices that constituted their various worlds
- class, racial, and ethnic considerations
- the role of empire in the development of British institutions and identities
- the Civil War
- industrialization
- Victorian morality
- twentieth-century suffrage
- the world wars
- second-wave feminism

Susan Kingsley Kent is Professor of llo at Boulder.

Gender and power in Britain, 1640–1990

Susan Kingsley Kent

London and New York

First published 1999
by Routledge
11 New Fetter Lane, London EC4P 4EE

Simultaneously published in the USA and Canada
by Routledge
29 West 35th Street, New York, NY 10001

Routledge is an imprint of the Taylor & Francis Group

Typeset in Palatino by Routledge
Printed and bound in Great Britain by TJ International Ltd,
Padstow, Cornwall

British Library Cataloguing in Publication Data
A catalogue record for this book is available from the British
Library

Library of Congress Cataloging in Publication Data
Kent, Susan Kingsley.
    Gender and power in Britain, 1640–1990 / Susan Kingsley
Kent.
    Includes bibliographical references and index.
    1. Great Britain–Politics and government–1485– 2. Political
participation–Great Britain–Sex differences–History.
    3. Gender identity–Political aspects–Great Britain–History.
    4. Masculinity–Political aspects–Great Britain–History.
    5. Power (Social science)–Great Britain–History. 6. Women in
politics–Great Britain–History. I. Title.
DA300.K46 1999
305.42'0941–dc21   99–19808

ISBN 0–415–14741–7 (hbk)
ISBN 0–415–14742–5 (pbk)

For my parents
Jack and Barbara Kent
with love and gratitude

Contents

Figures

Acknowledgments

A book of this nature relies upon the research and scholarship of other people; without their work it could not have been written. In its very conception, *Gender and Power in Britain, 1640–1990* derives from the theories of gender and identity put forth by Joan W. Scott in her seminal *Gender and the Politics of History* (New York, 1988). Scott defines gender as the knowledge, the understandings that various cultures produce about sexual difference – differences in the physical, mental, moral, and emotional complexions of men and women that are purported to come from nature and that prescribe their proper roles and activities. Gender, moreover, in her reckoning, serves as one of the most fundamental and vivid ways by which relations of power can be articulated and mobilized in any given society at any particular time. It acts to represent relationships of power that seem entirely unrelated to men and women: relationships between monarchy and parliament, for example; or between middle-ranked people and aristocrats; or between imperial Britain and its colonies. Utilizing images of masculinity and femininity in this way very often has an impact on how men and women are perceived by themselves and by society as a whole, and on the social relations they have with one another. This book seeks to demonstrate and explain how various political regimes in Britain from 1640 to the present both constituted and were constituted by gender as Scott defines it.

The work of Joan Scott, then, underpins this book. The research and writing of other scholars provides the substance, the content, and, in some instances, the argument of the individual chapters. I have noted in the text where this is the case and have included as "sources" all the books and articles on which I have relied, but in a book like this where I have tried to note as sparingly as possible in order to maintain a narrative flow, it is important to single out those particular individuals whose work has been central. Chapter 2, for example, is heavily dependent upon the work of Rachel Weil. Chapter 3 draws upon that of J.G.A. Pocock and Deborah Valenze. In Chapter 4, the books by Linda Colley, Kim Hall, Felicity Nussbaum, and Kathleen Wilson provide the bulk of the material; in Chapter 5 it comes from G.J. Barker-Benfield, Judith Lewis, and Claire Midgley. Colley and Barker-Benfield are key again in Chapter 6, where Anna Clark's ideas first appear as well; her book and articles form the crux of the arguments made in Chapter 7 and in the last section of Chapter 9. Much of Chapter 9 draws upon the many articles written by Catherine Hall. The research and scholarship of Anna Davin, Ellen Ross, Patrick McDevitt, and Margaret Ward figure prominently in Chapter 10; that of Laura Doan, Kelly Boyd, and Alison Light inform Chapter 12. To these and all the scholars cited in the notes and in the sources, I am wholly indebted.

The author and the publishers would like to thank all the copyright holders of material reproduced in this volume for granting permission to include it. The copyright holders of artwork included in the book are credited below the figure captions. Extracts from 'Blighters' and 'Yellow press-man' (p. 282), copyright Siegfried Sassoon, reproduced by kind permission of George Sassoon. 'Eloi, Eloi, Lama Sabachthani? (p. 282) by D. H. Lawrence, from *The Complete Poems of D. H. Lawrence* by D. H. Lawrence, edited by V. de Sola Pinto and F. W. Roberts, copyright © 1964, 1971 by Angelo Ravagli and C. M. Weekley, executors of the Estate of Frieda Lawrence Ravagli; used by permission of Viking Penguin, a division of Penguin Putnam Inc. 'Political Union' by Iyamide Hazeley (p. 342), from *The Heart of the Race: Black Women's Lives in Britain* by Beverley Bryan, Stella Dadzie and Suzanne Scafe (Virago 1985), reprinted with kind permission by Little, Brown. Every effort was made to contact authors and copyright holders, but if proper acknowledgement has not been made, the copyright holder should contact the publishers.

I'd also like to thank the people who have read and commented upon the manuscript in its various guises. Ava Baron, Tom Laqueur, Fred Leventhal, Jane Lewis, and a number of anonymous readers provided much-needed guidance on sources and interpretation early on and I am grateful for their suggestions. Steven Epstein, Carol Byerly, and colleagues and students at the University of Colorado and at Rutgers helped me think about the issues dominating Chapters 3, 4, and 9. Michael Adas, in particular, gave me terrific advice for Chapter 9. Bonnie Smith, Kathleen Noonan, and two unnamed critics read the first six chapters of the manuscript, offering ideas and criticism that have improved those chapters considerably. Anna Clark read the entire manuscript in its penultimate draft. Her observations, objections, comments, and cautions have made this a better book; I greatly appreciate her efforts. The errors that will inevitably arise in a work of this length should be attributed entirely to me.

My editor at Routledge, Heather McCallum, presided over the long process of producing this text with fine judgment, patience, and gentle handling. Fintan Power, Emma DeVita, and Tony Nixon ensured that the final product looked and sounded just right. My grandmother did not live to see the book completed, but she asked about it every time I called her, and her enthusiasm spurred me on. The rest of my family contributed in their own special ways; my nieces, Maggie Horvath, Jillian Kinton, Elizabeth Mendelsohn, and Erika Mendelsohn, actually helped compose a chapter. Anne Davidson gave me the emotional and moral support and the humor I needed to complete this project; she is a constant source of inspiration and sustenance. To all of you, and especially to my parents, to whom this – my best effort yet – is dedicated, my sincere thanks.

Part I

The seventeenth century

Gender and the crises of authority

GENERAL INTRODUCTION

The seventeenth century was marked by extraordinary change and upheaval. In every area of life – from the economy, to society, to religion, to politics, to the family – traditions, customs, and eternal verities faced challenge and resistance. On farms and in workshops, new capitalist methods of production and organization began to take hold, transforming the relations between landlords and tenants, masters and journeymen and -women. A new social grouping appeared – called "middling" because of their ranking between the landed gentry, who did no work, and the rest of society, who worked with their hands – which challenged the traditional exercise of power in society by the landed classes. In religion, puritans questioned the right of the bishops of the Church of England to organize religious life, and sought to implement their own godly order. In politics, many of these "middling" people, and puritans drawn from the gentry, resisted the efforts of the Stuart kings to rule absolutely, and fought a civil war in order to assert the supremacy of parliament. Within the family, sons challenged their fathers for the right to inherit property, and wives demanded more than mere spiritual equality with their husbands.

In every one of these areas, authority – the source of power in any given jurisdiction – came under direct assault. Throughout the seventeenth century, debates about the location of authority in the state, in the church, in society, and in the family raged, marking the period as, in the words of one of its most prominent historians, "the century of revolution."[1]

Protagonists involved in these struggles over authority – puritans, parliamentarians, royal supporters, men and women of all ranks – often argued their points using metaphors of gender. Contemporaries frequently framed their support for a particular position about monarchical power, for instance, by comparing it to the power of the father in the family. By drawing upon current – and often contradictory – ideas about masculinity and femininity, about the natures of men and women, about the roles they played, and about the state of the relationship between parents and children, and husbands and wives, spokespeople for one side or another could hope to ground their arguments in "nature," to justify them on the basis of what looked to society as the natural and, therefore, right and proper way to conduct affairs. By doing so, however, they often also forced a reconceptualization of the gender organization of their society; their opponents, disagreeing with their arguments about political authority, might be compelled to dispute the very premises on which the arguments were based – the ideas about masculinity and femininity, about the natures of men and women, about the roles they played, and about the state of the relationship between parents and children, and husbands and wives. Although new ideas about the family and about gender thrown up by struggles for power in the political, religious, economic, or social realm rarely had any immediate effect on the ways in which families, and men and women, went about their business on a day-to-day basis, they did operate to both open up and close down possibilities for individuals to rethink their place in the familial, political, and social order, which could produce longer-term changes in that order. By articulating the crises of authority of the seventeenth century in gendered and sexualized language, contemporary men and women also created crises of gender that would themselves have to be addressed as those of more conventional authority were resolved.

NOTES

1   Christopher Hill, *A Century of Revolution* (New York, 1975).

Chapter 1

Challenging authority at mid-century

State, family, and society in 1600

The lands that comprised the "British Isles," as they were known to map-makers and geographers in 1600 – England and Wales, Scotland, and Ireland – contained a vast array of peoples who perceived no common tie among themselves beyond that of geography. Differences of language, culture, history, law, customs, and religion divided the inhabitants of each kingdom. A single monarch, Queen Elizabeth, ruled over England and Wales; another, James VI, reigned in Scotland. During the twelfth century, Ireland had been conquered by Henry II and rendered a "lordship" of the English crown; in 1541, Henry VIII declared himself king of Ireland and commenced the process of bringing the country under the administrative purview of England. In a bid to secure their power in a now-protestant state, he and Elizabeth established "plantations" of loyal protestant followers in Ireland, massacring catholics, confiscating their lands, and granting them to English colonists. In 1608, the plantation of Ulster took place: James VI of Scotland, now also James I of England, ousted Gaelic landowners in five counties in the northern reaches of Ireland and transferred the land to Scottish and English protestants. More than 10,000 Scots ultimately came to settle there.

Early seventeenth-century Britons understood the world in which they lived to be fundamentally, properly, and irrevocably hierarchical. They imagined their social order to be a "great chain of being," with God the Father and the angels at the top, followed by monarchs, aristocrats, gentry, and everyone else. Women held their various positions on the chain by virtue of their relationship to men as wives or daughters; as women, they were inferior and subordinate to men, as God had demonstrated in making Eve out of Adam's rib. Moreover, Eve's transgressions had stained all women with her sin. Construed as insatiably lustful, with sexual appetites equal to or greater than men's, women of the seventeenth century were perceived to be potential agents of damnation and destruction, requiring the mastery of men to preserve their propriety and honor, and even the stability of the social order itself.

"Scientific" theories asserted women's defectiveness relative to men. Where men were composed of hot and dry humors, early modern medical treatises declared that women were made up of the less perfect cold and wet humors. Women were, the medical men asserted, lesser men, the weaker vessel. Their passive role in reproduction – the womb serving merely as the receptacle and incubator for the active male seed in which all of the elements of life were contained – offered a "physiological" justification for their social, political, and legal disabilities.

Hierarchies of gender mirrored those of status based on land ownership in rural areas and on guild structures in the towns. Just as subjects of the crown knew themselves to be subordinate to their monarch, farmers knew themselves to be fully subordinate to their landlords, and apprentices and journeymen and -women to their guild masters, so too women understood themselves to be subordinate to their fathers and their husbands. Patriarchal rule – whether it be of master to man or man to woman – prevailed.

Patriarchy in state and society as well as in the family rested on the ancient presumption that the male head of household held property not simply in his land and his animals, but in his wife and his children as well. That property was to be handed down to the eldest son, part of the inheritance system known as primogeniture. Although never legally classified as chattel – property – of men, married English, Welsh, and Scottish women faced restrictions in common law that rendered them, for all intents and purposes, the property of their husbands. At the very least, common-law doctrines institutionalized the inferiority and subordination of women to men. Under the law of coverture, unique to England, married women had no legal existence apart from their husbands: they had no legal rights to property, to earnings, to freedom of movement, to conscience, to their bodies, or to their children; all belonged to their husbands. If a woman was raped, the crime was perceived as a form of theft, not from her, but from her husband or male relatives; cases of adultery were prosecuted only in those instances where the woman involved was married. Women lost their names when they married. All of these circumstances combined to suggest that women were the property of men in fact if not in law. Certainly they meant that women did not enjoy the autonomy, the independence, that was a vital prerequisite for formal political participation (which, indeed, most men did not possess either, though not because they were excluded by law). By 1600, only in rare and exceptional cases did individual women vote for or hold public office. In the Gaelic areas of Ireland where English common law did not prevail, married women may well have enjoyed a higher legal status and greater property rights. Gaelic women, it appears, could hold property and administer it as they saw fit, independently of their husbands.

In practice, the facts of demography, the existence of four other systems of law, and the need to ensure the survival of all members of the family tended to mitigate against the inheritance and legal disabilities of English, Welsh, and Scottish women, daughters, and younger sons experienced under common law.[1] First, because death rates were so high and life expectancy so low compared to those in the late twentieth century, the inheritance patterns and legal disabilities enshrined in common law often did not come to pass as expected. Some 40 percent of marriages never produced a son; in that 20 percent of marriages that produced only daughters, they would inherit land jointly from their father. Even when marriages produced a son, it was very likely that he would not be of age at the time of his father's death; thus, the inheritance would, for some time at least, pass into the hands of his mother to be administered by her until he turned twenty-one. Because married women regained their own legal identity upon the death of their husbands, mothers negotiated their children's marriage agreements as often as did fathers.

Second, four additional systems of law enjoyed jurisdiction over property ownership and acted to ameliorate the severity of common law, especially as it pertained to women's property and rights to inheritance. Equity courts, ecclesiastical law, manorial or borough law, and parliamentary statutes could be resorted to for much of the seventeenth century to preserve women's and children's property rights that common law did not recognize. Through equity, a father could establish the marriage portion his daughter took into a marriage as her own separate property. Upper-class women such as Lady Anne Clifford or Mistress Alice Thornton defended their property rights in drawn-out court cases, confident that custom and law would uphold their claims. Ordinary women, too, made marriage settlements that protected their property interests. Ecclesiastical courts, regulating the division of personal property rather than land, recognized a form of communal property within marriage and the division of parents' wealth among all children equally. Manorial or borough courts determined the inheritance of land on a local basis, varying considerably according to location; in many places, all sons could expect to inherit a portion of the estate, a system known as partible inheritance. In London and other boroughs, married women could attain the special status of "feme sole trader," giving them for business purposes – as long as their business was separate from their husbands' – access to courts as if they were single women with their own legal identities.

Perhaps most importantly, the survival of individuals in the seventeenth century depended on the survival of the entire family; women's material contribution to the family economy made the difference between life and death. New households could not set up until couples had obtained the necessary financial resources to sustain themselves and the children they expected to have – the availability of a plot of land or a cottage, the completion of artisanal training, the inheritance of a marriage portion. Wives were expected to bring to the marriage a dowry, also called a marriage portion, equal to the contribution that their husbands made. Fathers, aware that the most significant component of wealth consisted of an inheritance, tried to ensure that the inheritances they left their children were equal and sufficient for them to marry and set up households; what the eldest son received in land was very often matched in value by the moveable household goods left to the other children, though those children had no legal claim on them and were at the mercy of their fathers' goodwill.

A lease to a cottage, a cow, a bed, clothing, utensils, tools – the inheritance of these items made it possible for daughters and younger sons to marry and set up independent households. They were not usually able to do so until relatively late in their life; men of ordinary rank married in their late twenties, women in their mid- to late twenties. Amongst the aristocracy, for whom marriage constituted a kind of alliance between powerful families, or the gentry, for whom it was the means by which family economic, social, and political interests were furthered, women and men married earlier, some in their mid-teens. They did not have to wait to amass the resources necessary to establish separate households.

The household was the site of economic activity; whether it be a farm or an artisanal workshop, work and family could not be separated from one another. The family economy characteristic of early modern society depended on the labor of all members of the household; marriage was above all an economic partnership. Within this economic enterprise, clearly demarcated spheres of activity for men and women provided the gender boundaries that ordered everyday life. In rural areas, men worked in the fields, free to travel fairly long distances from the household in order to farm and to labor for long undisturbed periods of time. Women tended to do work that was located closer to the house so that the constant interruptions of small children and the necessities of running a household could be accommodated. They looked after the raising of livestock, dairying, brewing, baking, and cultivation of vegetable gardens. Women sold the dairy and vegetable products at market and managed whatever household cash income there might be. This was so at all social levels, though in the case of the gentry and aristocracy, wives supervised rather than undertook these activities themselves.

In urban areas and those parts of the countryside where artisanal manufacturing took place, wives in workshops and small shops proved indispensable to the family economy. They sold the products of the workshop and provided for the needs of both family members and apprentices, who lived with the family as part of their apprenticeship agreement. In those families that depended primarily upon wages to survive, marriage age could be earlier, as the material prerequisites for setting up a household did not require waiting for a plot of land or a position in a workshop to come open. Because they married earlier, these parents might produce more children than those without waged income. The existence of wages might also mitigate against the companionship that must have developed among men and women as they worked together to sustain the enterprises that upheld the economic partnership that was marriage, as husbands and wives often had to work away from home. In professional families – the church, the law, medicine, teaching, the military, crown administration – where husbands worked away from home, women's family lives were not so closely integrated with work. As with more ordinary people who had to leave home to find labor, work and home might be separate worlds. Among gentry, where neither husband nor wife worked, both nevertheless had to co-ordinate their efforts to oversee the management of the estates and to protect the interests of the families. In law and in custom, women might be the subordinate, inferior sex; in practice, their contributions to the family enterprise and the management of whatever cash income came in, without which the family could not survive, provided them with economic leverage.

Households were generally nuclear, that is, consisting of parents and children. Most families, except for the very poorest, contained live-in servants. The number of people living in these households varied according to social class, the kind of work families did, and the extent to which families relied on the labor of children to survive. Among ordinary people, economic survival could mean a constant balancing act between producing enough children to fulfill the necessary labor of farm or shop and not producing too many children so as not to outrun the ability to provide for them. The wealthiest households usually contained the greatest number of people in them because they could afford more servants and to keep adult children at home. In the middle of the sixteenth century, wealthy merchant families in Coventry contained an average of 7.4 people; the gentry some 6.6 people. The poorest households were also the smallest, containing perhaps only three or four people.

Fertility in any given family was most often a consequence of that family's economic situation. Mortality rates, especially among infants under the age of one, were so high that women gave birth to a large number of children with the expectation that perhaps half of them would not live to see their twenty-first birthdays. Death rates among the infants of the upper classes were actually higher than among ordinary families: in upper-class families, parents sent their babies out to wet nurse, where they did not necessarily receive the care and attention that children who were nursed at home could expect from their mothers. Poor women who served as wet nurses for upper-class infants might neglect their own children in order to provide the milk for which they had contracted with upper-class parents. Because breast-feeding women are generally infertile, we can speculate that upper-class women, who did not generally nurse their children, and whose only other methods of contraception consisted of abstinence, *coitus interruptus*, or abortion, were not able to space their births as widely – between eighteen and twenty-four months – as the majority of ordinary women did. Upper-class women married earlier and were better nourished. Their birth rates, presumably, would have been higher, but we have little evidence that in fact they were any greater than those of ordinary people. Before 1650, across all social classes, women marrying before they reached the age of thirty had on average 6.4 children. Between 1650 and 1750, that number fell to between a range of 4.2 and 4.4; after 1750 it rose again to nearly six. We must remember that these figures represent only a static snapshot of families at any given time; they do not tell us how many children were stillborn, were born but did not live to adulthood, or how many women suffered miscarriages, a fairly common experience. Jane Josselin, for example, the wife of a seventeenth-century clergyman, miscarried fully a third of her pregnancies.

Marriage was the expected norm for all men and women, but the harsh realities of seventeenth-century life conspired to frustrate the realization of that ideal. Only some 10 percent of the English population did not ever marry (that percentage was higher for Scotland), but about one-third of the adult women at any given time were either single or widowed. High mortality rates among all age groups meant that the average marriage lasted no more than seventeen to twenty years, and although remarriage was common after the death of a husband, widows who did not have the resources to contribute to the setting up of another household, or who, conversely, had enough to live on without the contribution of a husband, tended not to remarry. Poor widows found themselves dependent upon their grown children, who, contemporaries believed, were more often than not reluctant to help them. In those cases where the support of children was not forthcoming, poor widows turned to parish relief, which could provide for only the most marginal existence. By far the greatest portion of those on poor relief were women.

Single women could anticipate few options. Because survival required membership in a household, most single women could not hope for an independent life. They contributed to their own household in the capacity of a dependent child, no matter what their age, or they joined another as a servant. Those who migrated to cities like London might find a wider array of opportunities; they could work as domestic servants, live with other women employed in such occupations as textiles or needlework, or earn money through prostitution. In any case, their wages were low and their situations precarious, and many women found it both economically and emotionally preferable to live with men without benefit of marriage. Cohabitation and pre-nuptial conception rates were far higher in cities than in the countryside, where familial and community watchfulness enforced promises of marriage and ensured lawful wedded unions. Servants who had migrated to London, because they lived in, could not expect any such freedom of action; they married even later than women in the countryside, probably after having worked long enough to save a marriage portion.

While marital unions were dissolved regularly through the death of a spouse, virtually no other mechanism existed whereby an unhappy partner could be freed from one marriage and enter into another, except in Scotland, where, after the

Reformation, divorce might be obtained on the grounds of adultery, desertion, and, in a few instances, of a husband's impotence. Annulments, which would permit the parties to remarry, were difficult and expensive to obtain. The Church of England did permit a form of separation "from bed and board," called divorce *a mensa et thoro*, in cases of adultery and extreme cruelty, but like the Roman Catholic Church it did not recognize divorce that permitted the possibility of remarriage, called divorce *a vinculo*. Only the very persistent and wealthy could undertake the procedures necessary to procure a separation, and only the most wealthy and well-connected individuals could obtain a divorce through an Act of Parliament. Those couples whose marriages were intolerable probably just separated illegally, like William and Mary Fuller, or Anne Hannah of Buckinghamshire. Desertion, usually by the husband, provided another way out of marriage; for women like Elizabeth Warner of Shrewsbury, desertion could spell economic disaster. For all but the most prosperous in the seventeenth century, the idea of separation meant severe economic difficulty and could not therefore be entertained by ordinary people.

The information we have about birth, death, and marriage rates, about the sexual division of labor or inheritance practices, does not necessarily enable us to draw reliable conclusions about the tenor of relationships between men and women. To note that marriages were economic relationships designed to ensure economic survival and propagation is not to say that they were loveless, or that real companionship did not grow up between husband and wife, or that parents did not love their children or, given the probability of their children's deaths, could not afford to love them as nineteenth- and twentieth-century parents did under much more prosperous circumstances. We have no shortage of evidence to show that they did, despite the material hardships they faced and the psychological trauma they experienced upon the death of a child. Moreover, as we have seen, the legal doctrines that upheld a rather draconian patriarchal order could be and were circumvented fairly often, testimony to the failure of ideology to accurately reflect the way men and women operated on a daily basis.

But it is also the case that the material and emotional lives of men and women unfolded within an ideological system of beliefs and values about the natures and roles of men and women that helped people to make sense of their world and to give it order. This ideological system, while it might not correspond to the ways individual men and women behaved or thought, did act both to offer possibilities for and to circumscribe the ways individuals could imagine they could live. For example, the belief that women were inherently sexual creatures made it imaginatively possible for them to take pleasure in sexual intercourse; religious thinkers recognized that the satisfaction of sexual desire was one of the purposes of marriage, while medical writers believed that conception – the primary function of marriage – could only occur if both partners experienced orgasm. On the other hand, the sexuality of women could readily be construed to cause all sorts of disorder and render them unfit for any kind of autonomy. The subordination and inferiority of women that was so central to seventeenth-century social, political, economic, and familial organization derived from ideas about women's sexual nature. Those ideas prescribed proper and improper behavior for women and thus helped to de-limit their activity.

Regardless of social class, women were expected to stay within the confines of the home, the realm of "within," as some ministers put it, as opposed to the world "without." Didactic literature enjoined them to keep themselves within the private sphere of home and family where they could best cultivate and exhibit the qualities of proper women. As we have seen, ordinary women did venture out of the private sphere to work their gardens, tend their livestock, and sell their goods at market; the wives of middling artisan households engaged in commercial activity from their front rooms. (They did not, however, join their husbands in the alehouse, where most lower- and middle-ranking men spent their leisure hours.) Upper-class women traveled for business and pleasure, and some for education, which they could not obtain from the grammar schools and universities attended by their brothers. These activities out of doors violated norms of female behavior, but at the same time, women's recognized obligations to contribute to the family economy necessitated their transgressions. This contradiction left women in a potentially precarious state: any misstep outside their prescribed private sphere could bring down on their heads the disapprobation of society. Few proper women were prepared to risk the displeasure of their communities, and displayed, at least in public, the traditional virtues assigned to them.

Proper women were expected to be modest, humble, obedient, pious, temperate, patient, silent, and, above all, chaste. This is not to say that they were all of these things; indeed, the very need to enjoin them to be so may suggest that they were not. Most likely, however, once these norms of femininity became accepted as part of the "natural" order, as was the case by 1600, it would be difficult for women to transgress them with impunity. To do so would be to call down upon their heads charges of immorality and unnaturalness, which most people could not have afforded. Observations that women did not enjoy the same legal, educational, or political privileges as men, such as those put forward by Margaret Cavendish, Duchess of Newcastle, were likely to provoke outrage, culminating in diagnoses of insanity.

In fact, women may well have served as the most forceful exponents and enforcers of the code of femininity. Most accepted and internalized the religious and scientific discourses that proclaimed their inferiority and need for subordination. Educated women, a tiny minority, might be even more likely to subscribe to doctrines about femininity: they would have read the learned treatises that credited the humors with causing the differences between men and women upon which women's subordination was based. No alternative authoritative theory emerged to challenge these scientific views until mid-century, when the Cartesian theories of the rational individual entered Britain from the continent. They were reinforced at the end of the seventeenth century by John Locke's *Essay Concerning Human Understanding*, which postulated that all human beings possess at the time of their birth a mind that is unformed – a *tabula rasa* or blank slate. As we will see below, his notions of human potentiality for self-fashioning offered women an opportunity to challenge the doctrines of female inferiority that underpinned virtually all relationships.

Ordinary women, by contrast, would not have read the conduct books or scientific treatises that proclaimed their inferiority and subordination. They would, however, have listened almost every Sunday to sermons that preached the same ideas. They embraced church teachings, about their intellectual defects and their exclusion from the masculine domains of politics and learning, as part of the religious doctrine that offered them the only source of solace in a harsh and horrific world that carried their children away from them on a regular basis. For much of the seventeenth century, just as élite men were becoming more secular in their beliefs, women steadfastly upheld the religious teachings that prescribed for them an inferior, dependent, subordinate place in society.

But the ideology of gender, like any other ideology, is never static. Changes taking place in the economy, or in politics, or society bring about changes in ideology as well, exposing inconsistencies and contradictions. Because ideologies are always uneven and often contradictory in their applicability to or effect on various people in society, they produce possibilities for resistance to them, possibilities for change. As we shall see, even the most extreme forms of protestantism, by proclaiming the *spiritual* equality of men and women, their equality, in other words, before God, opened up avenues for some women to make claims for other kinds of equality as well. By the middle of the seventeenth century, economic, social, and political change converged to produce a challenge to authority that would have profound implications for the relationships between men and women, ruler and ruled.

Economic, social, and political transformations

Already in 1600, England and the lowland areas of Scotland were societies in flux. Fueled by inflation and by new opportunities for long-distance trade, the medieval locally-based economy of communal, open-field agriculture and guild manufacturing had begun to give way to a nation-wide economy characterized by capitalist modes of production and organization. The gradual and uneven development of a capitalist economy had differential effects on people. As landowners began to farm their land according to more rational, efficient practices and to produce crops not simply for sustenance but to sell at market, many became prosperous; but those who had depended on common areas and non-arable acreage to grow or raise what they needed to live on could no longer provide food for their families. Many became migrants, seeking waged work where they could find it; others spun thread or wove cloth in their cottages in return for a wage. The enterprising individuals who circumvented guild restrictions on manufacturing and commerce in the towns, setting up these workers in rural cottages to produce cloth and paying them low wages, profited nicely from the greater efficiency of domestic industry and from expanding markets. Urban guild masters, faced with competition from domestic industry as well as from increasing numbers of artisans, introduced new impediments to gaining access to their ranks, shutting down the normal avenues by means of which apprentices and journeymen and -women established themselves and made their living. By 1600, at least one-third of the English population could no longer count on the plot of ground that allowed them to establish self-sustaining households, or gain entry to a craft that would enable them to become independent adults. They had become employees – men and women who worked for a wage.

Capitalism produced dramatic change in other areas of life. The simple social distinction of peerage and gentry (that 2 percent of the population who owned land and lived off the work others did on it) and non-gentry (those who did the work) that marked pre-capitalist society no longer sufficed to describe the complex ranking of groups thrown up by economic change. In both rural and urban areas, a more precise social measuring of the "degrees of men" was required, corresponding to new forms of wealth and the nature of the work they performed.

In the countryside, where the great majority of people lived right up until the mid-nineteenth century, a large group of substantial non-gentry landholders and farmers emerged. The famed yeomanry, as this group was called, owned their land and farmed it themselves; they were freeholders. On the strength of their wealth, many of them could be distinguished from the gentry only by their lack of "gentle" birth – that is, they did not descend from knightly or noble families. As was the case with the aristocracy proper (whose titles of nobility succeeded only to the eldest son), the sons and daughters of the yeomanry married into the gentry, replenishing and revitalizing the landed élite.

Husbandmen farmed land they did not own but leased from the yeomanry or gentry. Over the course of the seventeenth century, increasing numbers of these people lost their land to enclosure and fell into the ranks of agricultural laborers, who worked other people's land for wages, or cottagers, whose income derived from domestic manufacturing of textiles. Along with paupers, who had no source of income, cottagers made up perhaps a third of England's population. In 1688, the statistician Gregory King estimated that most people in England could not make ends meet and were judged by their contemporaries to be poor.

In towns and cities, whose populations were growing faster than the national rate (in 1700, 10 percent of England's population lived in London alone), the expansion of trade and commerce produced a group of wealthy merchants, men quite as rich as gentlemen who did not labor manually themselves but directed those who did. As their numbers grew, so did their significance and sense of importance. Independent artisans and smaller traders occupied the rung below merchants; journeymen and laborers working for wages the next. In terms of civic importance, though perhaps not social status, the great merchants of London in particular joined the group of professionals in the church, the law, medicine, education, the armed forces, and government administration, whose ranks were filled by the younger sons of the aristocracy and gentry who did not inherit their fathers' estates. In time, the sons and daughters of merchant and gentry families came to intermarry, bringing infusions of capital to struggling gentry and "gentle" social status to aspiring merchants. Some historians use the term "gentlemanly capitalism" to describe the economic, social, and political regime produced by this alliance of land and commerce after 1688, but that is getting ahead of our story.

Together, yeomen in the countryside and merchants and artisans in towns and cities constituted a "middling" strata of English society by the middle of the seventeenth century. Their material success, as well as that of enterprising élite rural families, in a newly developing and highly risky capitalist market economy depended in part upon the existence of a settled and consistent system of laws; unless they could be confident that their contracts would be enforced and their property secure, few would risk the investments necessary to engage in capitalist ventures, whether they involved improvements of land or long overseas voyages. Many, though certainly not all, "middling" people embraced puritanism, a version of protestantism whose notions of predestination tended to give spiritual approbation to worldly success, and which, among other things, sought to transform the hierarchical, ecclesiastical structure of the established Church of England with its bishops and archbishops. Some members of the new forces thrown up by economic, social, and religious change, following the lead of many prominent aristocratic and, especially, gentry families, soon found themselves alienated from a monarch seeking to assert his authority over law, church, and state.

When James VI of Scotland became king of England in 1603 as James I, he sought to rule absolutely, basing his claim for supreme power over the state, the church, and the law on the doctrine known as the Divine Right of Kings. James (1603–25) and his son and successor Charles I (1625–49) insisted that their power came directly from God and that it was a sin against God to resist it. Such an argument provoked a loud protest from members of parliament, who were seeking control of state policy; from lawyers, many of whom sat in parliament, looking to establish the independence and predominance of common law over the arbitrary decisions of the crown; and from puritans, whose disagreements with the Church of England extended to church governance. Increasingly during the reigns of James I, and especially Charles I, members of parliament asserted their right to challenge monarchical rule. In 1629, Charles dissolved parliament and ruled without it for the next eleven years, until in 1640 he was forced to call it by the need to raise revenue to fight off a Scottish rebellion provoked by his efforts to impose Anglican doctrine and organization on Calvinist Scotland. In 1641, Gaelic landowners of northern Ireland, fearful for their security of land and religious freedoms, rose against the protestant Ulster Scots, a rebellion that soon ignited catholics of all social orders against protestants throughout Ireland, and one that declared its explicit support for King Charles and the constitution of England. Pressing their advantage over the king in a time of financial emergency and alarmed by exaggerated reports of quite real massacres of protestants by Irish rebels, parliamentarians led by the puritan John Pym forced a dramatic transformation in government, upsetting the balance of power between monarchy and parliament. By 1641, parliament had become a permanent institution of government that met regularly and could not be suspended arbitrarily by the monarch; the crown lost its capacity to raise revenue without parliamentary consent; and the system of royal courts through which monarchs since the days of Henry VII had exercised prerogative power were abolished. Parliament also declared that catholicism in Ireland was to be officially outlawed. Charles consented to the impositions placed on his power only with great reluctance; within a year, forces under his command stormed parliament, demanded the arrest of its leaders, and provoked civil war.

Civil war

The English Civil War of the 1640s, or, as one historian, seeking to more accurately assess its nature, calls it, the War of the Three Kingdoms,[2] and the subsequent rule of Oliver Cromwell during the interregnum of the 1650s, convulsed the lands of England and Wales, Scotland, and Ireland. As we have seen, rebellion against the king in Scotland began in 1637, while the rising of Irish catholics in support of the king took place in 1641. Fighting between English forces in support of the king and those that backed parliament broke out in August of 1642. Charles enjoyed the backing of three-quarters of the titled nobility and a bare majority of the gentry. The small land-owning yeomanry more or less followed the gentry in their localities. Parliament could count on a sizable minority of gentry and the yeomen who lived nearby, the business classes of the commercial centers, and, most importantly with regard to financing the armies of parliament, London. The wealth of London ensured that parliament's armies would remain continually at full strength, while those of the king often suffered for lack of funds with which to pay his soldiers. Roughly speaking, the northern and western parts of England sided with the king; the southern and eastern portions with parliament. These are only the most crude of delineations, however, for the causes of king and parliament created divisions within many areas and even among individual families.

Charles fared well in the first year of the war, but by 1644 his forces had become bogged down and he was looking to Ireland for allies. Word of his intention to concede privileges to Irish catholics in return for their help in fighting against the parliamentary armies in England inflamed opinion against him. Parliament, for its part, had turned to Scotland for assistance, granting it a religious settlement in favor of Presbyterianism. Scottish armies marched south into England in 1644, routing the king's forces and loosening his hold on the north of England. Parliament's New Model Army, made up of disciplined and well-paid men led by the puritan Oliver Cromwell, defeated the king's army in 1645. Charles fled, and in 1646 gave himself over to the Scots in surrender.

The New Model Army contained many men whose particular puritan persuasion led them to reject virtually all forms of hierarchy and authority in religious affairs. Called "independents" after their vision of individual congregations conducting their own affairs independently of any ecclesiastical organization and determining their own beliefs and practices, men and women who embraced this form of protestantism – whether they be Congregationalists, Anabaptists, Quakers, or the more radical Diggers – very often projected their ideas about religious autonomy and independence on to politics, espousing a belief in democracy, or in the sovereignty of the people. Independents sat in parliament, too, but they were vastly outnumbered by Presbyterians, who cleft to a more definitively hierarchical religious structure and authority, and eschewed any notion of popular sovereignty. For them, parliament's authority, not that of the people, should prevail in matters of government and politics. Alarmed by the radical political views of the "Levellers" in the army, so-called because they sought to remove – or level – any distinctions of hierarchy among men, parliamentary leaders moved to demobilize the army upon Charles's surrender to the Scots. But soldiers organized themselves politically to make known their demands to parliament and refused to disband. Parliament turned to Scotland for help, seeking the use of Scottish troops to forcibly disarm the men who had fought and won a civil war on its behalf.

The New Model Army mutinied, and in June 1647 took Charles, who had been returned to England by the Scots, into custody. In August, Levellers presented an Agreement of the People to the House of Commons, a document that asserted that the current parliament would be dissolved and that a new one elected by universal manhood suffrage within equal electoral districts would be established. It called for equality before the law of all men and for freedom of religion within a republican form of government based upon a written constitution. In November 1647, having schemed with the Scots to establish Presbyterianism as the state religion in return for his restoration to the Scottish throne, Charles escaped from his English captors, and war resumed. The Scottish army moved south against the English in 1648, but Cromwell's forces quickly subdued it.

The New Model Army then turned its attention to parliament in December 1648, purging the House of Commons of its Presbyterian members, and leaving behind a "Rump" parliament of independents. That body tried Charles for treason in January 1649, and executed him on January 30. The Commons then abolished the monarchy, its prerogative courts, and the House of Lords, and set itself up as the "supreme authority of this nation, the representatives of the people in Parliament" under a commonwealth form of government. But political and religious divisions within the army and society as a whole were such that within three months, Cromwell moved to suppress mutinies by Levellers seeking even greater democratic reforms within his army. Four years later, in 1653, he rousted the Rump parliament from its house and abolished it. Lacking support from virtually every segment of society, despised by both revolutionary and conservative political forces, and dependent upon the army for its existence, the commonwealth constituted in reality a military dictatorship headed by Cromwell.

The beheading of Charles I provoked outrage from many quarters and turned him into a martyr. In Ireland, protestant royalists and catholics joined together in opposition to England's government, posing a threat that could not be ignored. Cromwell's forces invaded the island, stormed its walled towns, and massacred its inhabitants. By 1652 the land lay prostrate, fully one-third of the population destroyed. Cromwell's lieutenants seized Irish land held by catholics and settled them upon English protestants. The Act of Settlement of 1652 conferred upon some 36,000 of his soldiers much of the land of Ireland. Catholic peasants suffered eviction and resettlement, and found themselves landless and in terrible straits. By the time of the Restoration in 1660, almost 80 percent of the land in Ireland had been seized and occupied by English and Scottish protestants; Irish catholics, despite the fact that they comprised more than 80 percent of the population, possessed only a fifth of the lands that had once been theirs. English protestants in Ireland gained thirty seats in parliament and the right to trade freely with England. Irish catholics looked upon their English landlords and England itself with hatred and loathing.

The Scots reacted to the execution of Charles I by declaring his son, Charles II, king of Scotland, provoking an attack on the country by Cromwell's army in 1650 that resulted in a massive defeat of Scottish forces. The next year, Charles led another Scottish army into England, which Cromwell destroyed entirely at the Battle of Worcester. Charles fled to France, while the English conquered Scotland, abolished its parliament and general assembly, and brought it under the political and administrative control of England. The Scots, though they kept their lands and churches, unlike the unfortunate Irish, would not soon forget their treatment at the hands of the English, and, like the Irish, would constitute a source of threat to the British crown over the next century.

The years of civil war and revolution produced upheaval and tumult in nearly every area of life. Long-standing, traditional practices and ways of understanding came under fire from members of parliament, lawyers, merchants, businessmen and -women, religious radicals, political radicals, wives, and children – all manner and make of person. The questioning of authority in every place, whether it be government, church, army, society, or family, created the feel, as historian Christopher Hill put it, of "the world turned upside down."[3] Frequently, protagonists and antagonists cast their disputes in the language of gender, infusing their arguments with imagery drawn from contemporary understandings of masculinity and femininity, of the relationships between men and women as they understood them or sought to make them. The use of such language affected the lives of real men and women who inhabited the British Isles, some quite dramatically.

In the years leading up to 1642, for example, proponents of royal absolutism and of parliamentary supremacy in government developed a series of justifications for their respective positions. Supporters of Charles I put forward arguments based on divine right and patriarchy, but they also resorted, from time to time, to contract theory to make the case that the people of England, Scotland, and Wales had ceded all of their rights to the monarch when they made their original contract of subjection to the ruler. They compared this imaginary "social contract" with the monarch to that of the marriage contract between husband and wife, whose contractual nature, accepted by virtually all Britons without question, consisted only of the consent that the parties to it gave upon taking their vows. The marriage contract established a relationship of male governance and female obedience, and it could not be revoked. Royalists were on firm ideological ground in making such an argument about marriage; by drawing an analogy to it, they were able to insist that just as in marriage, the agreement to obey the social contract with the monarch, once entered into, was binding. Resistance to the monarch by his subjects was akin to a wife violating her marriage vows; both were a sin against God, no matter how egregious the abuse a husband might heap upon her. Just as there was a covenant "instituted by God betweene King and People," wrote the royalist Sir Dudley Digges in 1643, "so there is a contract between Husband and Wife, the violation of which on the man's part doth not bereave him of his dominion over the woman."[4] The idea that subjects might justifiably rebel against their monarch was as absurd as the idea that a wife might end her subjection to her husband either by their mutual agreement to divorce or because he abused her.

The use of this analogy to marriage to justify royal absolutism forced parliamentarians to answer in the same idiom. Their advocacy of parliamentary and/or popular checks on the monarch's power led them to reconceptualize the traditional view of marriage as hierarchical and irrevocable. To answer the king's arguments about his power over subjects being akin to that of husbands over wives, they began to present the relationship between husbands and wives established by marriage as one in which the authority of husbands might be weakened or even broken altogether. In this they were on shaky ground, as the possibilities for divorce, as we have seen, were extremely limited and did not permit remarriage. Some puritans, however, were prepared to advocate that husbands and wives should be free to divorce *a vinculo*, that is, completely and freely, with the possibility of remarriage, a position forced on them by the logic of their arguments against monarchical power. John Milton, in *The Doctrine and Discipline of Divorce*, issued first in 1643, embraced the possibility of divorce as a civic good. Just as "a whole people" might "save not only their lives but honest liberties from unworthy bondage" to "an ill Government," so too, he argued, should an individual be permitted to extract himself from a disagreeable marriage. More than the happiness of a single person was at stake, Milton insisted; that of the whole polity would be effected. "For no effect of tyranny can sit more heavy on the Common-wealth, then this household unhappiness on the family. And farewell all hope of true Reformation in the state, while such an evill as this lies undiscern'd or unregarded in the house."[5]

Most parliamentarians, puritan and Anglican alike, could not accept so radical a claim; their analogies to the marriage contract tended to be restricted to the argument that while husbands did enjoy God-given superiority in marriage, there were inherent limits on their power. Others went one step farther, maintaining that if husbands overstepped their authority, wives had the right to resist them and even, in cases of extreme abuse, to separate from them. As this was so for husbands and wives, so too was it for monarchs and their subjects: "if men, for whose sake women were created, shall not lay hold upon the divine right of wedlock, to the disadvantage of women," wrote Henry Parker in 1644, "much less shall Princes who were created for the peoples sake, chalange [sic] any thing from the sanctity of their offices, that may derogate from the people."[6] Abused wives had the right to defend themselves by separating from their husbands; abused subjects had the same right to defend themselves by raising an army against their king.

The debates over monarchical authority provoked questions, then, about the relationship of men and women in marriage. Royalist supporters called upon widely and deeply accepted ideas about the power of husbands and about the irrevocable nature of the marriage contract. Those who supported resistance to Charles I posited a more advanced notion of marriage than most Britons could entertain in the 1640s. Even they, however, could only go so far in advocating changes in the marriage contract. They believed, as did their adversaries, that women's inferiority to men, and wives' subjection to husbands, were natural and came from God. Nevertheless, questions about the nature, the origins, and the scope of men's authority in marriage had been raised (and would be raised again after 1670, as we shall see in Chapter 2, in debates about the power of the restored Charles II). While such questioning would translate into transformations in the lived experience of only very few men and women, it established the possibility of altered relations between men and women.

Some puritans, like Ralph and Jane Josselin, for example, pursued the suggestions raised by parliamentarian arguments and implemented in their own marriages a kind of conjugal relationship that historians call companionate. They viewed marriage as a broader partnership than most of their contemporaries, in which husbands and wives fulfilled the spiritual and emotional, as well as the economic needs, of one another, and in which a degree of equality might exist. In the 1640s and 1650s, as civil and secular authority collapsed in the face of civil war and revolution, some wives extended the idea of spiritual equality with their husbands to social and even political equality with men. Quakers did away with vows of obedience in their marriage ceremonies; other sects sought to implement a single standard of morality and equal grounds for divorce for men and women.

These challenges to patriarchy joined with new kinds of female behavior provoked by the exigencies of civil war to transform, if only for a while, traditional gender arrangements. Women broke out of their domestic realm to respond to situations thrown up by war and revolution. Quaker women like Margaret Fell, Elizabeth Hooten, Ann Camm, Elizabeth Williams, and Mary Fisher, and hundreds of female preachers of other sects took to the road to deliver their "testimony" to the righteous cause of puritanism. Women of all classes and persuasions – from the royalist ladies and women of London and Westminster, who in 1642 petitioned Queen Henrietta Maria not to flee the country, to the Leveller women who beseeched parliament to acknowledge their "equal share and interest with men in the commonwealth" in 1649 – partook of the pamphleteering and public politicking that marked the 1640s and 1650s. Royalist women like the Duchess of Newcastle entered the political fray to petition on behalf of their husbands, traveling the length and breadth of the country to insure the protection of their interests. Women in support of the parliamentary cause urged that body to move against the king in February 1642 so as to prevent the "savage usage and unheard of rapes" that had purportedly been committed against protestant women in Ireland from occurring at home.[7]

Women served as spies – "Mary the scout" earned £10 for "the special service done by her at Taunton" on behalf of the parliamentary cause in 1645, while Mrs Endymion Porter had to flee England in 1646 so as to avoid being tried by parliament for spying for the royalists. In Ireland, Lady Bellew of Castletown and a Mrs May apparently gave out information to enemy forces. Others raised funds for their respective sides, while more intrepid women in Ireland and England actually served as "she-soldiers." Irish women who fought in England on the royalist side at the battle of Nantwich were said to have used long knives against their opponents, "which are such bloody instruments, that the eye of man never beheld before, being about halfe a yuard in length, with a hook and point at the end of them made not only to stab, but to teare the flesh from the very bones."[8]

Many defended their homes and estates while their husbands fought. In Ireland, Lady Forbes defended against a siege of Castle Forbes for nine months and gave shelter to some 200 local protestants. Lady Elizabeth Dowdall described how she defended her castle in County Limerick against Irish troops by hiring and training her own soldiers. When the Irish forces, with the high sheriff, Richard Stephenson, at their head, stormed the castle, Lady Dowdall "sent him a shot in the head that made him bid the world goodnight," she claimed, "and routed the whole army."[9] Lady Blanche Arundell survived a weeks-long siege of Wardour Castle in England by parliamentary troops, as did Brilliana Harley at Brampton Bryan and the Countess of Derby at Lathom House. Tales of their heroism spread through the country. Parliamentarians referred to the exploits of these women to demonstrate the declining fortunes of the royalist cause: if supporters of Charles depended on the leadership of mere women, they must be desperate indeed. Alternatively, the king's enemies could charge that men commanded by women were no men at all. Gender and sexuality served as an effective ideological weapon in the war between royalists and parliamentarians, enabling protagonists to question the manliness of their antagonists and thus their right to rule. This was most saliently, if obscenely, articulated in a royalist standard on which a naked soldier, sword and genitalia unsheathed and outstretched, declared himself, in Latin, "ready to use both."[10]

Above all, women turned to writing, producing the first outpouring of published works that would, by the middle of the eighteenth century, transform the hitherto exclusively masculine world of literature into a feminine domain. Women did write and publish before the civil war, but their output was minuscule. Between 1616 and 1620, for instance, only eight new publications by women appeared; when reissues and later editions are added, the number climbs to a mere twelve. The 1630s saw a small increase, but in the 1640s the number of works by women mushroomed. Between 1640 and 1645, more than forty new writings appeared; in the next five years, another sixty-nine new editions by women were published. Inspired by the example of women behaving in new and untraditional ways and by the desire to engage in political and religious debate, women like Eleanor Douglas, Anna Trapnel, Katherine Chidley, Susannah Bastwick, Dorothy Burch, Jane Turner – most of them of gentry or aristocratic families – took up their pens to make themselves heard. Far many more, fearing the charges of immodesty and sexual immorality that dogged women writing for publication, hid their identities behind the appellation "Anonymous." Perhaps even more surprising, women of the middling classes participated in the writing of political, social, and religious treatises; they engaged in and expanded the political culture of the time by working as printers, publishers, bookbinders, and booksellers, despite the disapprobation of men like Elizabeth Avery's brother, who exclaimed in disgust that "your printing of a Book, beyond the custom of your sex, doth rankly smell."[11]

The nature of women's publications broadened during the decades of the civil war and interregnum to include polemical treatises, plays, poetry, prose fiction, memoirs, prophetic literature, and collections of letters. Later in the century, handbooks containing practical household advice, cures for illnesses, and recipes constituted a significant proportion of women's writings and found a welcome audience from women trying to keep up with the new fashions in food, clothing, housewifery, and child rearing thrown up by vast economic change (see Chapter 3). Women had found their voice, and with it a means of expressing their desires. Despite widespread attempts to silence them, they would not soon relinquish it.

The chaos and dissolution of traditional authority characteristic of the decades of civil war and revolution provided opportunities for women to challenge, at least in practice, the ideological strictures that exhorted them to passivity, inferiority, and the private sphere. By the late 1650s, a broad section of the public – élite and popular alike – could no longer tolerate the uncertainty and divisiveness that marked the interregnum. They looked to a restoration of the monarchy, and with it parliament and the Church of England, for relief from political and social upheaval and release from puritan cultural oppression. With the return of Charles II came a curious and even paradoxical combination of conservative reaction and cultural loosening. Both would have profound ramifications for women in their relationships with men, with work, with the law, and with the state.

NOTES

1 This section derives in great part from Amy Louise Erickson's *Women and Property in Early Modern England* (London and New York, 1993).
2 See J.G.A. Pocock, "The Atlantic Archipelago and the War of the Three Kingdoms," in Brendan Bradshaw and John Morrill, eds, *The British Problem, c. 1534–1707: State Formation in the Atlantic Archipelago* (New York, 1996).
3 Christopher Hill, *The World Turned Upside Down* (London, 1972).
4 Mary Lyndon Shanley, "Marriage contract and social contract in seventeenth-century English political thought," *Western Political Quarterly* XXXII(1), March 1979: 79–91.
5 Quoted in Roderick Phillips, *Putting Asunder: A History of Divorce in Western Society* (Cambridge, 1988), p. 120.
6 Quoted in Shanley, "Marriage contract and social contract," pp. 79–91.
7 Quoted in Sara Heller Mendelsohn and Patricia Crawford, *Women in Early Modern England, 1550–1720* (Oxford, 1998), p. 400.
8 Quoted in Mary O'Dowd, "Women and war in Ireland in the 1640s," in Margaret MacCurtain and Mary O'Dowd, eds, *Women in Early Modern Ireland* (Edinburgh, 1991), p. 95.
9 Quoted in O'Dowd, "Women and war in Ireland," p. 93.
10 Quoted in Mendelsohn and Crawford, *Women in Early Modern England*, p. 394.

11 Quoted in Phyllis Mack, *Visionary Women: Ecstatic Prophecy in Seventeenth-Century England* (Berkeley, 1992), p. 118.

SOURCES

Brendan Bradshaw and John Morrill, eds, *The British Problem, c. 1534–1707: State Formation in the Atlantic Archipelago*. New York, 1996.

Susan Cahn, *Industry of Devotion. The Transformation of Women's Work in England, 1500–1660*. New York, 1987.

Alice Clark, *Working Life of Women in the Seventeenth Century*. London, 1982. Reprint from original, 1919.

Patricia Crawford, "Women's published writings, 1600–1700," in Mary Prior, ed., *Women in English Society, 1500–1800*. London, 1985.

——, *Women and Religion in England, 1500–1720*. London, 1993.

Amy Louise Erickson, *Women and Property in Early Modern England*. London and New York, 1993.

Moira Ferguson, ed., *First Feminists: British Women Writers, 1578–1799*. Bloomington, IN, 1985.

John R. Gillis, *For Better, For Worse. British Marriages, 1600 to the Present*. New York, 1985.

Ralph Houlbrooke, *The English Family, 1450–1700*. London, 1984.

Anne Laurence, *Women in England, 1500–1760. A Social History*. New York, 1994.

Alan MacFarlane, *The Family Life of Ralph Josselin, A Seventeenth-Century Clergyman*. New York, 1977.

Phyllis Mack, "The prophet and her audience: Gender and knowledge in the world turned upside down," in Geoff Eley and William Hunt, eds, *Reviving the English Revolution: Reflections and Elaborations on the Work of Christopher Hill*. London, 1988.

——, *Visionary Women: Ecstatic Prophecy in Seventeenth-Century England*. Berkeley, 1992.

Sara Heller Mendelsohn, *The Mental World of Stuart Women. Three Studies*. Amherst, 1987.

Sara Heller Mendelsohn and Patricia Crawford, *Women in Early Modern England, 1550–1720*. Oxford, 1998.

Mary O'Dowd, "Women and war in Ireland in the 1640s," in Margaret MacCurtain and Mary O'Dowd, eds, *Women in Early Modern Ireland*. Edinburgh, 1991.

Lois G. Schwoerer, "Women's public political voice in England: 1640–1740," in Hilda L. Smith, ed., *Women Writers and the Early Modern British Political Tradition*. Cambridge, 1998.

Mary Lyndon Shanley, "Marriage contract and social contract in seventeenth-century English political thought," *Western Political Quarterly* XXXII(1), March 1979: 79–91.

Hilda Smith, *Reason's Disciples: Seventeenth-Century English Feminists*. Urbana, IL, 1982.

Lawrence Stone, *The Family, Sex and Marriage in England, 1500–1800*. New York, 1977.

——, *Road to Divorce. England, 1530–1987*. Oxford, 1990.

Louise A. Tilly and Joan W. Scott, *Women, Work, and Family*. New York, 1978.

Randolph Trumbach, *The Rise of the Egalitarian Family: Aristocratic Kinship and Domestic Relations in Eighteenth-Century England*. New York, 1978.

Chapter 2

Restoring authority, 1660–1715

The Restoration

By the time Charles II (1660–85) returned to the throne of England in 1660 following twenty years of civil war and revolution, Britons had witnessed the killing of a king; the implementation of a republican form of government; challenges to the economic and political power of the landed élites, first from upstart "middling" groups in the towns and then from an army of plebeians; a military dictatorship; resistance to patriarchy from female sectarians such as the Quakers, who advocated women's equality with men, women's right to preach, to vote on church matters, and to disobey their husbands in matters of conscience; and the establishment of a moral order governed by strict puritan principles of piety and sobriety. The entire political and social order had been shaken to its roots.

The restoration of Charles II involved, then, far more than the restoration of the monarchy, parliament, and the Church of England. It entailed the restoration of what was perceived to be the natural order of landed élites – aristocracy and gentry – ruling over subordinated middling and lower ranks, of fathers ruling over children, and of husbands ruling over wives. One way to restore the established patriarchal and hierarchical system that had nearly been shattered by two decades of civil war and revolution, it seemed to contemporaries, was to restore the familial order that seemed to undergird it. That would prove impossible, as we shall see below, but politicians, political theorists, economists, and jurists found ways to redefine and reconstitute relationships of power between men and women just as they did those between parliament and king in 1660 and again in 1688.

With the Restoration, developments in ideology and in law acted to tighten those strictures that had been loosened during the chaos of civil war, to close down certain possibilities that had acted to mediate women's legal, economic, and social disabilities. In 1662, for instance, the government sought to re-establish the patriarchal basis of political and family life by ordering the re-publication of Richard Mocket's *God and the King*. First published during the reign of James I, Mocket's treatise compared the divine right of kings to rule absolutely to the "natural" right of fathers to rule their children absolutely. Few people were prepared, so recently after the ending of so much strife and uncertainty, to contest such a declaration on the part of Charles. Indeed, even "dissenting" fathers, those who refused to conform to Anglican religious doctrines, who had embraced ideas of companionate marriage, operated according to the precepts of patriarchal power and even sought to strengthen it. They saw no contradiction in accepting the notion that children should not be coerced into marriage while insisting that fatherly consent must be obtained; likewise, they advocated affection and spiritual equality between men and women in marriage, all the while asserting that wives must be subordinate to husbands. Nonconformists also insisted upon a much stricter marital discipline than did the restored Anglican church. Congregants might be expelled not only for engaging in premarital sex but also for neglecting to attain the consent of their parents to marry. During the 1660s and 1670s, a familial ideology of more stringent patriarchy predominated. Especially among the middle ranks of prosperous businessmen and farmers, marriage continued to be a function of property transmission; the individuals who owned that property, husbands and fathers, maintained and even increased their control over wives and children.

We can see this occurring legally, where alternatives to the common law such as ecclesiastical and manorial courts, which acted to soften the harshness of coverture and primogeniture in inheritance and to increase women's economic security, gradually lost ground as the competition for jurisdictional predominance shifted toward common law. The arguments of parliamentarians as they mounted their challenge to absolute monarchy throughout the course of the seventeenth century privileged the common law over all others; ecclesiastical law suffered from the disestablishment of the Anglican church during the interregnum. Parliament's victory over the monarchy in 1649 led to the increasing centralization of government affairs and ensured that the national common law and parliamentary statutes would prevail over local law, a development that did not cease with the Restoration. Although the process of rationalizing the system of law in England and Wales (Scotland retained its own system when it joined in union with England in 1707) would take another two centuries to complete, its overall effect was to restrict the legal and inheritance rights of wives, daughters, and widows even further in favor of the male head of household. Parliament contributed to the process in 1670 with the misleadingly named Act for the Better Settling of Intestates' Estates. This statute, aimed at that particular segment of the female population – widows – that enjoyed significant legal and sometimes economic independence, and which, as a consequence, engendered a great deal of anxiety in society, halved the share of goods a childless widow could inherit from her husband.[1] This might reduce her economic independence considerably. Other statutes passed in the late seventeenth and early eighteenth centuries reduced women's ecclesiastical rights to "reasonable" portions of their husbands' and fathers' moveable goods.

The restoration of the Church of England in 1661 had serious repercussions for dissenting and nonconformist congregations, among whom the Presbyterians were now surprised to find themselves, and especially for the women within their ranks. Charles's failed attempts to impose toleration for catholics and nonconforming protestants through royal prerogative did little to soften the persecution against those who refused to swear an oath to the Anglican church. More importantly perhaps for our purposes, religious enthusiasm, so reminiscent of the 1640s and 1650s, and in which both men and women participated, took on the qualities of excess, instability, and irrationality. People who refused to adhere to Anglican doctrine adopted more sober religious practices so as to avoid calling adverse attention to themselves and to demonstrate their respectability and thus their right to worship without interference. Men of the upper ranks tended to distance themselves from enthusiastic, revealed religion, embracing the reason of "science" instead to explain the world around them. No longer a source of common cultural experience, enthusiastic religion, with its connotations of emotional instability and mental weakness, came to be identified with women generally and men of lower ranks, an identification that seemed to be validated by the experiences of two decades of civil war and revolution. Religion, with its emphasis on belief, seemed "natural" to women, seen to be the less reasonable sex.[2] During the course of the eighteenth century in particular, religion would increasingly be called upon to uphold ideas about women as pious, virtuous, obedient, and passive: appropriate characteristics for those who would be assigned exclusively to the private sphere.

The fears engendered by the civil war and interregnum that female disorder produced social disorder, and the need to eliminate the latter by curbing the former made it virtually impossible for sectarian women to continue their public activities. No longer could they preach or write publicly without provoking severe disapprobation. Within both dissenting and Anglican churches, ministers emphasized personal piety and morality for women, and exhorted them to their obligations as mothers to raise pious children. Anglican ministers urged élite women in their congregations to observe the social distinctions of rank, making an explicit connection between pious women and social order. Latitude in the ways women might behave and still be considered "proper" by society was narrowing, part of the process of restoring order to political, social, religious, and family life.

Legal and cultural developments that increased patriarchal control in the family were reinforced by demographic and economic changes that acted to reduce women's capacities to contribute to familial material well-being, thus reducing their potential influence. The age of marriage began to fall, probably a reflection of the increasing numbers of people whose livelihood now depended on wages. In the earlier part of the seventeenth century, when women married in their mid- to late twenties, they had an opportunity to experience a significant period of independence that may have helped to render them less pliable in marriage. Earlier marriage may have left them less certain of themselves, less psychologically able or willing to hold their own against their husbands. Because they married earlier, they bore more children, which would have multiplied their domestic obligations. Moreover, the number of women who never married dropped to less than half that in the earlier part of the century, exposing increasing numbers of them to the now harsher effects of coverture.

Economic changes that intensified during the 1640s and 1650s acted to significantly alter the economic role of women in élite and middling families. This is a story we will pick up in later chapters, but for now we should indicate that as upper and middling families prospered as never before with the expansion of the economy, wives and daughters in those families no longer played a vital role in production. More and more, the ability of a husband and father to keep the women of his family idle became a symbol of his success, and it was not long before the idea that women of élite and middling families worked would be unimaginable, a serious violation of the social code. Women became the chief and conspicuous consumers of the goods produced by capitalist methods and of the exotic items coming into Britain from overseas. The transformation of women's economic role from that of necessary economic partner in production to one of leisured, ornamental consumer reduced the real power they might exercise in the family.

A few educated élite women protested vociferously against the situation women faced as a consequence of these developments, and attributed their subordination not to any "natural" inferiority but to lack of economic rights and access to education. Mary More, writing in the 1670s, argued that economic dependence upon their husbands rendered women near slaves. The title of Aphra Behn's first play, *The Forced Marriage*, written in 1671, suggested the constraints women faced as they struggled to achieve economic survival; the play itself, as well as other works Behn published, dealt with themes of rape and of women's powerlessness. Her outrage over enslaved Africans, expressed in *Oroonoko: or, the Royal Slave*, published in 1688, implied a link between the condition of women and that of slaves, anticipating by over a century an association feminists would make throughout the nineteenth century. Behn, Margaret Cavendish, the Duchess of Newcastle, and Bathsua Makin advocated serious education for women, albeit élite women, urging them to develop and utilize their considerable mental powers. In 1686, *The Female Advocate*, written by a 14-year-old girl named Sarah Fyge, castigated misogynist tracts that flooded Restoration England, charging their authors with jealousy, incompetence, and a bald desire to exercise power over women. In all of these ways, some women of the Restoration resisted contemporary beliefs about women's natural weakness and inferiority, and their need to be obedient and subordinate to men. In so doing, they also challenged the assumptions about masculine privilege on which such ideas about femininity rested.[3]

We have seen one version of masculinity and masculine privilege espoused by puritan and middling spokespeople for a return to patriarchal ordering based on men's authority and women's obedience and silence. An entirely different vision of masculinity received valorization by the ethos surrounding the court of Charles II. Designed to signify a release from the crabbed, pious, sexually repressive, and hypocritical regime of puritan rule, the behavioral code of those surrounding Charles II emphasized appetite, sensuality, and earthly delights. Public revels, popular festivals, and folk customs banned by the puritans during the Interregnum were restored. Clerical rule was mocked by such aristocratic "rakes" as Lord Sackville and Sir Charles Sedley, who preached naked in 1663 to a crowd gathered at a tavern in Covent Garden. John Wilmot, second Earl of Rochester, best known of a "merry gang" of rakes surrounding Charles, embraced a philosophy of libertinism that placed the pursuit of pleasure above all others. His style, his outlook, his behavior, and his demeanor marked the appearance of a new kind of masculinity in post-Restoration England, one consciously defined by its contrast to puritan concepts of decency, sobriety, and propriety. The aristocratic rake engaged in public behavior that was loud, riotous, bullying, and frequently violent; he drank and ate to excess; he fornicated; he insulted women. Rochester and the "Ballers" he led in a series of "frollicks" – public displays of nudity, exposure of their own and women's genitals, and sexual assaults on women – sought to halt what they saw as "the strange decay of manly parts since the days of dear Harry the Second." Their rakish activity, according to one historian, constituted only the most egregious examples of a pervasive male culture, one defined by its defiance of public decency, public order, and its brutalization of women.[4]

Rochester's version of manliness involved a corresponding model of femininity that contained contradictory elements. On the one hand, Rochester believed in a kind of equality between men and women; he demonstrated respect for women's intellectual capacities and decried the injustices they faced in law and society. He took particular care to see that his wife had the use of the property she brought to their marriage although the law of coverture gave him ownership of it. He encouraged women like Aphra Behn and Anne Wharton in their writing; both of them wrote warmly of his efforts to assist them. His view of libertinism extended to women as well, and he urged women to "love you[r] pleasures." On the other hand, he believed in the "free use of Wine and Women," a misogynist philosophy that placed women at his service as mere objects of his desire. As we have seen in the "frollicks," those objects of his desire were not necessarily expected to give their consent. What Rochester might consider seduction could easily slide into rape.

The two dominant moral orders obtaining in later seventeenth-century England, what we might call those of puritan reformers and aristocratic rakes, offered rather unattractive alternatives to women. Rochester recognized women's intelligence and capacity for sexual pleasure, but also exploited and degraded them. Reformers offered women a patriarchal system that provided legal and moral protection against sexual exploitation while denying their intellectual capabilities, curbing their economic opportunities, and repressing their sexuality. In the absence of economic, political, or legal rights that offered them any hope of autonomy, few women could afford to take up the former vision of femininity. The protection of patriarchy in a world in which women could exercise only the most limited forms of power seemed by far the safer bet. As we shall see in later chapters, the aristocratic, rakish vision of masculinity would prove incompatible with the values and outlook of the fast-growing bourgeoisie. Their greater confidence in their social position, and their predominance in the life of the nation as a consequence of vast economic expansion, would render them capable of insisting on and imposing a reform of manners on men and women that dramatically transformed the way men and women looked, behaved, thought, and interacted in the eighteenth century.

The rakish circle around Charles II only exaggerated the Restoration court style exemplified by Charles himself. Restoration propaganda frequently represented Charles as romantic, sensual, and pleasure-loving, incorporating images of a lover and his mistress to portray the relationship between the king and his people, and describing the Restoration itself as a wedding between a bride, Britain, and her husband, Charles. The king's sexually promiscuous behavior, involving him in scandalous activity that engendered widely publicized gossip and criticism, however, often acted to subvert the intention of court publicists, who sought to represent his rule as a return to normalcy. Charles, "most blessed and most pious, most worthy of all the human race," as he was proclaimed by one coronation inscription in 1661, Charles the metaphoric father of his people, was in fact the father of fourteen of them, all illegitimate. The problem for someone who did not take pains to hide his sexual affairs from the public was that representations of Charles as an amorous husband to the nation could be easily parodied by people who opposed his rule. In a period when otherwise serious political treatises contained scurrilous and obscene sexual narratives, political opponents and even supporters often portrayed Charles as a rapist violating the honor of his subjects or an adulterer unfaithful to his marriage vows. Political pornography served as an effective way to frame political debate and to articulate profound political fears.

Those fears were many, and not simply for that minority of "fanatics" who hankered after the republican past. Moderate puritans who accepted the Restoration nevertheless worried that it might be but a prelude to "all licentious practices," as one of them put it, confusing again the political and the sexual. Protestants of all stripes suspected Charles of sympathy with catholicism and with catholic France; certainly the avowedly catholic James, Duke of York, next in line to the throne in the absence of any legitimate heir to Charles, provoked apprehension. Finally, a significant portion of members of parliament and their supporters outside believed that Charles harbored absolutist designs. Catholicism and political tyranny served as focal points for a wide outpouring of political commentary, much of it expressed in sexual terms.[5]

Bawdy stories about the king engaged in a variety of earthly pleasures began to circulate in the mid-1660s, after a series of disasters – a visitation of the plague, the great London fire, war with the Dutch – seems to have kindled a general anxiety about a rehearsal of "the world turned upside down." No inherent logic determined the relationship between political pornography and arguments for and against absolutism as they unfolded during the exclusion crisis. Unlike in France a hundred years later, where sexual libertinism was advanced as a means of undermining absolutism, late seventeenth-century English writers tended to associate libertinism with political tyranny and absolutism. Some polemicists represented Charles's attempt to rule without parliament in the guise of sexual excess: the author of "Sardanapalus," for instance, portrayed a king who had slept with or wished to sleep with every woman in the kingdom. At the most basic level, such a fantasy suggested that the tyrannical Charles sought to deprive his male subjects of their most fundamental rights, their manhood and their property in women. Other writers suggested that the king sought to establish absolutism by debauching his subjects through the example of his own behavior, rendering them unable to resist monarchical encroachments on their rights. Charles, insisted one such author, "set himself by his own persuasion and influence to withdraw both men and women from the laws of nature and morality, and to pollute and infect the people with all manner of debauchery and wickedness" so as to "weaken and make soft the military temper of the people by debauchery and effeminacy, which generally go hand in hand together."

The linking of debauchery and effeminacy, which in the seventeenth and eighteenth centuries referred to excessive "womanizing" rather than to homosexuality, was a common device in political pornography, used to suggest that the king's pursuit of pleasure dictated state policy. One of Charles's courtiers, the pleasure-hunting Earl of Rochester, noted in his infamous "Sceptre lampoon":

> his pintle and his sceptre are of a length
> and she may sway the one who plays with the other.

A connection to absolutism appeared in the need to raise enough money to support his mistresses, as the author of "On the Duchess of Portsmouth," one of Charles's paramours, noted:

> The nation must be taxed both land and gains
> Not to supply the public but his reins

And all the coin by harrassed subjects lent
Must through your conduit pipe of lust be spent.

Stories circulated that the duchess had persuaded Charles to dismiss parliament; others had it that the Countess of Castlemaine, another of Charles's mistresses, had urged him to rule by military force. Indeed, the royalist Samuel Pepys confided to his *Diary* his belief that the amount of money required to support his mistresses kept Charles in financial straits. Pepys and his associates privately speculated that the king would dissolve parliament and turn to extra-parliamentary taxation or look to the absolutist Louis XIV of France for financial support before he would consent to a parliamentary inquiry into the extravagant expenditure of the kingdom's revenues upon the royal mistresses.

By linking the king's efforts to rule absolutely to sexual excess, supporters and opponents alike referred to age-old notions of the sexual treachery of women and their pernicious influence on men. Some pornographic tales placed Charles in an oriental setting, likening him to a despotic Turkish sultan whose dependence on a harem of women sapped his energies and warped his powers of intelligence. In other stories, debauchery was used to connect Charles's tyranny with catholicism. Popular belief had it that catholicism gave its adherents the excuse to behave however they liked; anti-catholic writers charged that the pope managed brothels in Rome, drawing on a widespread image of the catholic church as the "Whore of Rome," a powerful, sexually promiscuous, indecently wealthy woman. Charles's mistresses, the "catholic whores," connected him to the "Whore of Rome," making it possible to equate a debauched king with a catholic king. Anglicans hoping to dissuade dissenters from siding with the monarchy against parliament in hopes of gaining toleration for their religious practices found this kind of argument effective.

References to Charles's excessive sexual desire were but one of many sexual images called upon to sustain arguments about his proclivities to political tyranny. Images of sexually domineering and devouring women were ever present, as we have seen in the charges that the king's mistresses were sucking dry the nation's resources. As one historian has pointed out,[6] Restoration debates about sexuality centered on power. While one cultural cliché had it that men conquered women in the act of sexual intercourse, a notion that appeared regularly in rakish concepts of a libertine masculinity, another posited that women's insatiability "defeated" men, who could never satisfy it. The ambiguity of sexual politics – the suggestion that the power in sexual relationships is elusive and unstable, and cannot be located in any given site – mirrored Restoration anxieties about political authority. In thrall to those whose pleasures he sought, the king had no real power; it resided in the hands of those who satisfied his desires. As one apologist for parliament put it in 1681, parliament was the only governing body that "hinders the subject from being given up as a prey, not only to the will of a Prince, but (which is ten times worse) to the unreasonable passions and lusts of favorites, chief ministers, and women."

These comments were made in the context of the exclusion crisis when, in the late 1670s and early 1680s, the king's inability to produce an heir and fears of a popish plot to assassinate Charles and place his catholic brother James on the throne, provoked debates once again over the relationship of the king and his subjects. Led by the Earl of Shaftesbury, a coalition of members of parliament, who came to be called Whigs, organized in 1679 a campaign to exclude the catholic James from the throne. Charles responded by dissolving parliament that summer; when he called two others, in 1680 and 1681, he found no way of compromising with the intransigent and increasingly inflammatory Whigs, and did not summon another parliament for the duration of his reign. The violent threats of the Whigs, who arrived armed at the parliamentary session of 1681, provoked a reaction in favor of Charles and James from people who feared another civil war. The king's supporters, called Tories, rallied to his efforts to remove Shaftesbury and other Whigs from local positions of power, and gave James their unwavering loyalty. Proclaiming the divine right of kings, they evoked earlier analogies of a monarch's power and that of fathers within families, particularly those contained in Sir Robert Filmer's *Patriarcha*, reissued in 1680, to justify their assertions. In doing so, they once again forced their opponents to rethink the relative positions of men and women within the family.

The best known and most influential of the works bearing on the family, John Locke's *Two Treatises on Government*, written in 1679 but not published until after the Glorious Revolution in 1689, placed familial relations on the firm ground of contract theory based in natural law. Leaving aside his momentous development of the concept that family authority and state or civil authority are not alike and should be kept separate from one another, whose implications for relations within the private sphere of family we will take up later, Locke's belief that marriage constitutes a contract went beyond that of parliamentarian arguments of the civil war period. Where they could not entertain the idea that the act of consenting to enter into marriage extended to other forms of consent once marriage was contracted, Locke argued that the parties to the contract might also stipulate the terms of their relationship within marriage. He further insisted that because all human beings – men and women alike – are free in a state of nature, there could exist no predetermined terms or conditions bearing on the parties to marriage, except that of producing and caring for children. As long as the obligations to care for the children born to a married couple continued to be met, that couple might terminate their marriage contract if the ends to which it had been directed were completed. Moreover, husbands did not, Locke claimed, enjoy any absolute sovereign power in marriage by virtue of their sex. He could not completely shrug off societal norms of male supremacy in marriage, noting that where husband and wife disagreed about how their "common Interest and Property" should be administered, "it naturally falls to the Man's share, as the abler and stronger," to make the final determination. Nevertheless, he qualified the exercise of a husband's power to areas of common concern, and argued that these, too, might be regulated by contract. Far in advance of other thinkers of his time in regard to marriage and the relationship of husband and wife within it, Locke's work did not immediately change the way society thought about, or the law regulated, marriage. It did, however, in conjunction with the acceptance of contract theory that accompanied and justified the removing of James II from the throne and replacing him with William and Mary in the Glorious Revolution, open the door to possibilities of divorce.[7] In the nineteenth century, as we shall see, reformers called upon his individualistic assumptions about human beings to effect changes in property law and marriage law that directly benefited women.

These changes would not materialize for generations. In the mean time, the traditional notions about the sexual treachery of women, their perfidy, and the pernicious influence they might have on men's exercise of power we saw articulated in political pornography continued to predominate in politics and culture. During the warming-pan scandal of 1688,[8] when Queen Mary, upon giving birth to a catholic son who would succeed James on the throne, was accused of having had him smuggled into her bedchamber in a warming pan, these sentiments were given full expression. Designed to call into question the legitimacy of the catholic heir and thereby to justify the ouster of James from the throne, these misogynist rehearsals of feminine evil had the paradoxical effect of creating a situation in which women were recognized as having authority to determine the course of political life.

The announcement of Mary of Modena's pregnancy in January 1688 after fifteen years of marriage came as a shock to James's subjects, who had expected the throne to succeed to one of his grown protestant daughters by his first marriage, Mary or Anne. A group of Tory and Whig leaders, induced to bury their political differences by the prospect of an unlimited catholic line of succession if the baby were to be a boy, began to hatch a plan to invite William, Prince of Orange, the husband of the protestant Mary, to invade England, oust James, and set himself upon the throne. At the same time, rumors that the Queen's pregnancy was fraudulent began to circulate, claiming alternately that her "great belly" was fake, or that the father of the child was not James at all but the pope's emissary, whose name, Ferdinand D'Adda, could easily be rendered Dadda. The Prince of Wales's birth provided a powerful justification for William's invasion of England. William had acted to defend the hereditary rights of his wife Mary to succession, he asserted in his *Declaration ... of the Reasons Inducing him to Appear in Arms in the Kingdom of England*, noting "the just and visible grounds of suspicion [that] the Pretended Prince of Wales was not born by the Queen."

The warming-pan scandal engendered discussions that both called on and dismissed women as sources of authority to determine the authenticity of legitimate succession. During the Queen's pregnancy, the idea that women had greater knowledge of matters of pregnancy and childbirth gave them an opportunity to speak out on an issue of political significance. Aphra Behn weighed in with her prediction that the baby would be male. Princess Anne, who along with Princess Mary had the most to gain from the scandal, kept her sister informed with regular reports of the Queen's condition and of the rumors purporting its falseness. Conveniently away at the time of the Queen's confinement, Anne did not witness the child's birth and could not confirm his authenticity. Her strategy, like that of others fanning the warming-pan scandal, was to make it possible for people to continue to believe in the pretense of the Prince of Wales by not providing them with any evidence to the contrary. Other women made depositions to the Privy Council in October 1688 declaring their conviction that the Prince of Wales was indeed the son of James, but the campaign to deny the prince's legitimacy had been effective, and, by that time, William's invasion had begun.

For years afterwards, the warming-pan stories continued to circulate; between 1688 and 1745, some fifty such works appeared, stimulated by concerns on the part of non-juring clergy who could not swear an oath to William and Mary, or to Anne when she took the throne, and by fears of Jacobite risings seeking to place the Stuart Pretenders, Old and Young, on the throne in 1715 and 1745 respectively. The accounts of women featured prominently in the recurrent tales, their privileged knowledge of matters of childbirth lending credibility and authority to one side or the other. In 1689, Lucy Armstrong recounted to the Earl of Nottingham that the midwife attending Mary of Modena's childbirth had confided to a woman of mutual acquaintance that the child was a fraud. Lady Isabella Wentworth and Margaret Dawson reported to the contrary to a number of non-juring clergy, while, in 1708, Mrs Frances Shaftoe declared in print that Sir Theophilus Oglethorpe, not James, was the real father of the Prince of Wales.

But if the warming-pan stories provided women with a forum and encouragement, even the authority to speak out on political affairs of great importance, they more often provoked negative commentary about women's essentially treacherous nature. Stories of other incidents of suppositious births circulated, calling upon age-old fears of women foisting illegitimate children on their unsuspecting husbands and perverting the proper course of paternal succession and inheritance. These stories evoked the same kind of anti-catholic bigotry mentioned above in connection with political pornography, conjuring up conspiracies between women and priests to change the course of kingly succession. The same beliefs about catholics' lax sexual morals appeared in the warming-pan stories, as evidenced in the designation of the pope's emissary as the Prince of Wales's father. Once again, the anti-catholic propaganda depicting the church as the Whore of Rome, this time in the guise of Mary of Modena, appealed to the sentiments of large numbers of Englishmen and women, and made the warming-pan stories credible. Popular beliefs about women's sexual treachery and thus their unfitness for political participation received reinforcement, enhancing other trends that were operating to confine at least élite women to a private role within home and family.

The revolution of 1688

An unusual set of circumstances excited even more commentary about women's fitness to rule in the years 1688 to 1714: for most of those years, a woman sat on the throne of England. Once again, troubling questions of authority in the political realm that dogged the settlement of 1688 and 1689 spilled over to and provoked discussion about the nature of men's and women's power and their relationships to one another. As was the case with the Restoration, the resolution of the problems in the political arena required the resolution of the questions raised about the gender order. There were differences, however. Whereas during the 1640s and 1650s, and again in the 1670s and 1680s during the Exclusion Crisis, arguments about political authority were articulated by means of *analogies* to familial authority, debates about the nature of monarchical authority that went on during the reigns of William and Mary (1689–1702) and Anne (1702–14), because the crown was held by a woman, were far more direct in their references to women and family authority.[9]

The revolution of 1688–89 has conventionally marked the establishment in England of constitutional monarchy and the rule of law, dramatically transforming the nature of the English constitution and the relationship of the crown to parliament. Parliament had asserted its authority to, in essence, remove one king from the throne and replace him with others. In combination with the Bill of Rights of 1689, which restricted the power of the monarchy by placing it under the law and asserted the sovereignty of parliament, the revolutionary settlement implied that a social contract between crown and subjects existed, one that could be revoked and a monarch removed if he failed to fulfill its terms. Hereafter, sovereignty, the source of authority in the state, it might appear, resided in the nation.

But as a number of historians have pointed out, those Whigs and Tories who made the Revolution of 1688/89 had profound reservations about what they had done. They did not wish to be seen as revolutionaries, nor could they come to any agreement about what their actions constituted. Crises of conscience compelled contemporaries to devise various stories to justify what was in fact the overthrowing of a legitimate monarch by his rightful subjects. Furthermore, all kinds of questions concerning the relationship of the monarchy to its ministers, to parliament, to political factions of court and country, and to the public arose, as did those seeking to inquire into the nature of loyalty and virtuous citizenship.

Because many of these problems could not be resolved by the law, they were often framed in terms of gender. In other words, the uncertainties about authority and the exercise of power thrown up by the revolutionary settlement found their most satisfying expression in stories about, or references to, gender and sexuality. In each case, the resolution of issues articulated in gendered terms had profound implications both for women's relationship to power and for the relationships of men and women outside the political arena.

We have seen this already in the case of the warming-pan scandal being used to explain William's invasion of England to oust James from the throne. This partic-ular justification for the Glorious Revolution could not be sustained for long, however, for it flew in the face of William's political ambitions. The warming-pan story gave rise to the claim that Mary's right to succession had been violated by the introduction of a suppositious son; the logical conclusion would have been for parliament to crown her as James's legitimate heir, as indeed a number of MPs asserted it must. William, however, would not accept a situation in which he would be but his wife's "gentleman usher," as he put it. Insisting that "he would hold no power dependent upon the will of a woman," he demanded full executive power, which he refused to share with Mary or relinquish in the event of her death. In the face of William's threats to withdraw his troops from England, leaving the door open for James's return, parliament capitulated to his demands. It placed the crown jointly in William and Mary's hands, and made him sole executive authority of the kingdom. In doing so, MPs eschewed accounts of the warming-pan scandal in favor of allusions to women's nature. These assertions about the nature of women better conformed to their decision and at the same time served to uphold a gender ideology that relegated women to private affairs. The dangerous times, some Williamites claimed, meant that it was not "safe to trust the administration of affairs to a woman," and called for "a vigorous and masculine" administration. "A Man, by nature, education, and experience, is generally rendered more capable to govern than a woman," wrote one of William's supporters in 1689, and thus "the husband ought rather to rule the wife, than the wife the husband." William would protect and defend his wife and her kingdom, removing all of the disturbing aspects of rule and enabling her to "enjoy all the pleasure of being queen without any thing of trouble." Others argued that Mary constituted a security risk to the country, fearing that the guilt that "will perpetually assault her tender breasts" would induce her to let her father James back in. Evoking notions of women as weak-willed, frivolous, emotional, and inconstant, these arguments purportedly drawn from "nature" about femininity enabled the revolutionaries to obscure the contradictions of their actions. Mary, the legitimate heir to the throne, would succeed in name only. The *de facto* power of the monarchy rested with her husband, who possessed few legal grounds for his claim.

Parliament dealt with William's lack of any constitutional claim to the throne by references to gender hierarchy within and legal strictures that pertained to marriage. Just as it was unthinkable for a woman to rule over her husband in marriage, so too was it unthinkable for William to subject himself to his wife's authority in the kingdom. "Does any think the Prince of Orange will come in to be a subject of his own wife in England?" scoffed one pro-William MP. "This is not possible, nor ought to be in Nature." The argument from marriage proved to be an effective one, for it also raised the issue of coverture, under which, as we have seen, a wife's property became the possession of her husband. Mary's property, including her estate in the crown, belonged to William. The law of coverture provided a legal coloration to William's claim to power, giving him, he insisted, "such a right as all the world knows to the succession of the crown." As it turned out, Mary herself invoked current thinking about gender to ratify the joint settlement of the crown. It was "unsuitable and ungrateful" and "not to be expected," she maintained, "that so generous and warlike a prince [as William] ... would suffer his wife ... to become his sovereign." "My opinion," she wrote later in her *Memoirs*, "has ever been that women should not meddle in government."

The unprecedented joint settlement of the crown on both William and Mary and the investing of William with exclusive executive authority created intractable constitutional problems necessitating additional invocations of gender to resolve them, or at least present the appearance of their resolution. By the terms of the settlement, Mary enjoyed royal authority without royal power, a situation that proved thorny during those periods when William left the country to fight James's forces in Ireland or to see to his interests in Holland. Parliament passed a Regency Bill that gave Mary power while William was away, but the bill raised as many questions as it answered. What if Mary's orders contradicted William's wishes? What if he issued a counter order from abroad? Whose power superseded whose in the event of such confusion? When there could be no satisfactory legal answers to these questions, MPs, ministers, and public commentators turned to gender ideology – to the notions of wifely submission and obedience – to provide them.

Mary, it was said, was so closely bound to her husband that his will was hers, and that she had no intention of doing anything but his bidding. "Her soul was married to her monarch's will," wrote one man after Mary's death in 1694. "Her love and admiration for him made her submission a delight to her." Moreover, because Mary lacked any political ambition, as would befit women in general, she could be no threat to the constitutional order. "While the Queen governed, still the wife obeyed," a Mr Hume reassured his readership. Writers continually noted the joy and relief with which Mary turned over the reins of power to her husband when he returned from abroad. Mary, for her part, was careful never to act in such a way as to upset the precariously balanced constitutional arrangement, affirming parliament's conviction that she was "the best woman in the world." Had she chosen to act otherwise, to seek to exercise power in her own right and to challenge thereby the authority of William as both king and husband, she would have called forth an entirely different assessment.

Mary's deportment as submissive, wifely queen ensured that the sexual hierarchy within marriage would be upheld, thus also insuring the revolution itself from association with, or charges of, sexual disorder that had beset the reigns of Charles II and James II. Rather, court propagandists and other commentators turned the political pornography of the Restoration to their advantage, using it as a foil against which to define the reign of William and Mary as virtuous. The post-1688 editions of the pornographic *Poems on Affairs of State*, for example, contained assertions that their material served to undermine Charles's corrupt court, rendering the contents of the work virtuous rather than obscene. The editor of the 1697 version avowed that the reissuing of the *Poems* would act to enhance moral and political rectitude by revealing a "just account of the true source of all our present mischiefs," which would enable Britons to "remove those pernicious principles which lead us directly to slavery." Slavery, in this account, appeared in the guise of a prostitute, an image consistent with the sexualized portrayals of Restoration politics, and a dramatic figure against which the reign of William and Mary, represented by supporters and by Mary herself as evidence of divine providence laboring to rescue the nation from the sins of the past, would be contrasted. But if the story of the revolution settlement as religious and moral regeneration was to work, the symbolism called for the appearance of a chaste, pious, and virtuous womanhood. The figure of Mary, in both her own actions and in representations of her, would come to stand in for that virtuous womanhood, casting out one version of femininity and replacing it with another within the dominant gender ideology that would develop over the course of the eighteenth century.

Mary believed that God desired the settlement that placed her and William on her father's throne, just as she saw His continued benediction in William's victory over James at the Battle of the Boyne. She feared, however, that providential goodwill would cease and the Glorious Revolution falter if the country continued the sinful behavior characteristic of the Restoration. She embarked on what has been called the Moral Revolution in an effort to secure the achievements of the Glorious Revolution for posterity.

As William could scarcely present himself as the model of morality and purity because of public knowledge of his extramarital affairs, it fell to Mary alone to place the stamp of piety and virtue on their reign. She persuaded William to enforce the laws against adultery, fornication, drunkenness, and blasphemy, and enthusiastically endorsed the societies for the reformation of manners that sprang up during her reign. Her assistance to the societies went beyond the merely rhetorical: she provided them with real power to alter individual behavior by commanding that justices to the commissions of the peace in Middlesex and Westminster be appointed from the ranks of the societies' members. In her own personal conduct she behaved with such propriety that Jacobite and Tory attempts to portray her as a sexual libertine or to charge that the court was "full of vice" failed to gain purchase among the public, thus eliminating from her opponents' armory a potent weapon.

Mary, in the judgment of a number of historians, cemented the success of the revolution settlement, reconciling alienated subjects in both pragmatic and symbolic ways. In the first instance, the presence on the throne of the daughter of James made it possible for thousands of people who would otherwise have supported James to swear their allegiance to William and Mary. As Aphra Behn expressed it in 1689:

> The murmuring world till now divided lay
> Vainly debating whome they shou'd obey
> Till you great Cesar's offspring blest our Isle
> The differing multitudes to reconcile.

Had William been crowned sole ruler, he would have faced opposition from perhaps half the nation of England. Mary's lineage could not stifle all Jacobite activity, but it certainly did cut down the number of attempts to replace James on the throne. By far the most serious efforts to overthrow the regime occurred after Mary died, by which time the revolutionary settlement was pretty well entrenched.

In more symbolic or imaginative ways, propagandists used the figure of Mary as both wife and queen, subject and monarch, to effect a reconciliation of political opponents to William's reign. Where Tories charged William and court Whigs with corruption, or of putting the private interest of individual politicians ahead of the public good, the private, wifely Mary – whose lack of political ambition and obedience to her husband was trumpeted far and wide – could be trotted out as the exemplar of virtue, thus attributing to Mary what William's opponents claimed for themselves. Alternatively, the court faction utilized the figure of the wife/queen to drum up support for William's military campaigns against Louis XIV on the continent, construing the isolationism of the Tories in terms that evoked softness and effeminacy. Poems portraying Mary in the guise of Britain depict her as a passionate bride who at first protests against William's ventures abroad, seeking to keep him safe at home. The figure of William's mother, Belgia, castigates her efforts, telling her that she stains the honor of her son:

> you Brittania have been found of late
> Soft to a scorn, nice, and effeminate,
> From your brave ancestors degenerate.

William points out to his wife that her desires to keep him with her play right into the hands of his continental enemies:

> My vows are jointly made to love and war,
> you seem to wish me as my Gallic foe
> He'd have me always stay at home with you.

These arguments persuade Mary/Britain to let William go, as they are meant to persuade the British public to come around and support William's war efforts abroad. The poems, by combining the figures of Mary the wife and Mary the queen of the British people, served as effective propaganda on behalf of William's foreign policy. They enabled court supporters to depict opposition to William as personal selfishness and to paint isolationists as effeminate. Tory efforts to present themselves as holding a monopoly on virtue in contrast to the corrupt, "foreign" interests of the court suffered mightily from such symbolic representations of Mary, thereby reducing the possibilities for political controversy and enabling large numbers of Britons to support the dual monarchy. Mary's symbolic powers of reconciliation continued after her death, when fears of renewed political division and of a return to the immorality and sin of the Restoration gripped many Britons. Eulogists presented Mary's death as a political threat to the hard-won unity and morality of the nation, thus identifying the Jacobite and even Tory opposition with enmity toward the beloved wifely queen and the virtuous regime she represented. By confusing the private woman with the public monarch, poets could effect a reconciliation of the political divisions they had defined through Mary's death: they ended their poems with a call for Britons to extend to William their affection for, and loyalty to, Mary.

Mary's symbolic utility resided in propagandists' abilities to conflate her private and public faces: what made Mary a good woman made her a good queen as well. This possibility existed only because of the nature of the dual monarchy; while Mary was represented as upholding the private virtues of love, morality, and obedience, William administered the kingdom with a firm hand. Such symbolic ambiguity was unavailable during most of the reign of Anne, who ruled in her own right from 1702 to 1714. What made her a good woman – her ostensibly passive nature, her easy temperament, her wish to please others – rendered her in the eyes of her detractors and some of her supporters an ineffective and even dangerous ruler. The image of Mary could be manipulated to defend both private and public virtue. After the reign of Queen Anne, women could be associated only with private virtue. Indeed, as we shall see, one of the most effective means of belittling or demeaning a political cause or position would be to associate it with women.

Anne and George

In the early years of Anne's reign,[10] individuals could still offer a variety of inter-
pretations of the nature of female rule. Some, like Mary Astell, sought to exploit
Anne's reign to challenge the idea of a natural sexual hierarchy, to contest the
notion that men were naturally superior to women. If that were so, she pointed
out in the 1701 Preface to *Reflections on Marriage*, "it would be a sin for any woman
to have dominion over any man, and the greatest Queen ought not to command
but to obey her footman." Others upheld the belief in a natural sexual order by
distinguishing Anne the queen from Anne the woman, and describing the former
in manly terms. "She possesses a masculine spirit beneath the softer body of a
woman," proclaimed the author of *The Prerogative of the Breeches* in 1702. "Alone of
all her sex," Anne enjoyed a kind of symbolic masculinity that accrued to her by
virtue of her sovereignty. Her masculine prerogative was expressed in the greeting
she received upon her royal entry into Bath in 1702, where some 200 "virgins in
two companies richly attired, many of them apparelled like Amazons with bows
and arrows, and some with gilt sceptres and ensigns of regalia in their hands"
welcomed her. A different connotation adhering to femininity and militarism
appeared in a clergyman's exhortation to his countrymen upon the death of
William to exploit Anne's womanliness in their war with the French. The defeat of
Louis XIV at the hands of a mere woman, he urged, would cause him and his
subjects profound humiliation.

The array of possible meanings attached to femininity and to female rule gradually narrowed during the course of Anne's reign as politicians and propagandists
for both Whig and Tory factions began to portray her as weak and pliable, unable to
assert her own will against that of her ministers and "female favorites." As was the
case during the Restoration, political opponents frequently articulated their
protests against Anne's policies in private and sometimes sexual terms. In Anne's
case, so-called "bedchamber narratives" that pretended to be factual accounts of
the queen's affairs by those in the know told of her physical health, her emotional
state, her dependence upon certain people, and her sexual behavior. While historians insist that Anne acted decisively and relied on her own judgment in making
policy, the bedchamber narratives attributed what their authors believed to be
poor decisions to the corrupt influence exercised upon her by whichever "female
favorite" enjoyed ascendancy at the moment: Sarah Churchill, the Duchess
of Marlborough; her cousin Abigail Masham, a commoner; or the Duchess of
Somerset. Some of the narratives, by ministers perturbed by Anne's refusal to
heed their advice, hinted that Abigail Masham's hold over Anne extended beyond
mere platonic friendship. One poem of 1708, probably penned by the private
secretary to Sarah Churchill, wife of the Duke of Marlborough, described Masham's
duties at court: Anne's

secretary she was not,
Because she could not write,
But had the conduct and the care
Of some dark deeds at night.

Insinuations of Anne's sexual involvement with Masham reinforced beliefs that she was in thrall to others, not capable of ruling on her own, and gave added weight to the conviction that female rule constituted misrule and corruption. But critics of Anne as a ruler were careful always to include praise for her as a woman; the characteristics that made her a good woman in a private setting – pliability, tractability, the wish to put the desires of others before her own – were precisely those that undermined her ability to act publicly as a ruler. The bedchamber narratives contributed to a developing split between public and private virtue in the minds of contemporaries, one corresponding to John Locke's theoretical formulations that separated civic or public authority on the one hand, and familial or private authority on the other, in his *Two Treatises on Government*. Men might exercise virtue in public life, women only in private life.

Written at the time of the Exclusion Crisis in 1679, but appearing in 1689, most likely in a campaign for the passage of the Bill of Rights, Locke's *Two Treatises on Government* explored the conditions in which a monarch might be overthrown by his or her subjects. As we have seen, Locke proclaimed that in a state of nature all men and women are free, thus undermining the arguments from nature for women's subordination. So powerful were Locke's philosophical formulations against domestic patriarchy that the Church of England felt compelled to alter its doctrine in 1705 to acknowledge the mutual and reciprocal rights and obligations of men and women in marriage. Such ideas left open the door to divorce, as Locke had anticipated in likening the contract that establishes civil society with the contract that creates marital union, and in claiming that both could be revoked in the event of nonconformance with its terms. Increasingly during the 1690s, wealthy aristocrats turned to parliament to obtain divorce; in 1753 the Marriage Act gave parliament jurisdiction over marriage law, making possible a slow liberalization of divorce laws. It would not be until 1857 that divorce could be obtained by other than the very rich, and even then working-class couples could not afford the procedures. Moreover, the double standard of divorce law for men and women seriously hampered women's efforts to escape bad marriages, but the opportunity for divorce did now exist, at least theoretically, and more and more individuals would avail themselves of it.

But at the same time, Locke's *Two Treatises* – which came to serve as the theoretical justification for the settlement of 1689 by establishing men's right to resist tyranny and which stands as a founding doctrine of liberalism – provided philosophical legitimation for closing down the possibilities women had to participate in political affairs. In rebutting earlier patriarchal arguments based on analogies of state and familial power, Locke distinguished between the state and the family as civic entities, relegating the family to a private sphere disconnected from politics. In separating the two, and in insisting that qualification for participation in the public political sphere rested on property ownership and independence of the control or influence of others, Locke effectively excluded women from political activity. Married women, we have seen, could not own property under common law. Moreover, even if women did own property, under an equity settlement or as a feme sole, they were considered dependent upon men within the family and therefore disqualified from public life. Henceforth, in ideological terms, women would occupy the private sphere of home and family, where they could best display the virtue expected of them; men would demonstrate virtuous behavior in the public sphere of work and politics. More concretely, in 1690, the jurist George Petyt produced a manual of parliamentary procedure, which, for the first time, explicitly stated that a woman, no matter how much property she might possess, would not be permitted to vote. What had long been custom necessitated rigid codification if the uncertainties about power and authority in the state were not to spill over to the family and put up for grabs power and authority between men and women.

Because of the ambiguity of Locke's formulations, he could be interpreted in at least two ways. Drawing upon his arguments for support, Elizabeth Johnson decried in 1696 the "notorious violations on the liberty of freeborn English women," while an anonymous author of *The Hardships of the English Laws*, published in 1735, castigated the government for withholding from women their constitutional rights. Mary Astell reacted differently, focusing not on the liberatory elements of Locke's message but on the consequences for women in Locke's separation of power in the state and power in the family.[11] She saw that the condition of the possessive individualism that characterizes liberalism and justifies political participation for men necessitated the concomitant narrowing of women's scope. She asked pointedly in 1700, "if absolute sovereignty be not necessary in a state, how comes it to be so in a family? ... Is it not then partial in men to the last degree to contend for and practise that arbitrary dominion in their families which they abhor and exclaim against in the state? ... If all men are born free, how is it that all women are born slaves?" Astell, a Tory who opposed the revolutionary settlement, sought to weaken its ideological underpinnings by demonstrating the hypocrisy of separating public from private authority; but she was no less astute about liberalism's disadvantages for all that.

What we can see from a distance of 300 years is society's desire to put a lid on the possibilities for upheaval created by a "century of revolution." The arguments against patriarchal kings and individualistic premises about government had the potential to effect profound changes in domestic organization and in the relationships of men and women within it. As patriarchal authority and control within the family became increasingly discredited in the second half of the seventeenth century, and as liberalism's assertions that "all men were created equal" might be interpreted to include women, as they were by many women after 1688, society had to find other ways to explain and justify men's continued control of and power over women. By confining women ideologically to a separate, private sphere, by attributing to them qualities and characteristics that disqualified them from participation in the public sphere, contemporaries hit upon a way to both contain women and the anxieties produced by uncertainties about the source and location of power.

This development had accelerated during the years after Mary's death in 1694, when the appearance of increasing numbers of women who sought to make their opinions heard in political debate prompted a backlash. During the Sacheverell trial for treason in 1710, Daniel Defoe remarked that "all manner of discourse among the women runs now upon state affairs," while others noted disapprovingly that women were meddling in politics by directing their husbands' thoughts away from looking after the public good and toward looking after their own selfish private affairs. A 1697 pamphleteer observed that disproportionate numbers of women, "who generally know little or nothing of state affairs," seemed to support the Jacobite cause, as against "the best and wisest statesmen in the nation" who "are on King William's side." He advised women that "silence becomes your sex ... especially in a matter so much above your reach" and urged that when it came to politics, the "most commendable quality in a woman" was to believe and speak as her father, husband, or brother did, and to keep her own opinions and judgments to herself if she had any. These comments and others like them came from men whose convictions spanned the political spectrum, men who had in common only the strategy of attacking their political foes by associating their cause with femininity. Drawing upon an ancient tradition of political virtue that positioned women as antithetical to it, politicians could slander a cause as illegitimate or corrupt merely by affiliating it with women.

Ideas about gender, about the differences between men and women, could be so readily mobilized as a means of legitimating or scorning a particular set of politics because their apparent grounding in nature offered one of the few seemingly stable bodies of knowledge, one of the few known absolutes in a period of extraordinary uncertainty. As we have seen in the reigns of both William and Mary and of Anne, contemporaries struggled to identify and locate sovereign power or authority. In the case of William and Mary, politicians had difficulty defining just who held what power at what times; in that of Anne, they attributed royal action as originating from someone other than herself. Questions about the origins of political authority and the nature of authority after 1688 abounded, and no consensus existed as to what constituted legitimate or illegitimate politics. In the absence of such a consensus, gender filled the breach; images of what comprised "natural" characteristics of masculinity and femininity could be called upon to give the appearance of resolution to questions that had none. In the process, real women and men found themselves bound in many ways by the gender ideology invoked by such notions.

When Anne died in 1714, the questions of legitimate political authority arose once more. Mary and Anne, although protestant, were nonetheless daughters of the deposed King James II, and thus could claim at least semi-legitimacy. Indeed, Tory supporters of the Glorious Revolution, who had only a few years before proclaimed their allegiance to the doctrine of the divine right of kings, overcame their reluctance to oust James only by investing Mary and Anne with legitimate sovereignty as the children of their hapless monarch. Whigs, by contrast, had called upon the social contract theory of John Locke to defend their actions, arguing that monarchs enjoyed their power only so long as they acted to protect the liberties of "the people." If they failed to uphold their end of a contract that stipulated certain conditions, the contract could be declared void and the monarchs overthrown. The death in 1700 of Anne's last surviving child and future heir to the throne, the 11-year-old Duke of Gloucester, meant that the question of legitimacy had to be revisited.

Once again, Tories reluctantly gave their approval to the notion that parliament, as representatives of "the people," enjoyed the right to name a legitimate king. The Act of Settlement of 1701 bypassed James II and his son, the potential James III, whose catholicism not even Tories could abide, and tapped instead the closest protestant members of the Stuart line, Sophia, granddaughter of James I, and her son George, elector of Hanover. Sophia's death early in 1714 left George the sole successor to the throne upon Anne's death later that year.

The accession of George I bode ill for Tory members of parliament and those holding local offices in the countryside (George believed that the Tory-backed Treaty of Utrecht, which ended the War of the Spanish Succession in 1714, had been achieved at the expense of Hanover's interests). Purged from national and local political office in 1715, many Tories, never comfortable with the idea that the crown was parliament's to bestow, began to agitate for the return of the son of James II, known as James Stuart the Pretender, to the throne as the only legitimate monarch of Great Britain. By summertime, Jacobite mobs (so-called because of the Latin appellation "Jacob" for "James") were rioting in the midlands, in the west country, in the north, and in Scotland. Without a competent leader to guide them, the English rebellions died down soon enough, but in Scotland, ancestral home of the Stuart dynasty, some 10,000 men took up arms. By the time the Pretender appeared to lead them in late December 1715, the passion had gone out of the cause, and James could not rekindle it. The rising of "the '15," as the invasion of the north of England by Jacobite followers came to be called, failed ignominiously.

But not before it had generated great anxiety on the part of the Whig defenders of the Hanoverian regime, who set out on a campaign to firm up support for George and for the Whig regime throughout the kingdom, where Tory popularity if not Jacobite sentiment and disaffection with the Whigs ran high. Whig propagandists in the press, the pulpit, and the theater constantly conflated Tories with Jacobites, playing up the theme of their advocacy for a catholic Pretender against the protestant cause, and raising the age-old specter of the catholic church as the Whore of Rome conspiring to alter the course of legitimate succession. Processions marking the anniversary of the Hanoverian succession or the defeat of Jacobite rebellions flourished warming pans, reminiscent of the warming-pan scandal that questioned the legitimacy of James III. Whig writers depicted the plebeian women who supported the Tories as "Oister-women" and "Cinder-wenches" who "gather about Bonfires … to scream out their Principles." Tories, characterized as unruly and rebellious, could readily be rendered effeminate and vain, degraded and inconstant, admirers of arbitrary power – womanish, in short, part of the "rabble" of "Basket-women, Ballad-Singers, Bawds, Whores and Thieves." George I, by contrast, appeared in Whig spectacles and theatrical presentations, in ballads and broadsheets, as the epitome of masculine virtue, the virile, patriarchal monarch who would preside over a moral nation and furnish his subjects with legitimate heirs for years to come. Jacobite propagandists sought to undermine this image of the virile, virtuous King George and question his fitness to rule by alluding to his being cuckolded by his wife's lover, Count Königsmark. "Make room for the Cuckoldy King and Send him to Hanover," sang one woman in Westminster, whose efforts landed her in jail. Supporters of James III rejected George I as lacking all the qualities of "manly" kingship, claiming those characteristics for the Pretender instead. From both camps, then, Whig and Jacobite alike, emerged an image of legitimate power as masculine, virile, and virtuous. Illegitimate power, by contrast, was represented as effeminate and emasculated.

With the death of Anne and the succession of the Hanoverian king, George I, the questions about authority raised continually throughout the seventeenth century appeared to be resolved. Constitutional monarchy governed by liberal principles of limited representative government and the rule of law seemed to be well established, despite the attempts in 1715 and again in 1745 to put a catholic Stuart on the throne. Because both the concerns about power and the solutions put forward to allay them had been articulated in gendered and sexual imagery, resolution of the public political questions required a resolution within the ideological system that defined the nature of men and women and governed their relations with one another. Locke's model of separate spheres of public and private, into which men and women could be comfortably fitted according to their "nature," made it possible for contemporaries to give order and stability to their world. This model would combine with other intellectual tendencies and with economic developments to dramatically transform society and the relations of men and women within it.

NOTES

1 See Amy Louise Erickson, *Women and Property in Early Modern England* (London and New York, 1993).

2 For this and the following discussion of religion, see Patricia Crawford, *Women and Religion in England, 1500–1720* (London, 1993).

3 For this discussion of early feminist impulses, see Moira Ferguson, ed., *First Feminists: British Women Writers, 1578–1799* (Bloomington, IN, 1985); Anne Laurence, *Women in England, 1500–1760. A Social History* (New York, 1994); Sara Heller Mendelsohn, *The Mental World of Stuart Women. Three Studies* (Amherst, MA, 1987); Ruth Perry, "Mary Astell and the feminist critique of possessive individualism," *Eighteenth-Century Studies* 23(4) (summer 1990): 444–57; Hilda Smith, *Reason's Disciples: Seventeenth-Century English Feminists* (Urbana, IL, 1982).

4 For this discussion of "rakes," see G.J. Barker-Benfield, *The Culture of Sensibility. Sex and Society in Eighteenth-Century Britain* (Chicago, 1992).

5 The following discussion of pornographic political comment is based on the path-breaking work of Rachel Weil. See her "Sometimes a scepter is only a scepter: Pornography and politics in Restoration England," in Lynn Hunt, ed., *The Invention of Pornography. Obscenity and the Origins of Modernity, 1500–1800* (New York, 1993), and "Sexual Ideology and Political Propaganda in England, 1680–1714" (Dissertation, Princeton University, 1991).

6 The following discussion is drawn from Rachel Weil, "The politics of legitimacy: Women and the warming-pan scandal," in Lois G. Schwoerer, ed., *The Revolution of 1688–89. Changing Perspectives* (Cambridge, 1992).

7 Mary Lyndon Shanley, "Marriage contract and social contract in seventeenth-century English political thought," *Western Political Quarterly* XXXII(1), March 1979: 79–91.

8 For discussion of the warming-pan scandal and its legacy, see Weil, "The politics of legitimacy."

9 For this discussion of the Glorious Revolution and its implications for gender relationships I have relied upon Howard Nenner, "Pretense and pragmatism: The response to uncertainty in the succession crisis of 1689," in Lois G. Schwoerer, ed., *The Revolution of 1688–89. Changing Perspectives* (Cambridge, 1992); Lois G. Schwoerer, "Women and the Glorious Revolution," *Albion* 18(2) (summer, 1986): 195–218; W.A. Speck, "William – and Mary?" in Lois G. Schwoerer, ed., *The Revolution of 1688–89. Changing Perspectives* (Cambridge, 1992); and Rachel Weil, "Sexual ideology and political propaganda in England, 1680–1714" (Dissertation, Princeton University, 1991).

10 See Rachel Weil's excellent "Sexual ideology and political propaganda in England," for a complete treatment of Anne's reign. The following discussion derives from her dissertation.

11 See Perry, "Mary Astell and the feminist critique of possessive individualism," 444–57.

SOURCES

G.J. Barker-Benfield, *The Culture of Sensibility. Sex and Society in Eighteenth-Century Britain*. Chicago, 1992.

Patricia Crawford, "Women's published writings, 1600–1700," in Mary Prior, ed., *Women in English Society, 1500–1800*. London, 1985.

——, *Women and Religion in England, 1500–1720*. London, 1993.

Moira Ferguson, ed., *First Feminists: British Women Writers, 1578–1799*. Bloomington, IN, 1985.

Paul Hammond, "The King's two bodies: representations of Charles II," in Jeremy Black and Jeremy Gregory, eds, *Culture, Politics and Society in Britain, 1660–1800*. Manchester, 1991.

Anne Laurence, *Women in England, 1500–1760. A Social History*. New York, 1994.

Sara Heller Mendelsohn, *The Mental World of Stuart Women. Three Studies*. Amherst, 1987.

Howard Nenner, "Pretense and pragmatism: The response to uncertainty in the succession crisis of 1689," in Lois G. Schwoerer, ed., *The Revolution of 1688–89. Changing Perspectives*. Cambridge, 1992.

Ruth Perry, "Mary Astell and the feminist critique of possessive individualism," *Eighteenth-Century Studies* 23(4) (summer 1990): 444–57.

Mary Poovey, *The Proper Lady and the Woman Writer*. Chicago, 1984.

Lois G. Schwoerer, "Women and the Glorious Revolution," *Albion* 18(2), summer, 1986: 195–218.

——, "Women's public political voice in England: 1640–1740," in Hilda L. Smith, ed., *Women Writers and the Early Modern British Political Tradition*. Cambridge, 1998.

Hilda Smith, *Reason's Disciples: Seventeenth-Century English Feminists*. Urbana, IL, 1982.

W.A. Speck, "William – and Mary?" in Lois G. Schwoerer, ed., *The Revolution of 1688–89. Changing Perspectives*. Cambridge, 1992.

David Underdown, *Revel, Riot and Rebellion: Popular Politics and Culture in England, 1603–1660*. Oxford, 1985.

Rachel Weil, "Sexual ideology and political propaganda in England, 1680–1714." Dissertation, Princeton University, 1991.

——, "The politics of legitimacy: Women and the warming-pan scandal," in Lois G. Schwoerer, ed., *The Revolution of 1688–89. Changing Perspectives*. Cambridge, 1992.

——, "Sometimes a scepter is only a scepter: Pornography and politics in Restoration England," in Lynn Hunt, ed., *The Invention of Pornography. Obscenity and the Origins of Modernity, 1500–1800*. New York, 1993.

Part II

The eighteenth century

Engendering virtue: politics and morality in the age of commercial capitalism

GENERAL INTRODUCTION

The revolutionary settlement of 1689 and the Hanoverian succession of 1714 seemed to put to rest questions about authority raised throughout Britain during the turbulent years of the seventeenth century. Parliament triumphed over would-be absolutist monarchs; the Church of England asserted its rightful ecclesiastical place over catholics and dissenters. The rule of law conferred legal equality on adult white men; the gentry secured their absolute rights to property and established political control over the nation through their monopoly in parliament and their entrenchment in the countryside. As MPs, justices of the peace, and magistrates, landed élites emerged as the undisputed champions from the explosive conflicts of the "century of revolution." The Glorious Revolution of 1688, historians claimed, following wishful contemporaries, made possible the "growth of political stability"[1] that characterized the eighteenth century.

The picture of order, liberty, and stability conjured up by this so-called Whig interpretation of history obscures the conflicts and disturbances that characterized the eighteenth century. Whatever assuaging of anxieties relating to property rights and political power the gentry achieved by means of the revolutionary settlement might easily be offset by many other sources of psychic distress arising from the residue of a "world turned upside down" and of the revolutionary settlement itself. Religious differences, foreign wars, overseas expansion, massive demographic change, radical politics, women's increased public visibility and political activity, disturbances within colonial territories, and revolution in America and in France — all these contributed to deep-seated and broad-based feelings of insecurity in eighteenth-century British society.

In politics, as we have seen, anxiety about the proper succession of monarchs monopolized political debate in the early part of the century as the health of childless Anne broke down. The transfer of power to the Hanoverian line of protestant George I in 1714, and the failure of the Jacobite rising seeking to place the catholic

Stuart Pretender James III on the throne in 1715, put an end to this particular question. After 1715, theorists and commentators seemed obsessed by the problems of corruption and virtue in a polity increasingly organized around commerce and empire. By the 1760s, the idiom of politics revolved around questions of natural right and of contract, and their corollary, the possibility of resistance to political authority – these issues took on intense interest in the 1790s in the aftermath of the French Revolution. As a consequence of the reforms implemented in revolutionary France in the 1790s, and of the outbreak of war with France in 1793, British political discourse tended to emphasize the state as a source of stability. In each of these successive debates, the notion of citizenship – of who represented the national interest and who should be permitted to participate in political affairs – rested on the concept of virtue, a concept that was itself transformed in the course of the eighteenth century.

The transformations in political discourse took place against a background that provided a particular source of acute anxiety: the challenges posed by commercial capitalist expansion to the political, social, and gender orders of landed society. Concerns about each of them were often conflated in the minds of British politicians, theorists, and moralists, and this very conflation provided a partial solution, at the end of the eighteenth century, for the problems about politics and morality they raised in a period of unprecedented economic and social transformation. By conflating gender with political and social anxieties generated by commercial capitalism, articulating those concerns through the idiom of "virtue," and then splitting them off by identifying women with private, sexual virtue in the home, and men with the public activities of the marketplace, contemporaries were able both to tame their fears about capitalism and contain the dangers created in their minds by what appeared to be, in the words of one historian, "a crisis in men's control over women."[2] In the process they developed a new ideology of justification for bourgeois, capitalist society, and a new evaluation of and set of expectations for men and women. The publication in 1776 of Adam Smith's *The Wealth of Nations* – considered the classic celebration of capitalist consumption – and the consolidation of the ideology of separate spheres for men and women in the quarter century following together served to herald the advent of modern British society.

NOTES

1 J.H. Plumb, *The Growth of Political Stability, 1675–1725* (London, 1967).
2 Anthony Fletcher, *Gender, Sex and Subordination in England, 1500–1800* (New Haven, 1995), p. xvi.

Chapter 3

Challenges to virtue

The economic revolutions, 1690–1780

The concept of virtue occupies a central place in eighteenth-century English and Scottish political and moral theory. Drawn from the Aristotelian and renaissance republican traditions of citizenship, which saw in participation in civic life the sole means through which men (and it was only men and men of independent wealth) could achieve their full human potential, virtue signified the capacity of human beings to govern themselves. Whether that capacity derived from God, from nature, or from reason, the self-knowledge and self-command articulated in the ideal of virtue enabled "political man" to subordinate private interests to the public good. For Aristotle, the *oikos*, or landed household, provided the requisite material basis upon which independence and thus virtue and citizenship rested. Machiavelli substituted the bearing of arms for the possession of *oikos*. Seventeenth-century English political theorists of all stripes regarded landed property, what they called "real" as opposed to "mobile" property, as the *sine qua non* of the virtuous citizen. This corresponded nicely, of course, with the predominance enjoyed by landed élites after 1688.

The gentry of England and Wales, Scotland, and Ireland justified their political power on the basis of and took their identity as men from neo-classical ideals of virtue. At the heart of virtue lay personal independence. Landed property enabled individuals to exercise what was regarded as their natural political capacity free from government patronage, a subject of great concern during the 1670s when the court of Charles II restored patronage as a political instrument. Mobile property, by contrast, rendered men "artificial," and made them subject to appetites and passions that could be manipulated or exploited by a corrupting sovereign and thus unfit to participate in political life. As ownership of land and possession of independence could be enjoyed only by men, citizenship and virtue were masculine entities; parliament further ratified the masculine nature of virtue and politics in 1711 when it passed a law limiting eligibility for election to the House of Commons to those owning substantial amounts of land. Those holding property in the form of stocks or bank deposits could not qualify. Moreover, the gendered nature of virtue and property logically entailed upon possessors of mere "mobile property" a feminine quality, to which the susceptibility to appetites and passions could be adduced.

The financial revolution

The revolutionary settlement of 1689 obligated England to assist William III in his war against Louis XIV, a commitment that had unforeseen consequences in a continued series of continental wars throughout the eighteenth century, as we shall see in the next chapter. In order to provide the troops and revenue necessary to prosecute King William's War (the War of the League of Augsburg, 1689–97), the government created a number of institutions of public credit that enabled it to tap the wealth of the country without resorting to taxation or short-term borrowing. Chief amongst the mechanisms developed by the government to facilitate access to private caches of money and treasures that were literally lying around in safes or buried underground were the creation of the national debt and of the agency charged with administering it, the Bank of England. By 1696, a system of permanent borrowing was in place whereby investors could buy annuities from the bank that would guarantee them an income from the state, thus transforming what had once been short-term loans to the state by individuals or corporate entities into government securities. These investments provided the government with ready cash with which to prosecute the wars with France that took place over the next century.

The financial revolution of the 1690s, but most particularly the creation of the Bank of England and the national debt, provoked heated political debate.[1] Early eighteenth-century political theorists argued not about "rights" but about "corruption," and corruption is a problem of virtue, not of rights. At issue was the question of personal independence of the sovereign power: the Bank of England, in establishing the means by which government could tap the wealth of the country by inducing investors to lend capital and, not incidentally, greater political stability to the state, rendered those investors captive to the state for their material survival. It also, by financing the creation of larger armies and permanent bureaucracies, enlarged the fund of patronage available to the court. As the volume of investment grew ever greater, the English – and then, after 1707 with the Act of Union with Scotland, the British – government expanded the scope and range of its activities beyond what that investment could cover, guaranteeing creditors that they would be repaid with revenues collected and investments made in the future. Mobile property in the form of government shares based on credit emerged as the engine of capitalist expansion; the financial revolution succeeded in enriching, enlarging, and stabilizing the post-revolutionary regime, making possible the commercial revolution and the pursuit of empire.

But the national debt – what contemporaries called "public credit" – also produced acute disquiet, especially for landed élites who saw it as constituting a threat to real property and thus to their political hegemony. The landed classes opposed not so much the development of a market in traded or manufactured goods – which, after all, could at least potentially be a route to achieving independence and therefore virtue – as a market in credit, which they saw as establishing a new form of property altogether: property not in land or tangible assets such as a shipload of tobacco or naval stores, but property in government office, in government stock, and, because of the expansion of the national debt beyond the amount of investment currently available, in government expectations to which the national debt had mortgaged Britain's future. In making government dependent upon its investors and those investors in turn dependent upon government, "public credit" established relationships between governments and citizens which citizens themselves could purchase and that governments could utilize to own citizens. The independence so crucial to virtuous citizenship in the classical mode could not be sustained in such a system.

The creation of the national debt, with its promises of future payment deriving from future growth, compelled contemporaries to devise a new belief system whereby they could impute to one another an ability to develop into someone other than or beyond what they were now. An ideology of progress and an image of a secular future was an essential ingredient in sustaining a commercial, capitalist society. Just what belief in that future could rest on, however, was not self-evident: experience of the future did not exist, and reason could provide no means of predicting what it would look like. What seemed available to those trying to conjure up the future were imagination, fantasy, passion, and desire.

Individuals who thought at all about the nature of their society recognized that one increasingly tied to the vagaries of financial speculation rather than to the solid, visible, seemingly eternal rhythms of life on the land entailed the dependence of all men upon all men, a situation that ran counter to classical notions of independence so vital to the exercise of virtue. Worse still, the stability of such a civic polity rested on very little more than hope on the part of all members of society that each could be counted upon to pay the debts he or she owed to the rest. The conduct of affairs in such a society required that individuals determine – on the basis of no more than mere opinion – if others, many of them yet unborn, would pay off at a future time that might not ever come to pass. In such a society, it appeared to political and moral theorists, men were governed by opinion, opinion that might be little more than fantasy about the future.

The unpredictability and instability of such a belief system generated intense efforts to bring it to heel. Those efforts more often than not involved the rendering of unpredictability and instability in the guise of the female: just as the Roman and renaissance virtu's opposite was the feminine *Fortuna*, so too, in early eighteenth-century journalism devoted to questions of public credit, neo-classical virtue's nemesis, Credit, was depicted as a goddess. The goddess Credit, in the writings of Daniel Defoe, Richard Steele, Joseph Addison, Bernard de Mandeville, and other apologists for the Whig commercial regime, stands in for fantasy, the passions, and wildly dynamic change.

In 1706, Defoe's *Review* described Credit as an inconstant, irrational creature:

> This is a coy Lass, and wonderful chary of her self; yet a most necessary, useful, industrious Creature. ... If once she be disoblig'd, she's the most diffi-cult to be Friends again with us, of anything in the World; and yet she will court those most, that have no occasion for her. ... 'Tis a strange thing to think, how absolute this Lady is; how despotickly she governs all her Actions: If you court her, you lose her, or must buy her at unreasonable Rates; and if you do, she is always jealous of you, and Suspicious; and if you don't discharge her to a Title of your Agreement, she is gone, and perhaps may never come again as long as you live; and if she does, 'til with long Entreaty and abundance of Difficulty.

Addison, likening Credit to a woman of alternately frail and robust health, wrote in the *Spectator*:

> She appeared indeed infinitely timorous in all her Behaviour; And, whether it was from the Delicacy of her Constitution, or that she was troubled with Vapours, as I was afterwards told by one who I found was none of her Well-wishers, she changed Colour, and startled at everything she heard. She was likewise ... a greater Valetudinarian than any I had ever met with, even in her own Sex, and subject to such Momentary Consumptions, that in the twin-kling of an Eye, she would fall away from the most florid Complexion, and the most healthful State of Body, and wither into a Skeleton. Her Recoveries were often as sudden as her Decays, insomuch that she would revive in a Moment out of a wasting Distemper, into a Habit of the highest Health and Vigour.

Both Addison and Defoe sought to justify and defend the Whig commercial regime of the early eighteenth century, and made heroic efforts to endow commerce with the attributes of virtue. To that end, they were keen to tie Credit's health and stability to public confidence, to embue her with the capacity to discern "the stock of real merit," in the words of Defoe. When public order faced threats from an anti-Whig mob, from popery, or from republicanism, Credit withered and collapsed. As Defoe put it in 1710:

Credit is too wary, too Coy a Lady to stay with any People upon such mean Conditions; if you will entertain this Virgin, you must act upon the nice Principles of Honour, and Justice; you must preserved Sacred all the Foundations, and build regular Structures upon them; you must answer all Demands, with a respect to the Solemnity, and Value of the Engagement; with respect to Justice, and Honour; and without respect to Parties – If this is not observ'd, Credit will not come; No, tho' the Queen should call; tho' the Parliament shou'd call, or tho' the whole Nation should call.

With public order restored and confidence returned to the land, Credit recovered and even thrived. The Whig apologists attempted to turn credit into opinion, to sever its ties to the wild fluctuations of hopes and fears, of imagination and fantasy, of passions and appetites, and to anchor it solidly to the day-to-day experiences of trade and commerce in real, if mobile, goods. Appealing to notions of public virtue, they argued that Credit responded generously to conditions of social and moral health, that she had the reasoning facilities to discern when those conditions prevailed and when they did not. By eliminating the fantasy and unreality that seemed to underpin the world of public credit, and replacing them with concrete experiences of real commodities, Defoe, Addison, and others sought to place commercial activity squarely within the realm of virtue. They were unable to do so persuasively, because opinion, or confidence, seemed no more capable of withstanding the extreme oscillations between hope and fear than credit had been. Opinion, contemporaries held, was enslaved to the passions of hope and fear. Moreover, the classical discourse of virtue would not admit of any kind of virtuous exchange relationship, seeing in exchange the conditions for dependence and corruption. The development of a bourgeois ideology that affirmed capitalism as conducive to the public good would have to await the transformation of passions into interests.

For contemporaries regarded exchange capitalism, especially in the aftermath of the disastrous South Sea Bubble, as a system based on speculation rather than on calculation, and as such, a system grounded not in rationality but in fantasy and passion, entities that in other contexts occupied the realm of the feminine. In early 1720, the South Sea Company, chartered in 1711 to trade with the Spanish colonies in the Caribbean, took over some three-fifths of the national debt, expecting to make substantial profits by converting government annuities to South Sea Company shares and selling them to investors. Success in these endeavors depended upon the willingness of investors to continue to purchase and to send up the price of stock, which they did for months of frenzied buying. When buying seemed to fall off a bit in mid-summer, the directors of the South Sea Company resorted to all kinds of questionable and dishonest tactics to keep share prices high. They failed, and the stock crashed in September, bringing ruin to thousands of stockholders. The South Sea Company's close ties to the state through its charter and its purchase of the national debt, and its bribes to ministerial and court politicians, meant that the government could not escape from the scandal unleashed by the bursting of the bubble. Government and politics, in the minds of many angry citizens, appeared to have been put in jeopardy by the irrational forces of passion, fantasy, and appetite, forces that contemporaries believed fed on themselves and knew no moral limits.

The commercial revolution

The financial revolution made possible an expansion of commercial enterprise and imperial trade unprecedented in Britain's history. The development of new capitalist techniques in agriculture and manufacturing, increased trade at home and with colonies overseas, and an explosion of population growth after 1750 produced vast economic growth and dramatic social change. Increased prosperity consequent upon the commercial revolution changed the character of Britain's social order, expanding the number of those people who comprised the middling ranks – shopkeepers, manufacturers, wealthier independent artisans, civil servants, professionals, and lesser merchants – people whose annual income of £50 to £2,000 enabled them to live with some degree of "independence." Some 170,000 middling people lived in English cities in 1700; by 1800, those numbers had swelled to 475,000. Many others populated smaller villages and rural towns, to say nothing of the Scottish and Welsh urban population who do not figure in these estimates. Middling people as a whole constituted perhaps 25 percent to 30 percent of the entire population of England and Wales, compared to the 1 percent of the population who made up the aristocracy and gentry, and the 70 percent to 75 percent of the population who, if they were fortunate, labored on the land or in the workshops of others in return for wages. Certainly the ranks of the middling enjoyed the fastest growth during the course of the eighteenth century.

The commercial revolution benefited from new and enlarged sources of trade, new means of financial exchange, and new techniques of production, but it was perhaps even more a phenomenon associated with consumption. Throughout the course of the eighteenth century, many Britons – the English and those Scots living in Edinburgh and the lowland towns – enjoyed a consumer boom after 1750 that amounted to a revolution in consumption. Individuals delighted in the purchasing of commodities as never before, buying not simply necessities or even decencies, but luxury items as well. Fashions that once only the very rich could afford now made their way into the wardrobes of the middling ranks, enabling those of "meaner condition" to clothe themselves in the garb of the aristocracy.

More people than ever before could afford the new goods appearing on shop counters: spices, sugar, coffee and tea, tobacco, cheeses of all kinds. Prosperity displayed itself in embellishments to and new arrangements within the home. Formerly modest dwellings became transformed into elegant homes with the addition of carpeting to wooden flooring, and wainscoting to plaster walls; and the replacement of stone hearths with marble, and of simple oak furniture with more fancy designs in walnut and mahogany. Houses became larger and space within homes increasingly differentiated, so that sleeping quarters were separated from kitchens and living rooms. Privacy became possible and then normative; ultimately, it became seen as a necessary component of middle-class life. The increased availability of domestic consumer goods such as furniture, chamber pots, trinkets and knick-knacks, table and bed linens, mirrors, carpets, wall-hangings, pictures and prints, dry goods, kitchen utensils and implements rendered homes far more comfortable, and gave domestic life an appeal it had not had before. Middling people, who made up at least a quarter of England's population by mid-century, could furnish their homes with items that would not have been found in aristocratic households fifty years earlier. Lower-ranked households benefited from the commercial revolution as well, though not nearly as fully or as widely as the middling sorts. Many plebeians, in fact, as we shall see below, found themselves displaced by the changes of the economic revolutions, forced into waged work or on to parish relief in order to maintain their families.

Women produced much of the consumer demand that helped to fuel the commercial revolution of the eighteenth century. Certainly men shopped for clothing and goods, but their forays into the shops of haberdashers and furniture- or carriage-makers tended to be occasional, in contrast to women's consumption patterns, which demonstrated a regularity consistent with the running of a household that required daily purchases of mundane items. Manufacturers and retailers recognized that consumer decisions rested largely with the mistresses of households and pitched their goods accordingly. Novels, themselves a new phenomenon linked to the creation of an expanded market system, testified to the pleasures women experienced in consumption, if only to condemn them, and helped to broadcast the possibilities for pleasure to thousands of readers throughout the country.

The commercial revolution and its concomitant revolution in consumption patterns excited much adverse commentary from critics and defenders of the Whig commercial regime alike. Tories and Whigs railed against "luxury," the former because of its inherent corruption of the virtuous citizen, the latter because of its potential to undermine the moral community. Like credit, luxury operated in a world governed not by reason but by passion, with all the connotations of the feminine carried by its counterpart. During the eighteenth century, luxury became politicized, exploited in a running political battle between Whigs and Tories on the one hand, and between the upper and middling orders on the other. The qualities of diligence, hard work, frugality, sobriety, and modesty, aristocrats and gentry claimed, justified their political control over the country. Whigs seized upon fashion to argue their case against the Jacobite tendencies of the Tories on the one hand and the upstart middling ranks on the other.[2] By displaying themselves not in the finery and ostentation of Restoration style, but in the modest dress of "a plain and uniform costum," they proclaimed their antipathy to and victory over the French-influenced courts of Charles II and James II, and their predominance over the middling and lower orders. Visitors to the courts of Charles and James had noted the elaborate French fashions worn by élite Englishmen and -women, but after 1688 commentary focused on the tendency for upper-class Englishmen, but not Englishwomen, to sport fashions "temper'd with becoming modesty." Louis de Muralt described Englishmen in 1694 as having "no great opinion of finery or dressing, ... or generally of any thing that serves only to set off the body; whether 'tis because they are not over handsome, or that they shun whatever requires much care, or puts them under any constraint. They have too good an opinion of themselves, to imitate other people; and, in a word, they are such great enemies to every kind of slavery ... that they depend but very little upon custom." Francis Mission concurred, writing in 1698 that "generally speaking, the English men dress in a plain uniform manner."

By the early eighteenth century, a much more restrained style of dress prevailed amongst men of the upper ranks. They sought to demonstrate their public virtue by deploying a modest and sober style in contrast to the conspicuous consumption that, they claimed, characterized the fashions of women and lower-ranked men with aspirations to greater status. By adopting a style of "noble simplicity" and denouncing the world of fashion and luxury, gentlemen trumpeted their virtue, asserting their claims to social, moral, and political leadership. As we shall see in Chapter 5, middling men would take up the same claims on the same grounds of plainness and virtue when they made demands for political participation later in the century. By that time, however, what constituted virtue had undergone a dramatic transformation.

Represented alternately as "French," "asiatic," or "female" – all of which denoted effeminacy, which, in the eighteenth century, referred not to homosexuality as it does today but the too frequent association of men with women, whose qualities of sensuality, pleasure-loving, and appetite were believed to weaken men's independence and resolve – luxury threatened not just the good order of polity and society, but the very masculine identity of élite Englishmen and Scotsmen as well. For luxury, like credit in the early years of the eighteenth century, had strong and long-lived associations with desire, passion, and disobedience.[3] From the time of Augustine right up through the seventeenth century, lust for money and possessions, lust for power, and sexual lust had comprised the three principle sins of fallen man, brought down by Eve's luxurious partaking of the fruit of the tree of knowledge. In 1644, a puritan moralist claimed that the adornment of hair would lead to "whoredom … drinking, stealing, lying, murder, and HELL." Until Francis Bacon rent them apart, enabling later moralists to advocate the pitting of one passion against another in the hope of countervailing it, these vices were regarded as indissoluble and synergistic, feeding on and inciting one another to sinful indulgence. "Wherever you see pride in the front, sure lust marches in the rear," asserted one writer in 1716. The passions that at one and the same time lay at the heart of, and were unleashed by, luxury promised to undermine the independence, the reason, and the personal autonomy of virtuous men, their very masculinity.

The commercial revolution, then, posed a number of threats to the social and gender order of Britain. First, given the representations of credit and luxury as female and the understanding of commercial society as founded upon the volatile passions, desires, fantasies, and appetites usually associated with women, eighteenth-century "economic man" constituted a feminized, even an effeminate being, subject to forces that undermined independence and virtue. Second, as middling persons would claim increasingly after mid-century, the prosperity produced by commerce made it theoretically possible for all to be independent. If the independence that enabled citizens to be virtuous and thus politically active no longer required landed wealth but could be construed in other ways, the categories that distinguished between the independent citizen and the dependent, disenfranchised citizen would have to be rendered on the basis of gender and, as we shall see in Chapter 4, race. Women's consuming activities were, and were seen to be by contemporaries, responsible for the home demand that drove the commercial revolution of the eighteenth century, making the redrawing of categories of political eligibility all the more urgent. In the realms of the political, the social, and the cultural, men's involvement in commercial economic activity served to call into question their manliness and thus their fitness for political power. It would be in the realms of both the cultural and the social that the solutions to this dilemma would have to be imposed and a rationale for middling participation in political life fashioned.

Turning passions into interests

The dangers of effeminacy deriving from speculation, evident in the early decades of the eighteenth century, joined those found to be inherent in "luxury" in the second half of the eighteenth century. Apologists for the Whig commercial regime thus faced two intricately related tasks: they had to devise some ideological means of rendering a commercial system based in credit virtuous on the one hand, and they had to subject the unruly, and potentially effeminizing, passions and appetites of commercial capitalism to masculine discipline and management on the other. The first necessitated the removal of the feminine, in representational terms, from the public arena; the second required transforming passions into interests. The combination of these moves, by the end of the eighteenth century, emptied commercial capitalism and women of their sexually desiring content, masculinizing and rationalizing the marketplace, and domesticating the female.

"Everything in the world is purchased by labor," wrote David Hume in "Of commerce," in 1752, the motivating force behind which is "the passions," the desire to obtain pleasure through the accumulation of objects.[4] In the realm of the cultural or ideological, the problem for apologists of the new commercial society was that, as contemporaries recognized, desire, whether it be for consumer goods or for sexual satisfaction, served as the linchpin of theories of capitalism. As we have seen, passion and desire were understood to be central to the new commercial society; contemporaries could discern no clear conceptual boundary between sexual passion and desire, and the appetite for items of consumption. Those boundaries had to be firmed up, a solution found to the dilemma produced by commercial capitalism: how does one create a moral community in a society that depends for its success on the unleashing of desire. English and Scottish moralists and philosophers debated this problem throughout the eighteenth century. Their solution involved splitting "the passions" into their component parts – passion for power, for goods, and for sex – and arraying one against the others as a means of controlling them and benefiting humanity as a whole. In a formulation that would go far to reconcile moralists to the capitalist regime, Hume asserted in "Of interest" that "it is an infallible consequence of all industrious professions, to … make the love of gain prevail over the love of pleasure."

Hume's thinking depended upon seventeenth-century treatises of philosophers such as Francis Bacon, Thomas Hobbes, and John Locke who sought to harness the "passions" of human nature by pitting against them the "interests" of men. Seventeenth-century usages of the term "interest" included a whole array of human aspirations, not simply material ones; the word connoted a mental process of thoughtful calculation as to how those aspirations were to be achieved. After 1688, with political stability assured and religious questions at least partially put to rest, "interests" increasingly came to describe a more exclusive *economic* aspiration, in keeping with other terms such as "corruption" and "fortune," whose meanings narrowed from broad political senses to refer to monetary conditions. With the narrowing of the word "interests" to a monetary sense, it was possible now to create an opposition between interests and passions in such a way as to suggest that one set of passions, which contemporaries referred to as greed, avarice, or love of lucre, could be mobilized against other kinds of passions such as ambition, lust for power, or sexual lust. This transition took time, and clearly had not been completed when Bernard de Mandeville's *The Fable of the Bees* appeared in 1714. Subtitled *Private Vices, Publick Benefits*, Mandeville argued that personal indulgence brought about prosperity. Vice, in the guise of luxury, fueled the engines of commercial enterprise, producing benefits for the public as a whole. The furious reception given to *The Fable of the Bees* when it appeared testifies to the power of the threat to morality and order from conspicuous consumption still felt by contemporaries. So bald a validation of luxury could not be tolerated by early eighteenth-century public moralists, who denounced Mandeville vociferously in newspapers, from pulpits, and in the courts.

Hume moved the debate further along. By referring to the "passion of interest" or the "interested affection" as synonymous with the "avidity of acquiring goods and possessions" or "love of gain," he equated commerce with the positive connotation of "interest" in its larger sense of the enlightened conduct of human affairs. He endowed trade and money-making with the capacity to stimulate the exercise of "benign human proclivities at the expense of some malignant ones," and in so doing, cause the destructive and disastrous elements of human nature associated with the passions to decline and fall away.

Transforming passions into interests emptied them of their feminine content. Eighteenth-century meanings of interest, like their seventeenth-century predecessors, connoted rational calculation and decision-making designed to improve one's position. Reason and calculation were pre-eminently masculine qualities, which women, contemporary wisdom had it, did not share. Removing passion – pre-eminently a feminine attribute – from the exchange mechanisms of commerce and money-making placed those activities much more securely within a masculine domain.

In transforming the passions – rendered as feminine – into the interests – depicted as masculine – these thinkers also brought about a transformation in the concept of virtue. Hume and Adam Smith recognized that commercial life and virtue in its neo-classical form could not be made compatible with one another, that to try to cobble together some accommodation between the two was not only not possible but perhaps undesirable. Rather, different social values more consistent with commercial society had to be found, a quest that resulted in the splitting off of morality from society. Society would be depicted in the writings of Hume and Smith as a kind of machine operating in such a way that the exchange of goods and the division of labor, by means of which those goods were produced and exchanged, worked to transform universal selfishness into universal well-being. This kind of thinking, finding its apotheosis in *The Wealth of Nations*, provided a way to explain how society must of necessity function on the basis of pursuit of self-interest, but it left both civic society and the individual who sought to uphold it without any systematic moral structure. That moral structure – provided by the ideals of neo-classical virtue in the old society – would be found elsewhere, in the private world of home and family, embodied in the figure of wife and mother.

During the second half of the eighteenth century, Hume, Smith, and other English and Scottish philosophers spoke frequently of "the polished nations" of

Western Europe, whose increased commercial activity and therefore increased wealth distinguished them from "rude and barbarous" nations characteristic of the ancient, feudal world of farmers and warriors. In an elaborate formulation of the transition from the agrarian to the commercial society, Adam Smith argued that the increase in wealth from exchange produced a far more just and secure polity than that possible under the reign of presumably virtuous feudal lords. Before the advent of commercial activity, great lords had no alternative but to share their surplus agricultural products with their tenants, who owned no property of their own and thus had no security, and with their retainers, who were entirely dependent upon their lords and provided them with private armies with which the lords felt emboldened to make war. "The king was … incapable of restraining the violence of the great lords," Smith explained. "They [made] war according to their own discretion, almost continually upon one another, and very frequently upon the king; and the open country … [was] a scene of violence, rapine, and disorder." With the introduction of commerce and manufacture, goods appeared on which the great lords might expend their surplus wealth: "a pair of diamond buckles, or … something as frivolous and useless." The lords found these "trinkets and baubles" so attractive that they chose to spend their wealth not on supporting armed retainers but on commodities. The desire for even greater wealth with which to buy manufactures led them to enter into longer-term leases with their tenants and to engage them in more business-like relations: "they gradually bartered their whole power and authority" away in return for the possession of luxury objects. "Having sold their birth-right," Smith recounted, "for … the playthings of children …, they became as insignificant as any substantial burgher or tradesman in a city." The trader, acting on the basis of self-interest, and the now-consuming great lord, motivated by the gratification "of the most childish vanity," produced a political society in which "the great proprietors were no longer capable of interrupting the regular execution of justice, or of disturbing the peace of the country."

In the writings of the Scottish Enlightenment philosophers in particular, then, commerce and capitalism took on the power to "civilize" individuals and whole societies. In introducing the exchange of property in goods between individuals, commerce provided the means by which men learned that they enjoyed things in common, that they shared interests with one another. Commerce acquainted individuals with the arts of social intercourse conducive to smooth social interaction; it helped them to refine their manners and behave "politely." "Commerce tends to wear off those prejudices which maintain distinctions and animosity between nations," insisted the Scottish historian William Robertson in 1769. "It *softens and polishes* the manners of men."

All of this amounted to a campaign to vindicate capitalism and to legitimate its practitioners as being engaged in a masculine, virtuous pursuit of wealth.

Commerce, endowed with the power to "civilize" barbarous society, was rendered virtuous and masculine by redefining virtue through the terms of politeness and manners. The relationships into which commerce propelled individuals were not political but social; consequently, the qualities they compelled individuals to develop in order to function well within them were not described as "virtues" – a political term – but "manners," a word connoting ethical mores. The so-called "sentimental school" of philosophers such as Shaftesbury, Hume, Ferguson, Hutcheson, and Smith declared that commerce in things led to commerce with people. Both called forth passions, to which the speculative, acquisitive man of the eighteenth century was highly susceptible, but both also had the power to moderate the destructive power of the passions by subjecting them to the "natural affections" of benevolence and generosity, by exposing them to the beneficent influences of sociability and "sensibility."

Through social and commercial intercourse, moral philosophers argued in a body of writings we identify with the rise of "sensibility," men and women could develop the "humane," warm feelings of pity, compassion, of "kindness through sympathy." By cultivating "temperaments" or "frames of mind" imbued with the sympathetic emotions, by steeping themselves in a new ethical system governed by the qualities of "sensibility," individuals could supply themselves with the moral compass necessary to negotiate a world in which luxury and credit threatened to corrupt the ancient virtues based on independence and personal autonomy.

Sensibility and manners, as guides to the development of virtuous behavior between individuals in these formulations, operated not in the public world of politicians but in what contemporaries called the "private" world of men outside of government and politics but within their communities, what we might identify as the realm of "the social." This private world was not the same, for eighteenth-century thinkers, as the "domestic" sphere of home and family. It was here, in the interstices between politics and government on the one hand, and home and family on the other, that virtuous friendships between men could be formed, that the development of feelings of benevolence, humanitarianism, and generosity could take place among small social groupings of men and women, which could then provide the foundations for a larger, public morality. Sensibility, the cultivation of "gentleness of manners" based on the ability to "feel for" others, would establish a private morality or virtue that would enable men in the public world of government and politics to act morally as well. The qualities of sensibility, observed Smith in his *Theory of Moral Sentiments*, published in 1767, endowed the individual with the "character" most appropriate to "the circumstances [of] ... one who lives in a very civilized society." It made him more humane, and his humanity contributed to and improved public life.

While men displayed their virtue, in the guise of sensibility and manners, in the realm of the "private sphere" as the eighteenth century defined it, it was in the domestic sphere, from women, that they learned it in the first place.[5] The family, moralists and philosophers insisted, constituted the site where "the natural affections," and the "habitual sympathy" required of commercial society were taught and experienced. A new emphasis on domesticity developed over the course of the eighteenth century as moralists struggled to find ways to render men and society more virtuous. Private morality imbibed in the home promised an effective safeguard against the corruption of public life. As one Scottish poet attested in his paean to "The married state" in a 1764 issue of *Scots Magazine*:

> If you ask from what source *my* felicity flows,
> My answer is short – From a *wif*,
> Who, for chearfulness [*sic*], sense, and good-nature, I chose
> Which are beauties that charm us for life.
>
> To make *home* the seat of perpetual delight,
> Ev'ry moment each studies to seize,
> And we find ourselves happy, from morning to night,
> By the mutual endeavour to please.

As the key figure responsible for the creation of domestic bliss in the midst of the vicissitudes of commercial society, women took on a new significance and importance over the course of the century. Because they enjoyed a natural "complacency," Scottish and English moralists believed, by which they meant a capacity for sympathy, women possessed the power to soften men and to encourage in them the development of the sensibility that would preserve morality and virtue in a public world fraught with selfishness, corruption, and dissipation. In the writings of many, women appeared to be the single greatest bulwark against moral disintegration, responsible for reforming the manners of men and for maintaining the integrity of the moral community as a whole.

The moral power imputed to women by the latter half of the eighteenth century was considerable, and it produced a far greater appreciation of women than had existed earlier. As we shall see more fully in Chapter 6, however, the efforts to elevate women to the status of angels contained another agenda as well. "Why are girls to be told that they resemble angels," noted Mary Wollstonecraft at the end of the century, "but to sink them below women?" Women's newly recognized influence with men was effective only insofar as women exercised it through example or through gentle persuasion, moralists insisted, and their behavior should in no way suggest that they were not fully subordinate to their husbands, functioning under their beneficent but watchful gaze within their proper sphere of the home. The new recognition of women's importance to society, in other words, carried with it many prescriptive constraints on women's behavior, and would have significant ideological power to contain their activities in later decades. Women should expect "to command by obeying," argued James Fordyce in the wildly popular *Sermons to Young Women*, published in 1765, "and by yielding to conquer." Only in this way could the reformation of male manners be brought about and sensibility inculcated in men.

But sensibility had to be handled carefully by eighteenth-century philosophers and moralists. "The man of feeling," "all serene, soft, and harmonious," could easily slide into excessive feeling, rendering himself unfit for public, political life. Although Smith declared that "our sensibility to the feelings of others" was not "inconsistent with the manhood of self-command," he conceded that the refinement of manners, the civilizing of society through commerce could go too far: "the delicate sensibility required in civilized nations sometimes destroys the masculine firmness of character," without which, novelists never tired of warning throughout the eighteenth century, men could not successfully conduct business. Smith's solution, in effect, was to distinguish in *The Theory of Moral Sentiments* between two kinds of moral qualities and to assign each category to a particular gender. He contrasted "the soft, the amiable and the gentle virtues" deriving from sensibility against "the great, the awful, and the respectable" virtues arising from the individual's success in mastering his feelings. The former were learned in the home at the hands of women; the latter "under the boisterous and stormy sky of war and faction, of public tumult and confusion," where men operated.[6]

> The propriety of generosity and public spirit is founded upon the same principles as that of justice. Generosity is different from humanity. These two qualities, which at first seem so nearly allied, do not always belong to the same person. Humanity is the virtue of a woman, generosity of a man. The fair sex, who have commonly much more tenderness than ours, have seldom so much generosity. ... Humanity consists merely in the exquisite fellow-feeling which the spectator entertains with the sentiments of the persons principally concerned, so as to grieve for their sufferings, to resent their injuries, and to rejoice at their good fortune. The most human actions require no self-denial, no self-command, no great exertion of the sense of propriety. They consist only in doing what this exquisite sympathy would of its own accord prompt us to do. But it is otherwise with generosity. We never are generous except when in some respect we prefer some other person to ourselves, and sacrifice some great and important interest of our own to an equal interest of a friend or of a superior.

In this formulation, women possessed the tenderness of feeling that compelled them to act virtuously and to inculcate in their children the qualities of sensibility; they lacked the self-denial and self-command that fitted them for public life. Men acquired those capacities in the tumultuous public arena of commerce; the exercise of self-denial and self-command enabled them to place a limit on the potentially effeminizing effects of the civilizing process. The vicissitudes of the commercial world help to preserve manliness in the face of the effeminizing threats emanating from women in the home.

The "corruption" of women's work

It is important to emphasize that the ideological development of what historians call "separate spheres" for men and women – for men the rough-and-tumble life of work and politics, for women the domestic realm of home, family, and the cultivation of morality – did not necessarily reflect how men and women behaved in the course of their daily life. Moralists, novelists, journalists, and politicians might prescribe for respectable women a highly circumscribed life of domesticity, but in many, many instances their pronouncements fell on deaf ears. Historians have assumed, following the prescriptive literature, that the commercial revolution brought about a reduction of middling women's employment; that it moved them out of economic production and/or commerce and into the home where they acted merely as consumers. While it is certainly the case that women's consumption helped to fuel the commercial boom of the eighteenth century, it is also true that significant numbers of respectable middling women worked throughout the eighteenth century, either in their own trades or in the shops of their husbands. They continued to trade in luxury goods like silks, tea, chocolate, or chinaware; they prepared and sold food and drink; they acted as nurses and midwives; they undertook all manner and kind of needlework; and took paying boarders into their homes. As it became increasingly less respectable for women to work, many status-conscious individuals, especially among the middling ranks, may not have reported the work the women in their families did, but it appears from all the data historians have been able to gather that not much changed in either the kinds of work women performed or in the proportion of women working over the course of the eighteenth century. What did change, and with profound consequences, was the *meaning* that was attached to women's work.

For while upper- and middle-class women were being transformed, ideologically speaking, into the embodiment of virtue over the course of the eighteenth century, representations of plebeian women were changing too.[7] These were not unrelated phenomena: the very processes of commercialization that compelled the imaginative creation of separate spheres for élite men and women involved the development of new understandings of women's work. From constituting the industrious, productive, invaluable contributors to family and national wealth at the beginning of the eighteenth century, plebeian women came by the end of the eighteenth century to be regarded as coarse, profligate, and degraded; portrayed as shameful, suspect, and even criminal, working women were depicted as posing a serious danger to the nation's moral, physical, and economic health.

Just as commercialization wrought dramatic changes in the social and physical landscape of urban areas, so too the commercialization of farming in the country-side brought about profound and often disastrous changes for people whose livelihoods came from the land. The commercialization of agriculture and the proletarianization of farmers, which, as we saw in Chapter 1, had been going on since the seventeenth century, received additional impetus after 1750 with the advent of more efficient, "scientific" methods of farming. The introduction of new crops, of new techniques of land use, crop rotation, and the increased enclosure of common lands had an adverse effect on rural families, most of them landless. Where in 1600, perhaps one-third of the English population worked other people's land in return for a wage, by 1750 these landless laborers and cottagers with little or no land of their own made up the bulk of the rural population.

Wages earned for working the land of others or for spinning or weaving within a system of domestic manufacture could not be counted upon to make ends meet. Most families relied upon customary "use rights" to uncultivated land, woodlands, common lands, and harvested fields to provide the food and fuel they needed to survive. Until mid-century, when improving capitalist landlords shut down such options, custom decreed that laboring families could gather firewood and hunt game within woodlands, grow crops such as vegetables or hay on uncultivated waste land, graze livestock on common lands, and glean the leftover wheat and other grains from fields already harvested. Such customary use rights often made the difference between subsistence and failure for laboring families.

As we saw earlier in Chapter 1, women took responsibility for work located around the cottage while men went off to labor in the fields some distance from home. Taking advantage of customary use rights to commons, waste, and woodlands fell to women as well. They spent long hours tending crops, looking for firewood, and gleaning fields, in addition to the never-ending and ubiquitous chore of spin-ning, labor that earned them the approbation of their neighbors and society as a whole. In towns and cities, women's work in spinning, knitting, weaving, stitching, and lace-making sustained a widespread, lucrative foreign and domestic trade in textiles; women provided the domestic labor force in thousands of homes and small workshops. The early eighteenth-century plebeian women of England, Scotland, and Wales were nothing, contemporaries agreed, if not industrious, and their productive value to the family, the community, and the nation was recognized and acknowledged.

This image of plebeian women as industrious, productive contributors to the commonwealth suffered numerous assaults after mid-century. After 1750, a combi-nation of increased unemployment, urbanization, and an intensification of conflict between classes acted to produce in the minds of élites a picture of laboring people, and especially laboring women, as immoral and even criminal. A steep rise in population after 1750 (in which the numbers of English and Welsh grew from 6.2 million in 1751 to 9.16 million in 1801) led to a marked increase in the price of wheat, causing great distress for plebeians. Widespread unemployment and poverty resulted in a decline of nutrition and living conditions for many laboring families, just as prosperity was improving those of middling and upper-ranked people. Crowds of urban and rural workers often protested their plight, leading to fears on the part of wealthier individuals that the poor constituted a threat to social order and well-being.

Plebeian women served as the object of many of the negative portrayals of the poor drawn by fearful élites. In cities like London, which were growing at a rapid pace, migrant rural women came to be regarded as responsible for burgeoning the ranks of thieves, beggars, and prostitutes. Rising rates of crimes against property by women during periods of acute distress, and a dramatic increase in illegitimate births and infanticide – these operated to close down much of the sympathy and sense of responsibility that rural and urban élites felt in the early eighteenth century for poor women who were regarded as significant and contributing members of society and therefore deserving of paternal assistance in the form of parish relief, and produced instead a vision of them as immoral and degraded by the latter part of the century. The numbers of poor women did not change appreciably over time – some 86 percent of those classified as poor in 1755 were women, a percentage that had not changed much by 1803 – but attitudes toward them did. Now they were regarded with distrust and suspicion as illegitimate burdens on the state.

Laboring women in virtually every area of work came to be depicted negatively in the second half of the eighteenth century as commercialization transformed the nature of agriculture and manufacturing. Rising agricultural prices provided a stiff incentive for agrarian capitalists to increase the efficiency of their farming in order to secure greater profits, and they did so by eliminating many of the customary use rights to land that laboring families depended upon. They enclosed their open fields, brought waste land into cultivation, and tightened restrictions on hunting and gathering firewood and on gleaning. In what historians have called the transformation of "custom into crime," improving landlords turned hunting into "poaching" and collecting wood and gleaning into theft and trespass. Those who engaged in these once customary activities now became criminals violating the law of property. Plebeian men as well as women suffered from this shift to more efficient use of the land, but as so much of the activity derived from customary use devolved upon women, they were particularly hard-hit. Moreover, improving landlords could point to women's agricultural practices as the epitome of wasteful, inefficient farming, enhancing the image of their own methods of modernization by comparing them to the traditional customs of women, denigrating women in the process as stubborn or ignorant. "How many days, during the harvest, are lost by the mother of a family and all her children," demanded one reformer scornfully, unmindful of the necessity that drove them to it, "in wandering about from field to field, to glean what does not repay them the wear and tear of their cloaths in seeking?" Persistence in the practice demonstrated conclusively that women were irrational, advocates of "scientific" farming insisted, a characteristic that in an age of "science," "improvement," and "efficiency" took on immoral connotations. Gleaning, asserted one agricultural expert, encouraged "idleness and loss of time" by tempting the worker "to gather his employer's corn in a careless and slovenly manner" in order to leave a store for women to recover later.

A similar process of undermining the work of women took place in dairying, an activity synonymous with women whether poor or rich, and a skill recognized to be exclusively female. As the demand for cheese grew in response to increased population growth and the concentration of more and more working-class people in cities, and that of butter to rising standards of living among middle-class families who counted it a measure of their prosperity, dairying for profit became attractive to improving farmers seeking to utilize their resources in the most productive way. Dairying, formerly an art practiced by individual women whose talents were regarded as secrets to be treasured, became a "scientific" business venture operated by men who sought to produce standardized quality and uniform quantities. Agricultural reformers and managers depicted women's ways of making cheese and butter as part of an occult practice relying on secret recipes, secret ingredients, secret techniques, and the women who produced them as old-fashioned, ignorant, and irrational. Their practices, by contrast, drew on empirical observations derived from scientific experimentation. Setting themselves up as men of reason against superstitious, silly females, these so-called experts established by 1780 a new hierarchy of authority within dairying that ultimately displaced women from their recognized positions and represented them as inessential to the processes of dairy production.

In virtually every area of women's employment, from cottage industry to domestic service to, as we shall see in Chapter 6, the earliest factories, the valuation placed on the work women performed dropped dramatically. At the beginning of the eighteenth century women were praised for their industry and diligence; they were acknowledged producers of national wealth. By the end of the eighteenth century, working women were excoriated for competing with men for jobs, pitied for their plight, or condemned for degrading themselves and their families by taking up employment. The middle-class domestic ideal called for women to stay at home to look after the needs of their husbands and children, and, after 1800, middle-class reformers engaged themselves in a concerted effort to impose their ideas about the proper roles for men and women on working people as well.

These new societal attitudes could not prevent women from working, for necessity was a harsh taskmaster, but they had enormous consequences nonetheless. If the definition of "worker" no longer included women, if "workers" were men, then men could easily displace women in areas of work traditionally theirs. Women who had to work in order to feed themselves and their families found it nigh impossible to command employment that paid a wage sufficient for them to do so. "Women's work," by definition, paid poorly, and was by its nature intermittent. The negative connotations attached to women's work also placed enormous pressure on men and women to live up to a standard of exclusively male breadwinning that few working families could afford. The psychic stresses resulting from the failure of working-class men to support their families on a single pay packet could be severe, helping to produce alcoholism, domestic violence, or desertion.[8]

The ideology of separate spheres, then, had a powerful, if uneven, impact on the men and women of various ranks. Where it depicted middling and upper ranked women as nearly divine in character and elevated them to a level of influence they did not have before, it reduced working women to nearly subhuman status. The picture of the virtuous "angel in the house," as the middle-class woman would be called in the nineteenth century, required her mirror image, the degraded, brutish, immoral working woman. The crystallization of these portrayals of femininity would not occur until the time of the French Revolution, but the process by which they emerged had begun long before with the advent of commercial society. It would continue over the course of the eighteenth century as British society faced the challenges of imperial acquisition and loss, a surge of popular disquiet after 1760, and the threat of republican France at the end of the century.

NOTES

1 This discussion is drawn from the work of J.G.A. Pocock: *The Machiavellian Moment: Florentine Political Thought and the Atlantic Republican Tradition* (Princeton, 1975); and *Virtue, Commerce, and History* (Cambridge, 1985).

2 This section on fashion depends on David Kuchta's "The making of the self-made man: Class, clothing, and English masculinity, 1688–1832," in Victoria de Grazia and Ellen Furlough, eds, *The Sex of Things: Gender and Consumption in Historical Perspective* (Berkeley, 1996).

3 For this section and the following discussion on passions and interests, see Albert O. Hirschman, *The Passions and the Interests. Political Arguments for Capitalism before its Triumph* (Princeton, 1977).

4 The following discussion of material and sexual desire derives from Thomas Laqueur's "Sexual desire and the market economy during the industrial revolution," in Domna C. Stanton, *Discourses of Sexuality From Aristotle to AIDS* (Ann Arbor, 1992).

5 See Jane Rendall, "Virtue and commerce: Women in the making of Adam Smith's political economy," in Ellen Kennedy and Susan Mendus, eds, *Women in Western Political Philosophy* (New York, 1987); and John Dwyer, *Virtuous Discourse: Sensibility and Community in Late Eighteenth-Century Scotland* (Edinburgh, 1987).

6 Quoted in Rendall, "Virtue and commerce."

7 The following discussion depends upon Deborah Valenze's remarkable book, *The First Industrial Woman* (New York, 1995).

8 See Anna Clark, *The Struggle for the Breeches: Gender and the Making of the British Working Class* (Berkeley, 1995).

SOURCES

Joyce Appleby, "Consumption in early modern social thought," in John Brewer and Roy Porter, eds, *Consumption and the World of Goods*. London, 1993.

Jeremy Black and Jeremy Gregory, "Introduction," in Jeremy Black and Jeremy Gregory, eds, *Culture, Politics and Society in Britain, 1660–1800*. Manchester, 1991.

John Dwyer, *Virtuous Discourse: Sensibility and Community in Late Eighteenth-Century Scotland*. Edinburgh, 1987.

Anthony Fletcher, *Gender, Sex and Subordination in England, 1500-1800*. New Haven, 1995.

Albert O. Hirschman, *The Passions and the Interests. Political Arguments for Capitalism before its Triumph*. Princeton, 1977.

Margaret R. Hunt, *The Middling Sort. Commerce, Gender, and the Family in England, 1680–1780*. Berkeley, 1996.

David Kuchta, "The making of the self-made man: Class, clothing and English masculinity, 1688–1832," in Victoria de Grazia and Ellen Furlough, eds, *The Sex of Things: Gender and Consumption in Historical Perspective*. Berkeley, 1996.

Paul Langford, *A Polite and Commercial People. England, 1727–1783*. Oxford, 1992 (First published 1989).

Thomas Laqueur, *Making Sex: Body and Gender from the Greeks to Freud*. Cambridge, MA, 1990.

——, "Sexual desire and the market economy during the industrial revolution," in Domna C. Stanton, *Discourses of Sexuality From Aristotle to AIDS*. Ann Arbor, 1992.

Neil McKendrick, John Brewer and J.H. Plumb, *The Birth of a Consumer Society: The Commercialization of Eighteenth-Century England*. Bloomington, 1982.

J.G.A. Pocock, *The Machiavellian Moment: Florentine Political Thought and the Atlantic Republican Tradition*. Princeton, 1975.

——, *Virtue, Commerce, and History*. Cambridge, 1985.

Jane Rendall, "Virtue and commerce: Women in the making of Adam Smith's political economy," in Ellen Kennedy and Susan Mendus, eds, *Women in Western Political Philosophy*. New York, 1987.

Adam Smith, *The Wealth of Nations* (1776). New York, 1937.

Deborah Valenze, *The First Industrial Woman*. New York, 1995.

Amanda Vickery, "Women and the world of goods: A Lancashire consumer and her possessions, 1751–81," in John Brewer and Roy Porter, eds, *Consumption and the World of Goods*. London, 1993.

Chapter 4

Manly dominions
War and empire, 1689–1793

The "European" empire

The "British empire" of the eighteenth century generally conjures up an image of Britain's colonization of territories in North America, the West Indies, and India. But that empire is "British" and not merely "English" because England, over the space of two-and-a-half centuries, conquered and incorporated into the United Kingdom of Great Britain the countries of Wales, Scotland, and Ireland. Each country came into the United Kingdom at different times, in different circumstances, and each experienced differential benefits from union with England. Over time, first the Welsh, who came into the United Kingdom of England and Wales in the early sixteenth century, during the reign of Henry VIII, then the Scots after 1707, and finally, after 1801, the protestants of Ireland came to identify themselves and to be identified with Britain.

The catholic Irish, on the other hand, who made up the vast majority of the population in Ireland, never ceased to consider themselves a colonized people whose fortunes were governed by a cruel imperial master of alien culture and religion. We have seen how English overlordship of Ireland was buttressed by the plantation of thousands of English and Scottish settlers throughout the first two-thirds of the seventeenth century. When, in 1688, James II fled to Ireland in advance of the armies of William of Orange, fought against him with the support of many catholics, and lost, William and Mary exacted harsh revenge from Irish catholics. Their penal code banished the catholic clergy from Ireland; forbade catholics to vote or to sit in parliament; banned them from teaching; from buying land, from leasing it for more than thirty-one years, from inheriting it from a protestant, or from owning a horse worth more than £5; and excluded Irish shipping from the colonies, prohibited Irish woolen and glass exports from Britain, and made it unlawful to levy tariffs against English goods coming into Ireland. In virtually all respects, Irish subjection to England was complete.

From the time of the Tudors onward, the English justified their depredations against the Irish by portraying them as barbarous, primitive, pagan people whose country it was the responsibility of the English to "inhabite and reform." One commentator described Irish society as a collection of people living like "beastes, void of lawe and all good order"; they were, he asserted, "more uncivill, more uncleanly, more barbarous and more brutish in their customs and demeanures, then [sic] in any other part of the world that is known." Just as the Romans had once brought civilization to a backward, uncivil, and uncouth England, declared Sir Thomas Smith, so too would the English persuade the Irish to engage "in vertuous labour and in justice, and ... teach them our English lawes and civilitie and leave robbyng and stealing and killyng one of another."[1]

Depicting the Irish as by turns savage yet subtle, warlike but lazy, proud and cowardly, primitive yet cunning, English conquerors and observers of Ireland demonstrated a complicated mixture of attraction to, and repulsion by, Irish people and their mores. The Irish were dirty, violent, dishonest, lazy people who lived under inequitable and unjust laws, the English claimed, but they had nonetheless seduced and "degenerated" many an Englishman with their "corrupt customs." The "wild shamrock manners"[2] of women, in particular, both shocked and titillated English travel writers, who saw in their refusal to wear corsets an intentional assertion of sexual invitation. Because Irish women partook of strong drink, presided over public feasts, and greeted strangers with a kiss; because their marriage laws permitted them to retain their names upon marriage and to divorce their husbands with relative ease and material support; because Irish custom permitted sexual relations within degrees of kin affinity far closer than those constituted by either English law or the catholic clergy, English writers concluded that the women of Ireland held positions of authority over men at home and in public. Unmanly men and aggressive, sensualized, licentious women, they insisted, characterized social relations in Ireland, undermining good order and necessitating English intervention if civilization were ever to be established there. English observations of Irish culture and society contained frequent mention of exotic sexual activities and unconventional gender arrangements; languages of sexuality and gender served to legitimate English conquest of foreign peoples. Long before Britain acquired an empire of people of different races, religions, and cultures in Africa and Asia in the late eighteenth and nineteenth centuries, Ireland served as a model of subject peoples in need of British "civilization." The Irish, wrote Phillip Luckombe in 1783, "seem to form a different race from the rest of mankind."[3]

The Acts of Union that incorporated Scotland and Ireland into Great Britain in 1707 and 1801 respectively resulted not from any logical or organic extension of domestic social, economic, or political development but from British fears of catholic France. In 1707, an Act of Union established the United Kingdom of Great Britain, joining Scotland, England, and Wales under a single protestant monarchy, a single legislature, and a single system of free trade. Scotland, which preserved its own systems of law and education as well as its own social structure and religious organization, stood to gain economically from such an arrangement. English motives for the union were more defensive in nature: English politicians acted out of the fear that the death of the childless Queen Anne might lead the Scots to support their catholic countryman, James, the Stuart Pretender, in a bid for the throne. A legislative union with Scotland would obviate such a possibility, and shut down as well any opportunity for Scotland to serve as a bridgehead for the forces of catholic France. Similarly, Ireland was brought into the United Kingdom in 1801 to ensure that French forces could not take advantage of anti-British Irish catholic sentiment to use Ireland as a staging base against England in the Napoleonic wars.

Empire abroad and war with France

The commercial prosperity of England, or so contemporaries believed, owed much to trade with areas outside of Europe, with the Far East and with what Europeans called the New World – colonized lands in North America and in the Caribbean islands, the so-called West Indies. Success in commercial endeavors depended upon the ability of English ships and traders to get around the monopolies and barriers to trade set up by Spain and by France, efforts that frequently involved England in wars that took place both on the continent and in the colonies. Throughout the course of the eighteenth century – from 1689 to 1697, 1702 to 1713, 1740 to 1748, 1756 to 1763, 1778 to 1783, and again from 1793 to 1815 – Britain fought a series of long, drawn-out wars with France. Obligated by the Revolutionary Settlement of 1689 to provide support to William in his battles with the French, Britain also had its own geo-political and geo-strategic reasons to engage in warfare against catholic France. France's aspirations to expand its borders promised to upset the balance of power in Europe; its commercial enterprises and naval operations in North America, the West Indies, and India created obstacles for English merchants who sought to increase their trade with these areas; and its support for James II in 1689, and for his successors, the Pretenders James Edward and Charles Edward, in 1715 and 1745 respectively, threatened the social, economic, political, and religious arrangements established by the Glorious Revolution. The enmity of catholic France and wars against the French ultimately helped to forge a sense of national unity and patriotism among the disparate Scots, English, Welsh, and even Irish peoples to produce a sense of Britishness that could transcend regional particularities or loyalties.[4]

This process of psychological nation-building in Britain received additional impetus from the acquisition of empire, in which significant numbers of Scots, Welsh, and protestant Anglo-Irish participated and from which they gained substantial material benefits. Here, too, France played a large part, for it was in competition with the French for colonial territory or naval dominance that the British gauged their wins and losses. Defeats at the hands of the French in the 1740s, 1750s, and 1780s caused the British to question the virtue, the legitimacy – the very manliness – of their rulers; and victory over the French in 1763 and again in 1815 vindicated British manliness and left Britain in control of a vast colonial empire that would inform its culture and its politics for the next two centuries. Issues of war and empire, then, dominated much of the thinking and the activity of eighteenth-century Britons, and as we have seen so often before, languages of gender and sexuality served as the means by which concerns, anxieties, and fears about them could be adequately articulated and even resolved. The uses of such languages to represent and work out the burning questions raised by war and empire had profound consequences for the ways in which men and women came to define their identities and their places in the nation.

Empire served as an important source of Britons' pride in themselves and in the principles that they claimed governed their social, economic, cultural, and political institutions. Although it was palpably not the case for all of those people whose liberty and freedom had been sacrificed to the material interests of their British rulers – native Americans, African slaves, Irish catholic peasants – supporters of empire depicted their enterprise as one in which notions of liberty and consent were central. (As we shall see later in the chapter, the ability to portray the colonies as bastions of freedom and liberty for white Britons depended upon the suppression, in real and in imaginative terms, of those who did not and could not enjoy such beneficence. New, scientifically systematized ideologies of race and of gender, oftentimes intertwined with one another, served as justifications for the rule of protestant Britons over subject peoples in Ireland, North America, and the West Indies, and women at home.) Portrayed as commercially prosperous colonies inhabited by free white British citizens, empire was regarded as the source of trade, wealth, military power, and political virtue for the mother country. When colonies flourished, apologists of empire asserted, it was because they reflected the legitimacy and health of domestic political institutions; when they failed to live up to contemporary standards of government and economic viability, it was because Britain's political institutions were in the hands of a corrupt, weak, even effeminate ruling class.

In the first half of the eighteenth century, British unease over, and envy of, French power, wealth, and cultural hegemony over Europe expressed itself in caricatures of the French as unmanly subjects of a despotic king, distinctly antithetical to the manly British whose Glorious Revolution had produced a virtuous government of restricted monarchical power. "Let France grow proud, beneath the tyrant's lust," wrote the satirist William Hogarth in 1749, in a caption accompanying his engraving, *Calais Gate*:

While the rack'd people crawl, and lick the dust:
The manly genius of this isle [by which he meant Britain] disdains
All tinsel slavery, or golden chains.

But Britain's losses to France in the early phases of the War of Austrian Succession in the 1740s and the Seven Years' War in the 1750s, coupled with the Rising of '45 from Scotland, caused the British to question their own political virtue and manliness. The moral corruption of Britain at the hands of its effeminate, foppish, luxurious, indolent, French-loving aristocracy had left it unable to protect its interests abroad and its political institutions at home from assault. The governing classes, so claimed poets, playwrights, and pamphleteers, echoing the sentiments of many men and women of the middling commercial ranks, had been contaminated by French fashions and French passions, and must be reclaimed for the nation by the moral, virtuous, patriotic citizens of Britain. "The public spirit of persons in the middling rank of this kingdom," asserted the Member of Parliament for York in 1753, "and the depravity and selfishness of those in a higher class, was never more remarkable than at present." Depravity and selfishness were French traits, it was understood, traits that had to be extirpated if British power was to be preserved and British imperial interests protected. "We are at peace, it is true, with the power," wrote one clergyman in 1754, during one of the short hiatuses when the British and the French were not at war, "but it would be well for us if we were at war with the manners of France."[5]

The Rising of '45, when supporters of the Young Pretender, Charles Edward, from the Scottish Highlands invaded England with the aim of restoring the Stuart monarchy there, reinforced British fears of French power. Charles's forces were defeated in 1746, and promised French support for the rising never materialized, but it was clear to the English just how easy it would be for French armies, which were far greater than those of the British, to invade from the north, where Highlander sympathy for the Jacobite cause had enabled the Young Pretender's troops to place him in the Stuart palace of Holyrood in Edinburgh and to defeat the only force of British soldiers in Scotland. Charles's armed invasion of England, moreover, took him as far as Derby, only one hundred miles from London itself. The machinations of France and the Scottish Highlanders in the '45 made it possible for English politicians and publicists to identify the Jacobite cause with hopes for the destruction of England as an imperial power and its subjugation to the French. Politicians and military leaders had long believed that the northern border of England opened up on to a barbarian frontier; the rising did nothing to alleviate their unease. From here on, only a certain kind of "Scottishness" would be acceptable in the British nation. The Highlander Scots, portrayed as an "unpolish'd Race" of barbarous, "ignoble savages" lacking in manners or civilization, did not demonstrate the qualities necessary for membership in the British nation. They more accurately resembled those early stages of humanity depicted by Adam Smith and others in their efforts to make commerce respectable and virtuous: Edward Gibbon characterized the followers of Charles as "some naked highlanders." The loyal Lowlander populations, by contrast, had embraced English culture and civilization as their own, and in consequence were virtuous, free, and prosperous Britons. Even these Scots, however, as we shall see in the next chapter, could make only tenuous claims on British citizenship in times of acute popular upheaval.

Although the Rising of '45 failed to unseat George II, and although the Treaty of Aix-la-Chapelle that ended the War of Austrian Succession in 1748 reinstated the British in their prewar colonial possessions, Britons' confidence in their power had been severely shaken. Many regarded the Scottish rising as an indication that God had abandoned the English, that He wished to punish England for its luxurious and corrupt habits; others believed that the loss of imperial possessions would follow naturally from Britain's inability to produce the leadership and character necessary to defeat France. These fears received additional impetus in 1756, when, once again at war with France, Britain lost the Mediterranean island of Minorca to them. Additional losses of territory in America and India, and the threat of a French invasion of the British Isles themselves gave rise to a crisis of nation-wide proportions, calling into question once again the character of the British nation and the fitness of the élite governing classes to lead it.

Defeat at the hands of the French led prominent and influential individuals and groups of men and women to believe that the moral corruption of the aristocracy by "alien" French habits of indolence and luxury had produced corruption in the political, imperial, and military realms of British life as well.[6] Worse, contemporaries feared, corruption at the top amongst the aristocracy had seeped down to all levels of society to produce a degenerate, effeminate nation, a belief fueled by many of the arguments against commercial society that we saw in the last chapter. Effeminacy promised to undermine the "manly" qualities of courage, military prowess, strength, discipline, and patriotism, characteristics that had once enabled the British to command a world-wide domination of the seas, but whose weakening by luxury and French fashions had contributed overwhelmingly to British humiliation by France. "The luxurious and effeminate Manners in the higher Ranks, together with a general defect of *Principle*," thundered Reverend John Brown in his 1757 *Estimate of the Manners and Principles of the Time*, "operate powerfully, and fatally … to have fitted us for a Prey to the Insults and Invasions of our most powerful Enemies." "A Nation which *resembles Women*," he warned, devoid of the manly attributes of courage, liberty, appreciation for the public good, and a willingness to come to its military defense, invited precisely the disasters that Britain had suffered at the hands of the French in 1756.

British national character could only be resurrected and Britain's losses at the hands of the French avenged, argued many middling ranked critics of aristocratic government, through the acquisition and preservation of colonies. The "spirit of liberty" evident among the middling commercial classes engaged in the manly, rigorous pursuits of trade with the empire could counter the aristocratic "cultural treason" that had enabled effeminacy to take hold and cripple the nation at home and abroad. Empire began to be portrayed in the commercial press as an arena where middling ranked individuals demonstrated their resolution, their independence, their political virtue, their initiative, their skill, and their capacity to create wealth for themselves and for the nation as a whole. Against the aristocratic governing classes, who were held responsible for British losses because of their supineness in the face of the enemy, their enervation by luxurious and indolent living, their failure to act with force and discipline at a time of national emergency, their "effeminacy," middling commercial men defined themselves as manly, patriotic merchants who had the interests of the country at heart. When, in the years 1758–62, the British won a series of battles against the French, these visions of imperial potency in the hands of the commercial middling orders appeared to have been borne out.

Victory in the Seven Years' War brought with it not only unprecedented material spoils of imperial possessions; it also vindicated a particular view of the British national character that was commercially inclined, aggressive, liberty-loving, virtuous, and, above all, manly. As the Reverend Brewster exulted in a sermon in 1759, victory over the French showed that "Britain will never want [be without, be in need of] a Race of Men ... who choose Dangers in defence of Their Country before an inglorious safety, an honourable Death before the unmanly pleasures of a useless and effeminate life." One of the consequences of presenting defeat as the result of "effeminacy" and imperial conquest as a "manly" pursuit was a corresponding devaluation of the "feminine" in the fashioning of ideas about citizenship. Despite the fact that thousands of British women served in a variety of ways to ensure British success over the French, their activities failed to register in the political imagination that counted up the contributions to the public good. References to the manliness of the commercial middling ranks and the effeminacy of aristocrats operated to define the nature of citizenship, as increasing numbers of middling people saw it. If those who were manly should and could become citizens, then those who were not manly, as men and women of the commercial orders identified them – catholics, aristocrats, non-whites, the foppish, the irrational, the dependent, the timid, and, not least, women – these people should be excluded from political participation. Empire, in other words, helped to establish the criteria for citizenship on the basis of gender. "Manliness" qualified certain men for public life; "femininity" disqualified all kinds of individuals from participating in the political arena, men and women alike.

Victory over the French also enabled Britons to regard their imperial ventures as beneficent, humanitarian endeavors whereby Britain, by taking on the overlordship of the tyrannous French and the cruel Spanish, generously made available to its colonial territories and the native peoples who populated them the fruits of progress, morality, freedom, liberty, and prosperity, all of them a function, pro-imperial Britons believed, of an empire based on trade rather than on conquest. In the 1760s, as we shall see in the next chapter, middling people used this kind of justification for empire in support for their claims to citizenship. At the same time, these justifications glossed over the fact that imperial prosperity rested on the forced labor of hundreds of thousands of Africans sold and born into slavery; the expropriation of land from native Americans and Irish peasants; and the exploitation of native peoples in parts of India.

The slave trade

The commercial revolution of the eighteenth century derived as much of its impetus and prosperity from the exchange of human beings as from trade in agricultural and manufactured products, and in raw materials. The slave trade constituted one crucial leg of the triangular trade between Britain, Africa, and the Atlantic colonies, and the use of slave labor in the West Indian and North American colonies made it possible for small populations of white colonists to exploit the resources – largely sugar and tobacco – of those areas profitably. Slavery stood at the crossroads of foreign trade, colonization, and the consumer demands – both domestic and foreign – that stimulated economic growth; it was central, in many ways, to the development of the British economy of the eighteenth century.

Trade in slaves began during the reign of Elizabeth I in the second half of the sixteenth century, and continued under her successor, James I. In 1618, James chartered the Company of Adventurers of London Trading into Parts of Africa (also known as the Guinea Company), one of whose ventures involved the buying and selling of slaves from Guinea. In 1663, another company, the Royal Adventurers into Africa, obtained a charter from the king that cited slave trading as its specific purpose. Including among its stockholders the king and queen, and other members of the royal family, as well as a generous sampling of the country's nobility, the Royal Adventurers declared "that the *English* Plantations in *America* should have a competent [i.e. sufficient] and a constant supply of *Negro-servants* for their own use of Planting, and that at a moderate Rate."[7] The Guinea Company and the Royal African Company, successor to the Royal Adventurers, brought many African children and youth to Britain, where landed and mercantile élites kept them as servants, pets, or exotic showpieces designed to provide striking testimony to their wealth. Many African slaves in England wore gold or silver collars around their necks that were inscribed with their owners' names, initials, or coats of arms, a practice that might aid in the recovery of a runaway slave but more often served to identify black servitude with élite status and wealth derived from overseas trade.

As lucrative as this kind of trading in human beings might be, Britons did not engage in widespread slave trading until the late seventeenth century when Spain, which controlled the slave trade, began to lose its hold on its monopoly. In 1713, the Treaty of Utrecht, which marked the end of the War of the Spanish Succession, gave to Britain the *asiento*, the right to supply slaves to Spain's colonies in America. In the years between 1700 and 1810, some six and one-half million African men and women were sold as slaves and carried across the Atlantic Ocean in the holds of slave ships. Until about 1750, by which time natural increase amongst the slaves in North America could be counted upon to meet the demand for their labor, British slavers sold their human wares to colonists in North America and the West Indies. After 1750, the slave trade was largely confined to the Caribbean and to Brazil, but despite the decline of North American markets for newly transported slaves, the trade flourished. Britons managed fully a quarter of the world's slave trade up to 1791, and more than half of it between 1791 and 1806. In the 1780s, more than 88,000 slaves arrived in the Americas, half of them in English ships hailing from the port towns of Bristol, London, and Liverpool.

Those same ships carried cargoes of spices, tobacco, rum, molasses, but especially sugar to the North American colonies and to Britain, where demand for the sweetener had risen astronomically by 1775. Markets for sugar could only be supplied, West Indian planters insisted, through the increased utilization of slave labor. "It is as impossible for a Man to make Sugar without the assistance of Negroes," declared a rich West Indian planter, John Pinney, in the 1770s, "as to make Bricks without Straw."[8]

Once in England, the ships took on cargoes of manufactured goods such as textiles, brass pans, copper rods, iron bars and bowls, beads, pots and pans, muskets, gunpowder, and beer, and sailed to West Africa, where agents traded them for slaves. African demand for manufactured items was considerable, accounting for about 25 percent of Britain's cotton exports in 1792; exports of wrought-iron goods to Africa were second only to those to the American colonies at mid-century. Demand for these items in Africa played a large part in stimulating English manufacturing, as did the demand of the Caribbean colonists, who consumed some 12 percent of English manufactured goods between 1748 and 1776.

Slavery produced great wealth. West Indian planters used slave labor to generate profits from the sale of sugar; slaves owned by the American colonists produced tobacco and cotton that was sold to manufacturers in England. With their profits, colonists purchased commodities from Manchester, Birmingham, London, Sheffield, Glasgow, and Leeds, enriching the manufacturers of those items. The ships that carried African slaves to the Americas and raw materials to Britain, and the manufacturers to Africa and the American and West Indian colonies realized generous profits from their carrying trade, as did the insurance companies that protected their cargoes and the banks that financed them.

Contemporaries recognized the centrality of slavery and the slave trade to their prosperity. In 1729, a merchant named Joshua Gee observed that "our Trade with *Africa* is very profitable to the Nation in general; it has this Advantage, that it carries no Money out, and not only supplies our Plantations with Servants, but brings in a great Deal of Bullion for those that are sold to the *Spanish* West-Indies. ... The supplying our Plantations with Negroes is of that extraordinary Advantage to us, that the Planting Sugar and Tobacco, and carrying on Trade there could not be supported without [t]hem; which Plantations ... are the great Cause of the Increase of the Riches of the Kingdom. ... All this great Increase of our Treasure proceeds chiefly from the labour of Negroes in the *Plantations*." A mercantilist put it more succinctly in 1745: "If we have no *Negroes*, we can have no *Sugars, Tobaccoes, Rice, Rum*, etc. ... consequently, the Publick *Revenue*, arising from the Importation of *Plantation-Produce*, must be annihilated: And will this not turn many hundreds of Thousands of *British Manufacturers* a Begging?" The slave trade, wrote another in 1772, constituted "the first principle and foundation of all the rest; the main spring of the machine, which sets every wheel in motion." "There is hardly any Branch of Commerce, in which this Nation is concerned," declared the Committee of the Company of Merchants Trading to Africa in 1788, "that does not derive some advantage from it."[9]

We should note that Joshua Gee used the term "servant" instead of "slave" to describe those men and women who performed the labor on plantations. This may have been an attempt on his part to make palatable or to disguise through misrepresentation a system that could not be rendered compatible with the principles of liberty so near and dear to British hearts after 1688. If so, his effort was undercut by his reference to selling them to the Spaniards. At any rate, far more ambitious efforts to reconcile slavery and the trade in human beings with British tenets of freedom and justice and the Enlightenment project of human progress got underway during the eighteenth century as "scientific" principles and practices of taxonomic classification were brought to bear on the subject of race.

These drew on earlier medieval and Renaissance understandings of race as a contrast of darkness and light, which in turn connoted good and evil.[10] Long before the English laid eyes on people whose skins were dark, they utilized terms of black and white that carried deep and portentous meanings for them. In a literary, religious, and cultural context, "black" signified such negative things as death, mourning, evil, sin, and danger. "White," by contrast, stood for purity, innocence, goodness, and beauty. As England entered into long-distance trading relationships with other states, engaged in military operations with its European rivals, and became involved in overseas colonization, the term "black" proved to be a ready means of distinguishing English "civilization" from "barbarism," a quality long associated with Africa. Moreover, blackness could be ascribed to virtually any group of people who fell under English control – native Americans, Indians, Irish, and even Welsh and Scots might become "black" as the English cast about for ways to justify coercive measures against them by rendering them different, inferior, unruly, and in need of English discipline and tutelage. Racial discourse provided a shorthand for rationalizing English and British colonizing efforts.

Because purity, innocence, and beauty were qualities often represented by women or, indeed, by women's noticeable lack of them, the use of blackness to characterize subordinated peoples contained a gendered and sexualized component right from the start. In fact, the earliest travel writings about Africa drew upon notions of gender, specifically those having to do with sexual chaos or disorder, rather than race, to convey the sense of difference and alienness experienced by European explorers as they came in contact with African societies for the first time in the fifteenth century. Blackness, in these early narratives, appears to be merely a physical curiosity for Europeans – West African men, wrote John Ogilby in 1670, possessed "large propagators," – but gradually, as it became increasingly enmeshed with the familiar yet still threatening signs of gender disorderliness, blackness began to stand in for the idea that difference, strangeness, diversity, or disorder could be construed as destructive to, or harmful of, the European social and cultural practices that constituted "civilization." A century after Ogilby's casual, even admiring, assessment of African genitalia, another English observer embedded his description of African sexual practices within a long list of qualities believed to be the antithesis of those characterizing the manly English gentleman and the proper English lady: the African was "proud, lazy, treacherous, thievish, hot and addicted to all kinds of lusts, and most ready to promote them in others, as pimps, panders, incestuous, brutish, and savage, cruel and revengeful, devourers of human flesh, and quaffers of human blood, inconstant, base, treacherous, and cowardly," noted an entry in *The Universal History* (1760); one could no more "be an *African* and not lascivious" than to "be born in *Africa* and not be an African."[11]

Africa, in the minds of the British, came to signify unalterable, fundamental difference from European social and gender roles, European morals, mores, customs, values, and traditions, difference usually expressed by means of a disordered gender system and promiscuous sexuality attributed to Africans, and especially to African women, by writers and explorers. In 1600, John Pory translated into English the writings of a converted Moor who came to be called Johannes Leo Africanus; Pory's translation, *A Geographical Historie of Africa*, served as the pre-eminent travel guide to Africa until the latter part of the nineteenth century, when the accounts of British explorers replaced it. *A Geographical Historie* referred often to the "principall and notorious vices" of Africans, which Leo identified as the outrageously erotic behavior of women who would not be controlled by their menfolk, as grounds for his condemnation of African societies. "The Negroes likewise leade a beastly kinde of life," he wrote, "being utterly destitute of the use of reason, of dexteritie of wit, and of all artes. Yea they so behave themselves, as if they had continually lived in a forrest among wilde beasts. They have great swarmes of harlots among them; whereupon a man may easily conjecture their manner of living." So overwhelming was the sexuality of African women in the minds of British men that it exceeded all bounds. In 1677, Sir Thomas Herbert claimed to have observed African women keeping "frequent company with" baboons as he traveled throughout "divers" parts of the continent. "If they meet with a [white] Man," William Smith averred in a 1745 account of his experiences in Guinea, "they immediately strip his lower Parts and throw themselves upon him."[12]

These descriptions reduced Africans and African societies to the level of primitive savagery, a state of being that excused British involvement in the slave trade on the grounds that Africans could hardly be counted as human and would come to justify later nineteenth-century British efforts to subdue and control the peoples of Africa and Asia by an imperial rule that promised to raise them up to "civilized" status. They drew upon a kind of geographical version of the humoral theory of hot and cold and dry and wet to explain racial and sexual difference, and different stages of societal and political development on the basis of habitation in one of three climatic zones, torrid, temperate, or frigid.[13]

In the writings of a number of Enlightenment figures, including those of Adam Smith, David Hume, and Edward Gibbon, hot climates – those found in the torrid zones immediately adjacent to the equator – stimulate inordinate sexual desire and behavior; the populations residing there display few inhibitions and in fact indulge in riotous sexual activity regularly. The further one moves away from the equator, toward Europe, say, in the temperate zone, the degree of sexual passion exhibited by populations diminishes, or at least is much more readily controlled. Further north, in the frigid zone, men and women are so indifferent to passion as to practically ignore each other. These various regimes of sexual desire and activity correlate with the extent to which the societies participating in them have developed their social, economic, and political systems. As Adam Ferguson claimed in his 1767 *Essay on the History of Civil Society*:

> The burning ardours, and the torturing jealousies, of the seraglio and the haram, which have reigned so long in Asia and Africa, and which, in the Southern parts of Europe, have scarcely given way to the difference of religion and civil establishments, are found, however, with an abatement of heat in the climate, to be more easily changed, in one latitude, into a temporary passion which ingrosses the mind, without enfeebling it, and which excites to romantic achievements: by a farther progress to the North, it is changed into a spirit of gallantry, which employs the wit and the fancy more than the heart; which prefers intrigue to enjoyment; and substitutes affectation and vanity,

where sentiment and desire have failed. As it departs from the sun, the same passion is further composed into a habit of domestic connection or frozen into a state of insensibility, under which the sexes at freedom scarcely chuse to unite their society.

For Ferguson, Hume, and John Millar, the climatic influences that determined sexual passion and the relations between men and women also established the nature of social, economic, and political relations. Civilization and political liberty scarcely existed, according to these thinkers, in the hot climates of the torrid zone, where heat and uninhibited sexual activity sapped the energies of individuals and rendered them lethargic and compliant. In the more temperate regions of Europe, climate and sexual restraint enabled the development of societies that enjoyed the energy, productivity, and discipline necessary to produce political liberty and civic virtue. The commercial society of Britain, noted these philosophers, characterized by wealth, industry, political freedom, polite social relations, and the benefits of domesticity and separate spheres; and the "backward" societies of Africa, populated by indolent, slavish, lascivious men and women, provided a vivid contrast of the differential effects of climate and geography on progress and civilization.

Enlightenment thinkers very often measured the level of progress and civilization of any given society by examining the status of women in that society. John Millar's 1771 *Origin of the Distinction of Ranks* argued that as societies moved through the hunting–gathering, pastoral, and agricultural stages of development to reach the final, optimal commercial stage, the treatment of women in those societies improved markedly. Hunter–gatherer societies, which Millar and others identified with contemporary societies in Africa and Asia, "entertain very gross ideas concerning those female virtues which, in a polished nation, are supposed to constitute the honour and dignity of the sex." These "savage" societies enslaved women, entailed ceaseless work upon them, and rendered them helpless before the whims and brutalities of men. During the second and third, pastoral and agricultural stages, greater social stability and then settlement increased men's competition for women, which in turn helped to stimulate the development of greater refinement and sentiment than was necessary in a hunter–gatherer society. Respect for virtuous women increased, although those women found wanting in sexual loyalty met with severe disapprobation. Writing of the feudal age Millar allowed that "a woman who deviated so far from the established maxims of the age as to violate the laws of chastity, was indeed deserted by every body, and was universally contemned and insulted. But those who adhered to the strict rules of virtue, and maintained an unblemished reputation, were treated like beings of a superior order."

As we have seen in the writings of the Scottish Enlightenment figures in the previous chapter, commercial societies benefited even further from the refinement of manners and cultivation of sensibility that women brought to them. In return, these latter-stage societies, like Britain, generated "great respect and veneration for the ladies," Millar exulted. Ensconced in the home, where they indulged in the domestic pleasures of family life most suited to them, women in commercial society, the highest stage of civilization, enjoyed the respect, the friendship, and companionship of men. But women's bodies contained a "torrid zone," too, an inconvenient feature that seemingly defied geographic location and which threatened to undermine the progress and civilization of European countries by its very existence. Because, as we have seen earlier, commercial society depended upon the cult of domesticity for its legitimation as a virtuous regime, sexual desire among middle-class women could not be tolerated, and it had to be displaced on to other women. Identified with "savage" women who inhabited societies of lesser development, sexual desire came to be regarded as the mark of primitive, uncivilized, degraded individuals, who in turn became the foil against whom virtuous British women would define themselves.

This kind of formulation served to persuade many women that British control over large areas of the world was not only legitimate but moral, too. With very few exceptions – such as Lady Mary Wortley Montagu, whose extensive travels convinced her that European ideas about sexual attitudes and behavior in the Middle East were grossly inaccurate – the upper- and middle-class women of Britain believed that the fortunate position they held relative to "primitive" women of the world obligated them to support efforts to lift up their less fortunate sisters of the seraglio and the harem where they were reduced to sexual slavery.

These racial and sexualized descriptions also worked to reinforce the two visions of "womanliness" we saw being created in the last chapter to distinguish British women of the middle and upper classes from those of the working classes. For just as sexual desire was being displaced from middle-class women on to "savage" women of Asia and Africa in the course of establishing the cult of domesticity, it was also being displaced on to working-class women at home, who were themselves identified as savage. It was here, in the conflation of female sexuality with racial difference, especially as it pertained to Africa but also, as we shall see, to India and Ireland, that differences among women of the middle classes on the one hand and the working classes on the other could so easily be established through the use of blackness to represent degradation, sexual immorality, and danger. In a formulation that would become far more prevalent in the second half of the nineteenth century as imperial and class tensions became acute, the West Indies planter Edward Long warned in 1772, "the lower class of women in *England* are remarkably fond of the blacks."[14]

Figure 4.1 "The Parricide. A Sketch of Modern Patriotism," engraving of 1776 for the Westminster Magazine

Source: Courtesy of the Print Collection, Lewis Walpole Library, Yale University

Losing America

Confidence in Britain's imperial destiny did not last long after 1763. Prior to the Seven Years' War, Britain's colonial possessions had been few enough and the Europeans who had settled them enough like Britons to be able to fit into the picture the English liked to draw of the unique values of liberty and freedom they represented. Limited largely to the thirteen colonies of North America, populated by white, protestant, English-speaking persons, an empire based on trade, pro-imperials could readily claim, brought significant material and moral advantages with it. The empires of France, Spain, and even the Romans, which were based on conquest and unwanted rule from the center, required constant military effort on the part of the mother country to maintain its control, and had ultimately destroyed the mother country, it was believed.

Now, however, the Peace of Paris of 1763 ceded to Britain enormous tracts of territory in Canada, the West Indies, West Africa, India, Cuba, and the Philippines formerly held by France and Spain and inhabited by non-white, non-Christian populations. Enslaved Africans, French catholics, Indians, Amerindians – how was rule over these "alien" peoples to be rendered compatible with the vision of empire as a beneficial product of liberty-loving commercial people? How could the British, and especially the English, who believed themselves to be uniquely free from tyranny after 1688, justify to themselves an empire that required the domination of those who inhabited it? In what ways was the British empire now any different from those of France, Spain, or Rome in its use of authoritarianism and brutal force as methods of rule? A small but vocal minority of anti-imperialists regarded empire as the source of luxury and corruption in the nation; much of that corruption, a number of journalists and politicians had argued shortly after the victories in the Seven Years' War, had been facilitated by Britain's imperial activities. By the late 1760s and early 1770s, a broad array of critics within and without parliament had begun to identify adventurers in India and planters in the West Indies as a source of moral contamination at home. "Bred for the most part at the Breast of a Negro Slave; surrounded in their Infancy with a numerous Retinue of these dark Attendants," charged Dr John Fothergill in 1765, West Indian planters "are habituated by Precept and Example, to Sensuality, Selfishness, and Despotism."[15] "Luxury, effeminacy and profligacy" amongst planters and "nabobs," as fantastically enriched agents of the East India Company were termed upon their return to England, had begun to contaminate the entire British political system with corrupt and authoritarian practices, it was asserted. West Indian planters, the *Daily Gazetteer* charged in 1767, "being bred the tyrants of their slavish blacks, may endeavour to reduce the whites [in Britain] to the same condition by an aristocracy."[16] As we have seen, a body of systematized racial thought emerged that portrayed Asians, Africans, native Americans, and, not incidentally, Irish, and Scots

Highlanders as childlike, feminine, or savage peoples in need of guidance, discipline, and control. The presence of a virtuous, manly British imperial master, under whose firm but gentle tutelage these benighted people might learn the attributes of civilization, the pro-imperial line went, would benefit colony and mother country alike. This kind of thinking about race and empire took on even greater intensity when Britain lost the thirteen American colonies in 1783, and at the same time, as we shall see below, acquired control over significant portions of India.

Britons' confidence in their right to rule over colonial territories received a serious blow with the revolt of the American colonies. At home, British opinion divided over the policies that had produced the war and the rightness of the colonists' cause. One small faction believed that the hyper-patriotic attitudes provoked by the imperial contest produced a dangerous kind of masculinity. Arguing in 1776 that "in every point of view, the laws of war, and the laws of thieving are exactly alike" in their affirmation of conquest, military coercion, and self-interest, all of which might place the state in moral and physical jeopardy, some of them went so far as to call for the substitution of a "feminine" for a "masculine" ethos. What they saw as the "weakness of women" promised a degree of safety for the nation, for it "hath not ushered in such a flood of calamities, as these fatal virtues of men." This, however, was a decidedly minority view, even among those who opposed the war.

Radicals seeking greater participation for middling people in the political process believed that the corruption of a government monopolized by landed élites – who, reformers charged, saw in politics the means by which to enrich themselves and their friends and connections – had established policies toward the American colonies that acted against the interests of the nation as a whole. In their view, the Americans' refusal to buckle under the tyranny of the king and his ministers demonstrated a manliness that Britons would do well to emulate. Apologists for the colonists argued that by resisting illegal authority, Americans were defending liberty, a practice that all manly and patriotic Englishmen should applaud. "Fighting like men – like ENGLISHMEN, for law and liberty supposed to be violated," as one newspaper put it, Americans appeared to many Britons to exemplify a "manliness of sentiment" lacking among Europeans, who had been afflicted with the "luxurious effects of a debauched, vitiated and enervated taste."

Against these claims of a manly resistance to illegitimate authority, supporters of the war against the Americans conjured an image of the colonists as a rebellious, unruly, disordered, insubordinate female and savage power that threatened the very existence of the British nation. One anti-American print published in April 1776 in the *Westminster Review*, titled *The Parricide* (which means the killing of the father), depicts America as a dagger-wielding woman in Indian head-dress (see Figure 4.1). She is cheered on by a dark-skinned man with snake-like hair, dressed in a loincloth and waving fiery torches in the air. The associations of "unnatural" femininity, distinctive racial characteristics, and "savagery" with the Americans' resistance to legitimate authority marked that legitimate authority as masculine, white, and civilized.

With defeat and the loss of the American colonies came an intense round of national soul-searching. Not surprisingly, given the gendered language through which the imperial enterprise was articulated, what was regarded as imperial failure came to be spoken of as a failure of manliness. Many eighteenth-century Scottish moralists, for instance, saw in British losses in the American Revolution the product of effeminacy brought about by too much refinement and luxury; they believed that the English, like the French, had begun the moral decline consequent upon luxurious living that accompanied prosperity. The *Caledonian Mercury* prominently displayed a letter from "An Old Fellow and an Englishman," who attributed Britain's military defeat in 1783 to "the loss of our ancient manners. Virtue is always connected with plainness and simplicity; effeminacy always with luxurious refinement. Our ancestors were men; we are, alas!, we are very despicable." Other letters and articles in the Scottish press identified the disgraced General Howe as being "debilitated by luxury and dissipation." The manliness of the nation, shaken by the successful challenge of the American colonists, would ultimately be redeemed through Britain's conquest of and control over India, whose non-white, non-Christian inhabitants were represented as in thrall to arbitrary and tyrannous rulers enervated by luxury and sensuality, subjects in dire need of a beneficent imperial master whose rule would expose them to enlightened principles of progress and civilization.

India

The British had been involved with India since the sixteenth century, when the East India Company received a royal charter that gave it the right to monopolize trade with India, which it did with great profitability throughout the course of the seventeenth and eighteenth centuries. India was not a colony or possession of the British government in the sense that the American colonies were until 1783, or Ireland, the West Indies, and Canada continued to be, and the British government had no official ties with, or jurisdiction over, affairs of the various Indian élites who ruled the continent after the disintegration of the Mughal empire in the first half of the eighteenth century. Rather, local East India Company officials, with the military assistance of a private army made up of mercenaries, established the company as an unofficial yet sovereign governing entity in a number of coastal towns of India like Bombay, Madras, and Calcutta, and took advantage of conflicts between indigenous rulers to annex large areas of territory over the course of the eighteenth century, first in Bengal, where they controlled vast resources of land, labor, and capital. These officials, men like Robert Clive, enriched themselves enormously by extracting huge fortunes from indigenous rulers who sought company protection and support as they vied with one another for power, and created an atmosphere and expectation of plunder among adventurers to, and traders with, India that could not be reconciled with the grand rhetoric of benefi-cence and progress that pro-imperialists insisted characterized their relationships with North America and the West Indies. When Clive and other so-called "nabobs" returned to England and showed off their great wealth to the opinion-makers of society, the envy and anger they provoked roused MPs to take action.

In 1773, parliament passed the Regulating Act, establishing some degree of control over the East India Company by creating the position of governor-general in Bengal, which had authority over Madras and Bombay as well. A council of five, made up of the governor-general and four other crown appointees, but paid by the East India Company, would be responsible for the company's affairs in Calcutta. This unwieldy structure lasted for eleven years, during which time Warren Hastings, the governor-general, increased the size and scope of the company's authority by developing systems of tax collection, administration, and civil and criminal law. He also fended off severe challenges to the company's rule in Bengal from a military alliance of three of the most powerful indigenous Indian states backed by the French, but in the process of doing so engaged in certain practices – violent and forcible extortion, seizure of treasuries, and the overthrow of princes and princesses – against his own Indian allies that raised outcries against him at home. Portrayed as the epitome of greed, corruption, and exploitation of naïve and innocent native peoples, Hastings provoked outrage among a number of MPs that was all the more heated for their conviction that the British government, through its relationship with the East India Company, was complicit in these sordid activities.

In 1784, the government of William Pitt, the prime minister, passed the India Act through parliament. By this legislation, which remained in force until 1858 when it was superseded by yet another regime of governance prompted by the Indian Mutiny of 1857 (see Chapter 9), the East India Company and the British government became partners of sorts. The company preserved its jurisdiction over the commercial affairs of those parts of India over which it had control, while the British government took over matters of governance and administration. The governor-general, appointed by and answerable to the crown, had the executive power necessary to carry out and enforce his initiatives; and the company, which could appoint its own officials, was free to conduct its commercial activities and control patronage. So as to insure that previous abuses would not be allowed to continue, the act included a provision that the East India Company clear with an oversight Board of Control in London, made up in part of cabinet ministers, any military or civil policies it wished to pursue.

In 1785, Hastings resigned his position as governor-general and returned to

England. There he faced the wrath of prominent MPs like Charles James Fox and Edmund Burke for his reportedly rapacious behavior in India; in 1786, Burke brought forward a bill of impeachment against Hastings for exercising "arbitrary power" in India, which caused "cruelties unheard-of, and Devastations almost without a name!"[17] In a theatrical performance that dragged on until he was impeached by the House of Commons in 1787, and then acquitted of the charges against him by the House of Lords in 1794, the question of Britain's culpability in an imperial venture gone all wrong was displaced on to Hastings and rehearsed over and over until a solution could be found that would render Britain innocent of any wrongdoing as well.

Burke and his Whig supporters, echoing the unease and anxiety felt about empire after the Peace of Paris in 1763, feared that the exercise of arbitrary rule over India threatened liberty at home in Britain. "I am certain," he declared, "that every means effectual to preserve India from oppression is a guard to preserve the British Constitution from its worst corruption." Although he was not a proponent of independence for India, Burke castigated the behavior of East India Company agents whose grabs for territory and riches shamed every freedom-loving, virtuous Briton; violated the integrity of ancient and long-civilized Indian states; and promised to stain the imperial project as a whole with their corruption and extortionate practices.

Hastings answered his critics by drawing upon a kind of "when in Rome do as the Romans do" notion of government. He argued that in a land long subject to the rule of "oriental despots," he could not expect to be an effective governor-general if he did not employ the tactics and principles that his Indian counterparts used against their subjects and against one another. The concept of "oriental despotism" referred to the belief that Asians – with the exception of "manly" warrior "races" in India like the Sihks, Marathas, and Rajputs, against whom the British were hard pressed to demonstrate their military dominance and who were ultimately co-opted into the Indian army by admiring British officials – by their very nature, submitted readily to absolute rule, almost as slaves submitted to their masters. It implied that Asian states possessed no system of laws, and their peoples no rights. These ideas tallied well with those about the effects of climate on civic society we saw earlier in the chapter, for India's heat and humidity explained what to Europeans appeared to be the supineness of Indians in the face of arbitrary, despotic rulers. "The labour of being free," wrote Alexander Dow in his 1770 *Dissertation on Despotism*, part of a larger history of India, required more than Indians could muster in a climate that produced overwhelming "languor" and ener-vation. It was much easier simply to give way "without murmuring" to the "arbitrary sway" of despotic rulers. Robert Orme asserted that the heat of India produced in its people an "effeminacy and resignation of spirit, not to be paralleled in the world." Noting that the fertility of the soil provided a wealth of produce, he claimed that "breathing in the softest of climates, having so few wants and receiving even the luxuries of other nations with little labour from their own soil, the Indian must become the most effeminate inhabitant of the globe."

If we keep in mind that the term "effeminacy" referred, in the eighteenth century, not to homosexuality among men but to a weakening of men too much in the thrall of luxury, sensuality, and pleasure, that is, to the qualities ascribed to women, we can understand better the association Europeans made between despotism and sexual licentiousness. "Oriental despotism" conjured up images of the harem, of polygamy, of jealousy, intrigue, passion, and cunning. Like the visions produced of African societies located in the "torrid zones" of the globe, representations of the licentious, immoral, despotic Indians who subjected their women to the worst kind of sexual slavery offered Britons a foil against which they then imagined themselves to be. Freedom-loving, independent, industrious, manly Britons who held their women in awe and treated them with respect – these were the individuals whose imperial ventures in North America had brought wealth, acclaim, and glory to Great Britain.

Reports of the East India Company's unrestrained greed and corruption, and Hastings' claim to have governed of necessity in the fashion of an Asian despot, threatened this image of the civilized British and caused people like Burke a great deal of anxiety over what could be easily construed as Britain's having acted no better than any other "oriental despot." Burke, following a well-known rhetoric of rapine and torture attributable to peoples of "lesser" civilization, catalogued the transgressions of Hastings and his followers through an inventory of sexual sensationalism, portraying India as an innocent virgin ravished by evil-minded Britons. "The treatment of females could not be described," he thundered to the House of Commons:

> dragged forth from their houses, which the religion of the country had made so many sanctuaries, they were exposed naked to public view; the virgins were carried to the Court of Justice, where they might naturally have looked for protection; but now they looked for it in vain; for in the face of the Ministers of Justice, in the face of the spectators, in the face of the sun, those tender and modest virgins were brutally violated. The only difference between their treatment and that of their mothers was, that the former were dishonoured in the face of day, the latter in the gloomy recesses of their dungeons. Other females had the nipples of their breasts put in a cleft bamboo, and torn off. What modesty in all nations most carefully conceals, this monster [Hastings] revealed to view, and consumed by slow fires.

Hastings and his men were Britons, acting on behalf of the greatest commercial company in the land, whose directors enjoyed vast influence over the financial and political affairs of Britain; many of them, indeed, sat in parliament. In order for Britain's grand imperial project to survive the conquest of India, Hastings and his agents would have to go down, and the East India Company and Britain itself removed from any participation in arbitrary rule, with all its connotations of sexual excess. For Burke and other Whigs, this meant that Britain must not only punish the wrongdoers and impose discipline on its officials in India, but also create a colonial government that would act in the interests of Indians, which, he claimed, were "in effect, one and the same" as those of the British. In short, Burke envisaged a form of colonial rule that could be made moral through proper, just governing of Indian people.

Under the governor-generalship of Lord Cornwallis from 1786 to 1793, Burke's vision of colonial rule was largely put into effect. Employees of the East India Company were no longer permitted to trade as private individuals, nor to exact through extortion from indigenous Indian rulers vast fortunes. Rather, they were paid salaries high enough to keep them from temptation. Cornwallis's Code of Regulations made the district tax collectors accountable for every sum they received and liable to prosecution if they exceeded even by a little their authorized amounts. District judges had authority over the police, and were charged with the impartial administration of a known and settled body of law, which, like its English counterpart, sought to protect property and maintain order. By establishing a colonial administration that looked much like their own in many respects, Britons could remove from themselves any taint of complicity in, and displace on to Indians themselves full and exclusive responsibility for the practices of "oriental despotism." While "every native of Hindustan, I verily believe, is corrupt," declared Cornwallis, Britons could congratulate themselves for what they saw as their "upright and humane intentions" for imperial power. Morally superior to the corrupt, dissembling, licentious native population, the British could go about their business of empire in India confident of their right and their duty to rule people who were fit only for subjection.

The gendered and racialized images of legitimate and illegitimate claims to power and authority had lasting effects. In the case of gender, as we shall see in the next chapter, they served to justify a full-scale campaign to eliminate women and what was regarded as "the feminine" from the public arenas of work and politics, and to restrict them to the private world of home and domesticity. In the case of race, they acted to diminish the doubts Britons had about their imperial control of millions of non-white subjects in Asia, and to excuse their widespread, enthusiastic participation in the transport of, and trade in, African slaves. The intersections of racial and gender attributes appeared regularly in efforts to uphold or resist various regimes of power throughout the eighteenth, nineteenth, and twentieth centuries. The impact they had on human beings, men and women of all races, classes, and ethnicities, would be profound.

NOTES

1 Quoted in Thomas Metcalf, *The New Cambridge History of India, III: Ideologies of the Raj* (Cambridge, 1994), p. 2.
2 See R.F. Foster, *Modern Ireland, 1600–1972* (London, 1989).
3 Quoted in Richard Ned Lebow, *White Britain and Black Ireland: The Influence of Stereotypes on Colonial Policy* (Philadelphia, 1976), p. 41.
4 See Linda Colley, *Britons: Forging the Nation, 1707–1837* (New Haven, 1992).
5 Quoted in Colley, *Britons: Forging the Nation*, pp. 34, 92, 90.
6 Much of what follows is drawn from Kathleen Wilson, *The Sense of the People: Politics, Culture and Imperialism in England, 1715–1785* (Cambridge, 1995).
7 Quoted in Peter Fryer, *Staying Power: The History of Black People in Britain* (London, 1984), p. 20.
8 Quoted in Fryer, *Staying Power*, p. 14.
9 Quoted in Fryer, *Staying Power*, pp. 17, 15.
10 This discussion on race derives from Kim F. Hall, *Things of Darkness: Economies of Race and Gender in Early Modern England* (Ithaca, 1995).
11 Quoted in Anne McClintock, *Imperial Leather: Race, Gender and Sexuality in the Colonial Contest* (New York, 1995), p. 22.
12 Quoted in Hall, *Things of Darkness*, p. 34; McClintock, *Imperial Leather*, p. 23.
13 The following discussion of "torrid zones" depends upon Felicity A. Nussbaum, *Torrid Zones: Maternity, Sexuality, and Empire in Eighteenth-Century English Narratives* (Baltimore, 1995).
14 Quoted in McClintock, *Imperial Leather*, p. 23.
15 Quoted in Fryer, *Staying Power*, p. 19.
16 Quoted in Wilson, p. 275. Much of the following discussion is drawn from her *The Sense of the People*.
17 The discussion of Hastings's impeachment is drawn from Metcalf, *Ideologies of the Raj*; and Sara Suleri, *The Rhetoric of English India* (Chicago, 1992).

SOURCES

C.A. Bayly, *Imperial Meridian: The British Empire and the World, 1780–1830*. London, 1989.

Linda Colley, *Britons: Forging the Nation, 1707–1837*. New Haven, 1992.

R.F. Foster, *Modern Ireland, 1600–1972*. London, 1989.

Peter Fryer, *Staying Power: The History of Black People in Britain*. London, 1984.

Kim F. Hall, *Things of Darkness: Economies of Race and Gender in Early Modern England*. Ithaca, 1995.

Pat Hudson, *The Industrial Revolution*. London, 1992.

Anne McClintock, *Imperial Leather: Race, Gender and Sexuality in the Colonial Contest*. New York, 1995.

P.J. Marshall and Glyndwr Williams, *The Great Map of Mankind: Perceptions of New Worlds in the Age of Enlightenment*. Cambridge, MA, 1982.

Billie Melman, *Women's Orients: English Women and the Middle East, 1718–1918*. Ann Arbor, 1995.

Thomas R. Metcalf, *The New Cambridge History of India, III: Ideologies of the Raj*. Cambridge, 1994.

Felicity A. Nussbaum, *Torrid Zones: Maternity, Sexuality, and Empire in Eighteenth-Century English Narratives*. Baltimore, 1995.

J.G.A. Pocock, "Political thought in the English-speaking Atlantic, 1760–1790," in J.G.A. Pocock, ed., *Varieties of British Political Thought, 1500–1800*. Cambridge, 1993.

Sara Suleri, *The Rhetoric of English India*. Chicago, 1992.

Kathleen Wilson, *The Sense of the People: Politics, Culture and Imperialism in England, 1715–1785*. Cambridge, 1995.

Chapter 5

Feminine encroachments
Women, culture, and politics, 1740–89

Commerce and imperial trade swelled the ranks of middling people in England, Wales, Scotland, and northern Ireland; the combination of their numbers and of the wealth they produced and consumed over the course of the eighteenth century helped to form them into an increasingly significant political force. Because few of them had direct access to parliament through the vote, which was denied to most of them on the basis of their lack of landed property, their influence remained "out-of-doors," as contemporaries would say. Through the commercial press and voluntary trade, philanthropic, and social associations, men and women of the middling ranks made known their political concerns and demands, and were joined in them very often by men and women of plebeian status, who could be rallied in support of, or opposition to, various causes.

The chief political issues of the 1740s and 1750s for middling people concerned the failure of what they saw as a corrupt, effeminate, Frenchified aristocratic government to set and carry out policies that furthered the national interest, which, as many middling people saw it, involved strengthening manufacturing and commerce at home and trade overseas. Virtuous government, argued men and women of the commercial ranks, could hardly be carried out by dissipated, indolent aristocrats who were slaves to French fashion and to their own appetites and vices. They sought rulers who could better preserve the principles of liberty-loving, independent Britons as they had been achieved through the Glorious Revolution, but they seemed little inclined to press for their own participation in governing. Beginning in the 1750s, middling people, joined by many from the artisan ranks, began to assert more forcefully a new political idiom of "social contract" and its corollary, "resistance to tyranny," drawn from the writings of John Locke, and to claim their "rights" to representation in parliament. As we have seen so often in past chapters, many of their demands, concerns, and causes – and the responses to them – were framed in terms of gender and sexuality, a circumstance that would have serious practical consequences for men and women with regard to their power, their opportunities, and their identities in the nineteenth century.

As we saw in the previous chapter, the qualities that defined citizenship by the middle of the eighteenth century, and which would confer "rights" on individuals in the second half, had become gendered as male. This was so despite – and because of – the considerable contributions made to the war efforts against France by significant numbers of women. Over the course of the century, women appeared with men in public spaces – themselves transformed and rendered appealing by the "urban renaissance" consequent upon the commercial revolution – more and more frequently; they began to make known their wishes and desires through the press, the reading and writing of novels, and the consumption of goods now available to them in unprecedented variety and volume; they participated in religious and humanitarian reform efforts; and some went so far as to demand increased access to education and political rights. Their visibility, their economic influence, and their political claims disturbed many people, prompting a concerted effort to more fully circumscribe them within the home. An intensification of separate sphere ideology – of the insistence upon distinct public and private realms for men and women that we saw being developed in response to the perceived need to remove the feminine from the public arenas of finance and commerce – followed, designed to counter and contain women's public activity.

Expanding the public sphere

The commercial revolution sparked a dramatic change in the organization of and degree of comfort in the homes of middling and upper ranked people, a phenomenon we associate with the rise of domesticity. It also wrought great changes in public spaces, stimulating the building of walks, streets, shopping arcades, tea houses, parks, public gardens, and other places of amusement and pleasure. Such traditional gathering spots for men as coffee-houses, pubs, taverns, and inns retained their exclusively masculine clientele; and many of them developed over time into private clubs or associations where urban middle-class men joined together for a variety of purposes. Associations dedicated to philanthropic or civic-minded service to the community; to educational and moral self-improvement; to commercial activities; and to the exercise of political influence "out-of-doors" sprang up. Patriotic and high-minded, these clubs, societies, and associations acted as vehicles through which men of commerce and the professions could contribute to the public good as they defined it. They did so confident in the belief that their possession of property and their status as heads of household entailed upon them the requisite independence that undergirded "virtue" and authorized political activity. Virtue, once the exclusive mark of independent country gentlemen of landed wealth, now extended to domestic, middle-class patriarchs, whose possession of a household, of children, and of virtuous wives constituted them, at least in their own minds, as citizens deserving of recognition by, and inclusion within, the political élite. Starting in the 1750s and 1760s, they demanded the "rights" that virtuous, rational, liberty-loving Englishmen had wrested from the crown in the course of the Glorious Revolution. Although women were formally excluded from the clubs and associations that characterized eighteenth-century middle-class male social and political life, they made their presence felt in the public arena through other means. Manufacturers and merchants recognized women's predominant influence in the demand for goods and services, and in the partaking of leisure activities that fueled commercial capitalism; they catered to women's desires and granted them considerable authority in matters of taste, choice, and consumption. As early as the 1730s a commercial market for commodities that expressed any number and variety of political positions had emerged, and women bought and sold objects like scarves, cockades, and tea caddies in large numbers. In 1787, capitalizing on a market produced by the high emotions surrounding the anti-slavery campaign, Josiah Wedgwood manufactured a china figurine of a slave on his knees, imploring his purchasers, who were many, "Am I not a man and a brother?" In the 1750s, women contributed time and money to the patriotic associations that sprang up during the Seven Years' War, and in the 1760s, 1770s, and 1780s, as we shall see below, they actively participated in public debates and campaigned on behalf of various politicians and causes. Women marched, demonstrated, protested, and rioted; they were mobilized by propagandists and prosecuted for sedition. Their presence in, and acknowledgment by, the public realm conferred upon them a tacit, if not a proper, claim to citizenship.

Commercial capitalism afforded large numbers of women a degree of self-fashioning and self-expression not available to them previously, and an aspect of control over their lives otherwise denied them by law and custom. Middle- and upper-class women presented themselves in the new public spaces attired in the latest fashions, outraging many observers with their pronounced bustles and daring necklines. More shocking still were those women who adopted the clothing of men so as to participate fully in the activities of a more robust social and public life of riding, sport, and travel. In donning men's riding habits and appearing at masquerades in masculine dress, these "women of the world" seemed to be aping men in their fashions and, more disturbingly, in their behavior and self-assertion. Ballads, poems, and novels told of female warriors seeking love and adventure, stories that sometimes had their counterparts in real life: Lady Harriet Acland, for instance, accompanied a corps of grenadiers behind enemy lines during the American war to reach her wounded husband; others such as Hannah Snell, Hanna Witney, and Susanna Cope dressed as men, enlisted, and served their country in the army and navy. Tales of these "amazons" circulated throughout popular culture, exciting great interest among female readers and audiences, and much adverse comment from male critics, who used the term disparagingly to castigate the spectacular rise of women writers that took place during the eighteenth century.

Print culture, through which middling people helped to define notions of national interest and citizenship, and kept themselves abreast of and engaged in national affairs, expanded rapidly throughout the eighteenth century, touching the lives, and broadening the scope, of women across Britain. Some 50 percent of urban women in England could read in the 1720s, a reflection of the need of many of them to conduct business. By the 1750s, 40 percent of all women in England could read and 60 percent of men; those numbers had increased by 1800 to almost all men and a majority of women. A third of the members of circulating libraries were women; many participated in the active dissemination of political journalism in their capacity as writers, printers, booksellers, and newsagents.

Women articulated their needs, wants, pleasures, and fantasies most vividly through the reading and writing of novels. As the term indicates, the novel was new to the eighteenth century, but it soon became the single most popular form of reading, especially among middle-ranked women. The market for novels, in other words, was large, and was made larger still by the availability of fiction through circulating libraries after 1740: those who could not afford to buy their own books, which were in great demand, could borrow them.

Through fiction writing and reading, women — and men appealing to an audience of women — explored questions of women's autonomy, roles, and status; the power of men; sexual danger; and morality and societal values generally. The exploits of courageous, heroic female characters who stood up to and bested their male antagonists while still maintaining a "feminine" appearance appealed enormously to readers. These stock figures competed with another, ultimately more compelling fictional character, the "Lady in Distress." In one of the most emulated accounts of women's treatment at the hands of men, Samuel Richardson's *Pamela*, the heroine staves off rape at the hands of an aristocratic rake by fainting dead away, and, through her innocence and purity, converts him into a virtuous husband. As Pamela wrote to her parents of her triumph over the predatory Mr B, "I … have reason to bless God, who, by disabling me in my faculties, empowered me to preserve my innocence; and, when all my strength would have signified nothing, magnified himself in my weakness." By endowing women with the capacity to reform rapacious men through the exercise of their exquisite delicacy and acute sensibility, sentimental novelists, most of whom were women, hit upon a formula that would endure through countless repetitions. From Frances Burney's *Evelina*, published in 1778, to *Virtue in Distress, The History of Miss Sally Pruen, and Miss Laura Spencer*, written "by a Farmer's Daughter in Gloustershire" in 1772, to Mary Wollstonecraft's *Maria, or the Wrongs of Woman*, unfinished at the time of her death in 1798, sentimental novels articulated women's grievances against men and made claims for a world in which their feelings, their sensibilities, their needs and values counted for something.[1]

Women in public

Because they had so few opportunities for leisure, even literate plebeian women could not indulge in much reading or writing of novels. They found a means of expressing their resentments and grievances and joys and pleasures through religion, specifically through the offshoot of Anglicanism known as Methodism. Begun by John Wesley, a clergyman, in 1738 in reaction against the established church, whose clergy catered to the socially respectable and cared little for either the lives or the souls of the poor, Methodism sought to bring salvation to all God's flock, rich and poor, men and women alike. Against the secular, rationalized, logical doctrine of Anglicanism, it appealed to the emotions of individuals, to "the hearts" of sinners seeking God's forgiveness. Traveling from parish to parish, Wesley and his followers brought their evangelical revival to all parts of England, conducting open-air meetings where passion and "enthusiasm" took hold of vast crowds of congregants who yearned to be saved. By the 1780s, Methodism constituted a cohesive religious sect with an ecclesiastical structure and coherent doctrine.

Until the 1790s, when the death of John Wesley allowed the new denomination to be taken over by a conservative, respectable male leadership, Methodism eagerly welcomed women to its ranks and even to its pulpits to bring the gospel of "heart religion" to as many people as possible. Many early Methodist societies owed their existence to the initiative taken by women such as Mary Aldersley of Macclesfield, Elizabeth Blow of Grimsby, and Martha Thompson of Rufforth. Women of means like Thompson, Elizabeth Clulow, and Henrietta Gayer donated funds to sustain societies and build chapels. Women of more modest resources led small "bands" of four or five persons in which deep examination of personal lives and confession of sin took place, and conducted larger "classes" of twelve or more who came together in fellowship to discuss more practical matters of finance and organization. They risked and sometimes gave their lives to defend Methodist preachers from angry mobs.

And they preached. Beginning in the 1760s, a small number of women who felt called by God began to proclaim from the pulpit the gospel as Methodists understood it. The first to do so, Sarah Crosby, experienced conflicting feelings of obligation and embarrassment when confronted by the necessity to speak to an unexpectedly large congregation in 1761, but she soon expressed confidence in the rightness of her actions. She described her address to another congregation two weeks later in no uncertain terms:

> In the evening I exhorted near two hundred people to forsake their sins, and shewed them the willingness of Christ to save: They flock as doves to the window, tho' as yet we have no preacher. Surely, Lord, thou has much people in this place! My soul was much comforted in speaking to the people, as my Lord has removed all my scruples respecting the propriety of my acting thus publickly.[2]

Other lay women preachers followed, despite the discomfiture it produced in Wesley and many others. During the 1770s, Grace Walton, Mary Bosanquet, Hannah Harrison, Eliza Bennis, Peggy Dale, Ann Gilbert, Elizabeth Hurrell, Margaret Davidson – these women and many others took to heart what they perceived to be the "extraordinary call" of God to bring His word to others. They preached in chapels and traveled throughout England, Wales, and Ireland as itinerant preachers. Their success was phenomenal. In the 1770s and 1780s, women's activities within Methodism flourished, prompting Wesley to give his sanction to their preaching and compelling the English Methodist Conference to officially recognize women preachers.

Methodism attracted many women to its fold because its bands and classes offered them an alternative to what could be the oppressive and unhappy conditions of marriage and family life. Wesley himself believed in the sanctity of marriage, but he taught that celibacy constituted a holy state that came from God. He urged men and women who felt called to leave their unbelieving families and to form bands, or what he termed "love-feasts," with like-minded believers. Many women did create what amounted to spiritual sisterhoods where they found material and emotional support and camaraderie; Sarah Crosby, for example, founded a group called the Female Brethren in Leeds in 1793.

Because it championed workers and the poor, and gave women opportunities to play unconventional roles and to understand that they enjoyed spiritual, if not political and social, equality within its activities, Methodism seemed to many élites to threaten the social and gender order of eighteenth-century England, the order represented by the Anglican church.[3] One duchess objected vehemently to Methodist teachings, describing them as "repulsive and strongly tinctured with impertinence and disrespect towards their superiors, in perpetually endeavoring to level all ranks and do away with all distinctions." Opponents sought to discredit Wesley and his followers by accusing them of sexual profligacy and unnatural acts. Critics transformed the prayer and confession of "love-feasts" into orgies, and depicted the emotional oration, the joyful audience responses, and the hallucinations, fainting, and crying out of congregants at the revivals as the expressions of wild sexual passions. Henry Fielding, the novelist who wrote *Tom Jones*, claimed that the notorious "female husband" who passed herself off as a man and married a number of women in order to gain control of their money had herself been seduced by a Methodist woman. Moreover, he insisted, when she masqueraded as a male Methodist preacher, another Methodist man had made sexual overtures toward her. An Anglican clergyman told of one James Stephen, a Methodist preacher who traveled around England with "a young woman in man's clothes" in tow, and who made advances toward female enthusiasts who had come to hear him speak the word of God. A London bookseller named James Lackington described some of Wesley's female adherents as "sour, disappointed old maids," while others were "of a less prudish disposition." Unattractive and unable to attract a husband, or carnal and promiscuous, Wesleyan women so portrayed by their detractors lived and acted beyond the confines of the conventional gender order.

Methodist women were accused of abandoning their husbands, avoiding their domestic duties, and neglecting their children as they partook of the societies' communions and prayer meetings. The *Gentleman's Magazine* castigated the "many silly women" who left early "every Morning" to go to prayer or class meetings, leaving "their children in Bed till their Return, which sometimes is not til nine o'Clock … without any Regard to the grand Inconveniences, to which they are exposed by such neglect, contrary to the Laws of Nature." The chronicler of an anti-Methodist riot in Staffordshire reported that it had been caused by "the wife of a certain Collier" who "was missing from his House about a Week, … and was found by him at one of the Class-houses." A parish vicar in Chester wrote to a young girl who had been attending Methodist meetings at the expense, her mother declared, of her domestic duties. The vicar lamented that Methodists caused "confusion and disorder among families," and warned her that "those who neglect their own households are worse than infidels."

Although much of the assault on Methodism was directed at women, critics declaimed against Methodist men by labeling them "feminine," a charge that accrued weight because of Methodism's association with the emotions and attitudes ascribed to women. Wesley saw his brand of Christianity as a "heart-religion," and sought to bring it to the masses by appealing to feeling, to "the reasons of the heart," to something akin to what contemporaries recognized as sensibility, which was identified as more natural to women than to men. Passion, enthusiasm, and deep feeling, expressed through the tears, groans, sighs, and tremblings of mass congregations, could readily be called upon to show that "womanliness" rather than "manliness" characterized the men who cast their lot with Methodism. Because Wesley opposed dueling, cockfighting, bear-baiting, drunkenness, bawdiness, profanity, and public violence; because he sought to reform the manners of men to make them more gentlemanly, especially with regard to their treatment of their wives; and, because he urged male chastity, it was easy to taint his male converts with the charge of "effeminacy." He retorted that the miners, farmers, and sailors he converted to Christ, who sang hymns and refrained from cursing, could on no account be called "unmanly." "Nobody dared molest them," a contemporary pointed out. One reporter, following Lord Nelson, noted of the Methodist sailors who fought at the battle of Trafalgar, "they did their duty as well as any men."

The efforts by Wesley and his followers to inculcate in the men of Britain a new culture of politeness, manners, and deep feeling, or sensibility, paralleled the work of those moralists and theorists, as we saw in Chapter 3, to make commerce respectable. By the 1790s, Methodism and the gentlemanly code it promulgated had become an accepted and respected part of British life. As they became increasingly respectable and established, Methodist ministers acted to purge their ranks of radical elements, including those women whose preaching and religious activities had built the denomination in its early days. Women of the Methodist church became "ladies," wholly embracing the ideologies of domesticity and separate spheres that developed among the middle classes.

Religion also provided an opportunity for middle-class women to bring their influence to bear on a world beyond that of home and family. The evangelical movement within the Anglican church, seeking spiritual reform within the church and social reform outside it, preached a doctrine of domesticity writ large, of the extension of the individual and private qualities of discipline, obedience, chastity, propriety, cleanliness, and temperance to society as a whole. Because these were characteristics associated with the home and family, and middle-class women were understood to be responsible for their inculcation, evangelical women could freely join in the wider efforts to bring them to the poor and downtrodden. Charity work enabled them to operate in the public sphere without violating the precepts that, ideologically at any rate, restricted their activities to the private sphere. Performing the selfless tasks of providing relief to poverty-stricken families or of teaching in Sunday schools elicited no adverse comment from contemporaries; rather, it gave scope for women to demonstrate their talents and expend their considerable energies in doing good, and vastly enhanced their sense of self-worth. As Hannah More, a prominent evangelical, observed of her women friends and co-religionists, "formerly there seemed to be nothing useful in which they could naturally be busy, but now they may always find an object in attending the poor."[4]

Women in politics

The conviction that women possessed a finer sensibility than men authorized many forms of public activity beyond charity work. The anti-slavery campaign of the last decades of the eighteenth century, part of a larger humanitarian movement that addressed concerns such as prison reform, protection for children, education for the poor, and the breast-feeding of infants, attracted many evangelical, Methodist, and Quaker women to its ranks.[5]

While some strands of anti-slavery thought emphasized the rights of slaves to

freedom and autonomy, a position that made it more difficult for women to participate in, as they had no such rights and most could not imagine claiming them for
themselves, the most successful arguments against slavery made Britons recall the
suffering and inhumane conditions imposed on slaves by their fellow countrymen and
-women. The moral basis of anti-slavery appeals – sympathy for others, pity, compassion, the so-called "feminine" qualities associated with sensibility – dovetailed nicely
with the traits purportedly possessed by women, rendering them the obvious targets
of reform efforts outside of parliament and effective propagandists with those inside
parliament. As an appeal in the Manchester *Mercury* observed in 1787,

> If any public Interference will at any TIME become the Fair Sex; if Their
> Names are ever to be mentioned with Honour beyond the Boundaries of their
> Family, and the Circle of their Connections, it can only be, when a public
> Opportunity is given for the Exertion of those Qualities which are peculiarly
> expected in, and particularly possessed by that most amiable Part of Creation
> – the Qualities of Humanity, Benevolence, and Compassion.

The campaign to outlaw British involvement in the slave trade began at the
initiative of John Hylas, an Afro-Caribbean slave brought to England by his owner,
a woman whose name is unknown, in 1754. In 1758, he married, with the permission of their respective owners, a slave named Mary, who had been brought to
England from Barbados by the Newtons in 1754. John Hylas then received his
freedom, and for eight years he and Mary lived together as husband and wife. In
1766, however, the Newtons ordered the kidnapping and transportation of Mary
back to the West Indies, where she would be sold as a slave. John appealed to
Granville Sharp, a clerk in the Ordnance Department who had earlier managed to
secure the release of a former slave from jail, where he awaited transportation
back into slavery in Jamaica. Sharp helped John Hylas successfully sue for Mary
Hylas's freedom from the Newtons, who were ordered by the court to return her
on the first ship heading for England. In 1772, Lord Chief Justice Mansfield ruled
in the Somerset case that slave owners in England could not force their slaves to go
out of England.

These rulings did not constitute the end of slavery in England – though in
Scotland, by the 1778 ruling in *Knight v. Wedderburn*, slavery was condemned as
contrary to the laws of Scotland – nor even the forced deportations of blacks,
which continued at least until 1792. But they did publicize the plight of slaves, and
galvanized many Britons into action and formal association for the abolition of the
slave trade. From the start, women gave of their time and their money to organize
petition drives; they boycotted goods produced by the slave-holding West Indian
planters; and they wrote and spoke out publicly against Britain's involvement in
the slave trade.

Heart-rending stories about the break-up of families through the sale of individual members, usually children, and lurid tales of physical and sexual violence against slave women served as one of the most effective means of gaining support from the general public, the popular press, and ultimately from MPs. In 1788, Hannah More, a prominent evangelical, published "Slavery, a poem," contriving to ensure that its appearance coincided with a scheduled parliamentary debate on abolition. Her polemical entreaties against slavery constituted an incursion into the public realm of politics and commerce, though she was careful to argue her case in exclusively sentimental terms. "See the dire victim torn from social life," she wrote:

> The shrieking babe, the agonizing wife!
> She, wretch forlorn! is dragg'd by hostile hands,
> To distant tyrants sold, in distant lands! …
> By felon hands, by one relentless stroke,
> See the fond links of feeling Nature broke!
> The fibres twisting round a parent's heart,
> Torn from their grasp, and bleeding as they part.

These were motifs that especially concerned women, as the gender ideology of the late eighteenth century would have it; propagandists insisted that it was incumbent upon them to bring these horrors to public view, even if – especially if – it depicted a particular kind of British male in an unfortunate light. The case of one Captain Kimber, a slaver who strung up and whipped a black woman when she refused to dance unclothed for him on the deck of his ship, aroused a great deal of outcry. A 1792 cartoon captioned "The ABOLITION of the SLAVE TRADE, or the Inhumanity of Dealers in human flesh exemplified in Cap't. Kimber's treatment of a young Negro Girl of 15 for her Virgin Modesty" captured the various themes the anti-slavery campaign advanced in support of their cause (see Figure 5.1). It portrayed a gleeful Kimber with whip in hand and a sword emerging phallically from his cut-away coat, preparing to flog the naked woman as she hung upside down from a block and tackle operated by a reluctant seaman, whose unease with the situation shows on his face as he mutters, "Dam me if I like it. I have a good mind to let go" of the rope. In the background, three other half-naked African women cower in the stern while another seamen whispers to a mate, "My Eyes Jack our Girls at Wapping are never flogged for their modesty." "By G-d that's too bad," replies the other, "if he had taken her to bed to him it should be well enough. Split me, I'm allmost sick of this Black Business."

Chaste, modest victims of lustful, brutal representatives of a vicious planter aristocracy whose commerce in human cargoes offended most upright, moral, manly Britons and brought tears of pity to the eyes of compassionate British women – these dominant themes of anti-slavery propaganda could readily be

Figure 5.1 "The Abolition of the Slave Trade," cartoon of 1792

Source: Wilberforce House: Hull City Museums and Art Galleries

embraced and promulgated by women, who themselves had a stake in reforming men's behavior. As the Manchester *Mercury* noted:

> If it be just and right; if it be what Nature requires, and what Mankind expects, that Women should sympathize with Women; that if the Brutality of the Male should at any Time reverse in his Practice the Obligation of the Species, a Female may meet, from the Pity of her own Sex, that assistance which the Inhumanity of the other may deny.

This kind of argumentation produced paradoxical effects. On the one hand, making a case for a sort of sisterhood across racial lines undermined depictions of African women as subhuman. If they were chaste, modest, maternal, and wifely, they were not unlike the British middle-class women who wrote about them in these terms, and for that reason, they deserved to be united with their husbands and children, and free of abuse from brutal slavers or plantation owners. Sentimental appeals on behalf of slaves by women engaged in reforming humanity proved effective. In 1807, parliament, responding to overwhelming pressure created by the popular campaign against slavery, in which women had played a vital material and propagandistic role, passed the Abolition Act, bringing Britain's involvement in the slave trade to a close. On the other hand, depictions of slaves such as those in More's "Slavery," which soon became an exemplar for other anti-slavery representations of enslaved women and men, produced an image of Africans as passive, victimized, simple, alien individuals who lived in a timeless place with no culture or history and who could not speak out or act for themselves, requiring the assistance of white Britons to lift them up to freedom and liberty. These qualities meshed exactly with those promulgated about Africans and Indians by apologists for empire. Slavery in the British colonies continued after 1807, and although it would serve as a target for further humanitarian and feminist efforts in the nineteenth century, the racial ideology that underpinned it remained long into the twentieth century.

The development of what one historian has called "the cult of sensibility"[6] – expressed through literature, religion, charity work, and humanitarian reform – afforded many women the opportunity to enlarge the scope of their energies, intellects, and activities in the late eighteenth century. But sensibility and sentimental fiction, although they might empower women, might also encourage in them the overstimulation of feeling to the detriment of reason. Intellectual women representing virtually all political tendencies, from the conservative "bluestockings", such as Elizabeth Carter, Hester Chapone, and Hannah More, to the republican Catherine Macaulay and the radical Mary Wollstonecraft, shared the conviction that women ought to cultivate their reasoning faculties through education. Their rationales for urging more rigorous instruction on women than the current fashionable curricula of ornamental "female accomplishments" such as music, drawing, or dancing, and the ends they sought for women's education differed markedly, but whatever their position on women's place in society and polity, all of the advocates for women's education feared that excessive feeling in women – what we have called sensibility – untempered by the restraints of reason might leave them susceptible to any number of negative influences, "the prey of their senses," as Wollstonecraft put it, "the plaything of outward circumstances ... blown about by every momentary gust of feeling." More particularly, supporters of women's education like Wollstonecraft and Macaulay feared that without the inculcation of reason women would become the "prey" of licentious men who had only their own selfish interests in mind. "This state of things renders the situation of females, in their individual capacity, very precarious," Macaulay warned; "for the strength which Nature has given to the passion of love, in order to serve her purposes, has made it the most ungoveral [sic] propensity of any which attends us. The snares, therefore, that are continually laid for women, by persons who run no risk in compassing their seduction, exposes them to continual danger."

But education for women, in the minds of its champions, served a more positive end for women. Hannah More, for example, believed that middling and élite women should be educated so as to "be useful to others." In keeping with the ideas promoted by domesticity, she advised that an educated woman could better serve as a companion to her husband and a teacher to her children. "When a man of sense comes to marry," she argued in *Strictures on the Modern System of Female Education* (1799), "it is a companion whom he wants, and not an artist. It is not merely a creature who can paint, and play, and dress, and dance; it is a being who can comfort and counsel him; one who can reason, and reflect, and feel, and judge, and act, and discourse, and discriminate; one who can assist him in his affairs, lighten his cares, soothe his sorrows, purify his joys, strengthen his principles, and educate his children." Where More advocated education for women in order for them to improve upon their domestic responsibilities toward others, Catherine Macaulay, by contrast, insisted that women should obtain *for themselves* the benefits that education had to offer, and that the education given to girls should be the same as that for boys. "There is but one rule of right for the conduct of all rational beings," she asserted in 1790. "True wisdom ... is as useful to women as to men; because it is necessary to the highest degree of happiness, which can never exist with ignorance."

Mary Wollstonecraft combined More's domestic argument for women's education with Macaulay's individualist focus, and carried both to a political end. She saw in study and the cultivation of reason the means by which women could meet their familial responsibilities and also gain status as autonomous individuals and citizens with rights. "Connected with man as daughters, wives, and mothers," she observed in 1792:

their moral character may be estimated by their manner of fulfilling these simple duties; but the end, the grand end, of their exertions should be to unfold their own faculties. ... In every circumstance of life there is a kind of individuality, which requires an exertion of judgement to modify general rules. The being who can think justly in one track will soon extend its intellectual empire; and she who has sufficient judgement to manage her children will not submit, right or wrong, to her husband, or patiently to the social laws which make a nonentity of a wife.

Questions about the sexual vulnerability of women to licentious males and about what kind of education women should be eligible for received a great deal of attention in the 1770s and 1780s from a more general audience of men and women in the form of public debates. In London alone, in 1780, debates weighing various concerns about marriage, sexuality, education, and politics took place in thirty-three different locations; open to women and men alike, they often drew audiences of some 400 to 1,200 people each night. Four all-women debating societies appeared that year as well, La Belle Assemblée, the Female Parliament, the Female Congress, and the Carlisle House Debates for Women. Men could attend but were not allowed to speak. A sample of the topics debated during 1780 indicate that questions about differences in male and female temperament and behavior tended to dominate discussion, but the societies did not hesitate to address concerns about men encroaching upon women's employment, the exclusion of women from civil society, and even women's right to vote. On 14 October, for instance, La Belle Assemblée asked its members, "Ought not the women of Great Britain to have a voice in the election of Representatives, and be eligible to sit in Parliament as well as the men?"[7]

Questions like these had become more and more vital in the second half of the eighteenth century, reflecting both a broader movement among a large portion of the middling ranks that sought to expand political participation and to curb what many saw as tyrannical abuses by the monarchy on the one hand, and, on the other, a more particular dissatisfaction with the state of affairs that denied women political rights altogether. Upon marriage women lost their identity as individuals and became submerged into their husbands as legal entities. They lost legal possession of their person and their independent property, a circumstance that rendered them, by definition, ineligible for citizenship and political enfranchisement. Despite this handicap, and despite a middle-class political culture that rendered politics and citizenship "male," women participated heartily in various political campaigns during the second half of the eighteenth century. In the 1760s and 1770s, they joined in the radical movement surrounding John Wilkes and made their presence felt in the domestic controversies thrown up by the American war. In 1780 they played a prominent role in the anti-catholic Gordon Riots. As we have seen, they attended and participated in debates about their rights; they waged a vigorous campaign against slavery; and with the outbreak of the French Revolution in 1789, they made eloquent claims that the "rights of man" included women as well. Their activities provoked a more intense ideological effort to masculinize the political sphere and to contain women within the private sphere of home and family.

The accession of George III in 1760 inaugurated a new era in British politics. At the élite level, it was signaled by a fusion of Tory and Whig politicians into a united ruling class whose political aspirations consisted of obtaining offices and patronage for themselves, their kin, and their friends. The patronage system – in the days before professional bureaucrats carried out the administrative functions of government on the basis of their talent, education, and expertise – provided the means through which the state and the church obtained the personnel necessary to operate. On the other side of the equation, through networks of wealthy and well-positioned patrons, clients, and the brokers through whom the latter worked, the patronage system provided opportunities to gain access to place, power, and preferment as well as avenues for social advancement. What we would regard as old-boy and -girl networks operating through practices of corruption and bribery, and according to the principle of "who you know," in fact constituted, in eighteenth-century terms, a central, if unofficial, political institution.

Based on personal contacts between individuals, familial and political connections, and the power of persuasion; and operating in the intermediate spaces between public and political life on the one hand and private and social life on the other, the patronage system lent itself to women's participation in it. Because face-to-face contact across dining-room tables and ballroom floors was as likely to yield results as audiences in the halls of Westminster or hearings at political meetings or at court, women could be and were active, thriving, successful players in their own right. More than 10 percent of the patronage requests of the Duke of Newcastle, for instance, came from women seeking pensions for themselves, places for themselves or their children, and/or seats in parliament for male kin or friends. Success in obtaining patronage usually depended upon the rank and the family status of the petitioner; the sex of the individual seeking patronage seldom mattered to the outcome. Moreover, although the titled aristocracy accounted, not unexpectedly, for a massively disproportionate number of women's requests to Newcastle, some 53 percent, the rest of them were spread across the social order right down to women of the artisan class. Fifty-seven percent of the requests from these women were granted and another 24 percent promised in the future when opportunities opened up.[8]

Within the patronage system most women acted as clients seeking the favor of a patron. Some, however, acted as powerful go-betweens for family members or friends. Such brokers as Lady Katherine Pelham, Newcastle's sister-in-law, enjoyed strong track records in this regard, though failure to obtain office or pensions for clients could prove frustrating. For despite the fact that brokers could bring the pressures of mutual obligation and promises of electoral support or other political services to bear – for without this kind of leverage they would hardly be useful as brokers, male or female – in the final analysis, the power to grant favors lay with the patron. Far fewer women could act as patrons than men, given their formal lack of access to political, administrative, and church offices, but where opportunities to dispense private patronage existed, women could be found. Elizabeth Grey, Lady Portsmouth, for instance, one of the heirs to the estate of her first husband, the Earl of Suffolk, gained the right to appoint the Master of Magdalene College at Cambridge University in 1752. When the office fell open in 1760, Newcastle, as Chancellor of Cambridge, approached Lady Portsmouth with his nominee for the position. She, however, had another client in mind, and despite Newcastle's obsequious plea for his man, placed her candidate in the job. Her right to do so seems never to have been questioned either by her husband, the Earl of Portsmouth, or by the Duke of Newcastle, who, indeed, recognized explicitly the power she possessed.

At the popular level, politics became marked by increasing radicalism amongst the middling ranks, whose taxes had financed the long and hard fought wars with France that secured empire for Britain. The commercial and trading classes of the urban centers became increasingly supportive of reform efforts seeking to curb the arbitrary actions of self-interested MPs and ministers and to make them accountable to the people. Many of their extra-parliamentary protests focused on the actions taken by the crown against the press; on the suppression of individual liberties in the form of general warrants; on the Townshend Acts that sought to augment royal authority in the American colonies by making governors less reliant on the colonial assemblies for revenues; and, most spectacularly, on parliament's interference in the election for Middlesex in 1768, when it voided John Wilkes's victory and gave the seat to his defeated rival, a ministerial candidate by the name of Colonel Lutterell.

By that time, Wilkes had become the centerpiece of a broad-based and deep-seated campaign amongst the middling ranks against what they saw as the tyranny of the crown and its attacks on liberty. Proclaiming for "Wilkes and Liberty," and drawing upon ideas of social contract, Wilkes and his supporters lambasted the "secret influence" of the king's ministers, claiming that the threats they posed to the constitution and to individual liberty could only be countered by the resistance of "the people" to tyrannous actions by the crown. Arguing that a man's patriotism should not be gauged "by the number of his acres" – a reference to franchise restrictions that limited voting (except in parts of London, where property-holding criteria enfranchised men owning freeholds worth forty shillings) to those holding substantial landed property – Wilkes's followers claimed that their love for liberty in fact made them better patriots, better Englishmen, and thus more deserving than landed élites of the right to active citizenship.

The presence of women in public at a time when middling and plebeian men claimed for themselves a larger role in the political nation generated acute anxiety. Demands for political participation in the 1760s and 1770s by property-owning and independent, but not landed, shopkeepers, professionals, and tradesmen, and for universal manhood suffrage in the 1780s and 1790s, opened up the possibility for single or widowed – and perhaps even married – women to make the same claims. If active citizenship no longer depended upon the possession of landed estates but could be extended to those who owned other kinds of property as well, what was to stop property-owning women from claiming citizenship for themselves? And if voting could be extended to all adult males on the basis of their "natural rights" regardless of their property-owning status, how would the exclusion of women be justified?

One solution was to render women utterly unlike men, to disqualify them from political life by highlighting the emotional, physical, and intellectual differences from men already suggested by separate sphere ideology. The very qualities that gave women their moral ascendancy in the domestic sphere made them unfit for political life. They possessed greater tenderness and humanity than men, we saw Adam Smith assert in Chapter 3, but lacked the self-denial and self-command required by public life. Women were emotional, passive, submissive, and dependent, proclaimed philosophers, theorists, and public moralists; these characteristics suited them in their role as moral guardian and inculcator of virtue, but would serve them – and the polity – ill if transferred to public life, which called for men's capacity for reason, action, aggression, and independence. Moreover, women who ignored their weaknesses, who abandoned their children and husbands in order to step out into the world of politics, demonstrated their unnaturalness and, worse, placed society in danger by their actions.

Another strategy was to aggressively masculinize the political sphere. In his assaults on the crown Wilkes utilized a rhetoric that juxtaposed the manliness and Englishness of his supporters against the effeminacy and foreignness of the aristocratic ministers surrounding the king. John Stuart, Earl of Bute (pronounced "Boot"), George III's first minister and one of his oldest advisers, received particular vilification on account of his Scottish heritage and connection to the Stuart line. Depicted in the press and in the streets as an effeminate "Scotch-Jacobite" who put French interests before those of Britain, who sought to fill the offices of state with his fellow countrymen – long reputed to enjoy a sexual potency and endowment beyond that of Englishmen – Bute was the object of rumors that charged him with sleeping with the king's mother. One cartoon portrayed the Princess Dowager with her hand under Lord Bute's kilt, saying, "A man of great parts is sure greatly to rise. "Crowds of Wilkes's supporters marched through the streets displaying a petticoat and a boot, representing the princess and Lord Bute respectively, to make the symbolic argument that in infiltrating the bedroom of George's mother, an alien and French-loving Stuart aristocrat threatened the very existence of constitutional government as it had been established in the Glorious Revolution. As was true of pornography aimed against the monarchy in the seventeenth century, these vivid tales of Lord Bute's sexual liaisons with the Princess Dowager expressed acute political anxieties and served pointed political ends.[9]

Resistance to the tyranny of absolute government, portrayed in the guise of the king's foreign, effeminate, corrupt ministers who threatened the hard-won liberties of Englishmen, came to be represented as "manly patriotism." Those who risked life and limb to defend the country against illegitimate usurpations of monarchical power, as Wilkes and his supporters would have it, displayed a love of liberty and a "virtuous and manly resistance" to tyranny. American colonists resisting illegal authority, Wilkes often claimed, expressed a "manliness of sentiment" unavailable to their European counterparts. They were "fighting like men – like ENGLISHMEN, for law and liberty supposed to be violated," as one publication in the Midlands put it in 1775. Those who did not resist, by the same token, who complied with and even furthered encroachments on the liberties of the people at home or abroad, demonstrated their "effeminacy."[10]

For Wilkes and his radical supporters, these liberties included sexual ones, as was exemplified by Wilkes himself through his overt and extravagant sexual libertinism. The author of the pornographic *Essay on Women*, a man who flaunted his affairs with married women and treated his wife abusively, Wilkes behaved much like the aristocratic rakes depicted in the most popular novels of the day. But where "aristocratical" libertinism was marked by what radicals saw as "extravagant submission" to women, and thus effeminacy, the sexual liberty so beloved of Wilkites was characterized by mastery over women. For Wilkite radicals, the political and the sexual could be one and the same; and "manly patriotism" required that the dominant influence of the "feminine" be eliminated from both the political and the sexual arenas of life. Although tolerance for sexual libertinism as part of the radical political program waned as the century wore on and middling ranked men increasingly embraced the domestic ideal of morality and patriarchy, the sharp antipathy to both the effeminate and the feminine contained within contract theory and radical ideas about resistance to tyranny had the effect of narrowing the gender identity of political subjects. As middling ranked men made their claims for an enlarged citizenship that expanded their rights to political participation, they closed down these same opportunities for those who were not male, aggressively heterosexual, or middle class. Indeed, during the 1760s and 1770s, at the height of the Wilkite campaigns of resistance, liberal political thinkers began to stress that men's claims for citizenship, for political subjectivity, rested as much on their ownership of their wives and children as on their owner-ship of property and their payment of taxes.[11]

This increased masculinization of political culture (as if to underscore its intent to remove women from politics altogether, the House of Commons in 1778 banned women from the gallery and the floor of the house, where they had, since the early part of the eighteenth century, gathered to listen to debates) did not prevent women from embracing radical principles or participating in political activities throughout the latter half of the eighteenth century. Indeed, the intensification of separate-sphere ideology, designed to shore up the boundaries differentiating men from women, occurred precisely because those boundaries between public and domestic had become so unstable and showed no signs of firming up. Women contributed heavily of their time and money to the Wilkite campaigns: the "patri-otic Ladies of Worcester" and the "lady freeholders of Middlesex," to name only two such instances, appeared at demonstrations and balls held in support of Wilkes and his radical cause. Others participated in debates and the dissemination of propaganda on his behalf. But women who did involve themselves in politics had to be careful to present themselves as "auxiliaries" to male citizens if they were to remain unmolested by press or public opinion. They had to conform to the middling ideals of domesticity and sexual virtue being consolidated in the second half of the eighteenth century, and if they did not, they faced ridicule and charges of disreputability, as did the objects of their support, which became tarnished and degraded by their association with "the feminine."

One such example of discrediting a political movement by equating it with "the feminine" took place during the Gordon Riots of 1780, when a large anti-catholic crowd gathered before parliament to protest legislation that would remove some of the legal disabilities suffered by catholics. For five days mobs rioted through the streets of London, attacking catholic chapels, the homes and businesses of wealthy catholics, and those who supported the cause, like Edmund Burke, or who tried to put down the riots. They burned tollhouses and prisons, made an assault on the Bank of England, and invaded the houses of the Archbishop of York, Lord North, the king's first minister, and the Lord Chief Justice. Observers were appalled by the frenzy of the populace, whose primitive fury and mindless destruction, as they saw it, caused even radicals like Wilkes to recoil. When he got up in the House of Commons to denounce the rioters, Edmund Burke focused his outrage on the women amongst the crowds, terming them degraded, ignorant "monsters." The apparent atavism and anti-catholic fanaticism of the Gordon mobs, in conjunction with Burke's singling out of the women among them, enabled élite and middling politicians to regard the riots as an example of just what the addition of "the femi-nine" to the public sphere might produce.[12]

The election for Westminster in 1784, when Georgiana, Duchess of Devonshire, campaigned on behalf of Charles James Fox – a prominent Whig whose support for democratic suffrage ultimately came to be extended to women – afforded a prime opportunity to castigate those women who presumed to step out of their expected roles and venture into territory reserved for men.[13] Aristocratic women often canvassed at election time in order to secure their families' political interests, and their electioneering up to this time had raised no eyebrows. In this instance, however, Georgiana's presence among the voters of Westminster provoked an unprecedented response. Because the Houses of Parliament were located there, because it was the largest borough in Britain, and because, as a scot-and-lot borough, it included a large quotient of artisans and tradesmen among the enfranchised, the duchess's electioneering was sure to draw the attention of the press, whose journalists accused her either of being Fox's lover or of acting out of political conviction rather than merely lending familial support to an individual politician. Georgiana's easy familiarity with crowds of shopkeepers and tradespeople, the evident pleasure with which she went about the business of canvassing the constituency, and especially her offers to butchers of rides to the hustings with her in her carriage, marked her out for special comment.

Having crossed the lines of class order by going among the people of low rank, the Duchess of Devonshire became vulnerable to charges of unnatural behavior. As was so often the case, these charges were levied through a sexual pornography designed to serve political ends. Scores of obscene satirical prints and cartoons appeared. A print entitled *Political Affection* depicted her clutching a fox to her breasts while a child hungrily demanded milk. Another (see Figure 5.2) showed her canvassing on the street, her hair and dress blown about by the wind, a staff of liberty holding Fox's head and two phallically-drawn fox tails in her hand, while her husband, the Duke of Devonshire, sat at home changing his baby's diaper, a portrait of him with the horns of the cuckold hanging on the wall behind him. Still other critics noted that his supporters considered Fox "The Man of the People." Were they to confer a similar title on his most aristocratic follower, they concluded, it would render the Duchess of Devonshire a prostitute, a charge given all the more valency by the location of the Westminster hustings in Covent Garden, a notorious hang-out of prostitutes.[14] One squib put out by Fox's opponents made explicit reference to this particular aspect of Westminster when it accused his campaign of securing votes through the sale of the duchess's sexual favors. "Beautiful ladies, in all future Elections," claimed the broadside:

> will be provided by all Candidates to assist them in seducing the Electors. Girls will be brought from Armenia, and the Grecian Islands; Covent Garden with its environs too, will supply females for electioneering. In short, since it

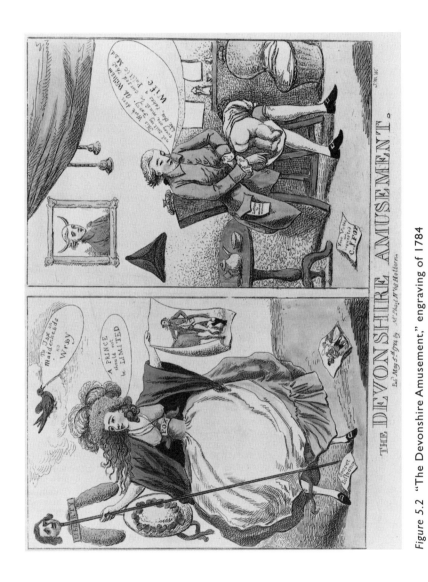

Figure 5.2 "The Devonshire Amusement," engraving of 1784

Source: Courtesy of the Print Collection, Lewis Walpole Library, Yale University

has become fashionable to seize the voters by this *handle*, there is no saying what may not be done.

Fox's Tory opponents protested that women had no right to "interfere" in elections, an argument that could not square with their own enlisting of the Duchess of Rutland, Lady Salisbury, and Mrs Hobart to canvas on their behalf. "The ladies who interest themselves so much in the cause of Elections are perhaps too ignorant to know that they meddle with what does not concern them," ventured one Tory broadside. Such assertions compelled Fox and his Whig supporters to defend the rights of women to citizenship and political participation, a claim that accorded well and resonated with the outcomes of various debates we saw taking place in debating societies during the 1780s. During the election for Westminster, an audience at Coachmakers' Hall decided heavily in favor of the proposition that it "is ... consistent with decency for the female sex to interfere in elections." Forced by Tory opposition to take a stand that they might not have otherwise, the Whigs' support for women's political rights went far beyond the traditional custom of aristocratic women campaigning to uphold, protect, and further their families' political fortunes.

It also enabled Tories to cast doubt on the manliness of Fox and his democratic voters. Long possessed of rakish appearance, habits, and reputation, Fox epitomized the effeminate aristocrat enervated by the luxury and licentiousness so loathed by radical critics of government. In the hands of the Tories, led by the cold, aloof, incorruptible, chaste, and misogynous William Pitt, Fox's enthusiastic heterosexuality and his reliance upon the Duchess of Devonshire to win elections for him made him unfit for public office. Liable to the corruptions of female influence, Fox, and by extension, those electors who, it was asserted, had been seduced by the duchess's charms to vote for him, could not lay claim to the manly independence required of virtuous public servants. Pitt announced in the House of Commons the day after the election that it could hardly have been indicative of real public opinion because Fox's victory had been "produced by the interference of female charms."

Georgiana's political activity, according to Tory cartoons and propaganda, rendered her unnatural and monstrous, responsible for undermining the social and gender order of Britain and bringing discredit to Fox's political principles. They did not keep him from winning the election in democratic Westminster – indeed, Georgiana's campaigning on his behalf is credited with securing his victory. Nor did they prove effective in the long run in curbing Georgiana's future participation in public political life. It is true that when Fox's supporters celebrated his victory in May 1784 with a procession (see Figure 5.3) , the Duchess's carriage made its appearance, though the duchess herself was nowhere to be seen; but during a by-election for Westminster in 1788, she once again canvassed the constituency

PROCESSION TO THE HUSTINGS AFTER A SUCCESSFUL CANVASS.

Figure 5.3 "Procession to the Hustings after a Successful Canvass," engraving of 1784

Source: Courtesy of the Print Collection, Lewis Walpole Library, Yale University

heavily. Her political activity continued for the rest of her life, tribute to the power of aristocratic status to overcome the disabilities of gender imposed on lower ranked women. But the campaign of disgrace and ridicule directed against her by Fox's opponents gave added weight to the convention that politics was no place for a lady.

Efforts to eliminate women and the feminine from the arenas of politics and public life, provoked by the very presence and participation of women there in increasing numbers after 1750, would intensify in the last decade of the eighteenth century and the first twenty years of the nineteenth under the impact of the political turmoil and economic upheaval created by the French revolution, early industrialization, and war with France between 1793 and 1815. A powerful gender system of separate spheres for men and women, informed by the ideology of domesticity and by notions of upper-class women's inherent passionlessness, emerged, as we shall see, from campaigns on the part of élites to contain revolution at home and abroad.

NOTES

1 See G.J. Barker-Benfield, *The Culture of Sensibility: Sex and Society in Eighteenth-Century Britain* (Chicago, 1992).
2 Quoted in Paul Wesley Chilcote, *John Wesley and the Women Preachers of Early Methodism* (Metuchen, NJ, 1991), pp. 121–2.
3 The following discussion is dependent upon Anna Clark's *The Struggle for the Breeches: Gender and the Making of the British Working Class* (Berkeley, 1995), ch. 6.
4 Quoted in Mary Poovey, *The Proper Lady and the Woman Writer* (Chicago, 1984), p. 9.
5 My treatment of the anti-slavery campaign depends on the work of Claire Midgley, *Women Against Slavery. The British Campaigns, 1780–1870* (London, 1992); and Moira Ferguson, *Subject to Others: British Women Writers and Colonial Slavery, 1670–1834* (New York, 1992).
6 Barker-Benfield, *The Culture of Sensibility*.
7 Donna T. Andrew, " 'The passion for public speaking': Women's debating societies," in Valerie Frith, ed., *Women and History: Voices of Early Modern England* (Toronto, 1995), p. 183.
8 I am indebted to Elaine Chalus for letting me cite from her as yet unpublished article, " 'To serve my friends': Women and political patronage in eighteenth-century England," in Amanda Vickery, ed., *Women, Privilege, and Power* (Palo Alto, forthcoming).
9 See Linda Colley, *Britons: Forging the Nation, 1707–1837.* (New Haven, 1992), ch. 3.
10 Kathleen Wilson, *The Sense of the People: Politics, Culture and Imperialism in England, 1715–1785.* (Cambridge, 1995), ch. 4.
11 See Clark, *The Struggle for the Breeches*, ch. 8.
12 Iain McCalman, "Mad Lord George and Madame La Motte: Riot and sexuality in the genesis of Burke's *Reflections on the Revolution in France*," *Journal of British Studies* 35(3), July 1996: 343–67.

13 On Georgiana, see Colley, *Britons*, ch. 6; and Judith Lewis, "1784 and all that: Aristocratic women and electoral politics," in Amanda Vickery, ed., *Women, Privilege, and Power*, (Palo Alto, forthcoming). My thanks to Judith Lewis for permitting me to quote from her as yet unpublished work.

14 This comment and the following quotes are from Lewis, "1784 and all that."

SOURCES

Henry Abelove, *The Evangelist of Desire: John Wesley and the Methodists*. Palo Alto, 1990.

Donna T. Andrew, " 'The passion for public speaking': Women's debating societies," in Valerie Frith, ed., *Women and History: Voices of Early Modern England*. Toronto, 1995.

G.J. Barker-Benfield, *The Culture of Sensibility: Sex and Society in Eighteenth-Century Britain*. Chicago, 1992.

Elaine Chalus, " 'To serve my friends': Women and political patronage in eighteenth-century England," in Amanda Vickery, ed., *Women, Privilege, and Power*. Palo Alto, forthcoming.

Paul Wesley Chilcote, *John Wesley and the Women Preachers of Early Methodism*. Metuchen, NJ, 1991.

Linda Colley, *Britons: Forging the Nation, 1707–1837*. New Haven, 1992.

Dianne Dugaw, *Warrior Women and Popular Balladry, 1650–1850*. Chicago, 1989.

Moira Ferguson, ed., *First Feminists: British Women Writers, 1578–1799*. Bloomington, 1985.

——, *Subject to Others: British Women Writers and Colonial Slavery, 1670–1834*. New York, 1992.

Valerie Frith, ed., *Women and History: Voices of Early Modern England*. Toronto, 1995.

Peter Fryer, *Staying Power: The History of Black People in Britain*. London, 1984.

Bridget Hill, *Eighteenth-Century Women: An Anthology*. London, 1984.

——, *The Republican Virago: The Life and Times of Catherine Macaulay, Historian*. Oxford, 1992.

Vivien Jones, ed., *Women in the Eighteenth Century. Constructions of Femininity*. London, 1990.

Paul Langford, *A Polite and Commercial People. England, 1727–1783*. Oxford, 1992.

Judith Lewis, "1784 and all that: Aristocratic women and electoral politics," in Amanda Vickery, ed., *Women, Privilege, and Power*. Palo Alto, forthcoming.

Iain McCalman, "Mad Lord George and Madame La Motte: Riot and sexuality in the genesis of Burke's *Reflections on the Revolution in France*," *Journal of British Studies* 35(3), July 1996: 343–67.

Claire Midgley, *Women Against Slavery. The British Campaigns, 1780–1870*. London, 1992.

Conor Cruise O'Brien, *The Great Melody. A Thematic Biography of Edmund Burke*. Chicago, 1992.

Mary Poovey, *The Proper Lady and the Woman Writer*. Chicago, 1984.

Kathleen Wilson, *The Sense of the People: Politics, Culture and Imperialism in England, 1715–1785*. Cambridge, 1995.

Chapter 6

Domesticating revolution, 1789–1815

During the era of the French Revolution and the wars with France (1789–1815), the conflict and anxiety that we have discussed in the last three chapters – over religious differences, foreign wars, overseas expansion, massive demographic and economic change, popular politics, women's increased public visibility and political activity, and disturbances within colonial territories – reached heightened proportions. Against the backdrop of actual revolution abroad and potential revolution at home and in Ireland, and threats to national survival posed by French armies, these political, economic, and cultural developments appeared all the more unsettling, and efforts to contain the disruptions they promised were redoubled. As we have seen, because so many sources of anxiety and sites of conflict had presented themselves or had been presented in languages of gender and sexuality, attempts to solve the problems these issues raised were depicted in those same terms, which were intensified and strengthened by fears of revolution and war, and the perceived needs of state in a time of extreme danger. The ideology of separate spheres, buttressed and rendered increasingly inflexible now by an insistent claim of women's inherent passionlessness, received additional impetus in the context of the French Revolution and industrialization.

The French Revolution

When, in the summer of 1789, France's King Louis XVI gave in to the principles of representative government and the sovereignty of the people by recognizing the existence of the National Assembly, Britons of nearly every political stripe cheered. Whigs and even Tories saw in the French Revolution the apotheosis of their own system of balanced government, achieved exactly one hundred years earlier with the ratification of the Bill of Rights, while radicals and religious dissenters, seeking reform of a parliamentary system dominated by "old corruption," a broader representation of citizenship, and religious tolerance, welcomed it as a harbinger of things to come in Britain. The words of Anna Leticia Barbauld nicely summed up the general attitude toward revolution in France in the earliest days (though she had an altogether different, and indeed more radical, concern in mind). "Millions of men exist there," she wrote, "who … hail with shouts of grateful acclamation the better birth-day of their country. Go on, generous nation, set the world an example of virtues as you have of talents. Be our model, as we have been yours."[1]

Radicals like Richard Price celebrated the French Revolution as a template for creating a new British civic polity. He regarded Britain's Glorious Revolution as incomplete, deficient, and in need of remedying by means of an overhaul of the franchise. On 4 November 1789, on the occasion of the birthday of William III, he told members of the Society for Commemorating the Revolution in Great Britain that the French revolutionaries had kindled a spark among Britons. "And now, methinks, I see the ardour for liberty catching and spreading, a general amendment beginning in human affairs; the dominion of kings changed for the dominion of laws, and the dominion of priests giving way to the dominion of reason and conscience." He congratulated the French revolutionaries for forcefully reminding Britons that among their natural rights were "the right to chuse our own governors; to cashier them for misconduct; and to frame a government for ourselves."[2]

Price's address, published as *A Discourse on the Love of Our Country* in 1790, implied a different meaning for the term "revolution" than that conjured up by references to 1688 or to the American colonists' claims in 1776. Those "revolutions" sought a return to an earlier state of virtue that had ostensibly been corrupted by a departure from ancient practices. The French "revolution," by contrast, as Price and other radicals portrayed it, sought not a return to an older order but the overthrow of the present one. It connoted dramatic, sudden, and unprecedented change in politics and society. Price's *Discourse* provoked outrage in Edmund Burke, who responded with a now classic condemnation of revolution as the embodiment of political and sexual violence, anarchy, irrationality, mob rule, and sexual licentiousness.

Burke drew upon his experiences of the Gordon riots ten years earlier to inform his polemic against the French Revolution, *Reflections on the Revolution in France*, published in 1790, a work that in its political about-face moved Thomas Jefferson to remark on "the revolution of Mr Burke."[3] In the *Reflections*, Burke, an ardent supporter of parliamentary reform, religious tolerance, and American liberty, castigated the French revolutionaries for their actions. He seized upon the events of 6 and 7 October 1789, when a group of working men and women marched to Versailles to bring the king and queen of France back to Paris, where revolutionaries could better keep an eye on them, to smear the political events of 1789 with the stain of irrationality and excess, terms, as we have seen earlier, associated with women and femininity. "A band of cruel ruffians and assassins," he wrote, "rushed into the chamber of the queen, and pierced with an hundred strokes of bayonets and poniards the bed, from whence this persecuted woman had but just time to fly almost naked." Dragged from their chambers, Louis XVI and Marie Antoinette were "forced to abandon the sanctuary of the most splendid palace in the world, which they left swimming in blood, polluted by massacre and strewed with scattered limbs and mutilated carcases." They were "slowly moved along" the road to Paris, "amidst the horrid yells and shrilling screams, and frantic dances, and infamous contumelies and all the unutterable abominations of the furies of hell in the abused shape of the vilest of women." Burke used the figure of the queen in stark contrast to those "vilest of women": "surely never lighted on this orb ... a more delightful vision, ... glittering like the morning-star, full of life, and splendour, and joy." He lamented the fact that so hideous a spectacle as plebeian women partaking in political events could even take place. "On this scheme of things, a king is but a man; a queen is but a woman; a woman is but an animal; and an animal not of the highest order. All homage paid to the sex in general as such ... is to be regarded as romance and folly." For Burke, the revolution threatened not just the political order of monarchy and the social order of ranks; it promised to destroy the natural and God-given gender order as well, and on all of these grounds should be opposed. "Never, never more," he lamented, "shall we behold that generous loyalty to rank and sex ... which kept alive, even in servitude itself, the spirit of an exalted freedom."[4]

In 1791, Thomas Paine answered Burke with *The Rights of Man*, in which he claimed that citizenship rested not on possession of property, whether landed, mobile, or personal, but on the capacity of individuals to reason. *The Rights of Man* landed like a bombshell, exploding Lockean notions of citizenship that carried with them the separation of public and private spheres and granted men citizenship in part on the basis of their status as heads of households. Instead, everyone, regardless of social rank, and, people like Mary Wollstonecraft and Mary Hays would soon assert, of gender, possessed the ability to reason and everyone, therefore, qualified for direct participation in the political nation.

Wollstonecraft made explicit what Paine had left abstract. In 1792, she published *A Vindication of the Rights of Woman*, in which she argued for women's full admission to the political nation, with all the rights and responsibilities accorded to men, on the grounds that women, no less than men, possessed reason and contributed to public virtue through the rearing of civic-minded children. She urged that women be educated in the "manly virtues" (just as men, she asserted, should become "chaste and modest"), and learn to become industrious, independent members of society rather than dependent parasites. She envisaged citizen-women taking to "the field" to "march and counter-march like soldiers, or wrangle in the senate to keep their faculties from rusting."

Mary Hays, a member of the radical dissenting circle to which Wollstonecraft belonged, contended that the aims of government – the happiness of individuals –

and the means by which they were to be realized – "the possession … of private virtue" – would come to naught if women were not admitted to its jurisdictions. In March 1797, she wrote to the editor of the *Monthly Magazine* that "till one moral and mental standard is established for every rational agent, every member of a community, and a free scope afforded for the exertion of their faculties and talents, without distinction of rank or sex, virtue will be an empty name, and happiness elude our most anxious research." Hays's *Appeal to the Men of Great Britain in behalf of the Women*, published in 1798, called upon her countrymen to "restore to woman that freedom, which the God of nature seems manifestly to have intended, for every living creature! Liberty, – rational liberty, – such as is consistent with the good order of every branch of society." A year later, Mary Robinson castigated politicians for having banned women from listening to parliamentary debates. "Why are women excluded from the auditory part of the British senate?" she demanded in *A Letter to the Women of England, on the Injustice of Mental Subordination.* "The welfare of their country, cannot fail to interest their feelings." Alluding to the Enlightenment notion put forward by men like Edward Gibbon and Adam Smith that the progress of civilizations could be measured by the degree to which women were honored within them, she noted with irony that "many of the American tribes admit women into their public councils, and allow them the privileges of giving their opinions, *first*, on every subject of deliberation. The ancient Britons allowed the female sex the same right: but in modern Britain women are scarcely allowed to express any opinions at all!" Robinson urged the women of Britain to educate themselves, and especially their daughters, to "expand their minds, and purify their hearts, by teaching them to feel their mental equality with their imperious rulers."[5]

We should recall that France had long been viewed by Britons as a "feminine" nation. Now, in the midst of a revolution in which large numbers of women participated and which became increasingly radical as months passed, Britons' anxieties about women's place in public life took on greater intensity. With the advent of the September massacres in Paris in 1792, the beheading of Louis XVI in January 1793, and Britain's declaration of war on France the following month, suggestions like Wollstonecraft's of women becoming autonomous of their husbands and fathers, of their acting openly and freely in political affairs, of their taking to arms produced enormous disquiet. Advice manuals, conduct books, sermons from clergymen, novels, and newspaper and journal articles issued forth in a flood, asserting more forcefully than ever before that social and political order – and, indeed, women's very safety – rested on the delineation of separate spheres for men and women.

Laetitia Hawkins, for instance, in *Letters on the Female Mind, Its Powers and Pursuits*, published in 1793, admonished her correspondent that the questions of "*A King or no King? A Nobility or no Nobility?* are not those, my dear madam, which I mean to discuss with you, I would rather convince you that they are points neither you nor I can discuss with propriety or success." This was so, she explained, because the intellectual powers of women were weaker than those of men, and "nature certainly intended a distinction." Women might study languages, arithmetic, or history, she conceded, but "the study ... where I place in the climax of unfitness, is that of *politics*; and so strongly does it appear to me barred against the admission of females, that I am astonished that they ever ventured to approach it."[6]

An Edinburgh man, in response to reports that women were preparing for a French invasion by practicing their shooting, wrote to *Gentleman's Magazine* in 1795 that in displaying their "natural timidity and amiable softness" women best served the interests of themselves and the nation. "Let them leave military duties and the defence of our national dignity to their fathers, their brothers, and their countrymen." Priscilla Wakefield's *Reflections on the Present Condition of the Female Sex*, written in 1798, declared that "there can be but one head or chief in every family. Nature and reason, as well as custom, have established this power in the hands of the men." "The profession of ladies," Hannah More reminded her readers in 1799, "is that of daughters, wives, mothers and mistresses of families."[7] Part of the emphasis on separate spheres for men and women derived from the fear that revolutionary passions and political violence would spill over into sexual violence against women. Men who had no respect for rank, it was feared, would have no greater respect for sex, and women would suffer abuse at their hands. Laetitia Hawkins echoed Edmund Burke's earlier conviction that assaults on the social order emboldened individuals to take liberties elsewhere as well. In a statement that betrays anxiety about her own personal safety, she revealed in 1793, "I feel it impossible, with any degree of comfort, or even security, to walk in London, unprotected by a gentleman. The levelling principle has rendered all persons, making an appearance at all above the common rank, [vulnerable] to the most galling abuse, and often to personal insult." Men and women of every political affiliation were shocked by the treatment of Marie Antoinette at the hands of the Paris crowds and her execution by the Jacobins appalled British public opinion. Accounts of her abduction from Versailles in 1789 called up images of rape, as in this description of it by Mary Wollstonecraft. "The sanctuary of repose," wrote the radical reformer, herself no fan of royalty, "the asylum of care and fatigue, the chaste temple of a woman, I consider the Queen only as one, the apartment where she consigns her senses to the bosom of sleep, folded in its arms forgetful of the world, was violated with murderous fury."[8]

James Gillray's 1792 engraving of the September massacres showed *sans culottes* feasting on the organs and limbs of their unfortunate victims (see Figure 6.1). As much a rendering of castration and rape as of cannibalism, the cartoon depicts a plebeian Parisian family – all of the male characters, including children, drawn, in a literal representation of *sans culottes*, without their pants, their naked backsides

Figure 6.1 "Un petit Souper à la Parisiènne; or A Family of Sans Culotts refreshing after the fatigues of the day", engraving of 1792

Source: © Courtesy of the Trustees of the British Museum

prominently displayed – engaged in various acts of physical and sexual violation. A woman lies spread-eagled beneath a seated revolutionary armed with an ax, his naked bottom transecting her bare breasts. A gentleman sprawls under the dining table, his severed head atop a platter, one of his legs chewed off, and his genitalia run through by a table leg. A child pierced by a skewer running lengthwise through its body is dangled upside down over a basting tray, ready for cooking. These scenes, and countless warnings of the rapine and torture that would follow upon a French take-over of British society, bombarded the British public.[9]

In 1795, the conservative Crown and Anchor Society published a broadside that contrasted the "Blessings of Peace, Prosperity and Domestick Happiness" familiar to Britons to the "Curses of War, Invasion, Massacre & Desolation" suffered by Flemish, Spanish, and Dutch victims of France's revolutionary armies (see Figure 6.2). The British domestic scene, located indoors before a warm fire and a bountiful larder, showed plump, comfortable, contented women ministering to their kindly and protective husband and father. The scene of desolation, taking place outside a burned-down cottage, depicted a family agonizing over the body of their murdered husband and father as French troops marched away in the background. The wife's state of semi-undress that reveals her bare breasts, and the nakedness of the baby at her feet, are meant to signify the violations of women at the hands of revolutionary forces.[10]

William Cobbett explicitly related republicanism to sexual violence against women in his 1798 Democratic Principles Illustrated by Example, in which he told of Jacobins raping and murdering noblewomen in France. "Pause here, reader, and imagine, if you can," he wrote:

> another crime worthy of being added to these already mentioned. –Yes, there is one more, and hell would not have been satisfied, if its ministers had left it uncommitted – Libidinous brutality!... The wives and daughters of almost all the respectable inhabitants, particularly such as had emigrated, or who were murdered, or in prison, were put in a state of requisition, and were ordered on pain of death, to hold their bodies (I spare the reader the term made use of in the decree) in readiness for the embraces of the true republicans![11]

The confines of the home, and decidedly not the arena of political strife, conservative propagandists asserted, afforded women protection from the depredations of men like those described above. Separate sphere ideology offered women a kind of implicit quid pro quo, an unspoken bargain whereby women traded freedom and equality in the public sphere for obedience, submission, and the protection of men in the private sphere. "The whole world might be at war," Laetitia Hawkins reminded her countrywomen in 1793, "and yet not the rumour of it reached the ears of an Englishwoman – empires might be lost, and states

Figure 6.2 "The Blessings of Peace, the Curses of War", anti-invasion propaganda print by the Crown and Anchor Society, 1795

overthrown, and still she might pursue the peaceful occupations of her home; and her natural lord might change his governor at pleasure, and she feel neither change nor hardship." Women who talked of "equal rights, the abjectness of submission, the duty of every one to think for themselves," on the other hand, as Hawkins put it, endangered "the national female character" by threatening the peace of that very home that provided women with security. "She who is taught the merit of resistance is taught to be obstinate," she insisted; "she who has early imbibed an aversion towards the kingly character, will easily be persuaded to consider her husband as an unauthorized tyrant, and fancying she has reason on her side, if he is not very easy to live with, she will applaud the spirit that turns inconvenience to misery." The rights of women, she feared, would compel women to challenge the authority of their husbands in the home, leading to revolt within the marriage and divorce to the couple, which in turn would leave women defenseless before the assaults of men who would no longer have any respect for them.[12]

The corollary to this bargain, then, held that women who strayed from the confines of home to partake in politics, especially radical politics, risked sexual violation and even death. French republican women had, after all, suffered violence at the hands of French revolutionaries. In November 1793, a month after Marie Antoinette's beheading, Madame Roland and Olympe de Gouges, author of *A Declaration of the Rights of Woman and Citizen*, went to the guillotine. Conservative women's fears for their safety at the hands of republican revolutionaries received impetus from Britain's own home-grown radical campaign, whose political demands, by 1792, were being matched by social and economic demands from some quarters of the movement. The older political alignments of radicals against the aristocratic established order, of "the people" against "Old Corruption," now took on the appearance, in the minds of conservatives and even of most moderates, of an all-out battle of poor against rich, of the lower classes against the higher classes.

In January 1792, a group of artisans and shopkeepers led by the Scottish shoemaker, Thomas Hardy, acting upon the Painite principle of the possession of reason as the sole criterion for citizenship, formed the London Corresponding Society, calling for the rights of citizenship for working men. The following month, Paine published the second part of his *Rights of Man*, in which he joined the demand for economic and social rights – minimum wages, universal education, poor relief, family allowances, old age pensions, public works for the unemployed, all to be paid for by greater taxation of the wealthy – to those for political rights. Paine's second pamphlet appealed to great numbers of plebeians, men and women alike, whose economic situations, as we shall see below, had deteriorated in the past decade as industrialization made its way into various regions of Great Britain, and contributed mightily to the momentum of the radical movement. Within six months of its founding, the membership of the London Corresponding Society, which disseminated Paine's pamphlet far and wide in its propaganda campaign, had grown from twenty-five to 2,000. Following its example, provincial corresponding societies sprang up in a number of industrial cities. In Ireland, the United Irishmen, a society made up of middling and élite protestants and catholics established in 1791 to seek political reform and catholic emancipation from legal disabilities, would be pushed into a far more radical and even revolutionary position by plebeian catholic "Defenders" in both rural and urban areas, whose economic discontent combined with hatred of the foreign English. By the end of the eighteenth century, the second part of *Rights of Man* had sold perhaps 500,000 copies.

Attacks on the social order seem to have posed a far greater threat to élites than the political claims of "the people." Even the moderate reformer, Christopher Wyvill, whose radical credentials dated back to the 1770s, expressed alarm at the prospect of lower-class participation. "If Mr Paine should be able to rouze up the lower classes," he wrote, "their interference will probably be marked by wild work, and all we now possess, whether in private property or public liberty, will be at the mercy of a lawless and furious rabble."

Coinciding as it did with the far more violent turn of events in France in the fall of 1792, working-class radicalism, now termed "Jacobinism," injected an element of panic into the thinking of authorities. Acting upon rumors that an insurrection of London working men would break out in December, the government implemented a series of repressive measures designed to contain popular radicalism. *The Rights of Man* was banned, and Paine was tried, convicted, and sentenced to death for treason *in absentia* in November. Scottish radicals meeting in December in Edinburgh at a "National Convention" called to express support for the French were arrested and transported to Australia. The outbreak of war with France in February 1793 and the subsequent execution of Louis XVI intensified anti-Jacobin sentiments, giving rise to the formation of private associations devoted to the protection of property and privilege amongst conservatives and to stamping out all evidence of popular radicalism. These, alongside the actions of the government such as the suspension of habeas corpus in 1794, the arrest and trial for treason of Thomas Hardy and two other radical leaders in 1795, and food shortages caused by high prices and the disruptions of war, spurred working-class "Jacobins" to even greater political activity. Waves of rioting broke out across Britain in the fall and winter of 1794–5. At the end of October 1795, some 200,000 Londoners took to the streets and pelted the king's carriage with stones as he drove in state on his way to Westminster to open parliament. Shouts of "Peace!," "No War!," "Down with Pitt!," "No King!" greeted him, while protesters carrying loaves of bread on staves decorated with black crepe sought to bring their grievances to his attention. By the end of 1795, radicals could organize mass meetings of 100,000 to perhaps 200,000 men and women calling for political reform and the end of war with France.

In response to such rallies and riots, the government passed the Seditious Meetings and Treasonable Practices Acts of 1795, outlawing political meetings of more than fifty persons; when members of the corresponding societies began to meet in groups of fewer than fifty, the government passed the Combination Acts of 1799 and 1800. These last proved successful in driving radical politics underground, though not before a wave of disorder and unrest, fueled by bad harvests and high prices, swept through many parts of Britain in the years 1799 to 1801.

More dangerous for Pitt's government was the situation in Ireland. By 1794, the United Irishmen, under the leadership of Theobald Wolfe Tone, had moved from a position advocating constitutional reform to one embracing revolutionary republicanism. Backed by thousands of catholic "Defenders" – peasants whose economic distress had led them to organize against protestant landlords, and workers in the cities – the United Irishmen began negotiating with France for aid and assistance in a revolt against England. In December 1796, a French invasion force of forty-three ships and 15,000 men, including Wolfe Tone, now a general in the French army, attempted to land at Cork, in the south-west of Ireland, but it was dispersed in a storm and compelled to return to France. In May 1798, following the arrest of United Irishmen leaders in Dublin, armed insurrection broke out in the south of Ireland. Initially successful against British troops, it nevertheless failed, but not before some 30,000 catholic and protestant antagonists perished in some of the bloodiest atrocities of Ireland's history. United Irishmen used images of women violated by rapacious Orangemen and members of the yeoman militias to slur the loyalist cause and recruit supporters to their own. The catholic newspaper, *The Press*, told of Orangemen attacking Dungannon, where they raped the daughter of a farmer named Ruddy. When Ruddy tried to stop them, they killed him, and upon satiating their "brutal lust," as the paper put it, they burned down his farmhouse. A handbill directed against the loyalist yeomanry depicted one of them in Turkish garb, waving his scimitar above his head, with the caption, alluding to long-standing associations of the "orientalist" with cruelty and excessive carnality, "only in destroying I find ease to my relentless thoughts … to hold women in common … [is] ever my most sincere wish."[13]

Using rape as a metaphor for British rule over Ireland on the one hand, and as the sign of their emasculation at the hands of protestant overlords, from whom they could not protect their womenfolk, on the other, Irish republicans presented their cause as a manly duty, as an imperative for the recovery and assertion of their manhood. Representations of protecting women in republican iconography, however, did not extend to including them within the bounds of republican citizenship, despite the insistence of women like Mary Ann McCracken of Belfast that "there can be no argument produced in favour of the slavery of women that has not been used in favour of general slavery." She called upon republicans "to strike out something new and to shew an example of candour, generosity, and justice superior to any that have gone before them." Few of them saw anything more than "absurdity," as an article in the United Irish newspaper, the *Northern Star*, expressed it, in the idea of women participating in politics.[14]

By the time a French naval force landed at Killala in county Mayo, on the north-west coast of Ireland, in August 1798, the insurrection had been brutally put down; the forces of General Humbert were captured by the British within two weeks. In October, British naval forces intercepted the French vessel carrying Wolfe Tone to Donegal in anticipation of another Irish rising. He was tried and sentenced to death but committed suicide before he could be executed.

Stunned by the degree to which France had insinuated itself into the politics of Ireland, and fearful of the possibility that a rebellious Ireland might provide a staging ground for French forces to invade Great Britain, the British government moved to contain the dangers that Ireland posed. Recognizing the political and material impossibility of establishing a permanent occupation force in Ireland, Pitt decided on a strategy that entailed reconciling both catholic and protestant factions to political association with Great Britain. He proposed that Ireland be joined with England, Wales, and Scotland in the United Kingdom of Great Britain, a union in which Ireland's parliament would be abolished and its representation in the parliament in Westminster determined by proportional representation. This solution appealed to protestants, who saw in the parliament at Westminster far greater protection of their interests than the parliament in Dublin, susceptible to catholic pressure, could afford them. To the catholics of Ireland, Pitt promised what is referred to as "catholic emancipation," the right of catholics to sit for and elect members to the parliament in Westminster. In 1801, the Act of Union achieved the goal of bringing Ireland into union with Great Britain. To his dismay, however, Pitt discovered that the second promise of emancipation could not be realized because of hostility to it from members of his cabinet and, more impor-tantly, the king. His inability to carry out the promise he had made to Irish catholics had two serious consequences: Pitt resigned his position as prime minister rather than repudiate his oath, and a mass movement of nationalists grew up in Ireland in the 1820s over the issue of catholic emancipation.

Early industrialization

Working-class "Jacobinism" and the fear evoked by it among middling and élite Britons received impetus from the economic and industrial changes taking place at the time of the French Revolution in many parts of Great Britain. As we have seen, transformations in finance, commerce, agriculture, and demography had been proceeding throughout the eighteenth century, producing anxiety among élite and middling groups, and a great deal of hardship for plebeian men and women whose livelihoods were often adversely effected by them. By the 1780s, the manufacture of cotton textiles had begun to undergo dramatic alterations in the way it was carried out, in the manner in which the work force was organized and supervised, and in the location in which all of this took place. The factory system of the nineteenth century, characterized by the large-scale organization of workers performing specialized functions on power-driven machinery according to a rhythm regulated by the clock, introduced enormous change into the lives of working people in many areas of England, Scotland, Wales, and northern Ireland. The factory became the emblem of industrialization: the symbolic locus of male workers' discontent and protest, in which the presence of working women was regarded as a threat to working men's manliness; the site of efficiency and productivity in the minds of political economists, who saw in the so-called "iron law of wages" the most effective means of controlling working-class sexuality, whose excess, they believed, brought about the poverty characteristic of this period; and the target of innumerable parliamentary and extra-parliamentary campaigns aimed at removing women from the world of work.

The application of power-driven machinery to manufacturing took place first in spinning. Spinning had long been an occupation of women. For poor women, especially those in agricultural areas where labor was seasonal, it served as a source of income that might often make the difference to a family's economic survival. For middling and élite women, spinning symbolized female industry. Spinning constituted so central a feature of life for all women that the word for the spindle on which it took place, the "distaff," came to stand in for the female half of the family.

Throughout most of the eighteenth century, laboring women earned income from spinning by selling the thread they spun on a wheel in their cottages to a "putter-outer" or a merchant, who paid them wages far below the value that thread commanded in the marketplace. Because they assumed that spinners operated within a family economy, where men's income provided the bulk of support for the family and women's contributions were seen to be merely supplemental, they paid women pitifully low wages for their work. These assumptions about women's work, and the wages paid for it, informed practices in factories as well when once they came into being after 1780 or so.

The first factories, spurred by the invention in the 1760s of a spinning "jenny," which increased the number of spindles on a wheel from one to eight, and later to sixteen and then to eighty, were modest affairs, often no more than a large room in a cottage or a workshop in which a number of people worked. Production of thread remained unspecialized, and, because the first jennies were small, women could operate them. These early factories operated as domestic industry had in the past, with no single form of organization or hierarchy of labor in place to establish a standard of production. Thus, in the first few decades of industrialization, women retained their traditional employment, and some degree of control over their lives within it, while increasing their output, and the wealth of their employers, dramatically.

By about 1800, a new kind of entrepreneur emerged, who saw in the new technologies of cotton manufacture the means by which greater economy, efficiency, and productivity could be achieved. Interested in maximizing their profits and in establishing greater control over their labor force, and cavalier about the displacement of workers that their methods might entail, these new industrialists set up large factories or mills in areas where labor, raw materials, and new steam-powered machines could be brought together and concentrated in one place. The new spinning machines, called spinning mules, were larger and heavier than the earlier jennies, requiring both skill and strength for their operation. Thus employers located their mills in towns where male artisans could be found in large numbers. All of this meant that textile production, formerly an occupation that employed all kinds of workers throughout all of Great Britain, now took place in a few specific regions, leaving plebeians in whole parts of the kingdom out of work, in poverty and distress. And spinning, which had once been the ubiquitous occupation of women, became the trade of men.

But because the costs of setting up these new mills were so great, factory owners sought the cheapest possible labor force. They turned to young women – often the wives and children of the mule spinners – to do the necessary work of piecing, carding, and reeling. Women had never been paid wages commensurate with those for men, and employers continued to pay them and children far below the "living wage" commanded by men, in the belief that they did not, because assumed to be dependent upon a male head of household, require subsistence wages. Moreover, mill owners believed that women and children, considered "naturally" subordinate to their masters, were more docile, more easily controlled, and far more likely to yield to factory discipline than men. As a consequence, the number of female and child workers in factories far exceeded that of men. In one Scottish county near Glasgow in 1809, for instance, cotton mills employed some 900 men, 2,500 women, and 17,800 children.

From its very inception, factory work for women offered them low-level positions, low pay, and few opportunities for advancement. But because it provided one of the few alternatives to domestic service, which often entailed humiliating and abusive conditions of work, women turned to it when and where it was available. In Scotland, where single women accounted for about 20 percent of the adult female population, compared to only 10 percent in England, women comprised 61 percent of the labor force in the cotton industry. They made up 50 percent of the labor force in Lancashire, where cotton textiles were concentrated in England after 1800.

As new technologies made machines smaller and easier to operate, especially after 1815 when industrialization picked up momentum following the end of the

Napoleonic Wars, employers turned to lower-paid women to operate them. Men saw in women's employment an attempt to undermine their own, and, as we shall see in the next chapter, sought ways to eliminate women from factory work. They would capitalize on the rhetoric utilized by political scientists and evangelical moralists to cast women as reproductive rather than productive beings, a phenomenon derived from and contributing to the intensification of the ideology of separate spheres during the era of the French Revolution.

Malthus and More: Discipline and Domesticity

Competition in the textile industry combined with bad harvests and the economic dislocations created by the wars with France to produce a great deal of poverty and distress throughout England, Scotland, and Wales in the years 1790 to 1815. Food riots, machine-breaking, and demonstrations in support of political reform on the part of working men and women alarmed a great many people, especially in the context of the excitement and fear provoked by the French Revolution. Efforts by political economists to explain poverty as a consequence of excessive births among working people rather than of unemployment and/or low wages joined with those of evangelicals who sought to defend the social order of ranks and hierarchy. In both instances, languages of gender and sexuality were mobilized to promote a social system characterized by deference to authority, morality, individualism, and separate spheres for men and women. Domesticity became the means by which revolution, whether political or economic, could be imaginatively contained and its protagonists disciplined to meet the needs of the modern industrial state.

Poverty, of course, was nothing new to eighteenth-century Great Britain. It had long been a staple of everyday life, acknowledged by contemporaries in theories of moral economy that understood society to be comprised of mutually interdependent groups of people and that made it the obligation of the better off to attend to the economic woes of the poor through such means as poor relief, wage subsidies, and bread price supports. Even Adam Smith, who we have mistakenly come to identify with the most negative consequences of individualism and political economy, recognized that the well-being of the larger community had to come before that of individuals. But in the 1790s, economists of a much more individualist stripe came to dominate understandings of the way society and the economy operated, and how poverty could best be addressed. In a spate of writings produced by such classical economists as Thomas Malthus and popularizers of political economy as Hannah More, poverty came to be regarded as the consequence of the behavior of idle men and irresponsible women for whose subsequent distress the larger society could not – indeed should not – be appealed to for amelioration.[15]

Malthus's *Essay on the Principles of Population* (1798) postulated two givens about human nature: "First, That food is necessary to the existence of man. Secondly, That the passion between the sexes is necessary and will remain nearly in its present state." Because, he believed, humans reproduced their numbers geometrically, and agricultural output could only be increased arithmetically, population would inevitably, in the space of some two generations, outrun the food supply, producing a diseased society characterized by material want, disorder, chaos, warfare, and ultimately starvation. Malthus assumed that for the most part working people, unlike men and women of the middle and élite ranks, could not or would not control their sexual desires, and that their inability to restrain themselves sexually – their vices – brought about their misery and want. He and other political economists like David Ricardo, whose thinking accorded with what he called "the iron law of wages," argued that if workers' wages were too high, they would encourage plebeian men and women to reproduce beyond the capacity of nature to provide for them. Only a reduction in wages – which, if too high, would encourage early marriage and the production of children among workers, driving up the size of the labor force and thus causing the supply of labor to outrun the demand for it, depressing wages only further – and the elimination of poor relief – which encouraged excessive population growth by allowing the poor to reproduce without experiencing the consequences of their acts – would enable society to avoid the disasters that were sure to follow if population growth were to continue unchecked. Their writings justified the much harsher attitudes toward poverty and the poor that had been developing throughout the 1790s as inflation and the need to finance the war against France took its toll on élite pocketbooks. In 1795, for example, parliament had voted to eliminate the minimum wage for workers that had been seen as a way of helping them out in times of difficulty, and in the years immediately following the Napoleonic Wars, talk of abolishing poor relief altogether ran rampant.

In his formulations about excessive sexuality, reproduction, population growth, and poverty, Malthus cast much of the responsibility for society's ills on to plebeian women, building upon assumptions of unreliability and immorality on the part of working women we saw being developed earlier in the century. Because they were much more visibly "idle" in times of economic downturn, because they, more often than men, sought poor relief without being able to work for it, women came to stand in for all the ills attributed to the poor by their upper- and middling-ranked critics. Their failure to limit their births and the resulting high rates of disease and mortality among their children, critics charged, were clear evidence of their irresponsibility. The problems of society, seen to be a consequence of excessive births due to uncontrollable sexual desire, could be laid at the feet of laboring women.

In these formulations, too, we see women represented as reproductive rather than productive beings. Malthus transposed on to working people the assumptions about separate spheres for men and women that informed the thinking of the middling and élite ranks. His writings depicted the plebeian man as producer and provider for his wife and children, and the plebeian woman as a mother who stayed at home to care for their children, a portrayal of the ideal of the male bread-winner that working people had no possibility of attaining. Working men, as we shall see in the next chapter, helped to advance this understanding of men as the sole providers, partially to boost their manly status within their homes and work-places, and partially to exclude women from competing with them for jobs and sufficient wages.

Moreover, having lost a productive role and having been assigned an exclusively reproductive role in the imaginations of such theorists, working women as "mothers" fared ill in comparison with their upper ranked counterparts. Middling and élite mothers, insisted separate sphere ideologists, cared for their children and educated them in the ways of civility and morality. Working women, by contrast, rendered culpable for the poverty, disease, and misery in which they and their chil-dren lived by virtue of their excessive reproduction, were regarded as immoral, irresponsible, improvident, and as failures as mothers. If they could be persuaded to follow the example of their social superiors, Malthus believed, to postpone their marriages and limit their births, to exercise moral restraint, in short, they too could enjoy the material fruits of such restraint that middling and élite families enjoyed. Better living conditions and a higher moral existence, Malthus and his supporters held, awaited those who adopted upper-rank practices.

Such depictions provided middling and élite women scope for what would become their project, and through it the source of their class and gender identi-ties, over the next half century: the civilizing – by inculcating the principles and practices of domesticity – of working-class and poor women, and, through them, of the working classes as a whole. Informed by the precepts of evangelical Christianity and political economy, and inspired by the disorders produced by industrialization and the French Revolution, a small but influential group of male and female reformers, organized in the so-called Clapham sect, set about the dual tasks of bringing spiritual renewal and social order to a nation that had, as they saw it, fallen into moral degeneracy. Under the leadership of Hannah More, the evan-gelical campaign to strengthen the social hierarchy and reform the "manners and morals" of the nation proceeded apace, attracting widespread support from men, and particularly women, of the mercantile and landed middling classes.

Moral regeneration, in the eyes of evangelicals, could be achieved only through individual faith in the grace of God, and the best place for such faith to be sustained, they held, was in the home. The social improvement of the poor, and a renewed respect for social hierarchy, it followed, required them to practice self-discipline in all aspects of their lives, whether it be refraining from alcohol consumption, gambling, or sexual activity. These were qualities that the poor would have to be taught, and it devolved upon women of the middling ranks, as guardians of the domestic sphere and of morality, to serve as their instructors. Calling upon middling women to "come forward with a patriotism at once firm and feminine for the general good," Hannah More urged them in 1799 to "contribute their full and fair proportion toward the saving of their country," to "raise the depressed tone of public morals, to awaken the drowsy spirit of religious principle, and to re-animate the dormant powers of active piety." But they were to do so, she insisted, in accordance with her position on women appearing in public, "without departing from the refinement of their character, without derogating from the dignity of their rank; without blemishing the delicacy of their sex." Social stability demanded that middling women eschew any claim to political or legal rights, that they sacrifice their personal aspirations to public activity or equality with men to the higher religious and social goals of deference, hierarchy, and authority. They must learn, and pass on to their working-class charges, habits of restraint. "They should, when very young, be inured to contradiction," More advised. "They should be led to distrust their own judgment; they should learn not to murmer at expostulation; but should be accustomed to expect and endure opposition. … It is of the last importance to their happiness in life that they should early acquire a submissive temper and a forbearing spirit."[16]

Disciplining themselves and others in the ways of submissiveness, self-denial, and dependence, More assured the readers of her wildly successful *Cheap Repository of Moral and Religious Tracts*,[17] of which several million were printed, sold, and/or disseminated among the plebeian classes around the turn of the century, would advance the cause of domestic purity and moral regeneration of society. In "The history of Charles Jones," the protagonist sought in a wife "a pious, sober, stay-at-home, modest young woman," who would "sooth his sorrows, calm his fears, / And help him thro' his vale of tears." The family, in the *Cheap Repository Tracts*, offered shelter from a world of sin and temptation: within the home, men received the care and attention of diligent, industrious, sober, pious, and honest wives; children learned the lessons that would guide them throughout the rest of their lives at the feet of their parents. These virtues promised all of them a peaceable, happy, harmonious, comfortable existence.

But beyond that, these were the qualities and values necessary to uphold the new industrial order of factories and disciplined work forces. One of the first lessons middling women would have to impart if morality and civility were to be attained by the working classes, More asserted, was the folly and the danger of women going out to work. They would have to be taught domestic "oeconomy," the art of keeping a home neat, orderly, and provisioned on a very small income. As her middle-class protagonist in "A cure for melancholy" (1798), Mrs Jones, points out to a squire who has questioned why she is not training the girls of her local parish in spinning or carding, there is a[nother] manufacture, which I am carrying on, and I know of none within my own reach which is so valuable. What can that be? said the Squire. *To make good wives for working men*, said she. Is not mine an excellent staple commodity? I am teaching these girls the arts of industry and good management. It is little encouragement to an honest man to work hard all the week, if his wages are wasted by a slattern at home. Most of these girls will probably become wives to the poor, or servants to the rich; to such the common arts of life are of great value.

This portrayal of working-class life in which the male bread-winner brings his hard-earned pay-packet to his stay-at-home wife mirrors that drawn by Malthus in his *Essay on Population*. An arrangement of separate spheres for men and women, in which men went out to work while their wives remained at home to maintain a decent, moral, disciplined, and well-regulated domestic life – these, in the minds of evangelicals and political economists, provided the building blocks upon which a stable, hierarchical, deferential social order could be constructed and sustained in the midst of industrial transformation and political revolution.

Separate sphere ideology became fortified by a new model of sexual difference in the last years of the eighteenth century, when, under the pressure of the panic generated by the French Revolution, by war with France, and by political upheaval in Britain and Ireland, sexual activity on the part of women became construed as being inseparable from radical political activity. Political revolution, in other words, constituted sexual revolution, and vice versa. One of the most effective ways of de-limiting the threat posed by women in the public sphere was to describe those who insisted on women's political rights as being "unsex'd." By this term, contemporaries meant that such women were unnaturally affected by sexual feelings, something that "normal" and "proper" British women did not experience, indeed, could not experience. Just as significantly, radical political activity could be tarred and discredited with the brush of sexual promiscuity and disorder. It was by conflating the sexual with the political that opponents of radicalism – called anti-Jacobins in Britain – could claim that radicalism threatened "the destruction of domestic, civil, and political society."

Ironically, the life of Mary Wollstonecraft played, at least indirectly, a prominent role in the developments by which this came to pass.[18] In 1798, Wollstonecraft's husband, the radical William Godwin, published his *Memoirs of the Author of the Vindication of the Rights of Woman*, in which he revealed that Wollstonecraft, who had died of puerperal fever following childbirth the year before, had engaged in a number of unconventional liaisons with men. Unsuccessful in her efforts to have an affair with a married man by the name of Henry Fuseli, she turned to Gilbert Imlay, with whom she had a child without benefit of marriage in 1794. Abandoned by Imlay, she tried twice to commit suicide in 1795. In 1796 she met William Godwin, and became pregnant by him. Married in March 1797, Wollstonecraft gave birth to a daughter on 30 August, and died eleven days later. Godwin's memoirs provided ammunition to those seeking to condemn radical politics and especially the involvement of women in them. As one historian noted, critics could use the life of Mary Wollstonecraft to ridicule the ideas that she put forward in *A Vindication of the Rights of Woman*. The *Anti-Jacobin Review* represented Wollstonecraft's call for women's rights to education and political citizenship as a demand for the elimination of "restrictions on adultery." "Here we must observe," declared the reviewer, "that Mary's theory, that it is the right of women to indulge their inclinations with every man they like, is so far from being new, that it is as old as prostitution." He went on to claim that the philosophy represented by the notion of the rights of man – and, clearly, women too – "by leaving women to the exercise of ... their natural and social rights, ... would take away powerful restraints on the promiscuous intercourse of the sexes ... dissolve the tie of marriage, one of the chief foundations of political society, and then promote Jacobinical politics." As, by that time, Jacobinical politics in France had been responsible for the execution of the king and queen, for the September massacres, and for the Terror under Robespierre, such an indictment carried fearful weight.

If political revolution constituted sexual revolution then one strategy by which it could be contained was a reconfiguration of sexual difference that made sexual feelings for women taboo by rendering them "unnatural." The gender system that assigned to men and women their respective habitations of public and domestic by the end of the eighteenth century was informed by an entirely different understanding of sexual difference from that which ordered the relations between men and women in the seventeenth century. The change from one to another was brought about by the need felt by men and women, made anxious by women's increased independence, activity, and assertiveness after 1700 – much of it a consequence of the economic and political revolutions we have been discussing – to establish patriarchy on a more secure basis than it rested on earlier.

Before the middle of the eighteenth century, gender difference was understood to be a cosmological phenomenon, rooted not in the body, as it would come to be by 1800 or so, but in the distinctions of hot and cold, moist and dry, central to the humoral theory of the universe. Women were regarded as different from and inferior to men on the basis of their lesser heat. The source of all strength – intellectual, physical, or moral – heat acted as a measure of gender. The subordination of women in sixteenth-and seventeenth-century England, demanded of them in retribution for Eve's sin, rested on the belief that women, being colder than men, were weaker than men. But the humoral theory on which this formulation was based depicted strength in relative terms, not incommensurate terms. Gender or sexual difference might well derive its meaning from the greater size and strength of men, but the system allowed for the possibility that exceptional women might display the same mental or moral strength as men and be praised for it. At the same time, this system of difference based on hierarchy and degree permitted movement in the opposite direction as well: manliness might easily slide into effeminacy.

Fears about effeminacy informed public discussion about virtually every aspect of eighteenth-century society; we have seen how riddled with those fears were the discourses of virtue under siege from commercial capitalism. Questions of war, empire, and politics, especially after mid-century, took up the themes of manliness and effeminacy with a vengeance. What seems to have been at stake was the need for society to shore up an aristocratic, patriarchal system facing challenge from all quarters by drawing ever sharper lines between men and women. It did so by calling upon the new mechanistic theories of the scientific revolution, which left the humoral theory of gender in shambles. In keeping with the intellectual developments associated with Descartes and Bacon, gender became understood not in terms of the relative strength and weakness of men and women, of the superior and inferior hierarchical status they occupied on the Great Chain of Being, but in terms of polarities, dichotomies, opposites. Women were not simply weaker than, inferior to men, they were completely unlike them, practically members of a different species.

The invention of sensational psychology, or nerve theory, identified with the writings of John Locke and the physician George Cheyne, helped to effect the transformation of gender from a system based on hierarchy to one based on incommensurability. At the core of nerve theory stood sensibility, which made itself known to the general public through the medium of the romantic novel and which, as we have seen, played a vital part in the legitimation of commercial activity. Sensibility came to be understood in the latter half of the eighteenth century as belonging exclusively to women as a consequence of women's finer "nervous" system. That nervous system, like the female skeleton and, most especially, the anatomy and physiology of the female reproductive organs, came to be described in bio-medical treatises as distinct from, as incommensurate with, those of men. Sensibility offered a representational language by which men and women could be rendered as entirely different from one another on the basis of their sexual and reproductive organizations. Male and female reproductive organs that had earlier been regarded as like one another in function and even shared the same name, such as ovaries and testicles for example, now became functionally distinct from one another and took on different appellations.

Differential capacities to experience sexual pleasure came to constitute one prominent component of the physiological and anatomical differences between men and women. Where orgasm by both men and women had earlier been regarded as a necessary element in successful generation, the necessity and then

even the possibility of female orgasm was dropped from the reproductive reper-
toire. By the early nineteenth century, physicians, scientists, and novelists had
instilled in society a conviction that women were naturally passionless. Where, in
the seventeenth and early eighteenth centuries, women had had to marshal all
their strength to control their passions and ensure their chastity, by the late eighteenth century, they had no passion, and their chastity could be taken for granted
as an outgrowth of their natural innocence, a product of their inherent virtue,
which in turn derived from their utter lack of sexual desire. Ensconced firmly in
the home, and de-sexualized by the beginning of the nineteenth century, middle-
and upper-class women embodied the qualities of virtue, as they were now
defined.

The proponents of evangelicalism and of political economy, many of them, like
Hannah More, one and the same person, helped to establish among the middling
and élite ranks, if not yet among the working classes and the poor, models of
masculinity and femininity that prevailed throughout the nineteenth century. Even
among aristocratic men, a new seriousness and moral earnestness began to take
hold, superseding earlier aristocratic disdain for work, for instance, and replacing
styles that emulated the "effeminate" French with those of a much more "manly,"
British, sometimes even military, cast. Wigs, powdered hair, the wearing of
brightly colored silks, brocades, and laces – these gave way to a more understated,
sober form of dress for upper-class men, characterized by breeches, boots, and a
riding coat for rural élites, and dark-colored suits for those gentlemen who
worked in London or other large towns. Their behavior, or at least prescriptions
for it, underwent change as well, as notions of hard work, self-restraint, duty, reli-
giosity, and faithfulness to marriage vows trickled upward into élite households.
By 1800, it was no longer possible for politicians holding office to flaunt their
keeping of mistresses, as it had been in the earlier part of the eighteenth century.
Rather, they had to keep up the appearance, at least, of dedicated family men with
a keen appreciation for their domestic responsibilities. By 1815, Britain's ruling
élites, whose fitness to rule had been called into question throughout the eighteenth century by claims about their effeminacy, most recently by Paine's
description of them as a "seraglio of males," had established themselves as the
manly embodiments of discipline and authority. Élite women, for their part,
espoused, even if they did not conform to, principles of domesticity that rendered
women dependent, submissive, and passive, the guardians of morality and civility
in a rapidly changing and increasingly dangerous world. The idea of upright,
manly, respectable males operating in the public sphere of work and politics,
supported and sustained in their endeavors by dependent, submissive, pure
women operating in the domestic sphere of home and family, where their
authority over all matters pertaining to morality and civility went uncontested –
this ideological formulation of domesticity and separate spheres consolidated itself

by the first decades of the nineteenth century, and would serve as the paradigm for normative gender relations until the first decades of the twentieth.

From an ideal that characterized the public, political male in neo-classical ideology, virtue traveled through an intermediate stage that attached to it notions of the civilized, mannered, social creature of sensibility, to arrive at a set of meanings in the nineteenth century that marked it as private, sexual, and female. As virtue made his difficult journey through the imaginations of such illustrious figures as Shaftesbury and Hutcheson in the first half of the century, and Hume and Gibbon in the latter half, he–she encountered numerous hazards and detours; eventually, the vehicles of Adam Smith's *Theory of Moral Sentiments* and *The Wealth of Nations* carried her safely into the arms of domesticity, where the corruptions of now-commercialized public life could not sully or unsex her, and where she could not contaminate masculinity with her passions or her femininity.

As a consequence, too, politics and public activity no longer need be concerned with the pursuit of virtue in neo-classical terms. After mid-century, citizenship came to be seen as a product not of virtue but of the rights, first contractual and then natural, of the individual. Moral fulfillment, as neo-classicists had seen it, could no longer be found in the public arena of politics, where virtue no longer operated. Instead virtue became located in the domestic sphere, in the life of the family and most especially in women.

No longer apposite to the activities of the male in public life, virtue denoted women's chastity and innocence of sexual matters. Possession and maintenance of the virtuous female in the home by middle-class men signaled their respectability, their manliness, their fitness to participate in political life, and it was on these grounds that they, and later generations of working-class men, would make demands for and succeed in achieving citizenship as it was manifested in the franchise. In a real sense, then, the possession of virtue still served as the criterion by which men qualified for political life. What had changed was what constituted virtue.

NOTES

1　Quoted in Clive Emsley, "The impact of the French Revolution," in Ceri Crossley and Ian Small, eds, *The French Revolution and British Culture* (Oxford, 1989), p. 33.
2　Quoted in George Woodcock, "The meaning of revolution in Britain, 1770–1800," in Ceri Crossley and Ian Small, eds, *The French Revolution and British Culture* (Oxford, 1989), pp. 19, 21.
3　See Iain McCalman, "Mad Lord George and Madame La Motte: Riot and sexuality in the genesis of Burke's *Reflections on the Revolution in France*," *Journal of British Studies* 35(3), July 1996: 343–67.

4 Quoted in Conor Cruise O'Brien, *The Great Melody: An Autobiography of Edmund Burke* (Chicago, 1992), pp. 406, 407.

5 Quoted in Moira Ferguson, ed., *First Feminists: British Women Writers, 1578–1799* (Bloomington, 1985), pp. 413–19; and Vivien Jones, ed., *Women in the Eighteenth Century: Constructions of Femininity* (London, 1990), pp. 231–42.

6 Quoted in Vivien Jones, ed., *Women in the Eighteenth Century: Constructions of Femininity* (London, 1990), pp. 117–20.

7 Quoted in Linda Colley, *Britons: Forging the Nation, 1707–1837* (New Haven, 1992), pp. 253–4; and Jones, *Women in the Eighteenth Century*, pp. 121–30.

8 Quoted in Mary Poovey, *The Proper Lady and the Woman Writer* (Chicago, 1984), p. 31; and Colley, *Britons*, p. 255.

9 See Dror Wahrman, *Imagining the Middle Class: The Political Representation of Class in Britain, c. 1780–1840* (Cambridge, 1995), p. 38.

10 Colley, *Britons*, p. 305.

11 Quoted in Katherine Binhammer, "The sex panic of the 1790s," *Journal of the History of Sexuality* 6(3), January 1996, note 11: 413.

12 Quoted in Colley, *Britons*, p. 256; and Poovey, *The Proper Lady*, p. 32.

13 Quoted in Nancy J. Curtin, "Women and eighteenth-century Irish republicanism," in Margaret MacCurtain and Mary O'Dowd, eds, *Women in Early Modern Ireland* (Edinburgh, 1991), p. 135.

14 Curtin, "Women and eighteenth-century Irish republicanism," p. 138.

15 Much of the following discussion is drawn from Deborah Valenze, *The First Industrial Woman* (New York, 1995), ch. 7.

16 Quoted in Poovey, *The Proper Woman*, pp. 33, 34.

17 See Susan Pederson, "Hannah More meets Simple Simon: Tracts, chapbooks, and popular culture in late eighteenth-century England," *Journal of British Studies* 25(1), January 1986: 84–113.

18 See G.J. Barker-Benfield, *The Culture of Sensibility: Sex and Society in Eighteenth-Century Britain* (Chicago, 1992), ch. 7.

SOURCES

G.J. Barker-Benfield. *The Culture of Sensibility: Sex and Society in Eighteenth-Century Britain.* Chicago, 1992.

Katherine Binhammer, "The sex panic of the 1790s," *Journal of the History of Sexuality* 6(3), January 1996: 409–34.

Anna Clark, *The Struggle for the Breeches: Gender and the Making of the British Working Class.* Berkeley, 1995.

Linda Colley, *Britons: Forging the Nation, 1707–1837.* New Haven, 1992.

Nancy J. Curtin, "Women and eighteenth-century Irish republicanism," in Margaret MacCurtain and Mary O'Dowd, eds, *Women in Early Modern Ireland.* Edinburgh, 1991.

Leonore Davidoff and Catherine Hall, *Family Fortunes: Men and Women of the English Middle Classes, 1780–1850.* Chicago, 1987.

Clive Emsley, "The impact of the French Revolution," in Ceri Crossley and Ian Small, eds, *The French Revolution and British Culture.* Oxford, 1989.

Moira Ferguson, ed., *First Feminists: British Women Writers, 1578–1799*. Bloomington, 1985.

———, *Subject to Others: British Women Writers and Colonial Slavery, 1670–1834*. New York, 1992.

Anthony Fletcher, *Gender, Sex and Subordination in England, 1500–1800*. New Haven, 1995.

R.F. Foster, *Modern Ireland, 1600–1972*. London, 1988.

Catherine Gallagher, "The body versus the social body in Malthus and Mayhew," in Catherine Gallagher and Thomas Laqueur, eds, *The Making of the Modern Body: Sexuality and Society in the Nineteenth Century*. Berkeley, 1987.

Vivien Jones, ed., *Women in the Eighteenth Century: Constructions of Femininity*. London, 1990.

Thomas Laqueur, *Making Sex: Body and Gender from the Greeks to Freud*. Cambridge, MA, 1990.

Iain McCalman, "Mad Lord George and Madame La Motte: Riot and sexuality in the genesis of Burke's *Reflections on the Revolution in France*," *Journal of British Studies* 35(3), July 1996: 343–67.

———, "Popular constitutionalism and revolution in England and Ireland," in Isser Woloch, ed., *Revolution and the Meanings of Freedom in the Nineteenth Century*. Palo Alto, 1996.

Conor Cruise O'Brien, *The Great Melody: An Autobiography of Edmund Burke*. Chicago, 1992.

Susan Pederson, "Hannah More meets Simple Simon: Tracts, chapbooks, and popular culture in late eighteenth-century England," *Journal of British Studies* 25(1), January 1986: 84–113.

Mary Poovey, *The Proper Lady and the Woman Writer*. Chicago, 1984.

E.P. Thompson, *The Making of the English Working Class*. New York, 1963.

Deborah Valenze, *The First Industrial Woman*. New York, 1995.

Dror Wahrman, *Imagining the Middle Class: The Political Representation of Class in Britain, c. 1780–1840*. Cambridge, 1995.

George Woodcock, "The meaning of revolution in Britain, 1770–1800," in Crossley and Small, eds, *The French Revolution and British Culture*. Oxford, 1989.

Part III

The nineteenth century

"The angel in the house" and her critics: virtue and politics in the age of bourgeois liberalism

GENERAL INTRODUCTION

Britain emerged from the French Revolution and the Napoleonic Wars with its political, social, and economic institutions intact. The state had asserted its authority over would-be reformers through repression, and established a greater hold on its citizens through an appeal to patriotism and a militaristic nationalism; ruling élites had recovered their "manliness" by waging a victorious war against France and embracing the moral seriousness attached to evangelicalism, thereby strengthening their claim to rule for, and on behalf of, the nation; the fledgling factory system had survived a furious onslaught of distraught workers. In the empire, Ireland had been subdued through the Act of Union with the United Kingdom of Great Britain, French threats to the British presence in India had been eliminated, and new holdings in the Mediterranean and in South Africa, ceded by the Congress of Vienna after Waterloo, secured the routes to India. At home and overseas, Britain appeared a much more powerful, aggressive, disciplined, even authoritarian nation than had been the case in the eighteenth century.

Hardly a year had passed, however, before the social, economic, and political institutions of a newly resurgent aristocratic Britain faced challenges from within: from working men and women who sought relief from high bread prices and unemployment following the wars; from radicals who claimed that working men's indispensability to manufacturing and industry qualified them for a place in the nation; from middle-class men who sought a political voice commensurate with their material contributions to the nation as the landed, agricultural sector of the economy began to give way to that of industry; from Irish catholics who demanded the fulfillment of promises made to them earlier by William Pitt; from Indians defending their religions, customs, and economic and social systems from the incursions of British "liberal" practices, and newly freed Jamaican blacks seeking the freedoms promised by the liberal state but denied them by white planters; and from women who could not – or would not – conform to the prescriptions for their lives laid down by the ideology of separate spheres.

The ideology of separate spheres, forged within and consolidated by the vicissitudes of eighteenth-century economic, social, and political life, informed virtually every aspect of life in the nineteenth century. As politicians crafted the legislation that would establish the classical liberal nation state between 1828 and 1846, they imbued society with the liberal ethos of individual freedom, legal equality, *laissez-faire*, meritocracy, and separate spheres for men and women that would prevail throughout most of the nineteenth century. Domesticity eliminated the economic function of middle-class women and created the notion of the perfect wife and mother, or the "angel in the house," as Coventry Patmore styled her in the mid-1850s. In the competitive, unsettling, and sometimes brutal world of nineteenth-century industrial society, it fell to women to provide a haven of peace and security, a repository of moral values. The home became a refuge from what one writer of domestic manuals called "those eager pecuniary speculations" and "that fierce conflict of worldly interests, by which men are so deeply occupied as to be in a manner compelled to stifle their best feelings." Inside the "walled garden" of home, women were to create a sanctuary from the harsh realities of the industrial world. Their virtues of gentleness, sympathy, purity, and piety were to provide their husbands and children with the emotional security necessary to face the hardships of modern life.

Separate sphere ideology underpinned and gave stability to the structures that constituted bourgeois liberalism at home and imperialism abroad, but its promises, inconsistencies, and contradictions also made possible and legitimated the multiple resistances to it that challenged the classical, bourgeois liberal order of Britain by the end of the century.

Chapter 7

The virtues of liberalism

Consolidating the domestic ideal, 1815–48

In the years between 1815 and 1848, Britain's social, economic, and political structures became transformed. Once a system characterized by ranks and orders, in which landed and commercial élites whose wealth derived from agriculture and commerce monopolized political power, it gave way to one in which frequently mutually antagonistic classes vied with one another for political power within an economic system dominated by industry. Between 1815 and 1832, middle- and working-class radicals joined together to push reform of the old regime, a union that broke apart when parliament offered middle-class men the vote, splitting them off from their erstwhile working-class and female allies. The Reform Act of 1832 signaled the triumph of liberalism over a more far-reaching, more democratic radicalism.

After 1832, a classical liberal political system derived from a franchise restricted by property qualifications and informed by the principles of meritocracy, individualism, free trade, and respectability supplanted the earlier regime comprised of patronage, deferential social relations, moral economy, and "old corruption". Apologists for the middle classes who gained political power with the Reform Act of 1832 explained their victory after the fact by referring to the so-called "inherent" bourgeois virtues of domesticity, drawing distinctions between the virtuous middle classes on the one hand, and the purportedly debauched aristocracy and equally immoral working classes on the other.

But working-class radicals, whose efforts to gain the right to vote continued long after their betrayal by former middle-class allies in 1832 in a movement known as Chartism, refused to cede to the middle classes an exclusive claim to domesticity and separate spheres. Although it would take more than a century for the majority of working-class families to attain the financial status necessary to actually implement an arrangement of separate spheres for men and women, the ideal of the male bread-winner and the stay-at-home wife and mother took hold among many working people before mid-century, and would serve to justify in the minds of political élites the enfranchisement of urban working-class men in 1867.

Queen Caroline and the flowering of radical protest, 1815–20[1]

The period immediately following the defeat of Napoleon at Waterloo saw much social distress as efforts to return to a peacetime economy produced severe dislocation, depression, and unemployment. Workers in virtually every sector of the economy suffered hardship, and it is likely that the real earnings of average working-class families in the years 1815 to 1819 fell below what they had been in the 1780s. Poor rates, which householders earning a certain income paid to alleviate destitution among the working poor, reached very high levels, an indication that more families than usual were unable to sustain themselves economically.

In 1815, too, parliament passed the Corn Bill, which restricted the importation of wheat from outside Britain unless the price of domestic grain rose above a level that ensured farmers a handsome profit. The Corn Law benefited landowners by limiting competition from abroad, but hurt working people by making the price of bread more dear. Riots protesting the high cost of bread broke out across England in the fall of 1815, followed by a rash of machine-breaking by so-called Luddites in many of the industrial areas in 1816.

The dismal economic conditions of postwar life contributed to the propensity of many working-class men and women to join with middle-class activists in demanding parliamentary reform. The Corn Law, in particular, symbolized for radicals and reformers the abuses of a parliamentary system made up of privileged, self-interested, landowning élites. The reform movement, a disparate group made up of Whigs sitting in parliament, of middling people outside of parliament seeking far-reaching reform along constitutional lines, and a number of popular radicals willing to engage in extra-legal and even violent means to bring about significant political changes, sought to eliminate the "old corruption" of aristocratic government and to replace it with annual parliaments elected on the basis of a wider suffrage. Only in this way, reformers believed, could cronyism, favoritism, corruption, and the influence of the House of Lords and the Anglican Church be stamped out, and good government designed to further the interests of the people as a whole be implemented.

Radicals often framed their attack on aristocracy and "old corruption" in the language of gender and sexuality, in ways not dissimilar to those we saw operating in the second half of the eighteenth century. In the early nineteenth century, "dandies" like the Prince of Wales and his hangers-on at court received the brunt of radical criticism. Because they paid careful attention to their appearance, wore extravagant clothing, and flaunted a lifestyle that eschewed work of any sort, they could easily be rendered "feminine" by their detractors. The radical paper, *The Black Dwarf*, for instance, attacked aristocratic manhood in 1818 by describing élites as "a new race of men" who "wear stays, and drink God to save the King, in dandy punch. Their gender is not yet ascertained," it proclaimed, "but as their principal ambition seems to be to look as pretty as women, it would be most uncharitable to call them men." The radical *Spirit of the Union*, in 1819, employed much the same image of effeminacy in the "Dandy corseteers":

> How exquisitely pretty,
> In whalebone armor cas'd
> Each dandy walks the city
> Exhibiting its waist.

One semi-pornographic squib had the prince regent proclaiming, as he indulged his various appetites:

> For the good of the people this carcase so brawny
> I fatten with Turtle and mullogatawney.
> For the good of the people I spend on a ——— [whore]
> What else would be wasted on ten thousand poor.

These attacks on aristocratic effeminacy sought to undermine the legitimacy of élite rule and to buttress the case for radical reform by associating it with "manliness." As one working man put it at a December 1816 reform meeting in Middleton, "it was impossible for a Reform to take place whilst the Leaders of the Constitution were going on in wantonness and lust."

The demand by some radicals like Henry Hunt for universal suffrage, however – justified on the grounds of the natural equality of all people – opened them up to ridicule from their opponents, who suggested that if all people enjoyed a natural equality then women, as well as men, should be entitled to vote. A few radical women and men did, indeed, support women's enfranchisement and political rights, but most responded to these ideas with disdain. The *Black Dwarf* in 1818 spun a tale of women lawyers and clergy as it contemplated the possibility of "female politicians." "Gladly," it quipped slyly, "we would embrace such legislative bodies." More seriously, in a passage that betrayed the editor's fears that female empowerment would come only at the expense of men's, the paper claimed that women with political rights would reduce men to the status of mere nurses or milkmaids. The vast majority of radicals, whether of the working or middle classes, sought not universal suffrage but enfranchisement of male householders, men who occupied a household and headed a family. They articulated their political demands in the language of ancient constitutionalism rather than that of

Paine's rights of man: they argued that their independence and their possession of property in the persons of their wives and children – their virtue, in civic humanist terms – qualified them for citizenship.

Radicals might dismiss the prospect of women sharing in the gains of political reform, but they could not conduct their campaigns without their participation. In order to gain women's – and broader community – support, they learned, they had to put forward a program that went beyond purely political reforms to encompass the social and economic problems faced by plebeian families, and they had to involve women in their activities of protest. In the northern textile cities in particular, in Glasgow, Manchester, Blackburn, and Stockton, women organized themselves into reform and friendly societies, wrote speeches and held meetings, petitioned for reform, and marched in mass demonstrations. Armed with "large brooms to sweep away corruption," as one witness to an 1819 Glasgow mass meeting described them, or crowning male leaders with caps of liberty that they had embroidered, these women, while acting politically on their own behalf and that of their families, served as symbols of purity and virtue that could be arrayed against aristocratic corruption.

Conservative opponents declaimed against radical women as "the most degraded of their sex," condemning them for their "disgusting and abominable" attempts to "ruin society." Their efforts compelled many radical men to rush to the defense of women's participation in the reform movement, a phenomenon that had the effect of undermining, to some degree, the association of women with effeminacy and ineffectiveness. Instead, women took on the symbolic function of demonstrating radical virtue. In prints and broadsides women were often depicted as larger-than-life heroes stamping out "old corruption." Such images recalled the separate spheres notions of purity and virtue urged upon middle- and upper-class women, but with a significant difference. For women of the upper ranks, purity and virtue hinged upon their remaining at home, out of the public sphere altogether. Radical women, by contrast, insisted that the very needs of women and their families in the private sphere – their want of food, clothing, warmth, and even shelter – must be addressed as political issues. They explicitly tied reform of the political system to the alleviation of the hardships forced upon them by postwar depression and dislocation. The *Black Dwarf* in 1818 had radical women asserting that their "oppressors and tyrannical rulers" had compelled them to engage in politics by making it impossible for them to care for their children adequately. As the Manchester Female Reformers put it in 1819, "we can no longer bear to see ... our husbands and little ones clothed in rags." The Blackburn Female Reformers echoed their complaint in a condemnation of the old "borough-mongering system." "We cannot describe our wretchedness," they lamented, "for language cannot paint the feelings of a mother, when she beholds her naked children, and hears their inoffensive cries of hunger and approaching death."

The mobilization of plebeian women as the embodiment of radical virtue standing in opposition to aristocratic corruption and the crown's trampling on liberties took on powerful proportions in the events that came to be called the Peterloo Massacre of 9 August 1819. Some 60,000 people had gathered on St Peter's Field in Manchester to listen to Henry Hunt's calls for parliamentary reform when they were attacked by the local constabulary and by regular government troops. Four hundred persons were wounded, over 100 of them women. Two women and nine men were killed. Across England, the public expressed outrage that the state would, as the political cartoons represented the scene over and over again, send armed men to ride down and slash open innocent women. This portrayal of helpless women killed and injured by the agents of the old, unreformed order did a great deal of damage to the moral authority of that old order and symbolically endowed the people with the virtue – in the guise now of a plebeian woman – necessary to govern Britain.

The Queen Caroline affair provided radicals and reformers with another opportunity to demonstrate their defense of, and claim to, virtue in opposition to what they regarded as aristocratic tyranny and oppression. In 1820, George IV became king after many years of ruling as prince regent on behalf of his incapacitated father, George III. His estranged and ill-treated wife, Caroline, who had been in self-imposed exile in Europe since 1814, when she agreed to leave England in return for an annual payment of £35,000, returned, demanding that she be recognized as queen. George responded with an action for divorce in the House of Lords, causing a "Bill of Pains and Penalties" to be brought against her that censured her for adultery and rescinded her queenly status. Coming from a man whom the radical press had denounced as a lecherous dandy, whose regency had been characterized by profligacy and debauchery, making it an irresistible magnet for charges of financial and political, as well as moral, corruption, the new king's charges met with an outburst of popular fury against what was perceived as the latest, most egregious, manifestation of "old corruption." In the melodrama that followed, Caroline, whose behavior while in Europe was hardly pristine, took on the trappings of the "poor wronged female," "a poor forlorn woman" whose virtue, sullied by an evil king and his equally evil ministers, must be defended by the "manly," "courageous" people of Britain.

The radical press exploited the scandal with ferocious and obscene satire, taking every opportunity to draw connections between "old corruption" and the campaign against Caroline. Pamphleteers published accounts of adulterous liaisons on the part of the king's men who had brought action against the queen, and noted the salaries and pensions of those in the House of Lords who opposed her as a means of bringing to light the sordid workings of unreformed government. William Benbow, a radical publisher, ran a print charging that the state's evidence against Caroline had been produced by bribing spies from Italy to lie about her behavior there, bribes financed from the money stolen from hard-working, honest English soldiers and sailors who had only five years before given their all to protect their country against foreign aggression. In *Fair Play, or Who are the Adulterers, Slanderers and Demoralizers?*, Benbow insisted that "there is not a jury in the United Kingdom, would believe the filthy testimony of the filthy witnesses, arranged by the filthy junta, employed for the base, unmanly and iniquitous purpose of dethroning a Queen."

The Queen Caroline affair, by linking the somewhat abstract constitutional concerns of radicalism – the role of the monarch in government, corruption and patronage, and the infringement by parliament on the liberties of the people – with the immediately personal and moral concerns of people in their everyday lives, gave radicalism a base of popular support that it had not enjoyed since the days of the civil war of the mid-seventeenth century. "The people all favour the Queen," noted Lady Palmerston, "including the respectable middle ranks." Anti-king feeling ran high, and the king's ministers feared for the survival of the throne. William Lamb, who would become Lord Melbourne, wrote to William Wilberforce "that there appears to be a great danger of serious popular tumult and insurrection." A confidant of the Duke of Buckingham reported that "one cannot calculate on anything less than subversion of all government and authority, if this goes on; how it is to end, no one can foresee." For men, the misuse of Caroline by George and his ministers resonated with the grievances plebeians and radicals experienced at the hands of "aristocratic government." Referring to the economic distress of the postwar years and to the recent events of Peterloo, the "Artisans, Mechanics, and Labouring Classes" of Manchester in September 1820 commiserated with the queen. "The same power which scourged us, is now oppressing you," they declared. In Nottingham, the *Black Dwarf* reported, the people "felt for the wrongs of the Queen as they felt for the various oppressions under which they themselves labored." By mixing the personal with the constitutional, the private with the public, working people were better able to internalize the more distant concerns of political reform and make them their own. As long-time radical Major John Cartwright observed, "the honor of the Queen is closely related with the constitutional rights of the people." Caroline exploited this sentiment regularly, telling an audience at St Pancras in London that "those who degrade the Queen have never manifested any repugnance in abridging the liberties of the people." "My loss of rank," she explained at another time, "would have been their loss of liberties."

Women of the plebeian and middling ranks rallied massively on behalf of Caroline. Addresses bearing the signatures of tens of thousands of women from London, Halifax, Exeter, Nottingham, Edinburgh, Bristol, and elsewhere proclaimed their support for the queen, and gave expression to the fear that if the action against Caroline succeeded then they, the virtuous women of Britain, could find no security against men in their own lives. Caroline told an audience of women that "if my matrimonial rights are illegally annulled, theirs eventually may be rendered less secure." A number of "Ladies of Edinburgh," agreed, proclaiming in an address:

> The principles and doctrines now advanced by your accusers, do not apply to your case alone, but if made part of the law of the land may hereafter be applied as a precedent from every careless and dissipated husband to rid himself of his wife, however good and innocent she may be; and to render his family, however amiable, illegitimate, thereby destroying the sacred bond of matrimony, and rendering all domestic felicity very uncertain.

As one widely heard ballad phrased women's concerns:

> Attend ye virtuous British wives
> Support your injured Queen,
> Assert her rights; they are your own,
> As plainly may be seen.

The rights of women referred to in this ballad were not political ones. Instead, they denoted the right to respect, safety, and security that women, because of their sex, deserved from men. The *Black Dwarf* reminded its readers that "no man would basely forfeit the love and esteem of his wife, his daughters, his sisters, or his mistress, by calmly suffering the violation of every female right in the person of his Queen." Radical William Hone exhorted working men to come to the aid of the queen on the grounds that "the beauty – the goodness – the very helplessness of the sex are so many ... sacred calls on the assistance of every manly and coura- geous arm." In urging plebeian men "To assert the Rights of Man/To avenge the Wrongs of Woman," radical leaders were not merely insisting on the relationship of politics to virtue; they were incorporating upper- and middle-class evangelical ideals of separate sphere ideology into their radical rhetoric and directing them at working men and women. In the process, they helped to occasion a significant shift in the ways radical working-class men defined and understood their masculinity. In defending the "virtue" of the wronged queen, plebeian men took on the chivalric role of protector of all women, an image that contradicted Burke's depictions of them as the "swinish multitude" and countered the picture of plebeians as libertine and immoral in the countless *Cheap Repository Tracts* put out by evangelicals.

Plebeian women did not necessarily accept the prescription of separate spheres without some revision of its terms. Calling upon their own experiences and upon earlier working-class traditions of female industriousness, courage, and competency, many working-class women celebrated Caroline as a fearless, reason- able, educated heroine, ascribing to her qualities that went far beyond those of helplessness, passivity, and sexual purity. Benbow's "Glorious Deeds of Women" placed Caroline in a pantheon of heroines that included Joan of Arc and Charlotte Corday. Anne Cobbett, daughter of radical leader William Cobbett, painted a portrait of the queen that combined the traits of the now conventional upper- and middle-class woman of domesticity with those of a larger womanhood. She is "a real *good woman*, kind, charitable, feeling and condescending toward every creature." At the same time, wrote Cobbett, "she possesses wonderful courage, presence of mind, fortitude, promptness in action. ... She is very industrious."

Despite the wider scope given to Caroline by working-class women's depictions of her, it was her traditional status as wife and mother that enabled her to serve as a rallying point for such diverse constituencies. Middle-class women saw in her a virtuous female in need of male protection. Support for Caroline constituted support for the institution of marriage and a rejection of divorce; it shored up the boundaries of separate spheres. Plebeian women identified with her mistreatment at the hands of her husband, and applauded her courage in resisting him; they also utilized her separation from her daughter, Charlotte, upon Caroline's exile in 1814, and Charlotte's death three years later, to articulate their concerns about the difficulty of sustaining their own families. To middle-class men she offered an opportunity for them to assert their morality against the libertinism of the aristocracy, thus buttressing their claims for political reform by playing on the age-old concepts of virtue against corruption. For working-class men, she represented their own political grievances against oppression and tyranny, and enabled them to demonstrate their respectability as "manly" defenders of innocent, downtrodden females.

As it turned out, the political agenda of radicalism became subsumed under the personal, moral, and domestic concerns raised by the Queen Caroline affair. The House of Lords did indeed pass a Bill of Pains and Penalties against Caroline in October 1820, but by so narrow a margin that the government withdrew it, acknowledging its defeat at the hands of the people. But the victory of the people in this sordid episode did not translate into governmental reform. Indeed, radicalism as a political force rapidly lost its vigor and its numbers, as middle-class reformers and Whigs in parliament abandoned their alliance with the popular classes, and as improving economic conditions after 1820 weakened the appeal of radical politics for masses of working people. Radicalism did not disappear, but just as its popularity had skyrocketed during the Queen Caroline affair, so too it plummeted back to earth with her "acquittal" and with her acceptance from the government in January 1821 of an annual pension of £50,000.

Although the political radicalism of the affair faded away, at least for the short term, the scandal nonetheless had a lasting impact on and consequences for all ranks of society. It marked a historical moment when one societal model of marriage and sexuality was decisively thrown over for another. The evangelical domestic ideal, with its concomitant emphases on separate spheres for men and women; the sanctity of marriage and family; passivity, morality, and purity for women; and sobriety and respectability for men, gained a hold over British life that prevailed for the rest of the century. At the very top, it would no longer be possible for royals, and by extension, aristocrats, to behave publicly in a debauched, libertine, profligate manner. Britons had made it clear that their king, if he was to be the father of the people, would be a husband to his wife as well, a true husband of devotion, fidelity, and morality. As the "Ode to George the Fourth and Caroline his wife," implored the king:

A *Father* to the *nation* prove,
A *Husband* to they *Queen*,
And safely in thy people's Love,
Reign tranquil and serene.

In the persons of King William, who followed George IV upon his death in 1830, and his consort Adelaide, Britain obtained a royal family that exuded domesticity. Victoria's accession to the throne in 1837 completed the domestication of the monarchy. The innocence and modesty of the young queen; her celebration of marriage to Albert, to whom she deferred in all matters, despite parliament's refusal to grant him the title of king; the births of her numerous children; her inconsolable grief upon her husband's death; and her vigil at the bedside of her son and heir, Bertie, the Prince of Wales, when he fell ill with typhoid fever in 1871 — these signaled to Britons of every class that the royal family was above all a family, embodying the characteristics of evangelicalism and what would come to be called bourgeois morality rather than those of a promiscuous aristocracy. Ironically, the Queen Caroline affair, which had threatened to bring down the monarchy in 1820, served instead to strengthen it in the eyes of the British people.

For the working classes, the rhetoric mobilized in support of Caroline acted to reconceptualize understandings of plebeian masculinity and femininity, and of the relations between working-class men and women in marriage. As noted earlier, plebeian men took on the role of chivalric protector and defender of women, eschewing earlier radical traditions of a misogynist libertinism. Moreover, in supporting the cause of the "injured queen," plebeian men acknowledged on some level at least that their own wives had rights as well. What had long been styled the "struggle for the breeches"[2] within plebeian marriages – the animosities and differences of interest that plagued the relationships between hard-pressed men and women – came to be addressed much more openly in the years following 1820. As we will see in the next chapter, this struggle within what was normatively described now as the private sphere took center stage in working-class politics, and would find its resolution in a working-class domestic ideal consolidated after 1848.

Upper- and middle-class women, if not yet working-class women, received overwhelming public affirmation of a way of life – domesticity and separate spheres – that promised them protection, respect, security, and an arena in which they could play an influential role. The country's "domestic virtue" – the defense of the private sphere of home and family, and, most importantly, the care of, and solicitation paid to, the women who inhabited it – supporters of Caroline claimed insistently, marked Britain as a civilization superior to all others. The treatment of women at the hands of men became a prime measure of civility in British eyes, and would be used to evaluate the credibility of claims to citizenship by middle- and working-class men and for self-government on the part of colonized peoples. The elevation of women's status to a criterion of national greatness, and of women to the position of "the angel in the house," did not meet the approval of everyone, as we shall see later, but it did reflect a societal transformation in attitudes about women that could have positive results. No longer the embodiments of evil and carnality, as they had been construed in the eighteenth century, upper- and middle-class women, at least, commanded the respect and concern of the nation.

For middle-class men, the attack on Caroline by her husband and his ministers served to point up in no uncertain terms the corrupt nature, the injustice, of aristocratic rule, undermining its authority considerably. Moreover, it enabled them to claim an active role for themselves in a reformed system of government on the grounds of their superior virtue, of the "manliness" of their men in defending the purity and honor of Caroline, and, by extension, of their own wives and daughters. In possessing virtue, now defined as the keeping of chaste, modest women in the private sphere of the home and family rather than the holding of a landed independence, middle-class men asserted their respectability, their fitness for participating in the politics of the nation.

The Reform Act of 1832 and the triumph of liberalism

Radicalism fell into decline after the Queen Caroline affair, and popular protest on behalf of political reform died away for nearly a decade. It re-emerged in 1830, in consequence of Daniel O'Connell's success in gaining catholic emancipation for Ireland in 1829. O'Connell, a devout catholic of radical principles, organized thousands of peasants in his Catholic Association, and turned a network of priests into an electoral machine that was able to challenge the political monopoly of protestant landlords in the elections of 1826 and 1828 in counties Waterford and Clare. Referring both to the virtues of the Irish nation – "Look at the Sisters of Mercy," he once declared of the figures who best embodied the traits of self-sacrificing Irish womanhood, "they are seen gliding along the streets ... to the abode of some poor sick person. ... Oh such a country is too good to continue in slavery"[3] – and to the threats of violence emanating from the countryside in the form of the

Whiteboy movement, O'Connell exploited English fears of Irish civil war to wrest emancipation from the die-hard Tory government of the Duke of Wellington. Wealthy Irish catholics could now sit in parliament, as could protestant dissenters, who, by the repeal of the Test and Corporation Acts, gained access to public office. Together, these actions served to split the Tory party and topple the government, and open the door to the Whigs, who saw in moderate political reform the only way to avoid revolution.

For by 1830, rural unrest in the Swing Riots of 1830–1 and the formation of hundreds of Political Unions among working and middle-class people in London and the industrial areas had combined with the revolutions of 1830 in Europe to persuade élites that revolution might indeed be at hand. Reformers of every stripe – radical artisans demanding universal manhood suffrage; middle-class moderates looking to enfranchise the commercial and industrial men of Britain, and to gain representation for cities like Manchester, Leeds, and Birmingham, which had none; and Whigs in parliament seeking rational administrative reforms – followed the lead of Daniel O'Connell and exploited the potential of massive popular unrest to promote their agendas. Bowing to the arguments of Whig MPs like Thomas Babington Macaulay that some measure of reform was necessary if revolution was to be averted, the Whig government of Lord Grey brought in a Reform Bill, which passed into law and received the royal assent in 1832.

By the Reform Act of 1832, the radical vision of universal manhood suffrage, and even of household suffrage, was supplanted by a narrower view of political reform and citizenship that historians call classical liberalism. In its political guise, classical liberalism conferred citizenship and participation in government upon independent property owners. Because married women could not own property under common law, and because unmarried women were considered the dependents of men within the family, citizenship, in liberal formulations, was denied them, as it was those men who did not own property or were dependent upon others, such as servants, laborers, or lodgers. James Mill's widely read "Article on Government," for instance, written in 1820 for the 1824 *Supplement to Encyclopedia Britannica*, and reprinted as a pamphlet in 1825, asserted that "democratic" political rights were necessitated by the "laws of human nature" that stated that "the ruling one or the ruling few, would, if checks did not operate in the way of prevention, reduce the great mass of the people subject to their power, at least to the condition of negroes in the West Indies." Having stated the utilitarian case that only the widest political participation could ensure "the greatest happiness of the greatest number," Mill went on to qualify his claim. "One thing is pretty clear, that all those individuals whose interests are indisputably included in those of other individuals, may be struck off" the roster of political rights "without inconvenience." Among these he included "children up to a certain age," and women, "the interest of almost all of whom is involved either in that of their fathers or in that of their husbands." Working-class men, he asserted, could count on being looked after by "the most wise and virtuous part of the community, the middle rank."

Indeed, the Reform Act of 1832 explicitly barred women from the franchise by using the phrase *every Male Person* to define those eligible to vote (though the Reform Act for Scotland in that same year delineated merely *every Person*), and by limiting it in the boroughs to those men who occupied premises that had an annual worth of £10, effectively insuring that the newly enfranchised voters were of the "respectable" middle classes. Working men in a number of cities lost the right to vote in 1832, though over time, as inflation rendered the £10 criterion easier to meet, the numbers of working-class voters increased. Prior to 1832, perhaps one man in thirty enjoyed the right to vote; after 1832 that number rose to one in seven. Middle-class men, "the possessors of the wealth and intelligence of the country, the natural leaders of the physical force of the community," as MP Charles Buller described them, men whose commercial, financial, and industrial wealth could no longer be ignored by the ruling élites of Britain, were co-opted on to the side of order and conservatism to defeat working-class radical claims. Macaulay declared in the debate over the Reform Bill in 1831 that the middle classes offered a moderate middle ground between two extreme parties vying for control of government: "a narrow oligarchy above; an infuriated multitude below; on the one side the vices engendered by power; on the other side the vices engendered by distress." The middle classes, whose intelligence, hard work, steadiness, and respect for property inspired "confidence" that reform of political abuses rather than destruction of all property would follow their enfranchisement, Macaulay claimed, could be counted upon to prevent a collision between the two "vicious" extremes and "to save both from the fatal effects of their own folly."[4]

When the reformed parliament next met, it became clear to working-class radicals that their economic and familial concerns would not be redressed by a governing body informed by what were now deemed "middle-class" values. Instead, in keeping with those aspects of liberalism identified with political economy and Malthusianism, parliament refused to entertain measures designed to alleviate conditions of work in factories, and passed legislation creating a harsh, mean-spirited, and denigrating system of poor relief. For in addition to establishing principles of political rights and political liberties, classical liberalism stressed the rights of the individual to possess things. This cast on individual liberty gave activities relating to commerce and industry, like the amassing of capital, the rational utilization of labor and resources, the pursuit of self-improvement through education and training, and the cultivation of personal temperance and self-restraint, a good deal of emphasis. Government's role, in the view of classical liberals, was to eliminate the barriers that hampered the exercise of these activities, to reform itself and to do away with practices, customs, laws, traditions, and ways of thinking that got in the way of the individual's right to have, and benefit from, his property, whether that property be material, moral, intellectual, or, indeed, in the form of wife and children. Commercial and financial people, intellectuals, professionals, manufacturers, but also landed gentry seeking to improve their holdings and increase their wealth, found liberalism compatible with their interests and their outlooks. Evangelicals such as Hannah More and William Wilberforce approved of liberalism's emphases on individual responsibility, self-improvement, morality, and self-restraint.

These concerns all came together in the New Poor Law of 1834. Informed by utilitarian fears that overpopulation would produce an overabundance of labor and Malthusian beliefs that poverty was the consequence of promiscuous working-class sexual behavior, Poor Law reformers sought to drastically reduce the number of poor who would be eligible for poor relief by requiring persons seeking relief to enter workhouses in order to receive it. In the past, within the conceptual framework of a moral economy in which the survival of the whole society was understood to necessitate looking after the needy, the poor could expect to receive aid in the form of bread and even wage subsidies from their local communities, enabling them to remain with their families and to continue to seek out work. The Poor Law Act of 1834, by contrast, operated within the conceptual framework of political economy, in which poverty was understood to be the consequence of a refusal to work, rather than the result of low wages or of cyclical downturns in the economy. Providing wage or bread subsidies, Poor Law reformers and their evangelical allies asserted, only encouraged the poor in their sinful habits of indolence and promiscuity. Making them enter prison-like, sex-segregated workhouses, on the other hand, where they would be separated from their spouses and children and compelled to perform demeaning and hard labor in order to obtain relief, would discourage the poor from propagating.

The Poor Law Act of 1834 had significant repercussions for all of society. It served to embed into liberal national consciousness the idea that the state had no responsibility for ensuring a minimum level of well-being for its people; that poverty was the fault of the individual; and that governmental attempts to ameliorate it would simply encourage the poor in their irresponsible behavior. The New Poor Law reflected and furthered the belief of political economists that the state played no role at all in the workings of the economy, despite the fact that the legislation served to ensure a large supply of cheap labor to employers by making it impossible for able-bodied men and women to find material assistance except in the workhouse, where they would have to give up their dignity, their freedom, and their family life. Perceived as a concrete, visible manifestation of middle-class antipathy toward working people and the poor, its terms provoked high emotion and helped to stimulate among the working classes a movement known as Chartism to gain the vote in order to overturn it and to prevent further depredations against them, as we shall see below.

The New Poor Law also served to underscore the ideology of separate spheres and to instill in the minds of working-class men and women a connection between manliness, employment, and the male bread-winner ideal.[5] In the past, women and children had been able to obtain poor relief from parish authorities independent of their husbands and fathers. Indeed, poor women were the greatest recipients of poor relief in the eighteenth century. After 1834, women and children were considered inseparable from their husbands and fathers: should a married woman require assistance, she could only obtain it if her entire family entered the workhouse. Conversely, should a man seek material help in supporting his family, all members would have to enter the workhouse with him. In effect, the Poor Law assumed, wrongly, that working-class men supported their families single-handedly, without recourse to wages earned by their wives and children. It had the effect of placing women under economic, as well as legal, *coverture*. They were not recognized as wage earners and contributors to family survival; those functions, in ideological terms, rested exclusively with men. Those men who failed to perform them adequately placed themselves in a dependent position *vis à vis* the state's Poor Law guardians, a position ideologically associated with femininity. Manliness, as informed now by the New Poor Law, demanded that men demonstrate their independence through employment and their ability to maintain their families. Men who could not make enough money to support a family should not, in the minds of Poor Law reformers, marry at all. Until the twentieth century, however, the bread-winner ideal placed enormous strain on the relationships of working-class men and women, because few men could actually command a wage that would enable them to keep their families without the assistance of their wives and children, or, in dire circumstances, the Poor Law authorities.

Few men and women were willing to forego marriage and family, as Malthusians and the "iron law of wages" insisted they should. The London Democratic Association, a working-class organization, denounced the Poor Law as the product of a "pretended philosophy that crushes, through the bitter privations inflicted upon us, the energies of our manhood, making our hearts desolate, our homes wretched." A poem attributed to a working-class woman in the *Spitalfields Weavers' Journal* pointed out that utilitarian reformers seeking to delay marriage and child-bearing among working-class people were acting against God's plans and would have to resort to forcible castration of men to accomplish their ends:

> Lord help us! This is a plan:
> Can a thing wearing breeches believe he is still a man?
> I hate all these brawlers of natural sedition,
> If children are curses, why don't they petition
> The God of all Nature to alter his creatures
> That man might till twenty-five shun women's features,

If heard not, and prone to continue such courses,
Better do by the men as they do by the horses.[6]

The Poor Law of 1834 reinforced the earlier Malthusian assumptions that
women played an exclusively reproductive role in society, that they depended
utterly on their husbands for income. It also sought to control women's sexual and
reproductive activities by holding unmarried women wholly responsible for
producing illegitimate children, imposing in the process a double standard for
men's and women's sexual behavior. The so-called bastardy clause of the New Poor
Law released the fathers of illegitimate children from their previous responsibilities under the old Poor Law system of contributing to their support, making
unmarried mothers the sole supporters of their children. If unable to provide for
them, these women would have to find relief in the workhouse. Under the "law of
God," one bishop put it, unmarried mothers should suffer far more than the
fathers of their children, who could not, at any rate, be legislated into sexual
restraint. "Shameless and unprincipled" women who preyed on men's weaknesses
by flaunting their sexual wares, on the other hand, as the Poor Law commissioners
saw them, should be punished for their sins and, it was hoped, deterred by the
Poor Law from sinning any longer.

The bastardy clause limited the range of sexual activity that working-class
women might engage in with relative impunity and reinforced earlier efforts to
define working-class men as chivalric protectors of virtuous women. In order to
defend themselves against Malthusian charges of animalistic sexual behavior
working people opposed to the Poor Law had to counter depictions of working-
class women as lustful and working-class men as seducers of unmarried women by
casting them in a different light. The *Poor Man's Guardian*, for example, denied the
Poor Law commissioner's claims that unmarried working-class mothers had
seduced unsuspecting men by insisting that women had few sexual impulses. "It is
their softness and affection alone which cause them to yield to their husbands,"
noted the writer, in a passage that could readily have been describing middle- and
upper-class women. As "the weaker vessels" who lacked the "great consideration,
reflection and resistance necessary to resist seduction," they should not be blamed
for having illegitimate children. Under the New Poor Law, "the frail, feeble,
confiding victim" found no protection from "the powerful assailant." This rhetoric
depicted working-class women, like their upper-class counterparts, as passive
victims of male license.[7]

But working-class men needed to be exonerated from accusations of seduction
if their protests against the Poor Law were to be credible. Radical leaders
declaimed against "vile seducers" who impregnated single women, and castigated
the Poor Law reformers who, by the bastardy clause, empowered men to "corrupt
and ruin our young female population." They named as "vile seducers" rural

laborers, "savage Irishmen," agents of the state – particularly policemen and soldiers – but, above all, aristocrats, whose libertine behavior, they insisted, stood in marked contrast to that of all manly working men. By locating culpability for working-class illegitimacy among the ranks of "foreigners" and men of different classes, radical leaders could lay claim to respectable sexual behavior and establish an identity for working men as honorable citizens defending their virtuous women and their homes against the "wicked intrigues" of the "despicable aristocrat." Working men's claims to morality and respectability in their private, domestic behavior served as the basis for their subsequent claims to responsible citizenship and the vote.[8]

Chartism and the working-class embrace of domesticity[9]

The grievances among working people produced by the limitations of the Reform Act, by the New Poor Law, by parliament's refusal to limit the hours of work in factories, by employers' determination to keep wages low and hours long, by the persecution and transportation to Australia of factory and rural workers seeking to unionize in order to challenge the power of employers, gave rise, by 1838, to a large and powerful movement to gain political power known as Chartism. So named because of the demand for a "People's Charter" that would establish universal suffrage, annual parliaments, vote by secret ballot, equal electoral districts, the elimination of property qualifications for those men who would sit in parliament, and the payment of MPs, Chartism dominated working-class politics for a decade and commanded the time, energies, and passions of working men and women across England, Scotland, and Wales. Many Irish people in England, notably Feargus O'Connor and Bronterre O'Brien, played a prominent role in Chartism, which in its 1842 petition called for the repeal of the 1801 Act of Union between Ireland and Great Britain. The first charter petition arrived in the House of Commons in 1839 bearing 1,280,000 signatures. It was voted down handily. A second petition placed 3,300,000 signatures before the house in 1842, with the same results. In 1848, in what would prove to be their final thrust, Chartist leaders presented to MPs a petition containing two million names. By that time, amidst somewhat better economic conditions and a parliament that had become more responsive to demands for improved working conditions, Chartism had begun to fade and its power to mobilize masses of workers to ebb. This petition, like its predecessors, also failed by a large margin. But as the first national, organized working-class movement in Britain, Chartism gave notice to middle- and upper-class élites that working men's exclusion from political power could not go on indefinitely and would have to be addressed in the future.

Chartist radicals sought the vote for working-class men in order to redress the grievances they believed resulted from their unrepresented status in parliament. In order to demonstrate the strength of their demand to political élites they had to mobilize *en masse*, which required the participation of huge numbers of women in Chartist rallies, riots, boycotts, and fund-raising and petition drives. Like Caroline Williams of Bristol, women sewed and embroidered products to sell in order to raise money for the families of men imprisoned for Chartist activities. "Owd Nancy Clayton," a veteran of Peterloo, hosted commemorations of that event in Lancashire, helping to educate young and aspiring radicals in the history of their movement. Women, especially in the textile towns of Lancashire and Scotland, and in the West Riding of Yorkshire, attended and addressed public meetings; they canvassed local tradespeople to determine their sympathies to the cause and organized their neighbors to avoid giving custom to those who were not supportive of Chartism. In places like Cheltenham, they participated in what we would call sit-ins in parish churches, occupying pews that belonged to others and forcing the clergy to deliver sermons that reflected their demands for relief from misery. Women demonstrated, agitated, and even rioted on behalf of the charter. In Wales, a number of women from Montgomeryshire joined in a violent attempt to rescue Chartists who had been imprisoned by the metropolitan police in 1839. They stoned the building where the prisoners were held, and were arrested and sentenced for their efforts. During the Plug Riots of 1842, they marched by the thousands to protest the working conditions of the Lancashire textile workers and to sustain them in their strike.

For the most part, women articulated their support of Chartism in auxiliary or complementary terms. They did not seek political rights for themselves but for their husbands, fathers, sons, and brothers so that they might redress the ills suffered by working people as a whole. The Female Political Union of Newcastle-upon-Tyne called out to their "Fellow-countrywomen" in 1839 "to help our fathers, husbands, and brothers, to free themselves and us from political, physical, and mental bondage." These Chartist women involved themselves in politics, they said, because the indifference and cruelty of the political and economic élites had made their domestic lives miserable, making it "impossible" for them to remain in "the province of … [their] home." "For years we have struggled to maintain our homes in comfort, such as our hearts told us should greet our husbands after their fatiguing labours," they declared, but "our wishes have no prospect of being realised, our husbands are over wrought, our houses half furnished, our families ill-fed, and our children uneducated." Chartist women sought political rights for working-class men, who, they expected, would utilize them to increase their wages and reform the conditions of work for men, and the home life of women and children. "What can be more piercing and heart-rending to a woman than to hear her offspring crying for food to satisfy the cravings of hunger, and she not to give them?" asked Chartist women in Manchester in 1841. In a modified version of the language of domesticity and separate spheres, they insisted that "we have a right to struggle to gain for ourselves, our husbands, brothers, and children, suitable houses, proper clothing and good food."

On the question of women's political rights Chartists generally fudged. As Elizabeth Pease wrote to acquaintances in 1842, "I *believe* that the Chartists generally hold the doctrine of the equality of women's rights – but I am not sure whether they do not consider that when she marries, she merges her political rights in those of her husband." Only rarely did Chartist women express the desire for the vote for themselves. The Ashton Female Chartist Association believed that intelligence alone qualified an individual for the vote, and expected that women's enfranchisement would follow on the heels of the acceptance of the charter. One Scottish woman, "A Real Democrat," as she styled herself, wrote to *The Northern Star* in 1838 urging fellow Scotswomen to pursue their rights. "It is the right of every woman to have a vote in the legislation of her country," she asserted, "and doubly more so now that we have got a woman at the head of the government." Chartist leaders had no intention, however, of including women in their call for universal suffrage, despite efforts by conservative opponents to ridicule the charter by pointing out that it would of necessity enfranchise women as well. Chartist leaders resolved the dilemma created by the need to gain the support of working-class women while at the same time denying them the vote by appealing to the rhetoric of domesticity. This strategy complemented and strengthened ongoing efforts to defend working-class families and the men and women within them from insults and assaults on their morality by middle- and upper-class reformers and evangelicals.

When Chartist leaders demanded the franchise for working men as a logical extension of the Reform Act of 1832, their upper- and middle-class opponents countered that while middle-class men had earned the right to vote on the basis of their virtue – that is, their possession and support of chaste, demure, innocent, passive wives and daughters within the confines of the domestic sphere, which required of these men a great deal of "self-denial" – working-class men, by contrast, could show no such virtues. Instead, as *Blackwood's Edinburgh Magazine* put it in 1839, they displayed "sensual indulgence," engaging in "excessive drinking, bastardy, and wife desertion." Lord Ashley, a Tory, regaled parliament in 1843 with tales of a "beer-shop [in Leeds] where there are rooms upstairs, and the boys and girls, old people, and married people of both sexes, go up two by two, as they can agree, to have a connection." Their profligacy and disregard for sexual mores caused overpopulation and poverty, conservatives asserted confidently in Malthusian tones, producing deplorable housing conditions ("I have met with upwards of forty persons sleeping in the same room," an agent reported to the Poor Law commissioners in 1842, "married and single, including, of course, children and several young adult persons of either sex"), and making it necessary for the women and children of the family to work, either in factories or mines, where heat and the proximity of male co-workers jeopardized their morality ("I have no doubt the debauchery is carried on," wrote one factory commissioner in 1842, "for there is every opportunity; for the girls go constantly, when hurrying, to the men. ... I think it scarcely possible for girls to remain modest who are in pits, regularly mixing with such company, and hearing such language as they do. I dare venture to say that many of the wives who come from pits know nothing of sewing or any household duty, such as women ought to know"), or in prostitution, where they seduced the sons of the respectable middle class. They beat their wives, violated their daughters, and schooled their sons in debauchery and wickedness. "In Hull," claimed the Poor Law agent, "I found in one room a prostitute, with whom I remonstrated on the course of her life. ... She stated that she had lodged with a married sister, and slept in the same bed with her and her husband; that hence improper intercourse took place, and from that she became more and more depraved." Working men's inability to control their appetites and impulses, as their critics would have it, disqualified them from the exercise of citizenship, which required careful deliberation, rational thought, self-mastery, and the capacity to put the good of the nation before one's own gratifications.

Against these descriptions of immoral working-class men and women, Chartists presented a picture of steady, sober, hard-working men trying their best to support and protect honest, decent, working-class women and children in their homes against the depradations of greedy, licentious capitalists and aristocrats, but lacking the means to do so. As a Chartist poet, Gerald Massey, explained the situation:

> Our Fathers are Praying for Pauper Pay
> Our Mothers with Death's Kiss are white;
> Our Sons are the Rich Man's Serfs by day,
> And our Daughters his Slaves by night.

Methodist minister J.R. Stephens depicted working men as chivalric defenders of hearth and home. "For child and wife," he promised, "we will war to the knife!" In narratives designed to appeal to women who struggled to feed and clothe their children by taking work in factories or mines; or who relied on pay-packets from which many husbands held back money for their own drink and other pleasures, leaving women unable to pay the rent or put food on the table; or who had been deserted by husbands who could not earn sufficient wages to support them, Chartist leaders blamed "the rich, the capitalists." The Scottish Chartist MacFarlane insisted that working-class ills derived from Toryism. "Toryism just means ignorant children in rags, a drunken husband, and an unhappy wife," he argued, and promised that Chartism would enable men to return to their broken homes and repair their relationships with their wives. "Instead of the old Tory system of the husband coming home drunk to his family, we will have him sober, contented, and happy." Armed with a vote, working men could protect their families from the misery and immorality of factory and mining life. Painting a picture of domestic bliss, the Scottish *Chartist Circular* claimed in 1841 that Chartism had already worked wonders on family life. "Our fair countrywomen," it enthused, "acknowledged the change for the better in the 'guidman,' as he comes home on Saturday evening to read his *Circular*, and watches over the interests of his family."

This "guidman" of Chartist domestic rhetoric constituted a new working-class ideal of masculinity. Sober, just, even-tempered, family-oriented, and, above all, the sole bread-winner, this new vision of manhood appealed to working women and men alike. To women, it represented the possibility of a better marriage than many of them currently enjoyed. To men it offered opportunities for self-respect that the upheavals of industrialization and urbanization, and the antagonisms of upper-and middle-class moralists, had deprived them of. But the respectable breadwinner ideal, however attractive it might be to working people, could not readily be attained. Most men could not command a wage that would enable their wives and children to stay at home; women continued to work in order to meet their family's material needs. In these circumstances, given a model of masculinity that endowed manliness upon those who could support their wives and children, and a model of femininity that conferred responsibility for the nurturance of children and home upon women, competition between men and women for jobs could be fierce, especially when factory owners regarded women as a source of cheap labor. In this contest, working-class men seeking to eliminate women from their places of work found allies in an unlikely bunch – among parliamentary liberals and Tories worried about the effects on women of work in factories and mines, and evangelicals eager to impose middle-class norms of behavior on working-class people.

The Factory Acts of the 1840s limited the number of hours women could work to ten and restricted the jobs they might perform. Such regulation of industry seems to fly in the face of the value placed on *laissez-faire*, or non-interference with the workings of the economy. Liberal reformers got around this problem by categorizing women, like children, as "unfree agents," individuals incapable of looking after their own interests and therefore in need of the state's protection. Adult men, legislators presumed, were "free agents," able to see to their own concerns and to contract out their labor under whatever conditions they might choose. As it turned out, the Factory Act of 1847 had the effect of reducing men's hours in textile factories as well, as textile manufacturers could not operate profitably without the labor of women and children.

Male workers organized in labor unions benefited from the Factory Acts by having to work fewer hours, but their motivation had been to eliminate women from work entirely. Working men had long seen their manliness deriving from their status as heads of households and from skilled employment; their artisanal unions had for decades sought to keep unapprenticed men, women, and Irish people out of work they considered skilled. With industrialization, formerly skilled jobs in textile manufacturing like handloom weaving could be carried out by women and children, and factory owners turned to them enthusiastically because of their traditionally lower wages; male artisans associated the de-skilling of their positions with the introduction of women into factories, with their attendant fall in wages. Their skills no longer their exclusive property, male trade unionists might consider themselves less manly as well. Many male Chartists justi-fied the enfranchisement of working men on the basis of their skilled employment. If they were to become citizens, then, they must exclude women from work.

They went about trying to do so by mobilizing the rhetoric of domesticity. Chartists borrowed the middle-class ideology of separate spheres for men and women and turned it toward their own ends. Factory and mine work degraded women, they asserted, wore them out, and harmed their health and that of their children. A Chartist placard asserted in 1842 that textile factories "reduced thousands of tender mothers to a worse state than brute beasts."

"Was it not enough for mothers to leave their infants at home, at five thirty in the morning, and to be exposed to the insolence of some domineering wretch, with only a half hour for breakfast, an hour for dinner, for eleven shillings?" demanded a Mr Leech in the columns of the Chartist *Northern Star* in 1840. His indignance resonated with many married women, for whom the possibility of staying at home and caring for home and family rather than having to combine paid factory work with the obligations of housework came as a welcome prospect. Chartist women in Aberdeen complained that "we find ourselves outworn by toil in keeping our offspring from a premature grave," while married cotton workers in Lancashire protested that they received treatment "worse than their master's horses." "We are wives – not slaves!" declared Mrs Wrigley. Working families, Chartists claimed, deserved the privilege of domesticity no less than middle-class families. As Robert Blakely put it in 1839, "I see no reason why working men, whose labor creates every necessary and luxury of life, should be denied the plea-sures and comforts of home." The language of domesticity appealed to many women forced to carry the double burden of wage earning and housework. Working women threatened men's very manliness, Chartists argued, echoing Friedrich Engels's assertion that industrialization "virtually turned [men] into eunuchs." Playing on the fact that mill owners preferred to hire women over men because they could pay them a lower wage, Chartist men denounced the factory system for turning husbands into "that crowd of women-men, inverting the order of Nature, and performing a mother's duties." "It is quite pitiable," lamented William Dodd in 1842, "to see these poor men taking care of the house and chil-dren, and busily engaging in washing, baking, nursing, and preparing the humble repast for the wife, who is wearing her life away in the factory." No longer independent heads of households, unemployed working men found themselves dependent upon their wives and their manliness called into question.

Chartist men frequently adopted middle-class moral rhetoric to pressure the state into removing women from factory work. It degraded women, they claimed, rendered them immoral, independent, and selfish. "In consequence of females being employed under these circumstances," testified Richard Pilling, "the overlookers, managers, and other tools, take the most scandalous liberties with them." Working men could not hope to find "virtuous" wives among such girls, who had been "contaminated" by licentiousness and criminality, and had no idea how to keep a house. One group of working men told Sir Robert Peel that women "who are … considered unfit even to fulfil the office of menial to the rich, are the only parties whom, ordinarily, the male factory worker has a chance of obtaining as a wife." The state owed women protection from the evils of factory life, Chartists insisted, drawing attention to the hypocrisy of middle-class reformers who sheltered their own women at home but refused to allow working men to do the same. The disruption and upheaval of family life following from industrialization, they cautioned, invoking images of striking and rioting women, would lead to outbreaks of violence and endanger the state. Lord Ashley affirmed their warning. "When the women of a country become brutalized," he intoned in 1843, "the country is without hope."

Following the Plug Riots of 1842 and strikes against cotton mills in Lancashire and Yorkshire, in which women played a significant role, the state responded to middle- and working-class efforts to remove women from work altogether with a compromise solution. In 1843 it banned women from mining underground; a year later, it reduced the number of hours women and children might work in factories to twelve. The 1847 Factory Act further reduced women's working hours to ten. The Factory Acts as a whole demonstrated to many working people that parliament had become more attuned and responsive to the needs and demands of working-class families, which helps to account for Chartism's demise after 1848. The Factory Acts, however, served yet another function: they identified working women as a threat to working men. The language of domesticity proved successful in gaining concessions for working people and ameliorating conditions of work, but in the process it limited the possibilities for a critique of the economic system itself by attributing the problems of unemployment, low pay, and harsh working conditions to women workers rather than to the employment structure of industrial capitalism. Finally, it cemented in the minds of the working classes the notions that women were mothers and not workers, and that politics were an exclusively male enterprise. Domesticity, the male bread-winner ideal, and separate spheres for men and women, however unattainable and problematic for most working families, became cultural norms amongst the working classes in the second half of the nineteenth century.

The Plug Riots had helped to persuade MPs that the demands of workers had to be addressed. They also frightened a great many working people, who shrank from the violence and chaos they engendered. Increasingly after 1850, radical working men turned their attentions to trade union organization and peaceable co-operation with liberals in parliament on issues of mutual concern such as municipal reform. Projecting an image of the working man as a moderate, reasonable, disciplined, respectable paterfamilias in firm yet gentle control of his wife and children, radical leaders gradually won support for the enfranchisement of working men from a considerable number of MPs. In what amounted to a reward for their virtue, as we shall see in Chapter 9, working-class men who headed households were granted the vote in 1867.

NOTES

1 This section relies on the careful research of Anna Clark, in her "Queen Caroline and the sexual politics of popular culture in London, 1820," *Representations* 31, summer 1990: 47–68; and her pathbreaking *The Struggle for the Breeches: Gender and the Making of the British Working Class* (Berkeley, 1995). See also Thomas W. Laqueur, "The Queen Caroline affair: Politics as art in the reign of George IV," *Journal of Modern History* 54, September 1982: 417–66; and Iain McCalman, *Radical Underworld: Prophets, Revolutionaries, and Pornographers in London, 1795–1840* (Oxford, 1993), ch. 8.

2 By Anna Clark; see above note.

3 Quoted in Catriona Clear, *Nuns in Nineteenth-Century Ireland* (Dublin, 1987), pp. 131–2.

4 See Dror Wahrman, *Imagining the Middle Class: The Political Representation of Class in Britain, c. 1780–1840* (Cambridge, 1995), ch. 9.

5 See Clark, *The Struggle for the Breeches*, ch. 10; and Sonya Rose, *Limited Livelihoods: Gender and Class in Nineteenth-Century England* (Berkeley, 1992), ch. 3.

6 Quoted in Clark, *The Struggle for the Breeches*, p. 190.

7 Quoted in Clark, *The Struggle for the Breeches*, pp. 192, 194.

8 Quoted in Clark, *The Struggle for the Breeches*, pp. 194, 195.

9 This section is drawn from Clark's *The Struggle for the Breeches*, chs. 12–14.

SOURCES

Barbara Caine, *English Feminism, 1780–1980*. Oxford, 1997.

Anna Clark, "Queen Caroline and the sexual politics of popular culture in London, 1820," *Representations* 31, summer 1990: 47–68.

——, *The Struggle for the Breeches: Gender and the Making of the British Working Class*. Berkeley, 1995.

——, "Gender, class and the constitution: Franchise reform in England, 1832–1928," in James Vernon, ed., *Re-reading the Constitution: New Narratives in the Political History of England's Long Nineteenth Century*. Cambridge, 1996.

Catriona Clear, *Nuns in Nineteenth-Century Ireland*. Dublin, 1987.

Linda Colley, *Britons: Forging the Nation, 1707–1837*. New Haven, 1992.

Leonore Davidoff and Catherine Hall, *Family Fortunes: Men and Women of the English Middle Class, 1780–1850*. Chicago, 1987.

Flora Fraser, *The Unruly Queen: The Life of Queen Caroline*. New York: 1996.

H.J. Hanham, ed., *The Nineteenth Century Constitution, 1815–1914: Documents and Commentary*. Cambridge, 1969.

Thomas W. Laqueur, "The Queen Caroline affair: Politics as art in the reign of George IV," *Journal of Modern History* 54, September 1982: 417–66.

Iain McCalman, *Radical Underworld: Prophets, Revolutionaries, and Pornographers in London, 1795–1840*. Oxford, 1993.

——, "Popular constitutionalism and revolution in England and Ireland," in Isser Woloch, ed., *Revolution and the Meanings of Freedom in the Nineteenth Century*. Palo Alto, 1996.

Peter Mandler, *Aristocratic Government in the Age of Reform: Whigs and Liberals, 1830–1852*. Oxford, 1990.

Frank Mort, *Dangerous Sexualities: Medico-Moral Politics in England since 1830*. London, 1987.

Mary Poovey, *Uneven Developments: The Ideological Work of Gender in Mid-Victorian England*. Chicago, 1988.

Sonya Rose, *Limited Livelihoods: Gender and Class in Nineteenth-Century England*. Berkeley, 1992.

Edward Royle, *Chartism*. London, 1996.

Jutta Schwarzkopf, *Women in the Chartist Movement*. New York, 1991.

Gareth Stedman Jones, *Languages of Class: Studies in English Working-Class History, 1832–1982*. Cambridge, 1983.

Dorothy Thompson, *Outsiders: Class, Gender and Nation*. London, 1993.

William Thompson, *Appeal of One-Half the Human Race, Women, Against the Pretensions of the Other Half, Men, To Retain Them in Political, and Thence in Civil and Domestic, Slavery*. London, 1825 (reprint, 1983).

Deborah Valenze, *The First Industrial Woman*. New York, 1995.

Dror Wahrman, *Imagining the Middle Class: The Political Representation of Class in Britain, c. 1780–1840*. Cambridge, 1995.

D.G. Wright, *Popular Radicalism: The Working-Class Experience, 1780–1880*. London, 1988.

Chapter 8

"The Sex"
Women, work, and politics, 1825–80

Liberalism, as we have seen articulated clearly in James Mill's writings and in the wording of the Reform Act of 1832, explicitly denied women political citizenship. The potential contradiction between, on the one hand, a liberal ideology that had legitimated the dismantling of aristocratic power and authority and the enfranchisement of middle-class, and later working-class, men and, on the other, the denial of the claims of women to full citizenship was resolved by appeals to biological and characterological differences between the sexes. Definitions of femininity evolved whose qualities were antithetical to those that had warranted widespread male participation in the public sphere. Men possessed the capacity for reason, action, aggression, independence, and self-interest. Women inhabited a separate, private sphere, one suitable for the so-called inherent qualities of femininity: emotion, passivity, submission, dependence, and selflessness, all derived, it was claimed insistently, from women's sexual and reproductive organization. Upon the female as a biological entity, a sexed body, nineteenth-century theorists imposed a socially and culturally constructed "femininity," a gender identity derived from ideas about what roles were appropriate for women. This collapsing of sex and gender – of the physiological organism with the normative social creation – made it possible for women to be construed as at once pure and purely sexual; although paradoxical, these definitions excluded women from participation in the public sphere and rendered them subordinate to men in the private sphere as well.

These arguments at one and the same time idealized women and expressed profound fear of them. On the one hand, women were aligned with morality and religion, whereas men represented corruption and materialism. Women were construed as occupying the ethical center of industrial society, invested with the guardianship of social values, whereas men functioned in a world of shady dealings, greed, and vice, values generally subversive of a civilized order. On the other hand, women were also identified with nature – wild, unruly, yet to be explored and mastered; whereas men belonged to culture – controlled, systematic, symbolic of achievement and order. Correspondingly, women were assigned an exclusively reproductive function, in contrast to men, who allegedly held a monopoly on productivity. In each case, notions of femininity, or female nature, ultimately rested upon the perceived sexual organization of women, who were construed to be either sexually comatose or helplessly nymphomaniacal. Whether belonging to one category or the other, women were so exclusively identified by their sexual functions that nineteenth-century society came to regard them as "the Sex." This in turn set up yet another dichotomy, which offered two possible images for women: that of revered wife and mother, or that of despised prostitute. Both roles effectively disqualified women from economic and political activity. At the same time, as middle-class feminists and working women argued, the characterization of women as "the Sex" created the potential for the sexual abuse of women.

The contradiction between the ideal wife and mother on the one hand and the degraded prostitute on the other was simply too extreme to reflect the real experiences of women. Nineteenth-century women were, indeed, participants in and agents of culture; they did operate in the material and productive world of industrial society; and their contribution to the economic sphere was not limited to the production of babies or the servicing of male sexual needs. Working-class women battled valiantly against enormous economic odds to bring in precious shillings to the household exchequer while at the same time maintaining a household in such a way as to affirm their families' respectability. Many middle-class women co-opted the vision of the angel in the house in order to justify stepping out of it and engaging in public campaigns to end slavery, increase education, or reform the lives of poor Britons at home or colonized subjects abroad. Other middle-class women protested the image of femininity assigned to them, and, borrowing the very terms liberals used to justify enfranchising men, embarked on a movement to gain recognition for their full and complete humanity, thereby eliminating the reductively sexualized definition of femininity that threatened their integrity and dignity.

The problem of women's work

Domesticity stressed women's roles as wife and mother to the exclusion of all other functions. The very concept of women's work had become, by the first half of the nineteenth century, an ideological anomaly; we have seen how working-class men joined with middle-class moralists to define work as a male activity in the course of debates over the Poor Law and the Factory Acts. By the time of the 1851 census, authorities regarded motherhood as the main occupation of women, gushing that "the child receives nurture, warmth, affection, admonition, education from a good mother; who, with the child in her arms, is in the eyes of all European nations surrounded by a sanctity which is only expressed in the highest works of art." As of the 1881 census, doing work at home, whether housework, home industry, domestic service, or assisting in a family business, no longer qualified as employment. New meanings attached to the idea of work that eliminated house-work from the criteria of an "occupation," combined with an increase in wages over the century and an improved standard of living, ultimately produced a situa-tion where far fewer married women appeared to "work" than had ever before been the case.[1]

For most middle- and upper-class women, whose husbands or fathers earned sufficient incomes to enable their wives to stay at home and manage the house-hold, working for wages outside the home simply did not enter into the picture at all. For working-class and poor women, bringing in additional wages to supple-ment the pay-packets of their menfolk constituted a vital necessity. They worked because they had to in order for them and their families to survive. With the consolidation of the ideal of the male bread-winner and the stay-at-home wife, however, in conjunction with male trade unionists' efforts to keep women out of factory jobs and many factory owners' inclination to support them on the grounds that women belonged at home, work for women could become fraught with diffi-culties. If they worked, they might be denounced by their peers for assaulting working men's manliness and be regarded as destroyers of other women's homes; if they did not, the ability of their own husbands and fathers to claim respectability, and therefore manliness, on the basis of a neat, orderly, organized household bearing certain material amenities might be compromised. At the farthest extreme, working women faced charges of immorality from both male trade unionists who sought to bar them from work, and from middle-class moralists who saw in their refusal to remain at home according to the precepts of domes-ticity proof of their inherently degraded character. It was not hard for the image of the working woman – that is a woman who stepped out of her private sphere into the public one in order to earn wages – to slide into the image of another public woman who earned wages in return for her services, the prostitute. As we shall see below, in fact, the Victorian ideologies of domesticity and separate spheres relied upon the presence of the prostitute for their existence.

Working women dealt with the dilemma presented by the bread-winner and domestic ideals in a variety of ways. In many instances, wives simply left their jobs. By the 1850s, only single women tended to work in factories; upon marriage, they ceased factory work and took up labor that they could perform at home. (Cotton textile manufacture in the Lancashire area proved an exception to this rule, for in these factories, men and women worked together for the same wage, and it was neither necessary for male workers nor possible for owners to play men against women in setting wages.) Taking in lodgers, doing laundry, but especially performing non-mechanized manufacturing or piece-work in their homes enabled married women to preserve the illusion that they did not work. Industrial home work paid extremely low wages and involved long hours of tedious labor, but it made it possible for women to continue earning a supplementary income that more often than not determined if their families survived and were able to project a respectable image to their neighbors.

Outside of textile manufacturing, which from the beginning had employed women in factories (almost 50 percent of all cotton textile operatives were female in 1835 and their numbers relative to men increased as the nineteenth century progressed) because employers believed they could pay them lower wages than men, working women tended to congregate in those sectors of the economy that were not mechanized. For example, in 1851, 45 percent of all employed women worked in manufacturing, but only about half of these, some 22 percent, were engaged in factory textile jobs. The other half performed non-mechanized functions associated, very often, with the garment trade in their homes, doing what came to be called sweated labor. They might finish lace on garments, or make cardboard boxes and paper bags, fashion artificial flowers, seam hosiery, embroider finished cloth, or carry out any number of other processes. They earned very little money, for sweated industries tended to appear in areas where large numbers of men were un- or under-employed, and where dire economic conditions created a plentiful supply of potential workers, thus driving wages down. But these home-based industries enabled women and their children to earn at least some additional income for their families, and it was work that could be undertaken by women who had to care for small children.

Married women's work tended to follow a pattern closely tied to their life cycles. Childbirth continued to be frequent during the first three quarters of the nineteenth century, except in Ireland, where the famine had the effect of reducing the marriage rate for women from 90 percent to 75 percent. Working-class women in England, Scotland, and Wales gave birth to large numbers of children, and might well be either pregnant or nursing from the time they married at a young age, eighteen or so then, until they reached menopause somewhere in their early forties. Knowledge about controlling fertility existed, but because death rates for infants in particular remained quite high, few working-class parents, who relied on the earnings of older children, could have afforded to maintain small families. The risk of losing a potential contributor to the family wage economy was simply too great, and the effects on family survival profound. Thus, married women without children worked in order to contribute a wage, but women with many small children, even in textile areas accustomed to their working in factories, discontinued work outside of their homes and took in piece-work under sweated conditions. Once their children had reached fourteen, the age at which they might legally obtain full-time work, women might be able to stop, at least for a while. Upon the illness or death of their husbands or the departure of grown children from the home, married women had to work once again in order to survive.

Forty percent of all working women in England and Wales served as domestic servants. Domestic service constituted the single largest occupation for women, but variation according to geographical area could be pronounced. For instance in York in 1851, where little industry was carried out, some 26.5 percent of the female population was employed, 60 percent of them in domestic service. By contrast, in Preston and Stockport, where most of the labor force worked in textiles, and half of the cotton operatives were women, domestic service employed very few. In Preston only 3 percent of the population over the age of fifteen in 1851 were in service. In Dundee, 79 percent of the female work force worked in textiles, and only 8 percent were employed as domestics. In Glasgow and Aberdeen, where about 38 percent and 32 percent of working women, respectively, worked in textile manufacturing, some 22 percent and 26 percent were engaged as domestic servants. Edinburgh enjoyed far fewer opportunities for women, so that almost 43 percent of women workers served as domestics. Metallurgy and mining towns and cities such as Birmingham, and commercial or administrative centers like London offered little employment outside domestic service and sweated labor for women. And in Ireland, where the famine of 1846–7 dealt a massive blow to the cottage industries in wool, cotton, and linen that had served as the main source of income for women, domestic service became virtually the only employment available to women outside of the northern counties of the Belfast region. In Belfast, women could find work in linen factories.

In the eighteenth century, when production, family, and household were intricately tied to one another, domestic service employed plebeian men and women of all ages, and servants were regarded as family members. By the beginning of the nineteenth century, as part of the industrial process of moving work outside the home, and contributing to the increasing cultural understanding of women as non-productive members of society and workers as male, domestic service employed mostly working-class girls in an "outsider" relationship to upper-class but increasingly to commercial and professional middle-class families seeking to demonstrate their material capacity to hire others to do the menial work of providing for their personal needs. As the numbers of middle-class families within the general population grew by leaps and bounds, and as the gentility of middle-class women depended more and more on their doing no work at all, the demand for servants expanded. The supply increased as well as occupations for women contracted. For the parents of poor and working-class girls who had few opportunities for finding sustaining work, domestic service seemed to offer security, shelter, food, and clothing for their female children.

Domestic service might provide a refuge from extreme poverty and insecurity, but it also subjected working-class women to often humiliating experiences at the hands of their employers. Vulnerable to the sexual predations of the male members of the household whose displeasure could result in the termination of their positions, servants also faced indignities heaped upon them by women whose very class status depended upon drawing distinctions between themselves and the female employees in their homes. Domestic servants often bore the brunt of middle-class contempt for and moralizing about working-class people. Castigated as lazy and dishonest, servants very often took on, in the rhetoric of their employers, the racial characteristics ascribed to African or Asian peoples. "The greatest plague of life," as a popular novel in the 1840s described them, domestic servants were regarded as dirty, immoral, uncivilized creatures who could be counted upon to steal their masters blind and end up, finally, as prostitutes.[2]

Domestic ideology rested upon the assumption that all women married and became mothers. Certainly, marriage became the norm for by far the majority of women in the nineteenth century, as wage labor enabled increasing numbers of young men and women to marry without first obtaining land or a skill. But for a significant number of women, marriage remained an undesirable or unattainable ideal. Working-class women who did not marry had a difficult time supporting themselves. They might readily find work, but their wages were insufficient to sustain an independent existence, and very often they attached themselves to males or formed households with other single women as a means of sharing the expenses of everyday living. Middle-class women without an income who did not marry had far fewer options than did working-class women if they were to main-tain their class position and sense of dignity. They might live with fathers or brothers until their deaths, or take up the genteel occupation of governess to a wealthy family, but rarely could they establish themselves independently. By the middle of the nineteenth century, as the numbers of single women increased, observers like industrialist W.R. Greg began to see them as "the problem to be solved, the evil and anomaly to be cured."

"Redundant" women, as Greg termed them in an 1862 article, following Harriet Martineau's initial use of the term in 1859, threatened to compete with men for jobs. Twelve years earlier, he had identified surplus, that is, single women as a contributor to the evil of prostitution, claiming that if their numbers were not reduced and "their value thereby increased," men would readily and cheaply resort to the "illicit" companionship of fallen women. Both a moral and an economic evil, the problem of surplus – unmarried – women had to be addressed and solved if the moral and social order were to survive. Greg's solution to what he saw as the problems created by surplus women was to "remove five hundred thousand women from the mother country ... to the colonies," where the disproportionate numbers of men to women created enormous demand for them. Redundant women would become the wives of colonists, and would cease to swell the supply of prostitutes that plagued British society.[3] In Greg's formulations we see a classic statement of the two possible roles for women in a culture informed by the ideology of separate spheres: wife and mother, or whore.

Passionlessness[4]

Domesticity invested in women the responsibility of maintaining morality and purity. "The angel in the house," as the ideology had it, was herself pure, without sexual feeling, passionless. Until the early eighteenth century, contemporaries believed that women's lust, as personified by Eve, was insatiable, but that women could become spiritual through God's grace, and hence less carnal. During the eighteenth and nineteenth centuries, the dominant definition of women as especially sexual was reversed and transformed into the view that women were less carnal and less lustful than men. As we have seen, in the process of masculinizing the marketplace, denigrating aristocratic excesses, disciplining the working classes, and limiting women's political behavior, the notion of the woman without passion came into being. Passionlessness was, in the eighteenth century, a product of women's purported superior moral and spiritual nature, and it helped to give women a higher status in society than they had enjoyed before. It undermined the identification of women with sexual treachery, and countered the notion that women were primarily sexual creatures at a time when their social, political, and economic disabilities rendered them vulnerable to predation.

Some of the most prominent nineteenth-century writers on domesticity, like Sarah Stickney Ellis, incorporated the notion of women's greater spirituality and morality in calling upon women to utilize their influence to effect reform outside the home. Following Hannah More, she identified the domestic sphere as the proper one for women, and eschewed the idea of women engaging directly in the political or economic sphere. But Ellis and others like Harriet Martineau also believed that women's influence could be felt far beyond the arena of home and family, and urged women to exercise their power in order to change things in the political, social, and economic realms. Women had a "mission," a duty to bring their special qualities to the immoral world outside, a concept that authorized women's activities outside the home that appeared to contradict the mandate that they remain within it. And like More, both Martineau and Ellis insisted that women required education if they were to use their talents for beneficial ends rather than simply fritter away their time in idle pursuits.

Convinced of their greater virtue and of their duty to bring their moral strengths to bear on the harsher aspects of society, women flocked to a number of campaigns that were in fact political in nature. They petitioned against catholic emancipation, for instance, in 1829, and participated in the movement for political reform in 1830 and 1832. Some of them organized to repeal the Corn Laws and others to obtain the People's Charter in the 1830s and 1840s. They joined missionary societies seeking to educate and civilize working-class Britons and Indian and African subjects, or, like Asenath Nicholson, toured Ireland dispensing relief to starving peasants and urban poor during the famine of 1846–7. For the most part, they conducted their activities behind the scenes, in support of their menfolk, but their presence and their input proved invaluable. Above all, women joined the anti-slavery campaign in huge numbers.[5]

Revived in 1823 after its eclipse by the French Revolution and the wars with the French, the anti-slavery movement appeared to be the perfect arena for the demonstration of women's greater spiritual and moral natures. Conceived not as a movement for rights but as an expression of women's philanthropy, the campaign could be shorn of its political coloration and be represented in religious and moral terms. The Anti-Slavery Society exhorted women to serve the "sacred cause" of abolition in the name of Christ. "Should they, for His sake," one of its publications read, "actively engage in this labour of Christian love, they cannot fail, whatever be the issue, to inherit 'the blessing of those who are ready to perish', and the richer blessing of Him who declares that even a cup of cold water given in His name shall not lose its reward." Women might go about "imbueing ... the rising race with an abhorrence of slavery" by passing out pamphlets, writing letters, and petitioning members of parliament "without violating that retiring delicacy which constitutes one of ... their loveliest ornaments." Regarded as an extension of women's domestic duties, anti-slavery permitted women to flex their moral muscles, stretch their spiritual legs, and have an impact on a matter of immense political and economic importance in Britain without appearing to transgress against the strictures that barred them from any such activities.

Their impact was, in fact, great. The first women's anti-slavery society appeared in Birmingham at the home of Lucy Townshend in 1825, two years after the national Anti-Slavery Society, run entirely by men, was formed. By 1833, when Britain emancipated slaves in its territories and possessions, seventy-three ladies' associations had been established. The women of these organizations like Elizabeth Heyrick, Rachel Lloyd, Anne Knight, and Marie Tothill furnished labor and funds; they held petition drives and letter-writing campaigns directed to members of parliament; and led boycotts against merchants dealing in slave-based sugar. In 1833, one petition they presented to parliament contained 187,000 signatures and extended half a mile in length. The efforts of these thousands of women made it possible for anti-slavery campaigners to achieve their goals. As George Thompson, a leader of the national effort, noted of the women's societies in 1834, "where they existed, they did everything. ... In a word they formed the cement of the whole Antislavery building – without their aid we never should have been united."

In its early manifestations, then, passionlessness seemed to offer positive rewards for women; women had a stake in its creation as an ideology and its acceptance and perpetuation by society. As physicians took up the notion of passionlessness in the mid-nineteenth century, however, they reduced it from its moral and spiritual connotations to a phenomenon involving scientific, biological principles. Their version of the passionlessness of women once again imposed an exclusively sexual characterization upon them; it placed them in a position of sexual vulnerability while at the same time justifying anew their exclusion from "male" pursuits.

In denying middle-class women sexuality, nineteenth-century bourgeois society paradoxically heightened an awareness of women as primarily reproductive and sexual beings. One aspect of the physicians' "science of sex" insisted upon women's utter lack of sexual feeling; the other asserted that women's bodies were saturated with sex. William Acton, in *Functions and Disorders of the Reproductive Organs*, published in 1857, declared that:

> the majority of women (happily for society) are not very much troubled with sexual feeling of any kind. What men are habitually, women are only exceptionally. ... There can be no doubt that sexual feeling in the female is in the majority of cases in abeyance, and that it requires positive and considerable excitement to be roused at all; and even if aroused (which in many cases it can never be) it is very moderate compared with that of the male.

Acton believed that women's "indifference to sex was naturally ordained to prevent the male's vital energies from being overly expended at any one time."

Not all British physicians accepted Acton's dictum concerning female sexuality. Dr George Drysdale, for one, believed that sexual pleasure was natural and beneficial to both sexes. In *The Elements of Social Science* (1859) he advocated more frequent sexual intercourse for married couples as a means to prevent disease. Of the "inherent" purity of the female, Drysdale wrote, "if we examine the origins and meaning of these singular ideas with regard to women, we shall find that they are based upon no natural distinction between sexes, but upon the erroneous views of man, and especially upon the mistaken ideas as to the virtue of female *chastity*." But Drysdale was a man ahead of his time. Acton's views of female sexuality rather than Drysdale's prevailed throughout both the medical profession and society as a whole.

In asserting the non-sexuality of women, doctors helped to encourage the establishment of prudery in social interactions among the middle classes, and encouraged the idea that ignorance of sexual matters was tantamount to innocence in sexual matters. They encouraged the development of a situation in which women had little or no knowledge of their sexual and reproductive functions. Moreover, the definition of women as pure and asexual, while men remained passionate and lustful, set up a potentially antagonistic relationship between men and women in which men were understood to be aggressive and women to be victimized by that aggression.

At the same time that the doctors announced that women had no sexual feeling they also insisted that women were governed by their sexual and reproductive organs. One English gynecologist, Dr Bliss, articulated in 1870 the general view of women as "the Sex" when he referred to the "gigantic power and influence of the ovaries over the whole animal economy of woman." Dr Horatio Storer, an American member of the Medico-Chirurgical and Obstetric Societies of Edinburgh, writing a year later, concurred. "Woman was what she is [*sic*]," he averred, "in health, in character, in her charms, alike of body, mind and soul because of her womb alone." Dr W. Tyler Smith warned in 1848 in the *London Medical Journal* that upon menopause, "the death of the reproductive faculty is accompanied ... by struggles which implicate every organ and every function of body [*sic*]."

So exclusively were women represented as "the Sex" in the nineteenth century that any behavior on their part that deviated from that of wife and mother – such as making political demands or seeking an education – was denounced as "unsexed." For women were not simply defined by their reproductive systems; they were, as nineteenth-century physicians saw it, controlled by them as well. Henry Maudsley, an eminent British psychiatrist, wrote in an 1874 issue of the *Fortnightly Review* that "the male organization is one, and the female organization another ... it will not be possible to transform a woman into a man ... she will retain her special sphere of development and activity determined by the performance of those [reproductive] functions." According to Maudsley, nature had endowed women with a finite amount of energy, and its proper use belonged to reproduction. Reproductive processes demanded all the energy a woman could muster; to spend it in another direction would inexorably undermine the very functions that gave women their only reason for being. If women foolishly attempted to undertake study, for instance, he concluded, they risked ruining forever their child-bearing capacities, thus endangering the future of the race. Maudsley sought to justify attempts to exclude women from education and the professions, and to limit their role to a reproductive rather than a productive one. He asserted that women, by virtue of their reproductive functions, could not stand up to the rigors of higher education or sustained cerebral activity.

Real education strain began to take place, insisted Maudsley, just at the time of puberty, "when, by the development of the sexual system, a great revolution takes place in the body and mind, and an extraordinary expenditure of vital energy is made." Education continued beyond puberty, "when by the establishment of periodical functions, a regularly recurring demand is made upon the resources of a constitution." Any interference with the development of the processes of reproduction, especially in the critical years during and immediately following puberty, threatened to destroy women's health completely, that is, destroy their ability to bear children. The healthy performance of women's reproductive functions, Maudsley maintained, determined that they could not succeed in following men's paths or striving for men's goals. "They cannot choose but to be women; cannot rebel successfully against the tyranny of their organization." He concluded that a woman should not be permitted to undertake any form of education that would "unsex her," for "sex is fundamental, lies deeper than culture, cannot be ignored or defied with impunity … if the attempt to do so be seriously and persistently made, the result may be a monstrosity – something which having ceased to be woman is not yet man." Conceived as sexual beings and determined by reproductive functions, women who deviated from their assigned roles as wife and mother stripped themselves of personhood.

The development of the reproductive system in women was so delicate a process, according to the doctors, that the smallest complication rendered them susceptible to mental and physical disease. Maudsley advised that "their nerve-centres being in a state of greater instability, by reason of the development of their reproductive functions, they will be more easily and the more seriously deranged." Almost every female disease, claimed physicians, derived from some disorder of the reproductive system. Usually the "disorder" consisted of a refusal on the part of a woman to perform her duties as wife and mother, or, conversely, a tendency on the part of the woman to exhibit an unwomanly interest in sex. It was a short distance from defining all female illness as a disorder of the reproductive system to using gynecological surgery to cure those ills. Clitoridectomy, or excision of the clitoris, was performed to cure dysuria, amenorrhea, sterility, epilepsy, masturbation, "hysterical mania," and various manifestations of insanity. The source of these diseases, doctors believed, was sexual arousal; the termination of sexual arousal through clitoridectomy cured the disease. Some 600 such operations were performed between 1860 and 1866, at which time they were discontinued in England and did not resume. Ovariotomies, the removal of the ovaries, may have been performed even more often, for the cure of diseases that were non-ovarian in nature.

Isaac Baker Brown, a London gynecologist, reported in 1866 a number of successes in curing various illnesses through clitoridectomy, or the excision of the clitoris. In the case of a young woman of twenty, who had for two years "suffered from almost constant menorrhagia, during which time she had suffered great irregularities of temper, been disobedient to her mother's wishes, and had sleep-less nights," Baker Brown discovered that "all these symptoms arose from peripheral excitement" – a euphemism for masturbation. He prescribed his "usual plan of treatment" – clitoridectomy – which resulted in "the most rapid and marked success" in ridding the woman of her ills. Another woman came to him suffering from menorrhagia, which manifested itself in a "great distaste for her husband." This, too, Baker Brown found, resulted from "peripheral excitement." "I pursued the usual surgical treatment," he reported, "which was followed by unin-terrupted success, and after two months treatment, she returned to her husband, resumed cohabitation, and stated that all her distaste had disappeared; soon became pregnant, and resumed her place at the head of the table, and became a happy and healthy wife and mother."[6]

Victorian ideology finally offered only two possible images for women. They might be either the idealized wife and mother, the angel in the house, or the debased, depraved, corrupt prostitute. The image of the respectable, passionless middle-class lady, in fact, depended upon a contrast with the other image of the "fallen" woman. In his discussion of pure women in *Functions and Disorders of the Reproductive Organs*, for instance, Acton asserted that motherhood provided the only motivation for women's sexual activity, whereas natural desire propelled men. "There are many females," he claimed, "who never feel any sexual excitement whatever. ... Many of the best mothers, wives, and managers of households, know little or are careless about sexual indulgences. Love of home, of children, and of domestic duties are the only passions they feel." While desiring little or no sexual gratification for herself, the modest woman "submits to her husband's embraces, but principally to gratify him; and, were it not for the desire of maternity, would far rather be relieved of his attentions." Some women "evinced positive loathing for any marital familiarity whatever." In such cases, Acton stated, "feeling has been sacrificed to duty, and the wife has endured, with all the self-martyrdom of womanhood, what was almost worse than death." Other women, "who, either from ignorance or utter want of sympathy ... not only evince no sexual feeling, but, on the contrary, scruple not to declare their aversion to the least manifestation of it." Men who found themselves married to such women complained, "and I think with reason," Acton reported, "that they are debarred from the privileges of marriage, and that their sexual sufferings are almost greater than they can bear in consequence of being mated to women who think and act in the above-cited instances." He warned readers that lack of a sexual outlet "might be ... highly detrimental to the health of the husband," a problem "ultimately too often ending in impotence."

Although nineteenth-century physicians preached the desirability of restricting or controlling the expenditure of male sexual energies, they believed the male sex drive to be "innate." One "expert" on prostitution regarded sexual indulgence for men as natural. "In men, in general," observed W.R. Greg, "the sexual desire is inherent and spontaneous." Acton believed that male sexual impulses could be controlled but not entirely repressed. The equation of respectable, pure women with motherhood, and that of men with sexuality, required a construction of female sexuality that posited its dual nature. Masculinity and male sexuality rested on the twin pillars of motherhood and prostitution. For at a time when masturbation was perceived to be the agent of a whole slew of physical and mental pathologies, the only recourse for men in a society that separated maternity from sexuality was the creation of another class of women: prostitutes existing exclusively for the gratification of male sexual desires. William Lecky, in his *History of European Morals* (1869), recognized that prostitution served as an essential sexual safety valve for Victorians. "Herself the supreme type of vice," he wrote of the prostitute:

> she is ultimately the most efficient guardian of virtue. But for her the unchallenged purity of countless happy homes would be polluted, and not a few who, in the pride of their untempted chastity, think of her with an indignant shudder, would have known the agony of remorse of despair. On that degraded and ignoble form are concentrated the passions that might have filled the world with shame.

As we shall see below, the general and pervasive acceptance of male sexual license in Britain required the official recognition and institutionalization of prostitution.[7]

Challenging separate spheres: the women's movement, 1850–80

Under the regime of domesticity, marriage and the family were firmly based on ideals of romantic love, companionship, and a spiritual equality between men and women, but the legal, economic, and social position of women had yet to affirm that fact. Under the law of coverture, married women had no rights or existence apart from their husbands. The popular aphorism "my wife and I are one and I am he" described a situation in which a married woman had no legal rights to her property, her earnings, her freedom of movement, her conscience, her body, or her children; all resided in her husband. Throughout the nineteenth century women and their male allies challenged these holdovers of aristocratic patriarchal society, insisting that rather than protecting women in the domestic sphere of home and family, these legal disabilities exposed them to the brutalities of the world at large. The contradictions of separate sphere ideology opened up space within which women could contest their positions of powerlessness, often utilizing the very language of women's special qualities to make their case for fundamental legal and political reform.

The first challenge to property in women occurred in the 1830s, when Caroline Norton sued for control over her children after her husband absconded with them. The Custody Act of 1839 gave women custody of their children under the age of seven in cases of divorce or separation. Thereafter, the husband resumed control, though visitation rights were secured for his wife. The act modified but did not overturn paternal control, for any father had complete authority over his children, determining their domicile, the extent and location of their schooling, their religion, and their guardianship, but it served to crack the legal edifice within which women existed as chattel, as the property of husbands or fathers.

The early supporters of women's rights frequently characterized women's position in society as analagous to slavery; many of them, in fact, like Anne Knight and Harriet Martineau, had come to their feminist positions after having served at length in the anti-slavery campaign. Without the means to become financially independent of men, women would forever be locked into the same situation of vulnerability to abuse from men as African slaves experienced at the hands of their masters. For women such as Bessie Raynor Parkes and Barbara Leigh Smith Bodichon, women's inability to find respectable work by which they might support themselves, and, indeed, to actually end up owning for themselves any wages they might earn, rendered them unable to leave abusive or potentially abusive situations. Bodichon's *A Brief Summary in Plain Language of the Most Important Laws Concerning Women*, published in 1854, laid out in a systematic fashion the legal situation that condemned women to a position of chattel of men. The solution to these problems lay in increasing educational and employment possibilities for women and obtaining the passage of bills that gave married women the right to own property and retain their earnings, just as a feme sole might currently do. To this end these "ladies of Langham Place," as they came to be called after the location of their office in London, founded the *English Woman's Journal* in 1858. In its pages contributors publicized "the cause" of women throughout Britain, raising issues of concern for women such as property rights and divorce laws.

Langham Place also provided space for the Society for Promoting the Employment of Women, founded by Jessie Boucherett in 1859 to provide a kind of clearing house of employment opportunities for mostly middle-class women without means of support outside the overcrowded, low paying, and humiliating profession of governessing, which was currently the only work they might obtain without compromising their class position. The society argued that middle-class parents must recognize that their daughters might not be able to marry, given the "redundancy" of women relative to men, and must be educated for work beyond governessing or teaching. They recognized that for women to become economically independent of men they must break down the barriers that kept them from being educated in sound educational institutions for work that was remunerative. Queen's College had been founded in 1848 and began to grant degrees to women. In the 1850s, Mary Frances Buss and Dorothea Beale had opened the North of London, and Cheltenham, Collegiate School for Ladies, respectively, so that single middle-class women might qualify for employment that would provide an income to support them. But the ladies of Langham Place had their sights set on bigger targets: the British universities and medical schools. Their activities on behalf of women's higher education ensured that Girton College at Cambridge in 1871, the University of London in 1878, and Newnham College at Oxford in 1879 admitted women to examination. Anna Jellicoe, an Irish advocate for women's education, helped found Alexandra College in Dublin. The University of Edinburgh admitted five women to its medical school in 1869, and, in 1874, the London School of

Medicine for Women opened its doors and matriculated fourteen women. The ladies of Langham Place also helped to set in motion the campaign for women's property rights. With the passage of the Married Women's Property Acts of 1870 and 1882, married women secured the right to retain and own any property or earnings they might bring to their marriage; husbands no longer enjoyed full and free access to their wives' assets.

Women obtained some amelioration even from the law that most symbolized their status as property – that of divorce. Until 1857, divorce in England could be obtained only by act of parliament and was available only to the wealthy élite. The Matrimonial Causes Act of 1857 created a court for divorce and established grounds for the procedure. Men could divorce their wives, as before, on the basis of adultery alone; women, however, had to prove their husbands' adultery *and* cruelty, desertion, incest, rape, sodomy, or bestiality. The Royal Commission on Divorce, reporting in 1850, had recommended that adultery was much more serious on the part of the wife than of the husband. The Matrimonial Causes Act, however much it incorporated a double standard of behavior for men and women in England and Wales (in Scotland, a single standard of infidelity for either spouse prevailed, and, in Ireland, adherence to catholic doctrines prohibiting divorce by the vast majority of the population rendered laws made in Westminster moot), did allow divorce for women.

The most radical challenge of the women's movement to patriarchal control consisted of demands for enfranchisement on the same lines as men. The campaign for the vote was designed to eliminate the notions of separate spheres and natural differences between the sexes insisted upon by domestic ideology. The women's suffrage campaign as an organized movement began in April 1866, when Barbara Bodichon, Jessie Boucherett, Emily Davies, and Elizabeth Garrett set out on a petition drive to demand votes for women. By June they had collected 1,499 signatures. John Stuart Mill, who had stood for election to parliament from Westminster on a platform that had included the enfranchisement of women, presented the petition to the House of Commons.

In October 1866, Bodichon read a paper on women's suffrage before the National Association for the Promotion of Social Science in Manchester. In the audience that day sat Lydia Becker. Moved by Bodichon's words, Becker decided to act. In January 1867, she formed the Manchester Women's Suffrage Committee. Shortly after its formation, suffrage societies in London, Edinburgh, and Bristol were organized. The four societies existed independently of one another, but participants soon recognized the need for a central body to co-ordinate activities and policy. The London National Society for Women's Suffrage served this purpose. In Ireland, Isabella Tod established the Irish Women's Suffrage Society in Belfast in 1872; four years later in 1876, Anna Haslam founded the Irish Women's Suffrage and Local Government Association in Dublin.

Mill's election to the House of Commons made votes for women a distinct possibility. When, in 1867, Benjamin Disraeli's government introduced a bill to enfranchise a large portion of the working classes, Mill seized upon the opportunity to enfranchise women as well. He introduced an amendment to the bill, proposing to replace the word "man" with "person," and thereby admit women to the franchise on the same basis as men. The motion was defeated handily. Surprisingly, however, another amendment to replace the word "man" with "male" also went down to defeat, leading suffragists to hope that, on the basis of Lord Romilly's Act of 1850, the word "man" applied to women as well. Lord Romilly's Act had mandated that, unless explicitly stated otherwise, the term "man" in parliamentary statutes was to be used generically, including women as well as men under the jurisdiction of the law. After some debate in parliament as to the relevance of Lord Romilly's Act for the Reform Act of 1867, Disraeli ruled that it was a matter for the courts to decide. In the midst of the debate, one MP argued that "if a woman could be brought in under Lord Romilly's Act, so might a cow!!" The courts ruled that Lord Romilly's Act did not apply to the Reform Act of 1867, one of the magistrates indicating that it could also be used to enfranchise a dog or a horse.

Mill's role in the suffrage movement went beyond that of parliamentary champion of the women's cause. His writings, and those of his wife, Harriet Taylor Mill, provided a theoretical foundation for the arguments suffragists advanced throughout their fifty-year campaign. Harriet Taylor Mill's "Enfranchisement of women," published in the *Westminster Review* in 1851, was widely read and then circulated by the members of the Women's Suffrage Society in 1868. To her, John Stuart Mill attributed most of the ideas he presented in *The Subjection of Women*, published in 1869 but written eight years earlier. The Mills pointed out that the distinctions between the sexes imposed by society were purported to be those delineated by nature, that the private sphere belonged to women, and the public sphere to men, because of biological differences between the two. Separate sphere ideology, encompassing the notion of natural differences between the sexes, justified the exclusion of women from power and reinforced and perpetuated the stereotype of women as "the Sex," making them vulnerable to abuse by men. As Harriet Mill noted, "many persons think they have sufficiently justified the restrictions of women's field of action, when they have said that the pursuits from which women are excluded are *unfeminine*, and that the *proper sphere* of women is not politics or publicity, but private and domestic life." She insisted that cultural constructions of masculinity and femininity bore no relation to the reality of male and female character, stating "we deny the right of any portion of the species to decide for another portion, or any individual for another individual, what is and what is not their 'proper sphere.' The proper sphere for all human beings is the largest and highest which they are able to attain to."

Harriet Mill did not attempt to deny that male and female natures, as evident in her society, differed markedly. She would not, however, concede that these differences were necessarily natural or inherent to the two sexes. In the case of sexuality, for instance, she noted that "whether nature made a difference in the nature of men and women or not, it seems now that all men, with the exception of a few lofty minds, are sensualists more or less – women on the contrary are quite exempt from this trait, however it may appear otherwise in the cases of some." She thought that the most likely explanation for these differences derived from the socialization of boys and girls, "that the habits of freedom and low indulgence on which boys grow up and the contrary notion of what is called purity in girls may have produced the appearance of different natures in the two sexes." "What is now called the nature of women is an eminently artificial thing," insisted her husband. "What women are is what we have required them to be."

Harriet Mill suggested that separate sphere ideology camouflaged and made palatable a system of unequal power relationships. The designation of "self-will and self-assertion" as "manly virtues," and those of "abnegation of self, patience, resignation, and submission to power" as "the duties and graces required of women," she maintained, meant in reality "that power makes itself the centre of moral obligation, and that a man likes to have his own will, but does not like that his domestic companion should have a will different from his." The so-called influence of women within the private sphere, stemming from their special morality and purity, Mill contended, concealed a distinct lack of power to determine their lives. "What is wanted for women," she declared, "is equal rights, equal admission to all social privileges; not a position apart, a sort of sentimental priesthood." Women's dependence upon men, John Stuart Mill argued, rendered them vulnerable to them; it produced a situation "which in nine cases out of ten, makes her either the plaything or the slave of the man who feeds her." He emphasized the links between power in the public sphere and that in the private sphere. He believed that society insisted upon the continued exclusion of women from public power because men feared the corresponding power that they would obtain in the private sphere. "I believe that their disabilities elsewhere," he stated, referring to the law of coverture, "are clung to in order to maintain their subordination in domestic life." Men's "antipathy to the equal freedom of women," he charged, concealed the real fear "lest they should insist that marriage should be on equal conditions."

Following the Mills, advocates of women's suffrage repeatedly articulated their belief that separate sphere ideology masked fundamental relations of power. In an address to the third annual meeting of the Edinburgh branch of the National Society for Women's Suffrage in 1872, Helen Taylor, Harriet Taylor Mill's daughter, argued that the position of women in society had nothing to do with what were supposed to be natural differences between the sexes. Physical power had determined male supremacy. "In the beginning," she asserted, "man and woman were created equals, made in the same divine image. God blessed them unitedly, and gave them conjoint dominion over the world." The superior size and strength of men naturally conferred upon them the role of protector of women. Gradually, she maintained, what had been a matter of expediency developed:

> into a sovereignty that increased with exercise, until more physical power established a supremacy that has existed in greater or lesser degree until now. Under this arbitrary rule woman has been more or less degraded to the position of slave; been treated in many respects as a mere chattel, and she has rarely, if ever, been in a position fully to develop and freely to use the powers which God has gifted her.

Men had determined what women were and were not, what women were and were not to do, Taylor stated; woman was now demanding for herself "the right to perfect liberty in fulfilling her duties to the world in accordance with nature's teachings and her own convictions."

Five years later, in 1877, in a speech delivered to the London National Society for Women's Suffrage, Arabella Shore again drew the connection between so-called scientific justifications and the political arguments against women's suffrage. As women possessed in many cases the requisite criteria for voting, politicians were compelled to come up with other reasons for their exclusion. The "great Nature argument," as Shore termed it, effectively dehumanized women, making them politically ineligible. "We are told of the peculiarities of our nature, our conditions, our duties, and our character; that is, in other words, our physical and mental inferiority, our home sphere," she observed. Challenging the "great Nature argument," she insisted on knowing "what is meant by Nature. Is it ancient usage or established convention, the law or custom of our country, training, social position, the speaker's own particular fancy or prejudice, or what?" She refused to accept the separate sphere argument, the idea that private and public issues had nothing to do with one another. "We cannot separate domestic politics from social conditions of life," she stated. "If then we are told that we have nothing to do with politics, we can but answer that politics have a great deal to do with us." Finally, Shore declared that public powerlessness meant for women powerlessness in the private sphere as well. "With respect to the home as woman's natural sphere," she maintained, "it is by no means her domain, for as wife and mother she has no legal power, hardly any legal rights. ... So that this distinction seems to result in man's keeping the supremacy in every sphere to himself."

The pioneer suffragists and their supporters expected an early victory. The defeat of Mill's amendment of the Reform Act of 1867 compelled suffragists to rely on private bills introduced by their parliamentary allies, bills that lacking government support had little chance of passing. In each year from 1870 to 1879, suffrage measures were introduced, and in each year they were defeated. Suffragists began to realize just how great was the opposition to their cause, and after 1870 they tended to give their time and energy to other campaigns to improve women's position in society. The movement to obtain property rights for women, to gain entrance to universities and medical schools, and, most of all, the campaign to repeal the Contagious Diseases Acts commanded women's attention in the decade following 1870. Together, these discrete movements and that for votes for women sought to challenge the ideology of separate spheres that, they asserted, contrary to its promises of protection and security for women, restricted their rights and left them vulnerable to oppression and abuse.[8]

The Contagious Diseases (CD) Acts,[9] an appellation generally given to legislation pertaining to animals, were passed by parliament – in the middle of the night and without discussion – in 1864 and 1866 to regulate prostitution and to reduce the incidence of venereal disease in garrison and port towns of Britain. They gave police the authority to arrest any woman suspected of being a prostitute and compelled the woman to submit to an examination by speculum for venereal disease. If found to be infected, the woman was required to stay in a lock hospital (a hospital treating venereal disease) until she was deemed to be disease-free, at which time she would be given a certificate verifying her status. In 1867, medical and civil authorities began an effort to extend the acts to civilian towns and cities as well. The controversy surrounding the proposed extension of the acts brought the acts into public view, and set off a mighty campaign to repeal them.

Led by the eminently respectable Josephine Butler, an organization called the Ladies National Association for the Repeal of the Contagious Diseases Acts (LNA) formed in 1870. For the next sixteen years, until their repeal in 1886, its members dedicated themselves to ridding the nation of the laws and attitudes that conspired, they claimed, to make women "safe" for male vice and to subject women to the "instrumental rape" of the compulsory examination.

State regulation of prostitution through the CD Acts contained an implicit recognition of the double standard of morality for men and women. With one segment of the female population segregated and ensconced safely within the fortress of home, family, and domesticity, the understanding of male sexuality as an insistent urge that could not long be denied made it necessary for Victorians to target another class of women, the "fallen," as the proper outlet for male sexual drives. The prostitute was perceived to be a depraved individual, lacking all self-respect and decency, and therefore deserving of all the iniquities heaped upon her person by the exigencies of male sexuality, including the compulsory examination by that "instrument of hell," as Butler termed it, the speculum.

The attempts to create two classes of women, the pure and the impure, and in effect to legalize prostitution by means of the CD Acts, in many ways paralleled the conception of separate spheres for men and women. Pure women remained within the private sphere of home and family, where sexual relations between men and women assumed the existence of love, companionship, and, above all, procreation, all consistent with the ideology of woman as the angel in the house. The impure woman operated in the public sphere, where she sold sex for material gain. The one realm had no relation to, or connection with, the other, proponents for the extension of the acts argued. Victorians regarded the prostitute as the seducer of young men, the corrupter of morals, and the carrier and personification of disease, who entered her profession out of vanity, pleasure-seeking, and greed. The private woman, whose sexual feelings could be aroused, if at all, only in anticipation of motherhood, would have nothing to fear from the institutionalization of prostitution and would continue to enjoy the respect and chivalry of all good and true men, women were assured.

Butler and the LNA refused to accept the dual concept of womanhood. They objected, stating instead that the prostitute implied social acceptance of an insistent male sexuality. The safety and dignity of respectable women rested upon the existence of "a slave class of women for the supposed benefit of licentious men," as Butler expressed it. They opposed the acts not simply because they singled out one sex for punishment and obloquy, but because they sanctioned the notion of woman as the acceptable object for male usage. The repeal campaign provided feminists with an opportunity to attack ideas about male sexuality, for state-regulated prostitution effectively constructed a particular vision of a natural, uncontrollable male sex drive. By separating motherhood and sexuality, the ideology of separate spheres presented a single view of male sexuality as natural and a double view of female sexuality. Feminists insisted that if there existed one male sexuality, there was also only one female sexuality.

At the heart of the LNA's campaign lay the argument by the leadership that the creation of a slave class of women, while ostensibly protecting the purity and chastity of respectable middle-class women, made every woman a potential victim of male sexual abuse. Feminists refused to accept the men's argument that modest, respectable women had nothing to fear from the acts. They regarded prostitution as the product of male lust, fueled by hatred of and contempt for women. In a society that forced women into a position of economic dependence upon men, only an accident of birth prevented women of the middle classes from resorting to prostitution to support themselves and their children. Their analysis of the causes of prostitution and the purposes it served led them to identify with the prostitute as a victim of patriarchal society. Respectable women were vulnerable to the same forces that were responsible for the existence of prostitution – "the unrestrained passions of men," as the *Shield*, the official newspaper of the LNA, charged in 1872, and the lack of employment opportunities for women. "So long as men are vicious and women have no employment," Butler told the Royal Commission investigating the operation of the CD Acts in 1871, "this evil will go on." Mary

Hume-Rothery wrote to the prime minister, William Gladstone, in 1870 that "there is not one of us – no, Gentlemen, there is not one of the mothers, wives, sisters, or daughters whom you cherish with proud affection – who dare safely assert that, had she been born in the same unprotected, unfenced position, in the very jaws of poverty and vice … she, too, in the innocent ignorance of her unfledged girlhood, might not have slipped, like them, into that awful gulf from which society at large has long done its best to make escape hopeless." Butler accused the government of conspiring to force large numbers of women into the trade of prostitution by prohibiting them from factories and the professions. She noted that prostitution was "the one trade or profession which our Government appears anxious to throw open freely to women."

In refusing to accept the distinction between pure and impure women, feminists also challenged the notion that respectable ladies need have nothing to do with a subject as distasteful as prostitution. They recognized that the very existence of two classes of women depended in part on the convention that preached ignorance of sexual matters on the part of women. They set out to subvert that convention, insisting that prostitution was an issue of great importance to all women. Butler wrote to an MP that "at the very base of the Acts lies the false and poisonous idea that women (i.e. Ladies) have 'nothing to do with this question,' & ought not to hear of it, much less meddle with it." Such "propriety & modesty" insisted upon by the ideology of the angel in the house, she charged, had been "the cause of outrage and destruction to so many of our poorer fellow women. … I cannot forget the misery, the injustice & the outrage wh. have fallen upon women, simply because we stood aside when men felt our presence to be painful."

Members of the LNA identified with prostitutes, though usually in a removed and distant fashion. The LNA leadership referred to themselves as "the representatives of the women actually oppressed & insulted by the Acts." Their identification was most often circumscribed by issues of class to a spiritual level or one of sisterhood. "Womanhood is *solidaire*," cried Butler. "So long as they are bound, we cannot be wholly and truly free." "We have cast in our lot with the outcast," she announced, "determined to know no rest until this wrong be avenged, determined to … declare in the face of parliaments, and of insolently-proclaimed masculine necessities – 'she is my sister, and you shall not use her so'; determined to prove that it is not a law of nature, though these men have declared it and ratified it by act of parliament, that women must be preyed upon by men."

The identification of respectable middle-class ladies with women who were perceived by society to be the lowest, most degraded forms of life, however removed by circumstances of class and experience, was a remarkable phenomenon in the nineteenth century. Sometimes feminists went even further, and expressed their identification more immediately and personally. They intimated that what men could do to "fallen" women they were perfectly capable of doing to respectable women as well, that the demarcation between pure and impure was false. "Sirs," Butler declared flatly, "you *cannot* hold *us* in honour as long as you drag our sisters in the mire. As you are unjust and cruel to them, you will become unjust and cruel to us." The women of Britain, she maintained, "are conscious that in fighting for the injured class they are fighting for themselves, for their own liberties, their own honour."

Prostitution, the LNA leadership asserted, resulted from "the dependent position of women." What society defined as women's natural sphere, the home, feminists regarded as a training ground for dependence and subservience, eventually leading to prostitution in the case of those more unfortunate women. "That dependence of women upon men," reported the LNA in 1877:

> was taught and maintained by early training in the family, by unequal means of education, by the limited field of industry, whether of brain or hand, yet open to women ... by every fresh law which assumed or implied the inferior fitness or right of a woman to order her own life; by unequal laws between the sexes as to marriage, property, and other matters; by the acceptance of that unequal moral standard which pardons vice in a man, but almost shuts the door of hope on a woman who has erred; and lastly, by political subjection or extinction of women, which deprives them of any direct means of altering the laws which affect them unjustly.

For these feminists, the double standard, prostitution, and especially the CD Acts encouraged the view that all women were the chattel, slaves, and playthings of men and legitimate outlets for male sexual urges. They made a mockery of the notion of the angel in the house and negated ultimately both the separation of public and private spheres and the demarcation of pure and impure women. Prostitution served as a metaphor for the predicament of women under patriarchal society, carried only to a more extreme degree, they asserted. In the 1880s, after having succeeded in persuading parliament to repeal the Contagious Diseases Acts, many of them turned their attention to marriage, where, they declared, as we shall see in Chapter 10, many similarities to prostitution flourished, and then to gaining the vote, by means of which they hoped to redress women's lack of power to deal with the grievances they experienced under a regime of separate spheres.

NOTES

1 Sonya O. Rose, *Limited Livelihoods: Gender and Class in Nineteenth-Century England* (Berkeley, 1992), p. 80.

2 Deborah Valenze, *The First Industrial Woman* (New York, 1995), p. 172.
3 Mary Poovey, *Uneven Developments: The Ideological Work of Gender in Mid-Victorian England* (Chicago, 1988), pp. 2, 5.
4 The term "passionlessness" appeared first in Nancy Cott, "Passionlessness: An interpretation of Victorian sexual ideology, 1790–1850," *Signs* 4, 1979: 219–36.
5 This discussion of anti-slavery depends on the work of Claire Midgley, *Women Against Slavery: The British Campaigns, 1780–1870* (London, 1992).
6 See Susan Kingsley Kent, *Sex and Suffrage in Britain, 1860–1914* (Princeton, 1987), ch. 1.
7 See Kent, *Sex and Suffrage*, ch. 2.
8 See Kent, *Sex and Suffrage*, ch. 7.
9 See Judith R. Walkowitz, *Prostitution and Victorian Society: Women, Class, and the State* (Cambridge, 1980); and Kent, *Sex and Suffrage*, ch. 2.

SOURCES

Louis Billington and Rosamund Billington, " 'A burning zeal for righteousness': Women in the British anti-slavery movement, 1820–1860," in Jane Rendall, ed., *Equal or Different: Women's Politics, 1800–1914*. Oxford, 1987.

Barbara Caine, *English Feminism, 1780–1980*. Oxford, 1997.

Nancy Cott, "Passionlessness: An interpretation of Victorian sexual ideology, 1790–1850," *Signs* 4, 1979: 219–36.

Eleanor Gordon, *Women and the Labour Movement in Scotland, 1850–1914*. Oxford, 1991.

Lee Holcombe, *Victorian Ladies at Work: Middle-Class Working Women in England and Wales, 1850–1914*. Devon, 1973.

Susan Kingsley Kent, *Sex and Suffrage in Britain, 1860–1914*. Princeton, 1987.

J.J. Lee, "Women and the Church since the Famine," in Margaret MacCurtain and Donncha O Corrain, eds, *Women in Irish Society: The Historical Dimension*. Westport, CT, 1979.

Maria Luddy, "Women and politics in nineteenth-century Ireland," in Maryann Gialanella Valiulis and Mary O'Dowd, eds, *Women and Irish History*. Dublin, 1997.

Claire Midgley, *Women Against Slavery: The British Campaigns, 1780–1870*. London, 1992.

Cliona Murphy, "A problematic relationship: European women and nationalism, 1870–1915," in Maryann Gialanella Valiulis and Mary O'Dowd, eds, *Women and Irish History*. Dublin, 1997.

Maureen Murphy, "Asenath Nicholson and the Famine in Ireland," in Maryann Gialanella Valiulis and Mary O'Dowd, eds, *Women and Irish History*. Dublin, 1997.

Mary Poovey, *Uneven Developments: The Ideological Work of Gender in Mid-Victorian England*. Chicago, 1988.

Sonya O. Rose, *Limited Livelihoods: Gender and Class in Nineteenth-Century England*. Berkeley, 1992.

Louise A. Tilly and Joan W. Scott, *Women, Work, and Family*. New York, 1978.

Deborah Valenze, *The First Industrial Woman*. New York, 1995.

Judith R. Walkowitz, *Prostitution and Victorian Society: Women, Class, and the State*. Cambridge, 1980.

Chapter 9

Imperial manliness, colonial effeminacy

The gender of empire, 1823–73

In the years following the Napoleonic Wars, Britain established control over huge areas in South Africa, Asia, the West Indies, and Canada. In the decades between 1840 and 1870, it expanded its holdings by adding new colonies in Australia, New Zealand, British Columbia, Hong Kong, Lower Burma, Natal, the Transvaal, parts of what would become Nigeria and Sierra Leone, the Gold Coast, and the Punjab, Sind, Berar, and Oudh in India. While it granted various measures of representative government to the white settlement colonies in Canada, South Africa, Australia, and New Zealand by 1860, it progressively tightened its control over millions of peoples of color.

Britain's possession of vast territories in south Asia, Africa, and the West Indies, its rule over the subject peoples inhabiting these areas, and, above all, the continued existence of slavery could not be easily reconciled with liberal principles of constitutionalism, representative government, individual rights, and *laissez-faire*. As we saw in Chapter 4, apologists for slavery and empire utilized languages of gender and sexuality to explain racial differences and to justify Britain's actions: lacking the proper attributes of civilization as evidenced by their enslavement to "oriental despotism" and by the dismal state of their domestic affairs and their treatment of women, Indian peoples required the tutelage of their British masters if they were to be raised up to the point where they might govern themselves. Lacking any visible resemblance to manliness and womanliness as Britons defined them, exhibiting through their sexual behavior and their gender relationships, as Britons saw them, the characteristics of savage beasts, Africans could be stripped of their humanity and reduced to the level of slaves.

Throughout the first half of the nineteenth century, British officials set about reforming along liberal lines many of the institutions through which they ruled India. During the 1820s, 1830s, and 1840s, anti-slavery crusaders effectively countered the image of African men and women as bestial and succeeded in bringing about the abolition of slavery in 1833. In both instances, reformers called upon and referred to notions of domesticity and the ideology of separate spheres to explain and justify their actions, endowing the subjects of their campaigns with a humanity that differed from that of Britons only in degree. African and Indian men, like children, needed to be nurtured and taught before they could grow into manhood, liberals, missionaries, and abolitionists explained. They utilized an ideology of similarity to themselves to make the case for emancipating Africans from slavery and for establishing what they saw as enlightened practices among Indians. With the elimination of slavery, however, racial thought, paradoxically, became far more rigid and racism much more virulent. During the late 1850s and 1860s, racial and ethnic differences became increasingly characterized in absolute, biological terms, so that people of non-British, and even of non-English stock in the case of the catholic Irish, were construed as utterly unlike their British over-lords – indeed, unable to ever become like them. Under both regimes – of similarity before mid-century and of difference afterwards[1] – dissenting voices made themselves heard, but they were decidedly minority voices that did not express the spirit of the culture as a whole.

These ideologies of similarity and difference depended upon notions of gender for their articulation; the transformation from one to the other after 1850 corre-sponded to changes in dominant norms of masculinity among Britons as well. From an understanding of manliness that prized moral seriousness, earnestness, and rationality, Britons came to embrace a notion of masculinity that emphasized the body over the mind, action over thought, and feeling over reason. As justifica-tions for empire moved from the imperative felt by Britons to educate lesser peoples in the ways of civilization and self-government to their conviction after 1857 that Irish, African, and Asian peoples were inherently incapable of exercising the self-control necessary for governing themselves, and required the strong arm of British law and might to keep order, the model of manliness embodied by the evangelical Christian gentleman of liberal sentiments gave way by the end of the century to that of a much more conservative imperial pioneer and hunter. Concomitantly, and in accordance with the polarities of masculine/feminine, colonized and non-white peoples became increasingly depicted as feminine until representations of empire took on the image of masterly, manly Britons exercising control over irrational, impulsive, weak-willed, effeminate colonial peoples.

"Emancipated sons": Indians, Africans, Irishmen, and liberal imaginings of manliness, 1823–57

Classical liberalism contained within it a number of potentially incompatible elements, making it possible for individuals of vastly disparate beliefs to band together under its rubric. As we have seen, the thinking of political economists who emphasized the individual's right to possess things could readily come into conflict with notions of justice and equality stressed by others. But liberals of all stripes did share a number of tenets in common that gave the doctrine a coherence that transcended all differences. Underlying the principles of liberalism as various thinkers understood them was a fundamental belief in the universality of human nature, and complete faith that the influences of law, education, and free trade could dramatically transform human beings. These liberal assumptions about human nature held true for peoples as far afield as Asia and Africa, and informed liberal approaches to British imperial rule in the 1830s, 1840s, and early 1850s, especially in India.

Liberalism made its triumphant appearance on Britain's home stage with the Reform Act of 1832. It appeared earlier in India, with the arrival in 1828 of Lord William Bentinck as governor-general, who proceeded to implement reforms in law, education, and administration that would excite the envy of liberals at home. Employees of the East India Company like John Stuart Mill and Charles Trevelyan, and governmental officials like Thomas Macaulay, looked forward with confidence to the day when enlightened and just government, free trade, and education would so change Indian peoples – who for the most part they, like their eighteenth-century predecessors, regarded as indolent, sensual, wanting in "mental liberty and individuality," and in thrall to despotic rule – that they would be ready for self-government. For example, in his "Essay on Robert Clive," the conqueror of Bengal in the 1750s, Macaulay likened Bengali men to "women," "enervated by a soft climate and accustomed to peaceful employments." "The physical organization of the Bengalee is feeble even to effeminacy. … During many ages he has been trampled upon by men of bolder and more hardy breeds. Courage, independence, veracity are qualities to which his constitution and his situation are equally unfavorable." "There never," he lamented, "perhaps existed a people so thoroughly fitted by habit for a foreign yoke."[2]

But with British examples of firm but just government before them, and education in the ways of British law, thought, and morality, even these poor specimens of manhood could aspire to manly self-rule. "Trained by us to happiness and independence," Trevelyan exclaimed, "India will remain the proudest monument of British benevolence." Macaulay echoed him in a speech in 1833 upon the renewal of the East India Company's charter. India, he noted, might someday, having "become instructed in European knowledge," "demand European institutions" of self-government. Such a development was only to be hoped for, he insisted, and "never will I attempt to avert or retard it. Whenever it comes, it will be the proudest day in English history."[3]

Making self-governing Indians out of the existing population, "sunk in the lowest depths of slavery and superstition," required a wholesale reconstruction of Indian culture and society. Indians would have to be turned into Englishmen, in effect. The evangelical leader of the anti-slavery movement, William Wilberforce, believed that anglicizing India constituted "the greatest of all causes," exceeding even that of ending slavery. "Let us endeavour to strike our roots into the soil by the gradual introduction and establishment of our own principles and opinions; of our laws, institutions, and manners; above all, as the source of every other improvement, of our religion, and consequently of our morals." As Macaulay's "Minute on education" put it in 1835, the British must not simply educate a discrete group of Indians in English language and law so that it might help to govern the subcontinent; rather, they must create Indians who were "English in taste, in opinions, in morals and in intellect." Self-governing Indians would be those who had imbibed "our arts and our morals, our literature and our laws." Indeed, in the 1830s and 1840s, the British trained a cadre of Indians, many of them Bengali hindus, in English literature, law, history, and philosophy. Western in thought and customs, these educated Indians were often more British than the British, whose élites were educated in classical Latin and Greek rather than in English languages and literatures.[4]

Instituting reform of legal procedure; tax collection; land ownership, usage, and tenure; education; and administrative practices proved far easier than implementing religious or cultural change, but efforts to raise Indian "morality" to a level approximating that of the British proceeded apace nonetheless. These revolved around British outrage at what they considered the "degraded" state of Indian women at the hands of Indian men, in keeping with the widespread European belief that the treatment of women in any given place provided the measure of its civilization. Closed off and confined in the zenana, covered by the veil, Indian women, regarded by the British as especially sexual and passive, served as the marker by means of which Indian immorality was gauged. Since Indian men would do nothing to lift up their women to the levels of modesty and purity demanded by domestic ideology, Britons declaimed, it was left to the British to "rescue" them from their own men.

The practice of *sati*, or widow burning, offered the most egregious example of Indian savagery to Britons and provides a clear instance of Britons' efforts to erase crucial elements of Indian involvement in its abolition so as to present themselves as heroic defenders of Indian womanhood against Indian men. The spectacle of a living woman being burned to death upon the funeral pyre of her dead husband, despite the relative infrequency with which it took place, excited condemnation among reformers and evangelicals at home and in India. Indians themselves, led by the liberal reformer, Ram Mohan Roy, played a central role in the initiative that led Britain to outlaw *sati* in 1829, but credit for ending what Indians no less than Britons regarded as an abuse of women was placed exclusively in the hands of Britons. A statue of Bentinck, designed by his English supporters to honor his efforts to "elevate the moral and intellectual character" of Indians, stands on a pedestal containing a scene of *sati*, in which a bare-breasted woman, her sari draped down below her hips, is being dragged from her children to the funeral pyre by a man wearing a distinctly phallic sword. Not intrinsically an act containing sexual implications, *sati* was nevertheless depicted using sexual imagery in order to demonstrate British highmindedness. The juxtaposition of a sexualized woman and the violence of sword and fire, over which stood the man responsible for "abolishing cruel rites," served as a vivid illustration of Britain's superior morality to an "uncivilized," "unmanly" people steeped in blood and barbarism. Liberals and evangelicals could dramatically demonstrate their own "manliness" and "civilization" by stamping out such "ungodly" practices and bringing enlightened, Christian, liberal reforms in their wake.

In 1823, the anti-slavery campaign, moribund since 1792 when it was overcome by concerns about the French Revolution, reappeared on the public stage. The government had abolished the slave trade in 1807, in consequence of which Jamaican planters, lacking now a continual resupply of slaves, began to treat their slaves far more harshly. The anti-slavery leader in parliament, Thomas Fowell Buxton, sought gradual abolition of slavery, but his position was soon overrun by one of immediate and full emancipation held by the women supporting the movement. In 1823, a slave revolt had broken out in Demerara in British Guiana, and a white missionary named John Smith had been imprisoned for helping to incite it. His death in prison in 1824 set off a fury of full emancipationist activity in Britain that lasted until parliament abolished slavery in 1833. After that time, evangelical missionaries and former abolitionists continued to act to end the system of apprenticeship that had been set up in place of slavery to provide labor to Jamaican planters and South African farmers, a system that could not be regarded as having appreciably changed anything for formerly enslaved people.

Anti-slavery activists came to their beliefs from a variety of philosophic positions. Some radical men and women took a political stand on slavery, seeing it as a violation of fundamental rights to freedom that all persons enjoyed, regardless of class, race, or gender. After the outbreak of the French Revolution, and the revolt of slaves in San Domingo in Haiti in 1791, this particular strand of anti-slavery belief lost popularity, certainly among middle- and upper-class white men and women. Political economists and utilitarians such as Harriet Martineau saw in slavery an inefficient use of labor that stood in opposition to principles of *laissez-faire* and unnecessarily drove up the cost of commodities. John Stuart Mill, the pre-eminent spokesman for classical liberal thought, objected to slavery on the grounds of justice; he believed that education could render all men, and, as we saw in the last chapter, women, capable of the reasoning necessary for the exercise of personal freedom. At different times, such perspectives on anti-slavery came to the fore, but the single most dominant strand of anti-slavery thought derived from evangelical religion. Slavery was sinful, believed evangelicals of every stripe, a crime against God's law, and, on moral and spiritual grounds, must be extirpated. Humanitarian sentiments about the cruel fates experienced by others of God's creatures often prevailed over more abstract liberal notions of utility, reason, or justice.

Parliament abolished slavery in 1833 because it could no longer be tolerated by the vast majority of Britons. For a brief period in the 1820s, 1830s, and 1840s, eighteenth-century notions of absolute racial difference were driven underground by liberal and humanitarian sentiments expressed through the anti-slavery movement. Britons found slavery incompatible with their sense of rightness, their sense of themselves. To be "British" in the 1830s and 1840s entailed holding an abolitionist position, whether for political, economic, or sentimental reasons, as much as it involved embracing liberalism and the concept of separate spheres for men and women. For British women, anti-slavery sentiments dovetailed precisely with their purported greater sensitivity to cruelties and injustices, their greater morality and higher spiritual natures. For British men, devotion to Christian precepts as much as to liberal principles of justice and legal equality meant that no respectable middle-class male could turn a blind eye to the brutalities of slavery. Notions of manliness contained a strong element of abolitionism, of ending the oppression of African men, women, and children at the hands of British planters and overlords.[5]

Evangelicals and liberals understood slaves to be part of the human family of man. James Phillippo, a Baptist missionary to Jamaica, asserted that slaves were "men of the same common origin with ourselves, – of the same form and delineation of feature, though with a darker skin, – men endowed with minds equal in dignity, equal in capacity, and equal in duration of experience – men of the same social dispositions and affections, and destined to occupy the same rank with ourselves in the great family of man." The model of a universal human family enabled abolitionists to think in terms of equality before God and to see slavery as an abomination, but this imagined family structure closely resembled that of British families, in which a patriarchal father ruled over his dependent wife and children. Within it male slaves and men of color more generally – and, indeed, at various historical moments, white working men and Irishmen – occupied the position of children who would have to be guided and educated into manhood, which could not be attained until they enjoyed property in themselves and thus independence. Slave women and women of color required schooling in the ways of separate sphere ideology; they would have to learn to depend upon, serve, and be subservient to their husbands and fathers.

Within the evangelicals' family of man rhetoric, white Britons positioned themselves as older brothers and sisters, teachers and defenders of their younger siblings who needed education in the ways of civilization and morality, reason and domesticity, and protection from the depredations of ungodly planters. Frequently, the language of older brother and sister merged with that of father and mother, so that the hierarchies of power and inequality between whites and people of color might become even more pronounced. "Sons of Africa," "babes in Christ," as black Jamaicans were styled by white missionaries in a relationship of children to parent, "are willing to be taught," noted Willam Knibb, another Baptist missionary, "and where there is sympathy with them, they love those who instruct them." John Candler wrote in 1840 that "the Negroes, with all their shrewdness, have much of the child about them, and need to be humoured." While British men saw themselves as emancipators of the poor and downtrodden in the 1830s and 1840s, they did so in a paternalistic way. Jamaican freemen and women might enjoy the potential for equality with Europeans, but by no means had they attained even a small measure of the qualities that would bring them up to the level of their white saviors. White, but especially English, superiority to people of color had never been called into question by the anti-slavery campaigners.[6]

Between the early 1830s and the late 1840s, white missionaries focused their efforts in Jamaica on "raising" black Jamaican men to adulthood as they understood it within their own British context. Phillippo exulted that Christian teachings were helping to eliminate the traits ascribed to Africans, which he saw as a product of slavery. "That cunning, craft, and suspicion – those dark passions and savage dispositions before described as characteristics of the negro," he wrote, "if ever possessed in the degree in which they are attributed to him, – are now giving place to a noble, manly, and independent, yet patient and submissive spirit." Missionaries looked to create a society among Africans that looked very much like their own at home, complete with its gender sensibilities. Phillippo invoked eighteenth-century notions of a society's progress being measured by the treatment of its women when he noted that after emancipation black Jamaicans, "like the inhabitants of all uncivilized nations, … treated the women as inferior in the scale of being to themselves." Men preyed upon young girls, noted Knibb, who sought to establish separate schools for girls where they would be instructed by female teachers in the ways of decency and morality. "I know full well," he declared, "that until the female character is raised, we shall never far advance in civilization and virtue." In later years, both he and Phillippo counted their moral victories by the numbers of couples they had united in marriage and domesticity, judging their success in civilizing black Jamaicans by "the cottager's comfortable home, by the wife's proper release from toil, by the instructed child," as Knibb put it in decidedly English imagery.[7]

Missionaries in Jamaica sought to develop a class and gender system much like that of England's, in which they occupied the role of the prosperous professional middle class and black Jamaicans became part of a free labor force comprised of industrious workers. For black men they sought "a fair day's work for a fair day's wage." For black women who had to earn, domestic service appeared to missionaries to be the most appropriate kind of work for them, for it did not appreciably subvert the emphasis on domesticity for women in the way that work in the fields of a plantation might. "Domestic servants are beginning to be eminently trustworthy," wrote Phillippo approvingly, "and, when properly treated and confided in, do not suffer by comparison with the great bulk of the same class in England." Such progress, he celebrated, indicated that the post-emancipation project of raising up a civilized society of black Jamaicans was succeeding, for black Jamaican women were "advancing to that high moral standard which is fixed in the great Christian code." The degree to which black Jamaican families resembled the ideal family of white, middle-class Britons denoted exactly the degree to which they had become civilized.[8]

The anti-slavery campaign had broad-based and long-lasting ramifications. As we shall see in the next chapter, the situation of slaves appeared to many people to resemble that of white women at the hands of white men and helped to galvanize large numbers of mostly middle-class British women to demand their own freedoms and rights. More immediately for our purposes, the abolition of slavery led Britons to draw firmer lines between black and white peoples so that hierarchical relations of power could be sustained in the absence of legal differentiations based on race. Moreover, the end of slavery helped to further the imperial project. Once Britons could no longer be regarded as responsible for slavery in their own territories, blame for the continuation of the institution could be shifted onto others, particularly Americans, and, more and more, onto Africans, who, moralists asserted, relied on the slave trade to sustain their economies. In 1841, combining missionary zeal with political economy, Thomas Fowell Buxton, with the strong support of Prince Albert and the approval and financial backing of the British government, launched an expedition to Niger in West Africa to end slavery and establish "proper" commercial undertakings there. As depicted by Buxton's campaign literature and publicity, Africa was a place of darkness and barbarism. "Bound in the chains of the grossest ignorance," he wrote, its people fell "prey to the most savage superstition." Slavery, torture, butchery, human sacrifices, cannibalism, dismemberment, infanticide – these practices could be ended and African peoples redeemed by showing Africans alternative methods of using their material resources, by establishing commercial ventures in agriculture and trade in commodities, and by setting up schools and missions through which to educate Africans in European and Christian ways. Harriet Martineau's protagonist in *Dawn Island*, a novel written in 1845 on behalf of the campaign to repeal the Corn Laws in Britain and establish free trade throughout the empire, expressed the confidence of many influential Britons about the possibility of civilizing "barbaric" peoples by preaching to them the gospel of Christ and *laissez-faire*. "It warmed my heart and filled my head," he declared, "to see how these children of nature were clearly destined to be carried on some way towards becoming men and Christians by my bringing Commerce to their shores."[9]

The Niger expedition failed spectacularly. Of the 150 white Britons who set out to stamp out slavery at its source in the hinterlands of West Africa, forty-four died of malaria. The remaining Britons, themselves ill with fever, withdrew from a model farm they had set up with 150 Africans from the coast, leaving the African members of the expedition in control of the enterprise. When Britons returned the next year to bring relief to the settlers, they found the farm in disarray and fields planted with cotton and maize barren. Tribal warfare in the area had produced refugees looking to escape the bloodshed; these had been put to work by the settlers, who, it was reported, would do no work themselves. "I found them indolent and lazy," reported Lieutenant William Webb, the head of the relief expedition, "not one willing or even disposed to manual labour, but ready enough to exercise authority over the negroes they hired." Reports of settlers molesting the refugee women circulated, as did a story about the settlers using whips "apparently for the purpose of urging the natives to greater exertion." What had begun as a great moral undertaking to bring salvation and enlightenment to the "savage" peoples of Africa had turned into a débâcle. Not only had the trade in slaves not been abolished, but the settlers charged with establishing alternative forms of commerce had apparently resorted to slavery themselves. As *The Times* put it scathingly upon hearing the accounts of Webb and others, "the Niger ANTI-Slavery Expedition has ... planted a *very* 'model' of the most cruel and iniquitous SLAVERY, and that in a spot where such, as at least such systematic scourge-bearing slavery, was probably unknown before."[10]

The disaster of the Niger Expedition combined with other developments to help transform British racial thought after 1850. Charles Dickens sounded one of the first blasts against the prevailing liberal view that all races were equal in capacity and could be raised up to European levels in his excoriation of the anti-slavery campaigners in an 1848 article entitled "The Niger expedition." "Between the civilized European and the barbarous African," he insisted, "there is a great gulf set. ... To change the customs even of civilized ... men ... is ... a most difficult and slow proceeding; but to do this by ignorant and savage races, is a work which, like the progressive changes of the globe itself, requires a stretch of years that dazzles in the looking at." Only fools could expect to "railroad" savages into Christianity and civilization, he asserted, and they should not waste their efforts in a land as dark and benighted as Africa.[11] Thomas Carlyle, a celebrated intellectual and man of letters, followed suit the next year, when he denounced the abolition of slavery as a ruinous failure for the economies of the West Indies and declared blacks an inferior race of peoples fit only for the yoke of compulsory labor. During the 1840s, sugar exports from the West Indies to Britain dropped as competition from other sugar cane producers and from the production of sugar beets in Europe increased. In 1846, when parliament repealed the Corn Laws, removing protective tariffs on grain entering Britain, and ushering in the era of free trade, planters in Jamaica feared for their economic livelihood. They turned to Carlyle to plead their cause before the British public. His "Occasional discourse on the negro question," published in *Fraser's Magazine* in 1849 and reissued in 1853 as "Occasional discourse on the nigger question," established many of the basic elements that would characterize British racial thinking in the years after 1850.

In "The nigger question,"[12] Carlyle railed against the "troublous condition" of Jamaica caused by the abolition of slavery and called for a version of it to be reintroduced in order to save black and white Jamaicans alike from destitution and degradation. Blacks would not work, he asserted, repeating the allegations of Jamaican planters who saw in blacks' preference to cultivate their own plots to sell crops at market rather than work on plantations for low wages a manifestation of their "laziness," a refusal to work. He depicted them "sitting yonder with their beautiful muzzles up to the ears in pumpkins," by which he meant melons or tropical fruit like papaya or mango, "imbibing sweet pulps and juices; the grinder and incisor teeth ready for ever new work, and the pumpkins cheap as grass in those rich climates: while the sugar-crops rot around them uncut, because labour cannot be hired, so cheap are the pumpkins." Compel them to work, Carlyle exhorted his audience, for no man had the right "to eat pumpkin" who would not labor on the plantations. "If Quashee," as Carlyle styled Jamaican blacks derisively, "will not honestly aid in bringing-out those sugars, cinnamons and nobler products of the West-Indian Islands, for the benefit of all mankind, then I say neither will the Powers permit Quashee to continue growing pumpkins there for his own lazy benefit; but will shear him out, … perhaps in a terrible manner." The gods had ordained that "spices and valuable products be grown in their West Indies," Carlyle explained; even more, "they wish, that manful industrious men occupy their West Indies, not indolent two-legged cattle." Compel them to work with the whip, if need be, he continued, for it was unlikely that "Quashee" would be induced to labor as white men had been by the promise of delayed gratifications. "Quashee, if he will not help in bringing-out the spices, will get himself made a slave again, … and with beneficent whip, since other methods avail not, will be compelled to work."

Carlyle saw in slavery, or its preferred alternative, a system of "servants hired for life," the proper and divinely ordered relationship of "wise men" to foolish others, of the industrious to the "lazy," of the "strong to the weak; of the great and noble-minded to the small and mean!" He applied his condemnations to all men who would not work, but coded such people as "black." "They also," he observed of "rich white men," "have long sat Negro-like up to the ears in pumpkin." "Negroes" for Carlyle served as the model for all manner of indolence, insolence, corruption, and savagery, and their very inferiority demanded that they serve whites. "Decidedly you have to be servants to those that are born *wiser* than you, that are born lords of you; servants to the Whites, if they *are* (as what mortal can doubt they are?) born wiser than you." Carlyle's "The nigger question" represented blacks in feminine terms, as entities with feminine qualities in need of manly mastery.

"I decidedly like poor Quashee," he wrote in the 1853 edition, "and find him a pretty kind of man … a merry-hearted, grinning, dancing, singing, affectionate kind of creature, with a great deal of melody and amenability in his composition." For Carlyle, in fact, the great problem was not poor "Quashee" at all, but the effeminate, soft evangelical philanthropists and liberal political economists who had emancipated him in the first place. "Windy sentimentalists," he called them, lumping them in with "women and children and stump-orators" who "weep over" trifles like slavery, while "serious men who have work to do in this Universe" recognized that wise men, "superior" men must rule over others, over the "inferior" if order and governance were to prevail. "Well, *except* by Mastership and Servantship, there is no conceivable deliverance from Tyranny and Slavery," he declared with exasperation. In his formulations, which cannot be considered mainstream at the time they were written, but did become so in the second half of the nineteenth century, the concept of manliness did not embrace abolitionism and liberal understandings of human equality across lines of race. Rather, people who held such positions demonstrated effeminate qualities, as did the objects of their concerns, slaves and other people of color, and their projects would serve only to corrupt the proper ordering of British society. The "wedding" of evangelical philanthropists and political economists in the cause of "Black Emancipation, or the like," Carlyle promised, invoking gendered and perverse sexual imagery, "will give birth to progenies and prodigies; dark extensive moon-calves, unnamable abortions, wide-coiled monstrosities, such as the world has not seen hitherto!"

Carlyle linked what he saw as the parlous state of Jamaica to the situation in Ireland, from which he had just returned when he first wrote "The nigger question." He accused liberal politicians of having produced there what he feared would occur in Jamaica if blacks were not forced to work, "a *Black Ireland*; 'free' indeed, but an Ireland, and Black!" Their free-trade policies, in conjunction with Irish "laziness," he charged, referring in racial and sexual terms to the millions of people suffering from the potato famine, had given rise to not a white but to a "sallow Ireland, sluttishly starving from age to age on its act-of-parliament 'freedom.'" The Irish, like blacks in Jamaica, he declared in a letter to Ralph Waldo Emerson, would "have to learn that man does need government, and that an able-bodied starving beggar is and remains … a SLAVE destitute of a MASTER."

In 1845, Ireland suffered a potato blight, which worsened in 1846 and again in 1847–8. By the 1840s, the potato had become the staple crop for millions of Irish peasants, and when it failed, those peasants had very little else to turn to. In the years 1845 to 1851, the country lost some 2.25 million people, perhaps half of them to death by starvation or disease, the other half to emigration to England, Australia and New Zealand, and the United States. While Irish liberals and nationalists attributed the disaster of the Great Famine to English land tenure policies and the existence of an absentee Anglo-Irish landowning class, English and Scottish liberals in parliament and conservatives in and out of government believed the famine to have come about as a consequence of Irish character and morality. As *The Times* asserted in 1843, before the famine broke out, "Ireland and the Irish have, in a great measure themselves to thank for their poverty and want of capital. … It is by industry, toil, perseverance, economy, prudence, by self-denial, and self-dependence, that a state becomes mighty and its people happy." The English and northern Irish protestants had demonstrated such national traits, and the Irish catholics, by contrast, suffered from the lack of them. They would not work, it added in 1845. "Of all the Celtic tribes, famous everywhere for their indolence and fickleness as the Celts everywhere are," intoned *Fraser's Magazine* in 1847, "the Irish are admitted to be the most idle and most fickle." The satiric magazine *Punch* reported them to be the laziest and dirtiest people in the world, descended from "generations of beggars. You can trace the descent in their blighted, stunted forms – in their brassy, cunning, brutalized features."[13]

The Irish became the "white negroes" of Europe. Like Africans, black Jamaicans, and people of color throughout the world, the Irish – when acting peaceably and not making demands for repeal of the Act of Union of 1800 and the establishment of their own legislature, or setting the countryside ablaze in agrarian riots protesting lack of land security and food – were depicted in somewhat benign but decidedly unmanly terms. They were "a people of acute sensibilities and lively passions," asserted *The Times* in 1843 in terms usually applied to women, "more quick in feeling wrongs than rational in explaining or temperate in addressing them – as easily roused into outrage by supposed oppression as subdued into docility by felicitous kindness." Like women, they were impulsive, inconsistent, contradictory, passionate, and prone to exaggeration, and until they demonstrated a manly kind of behavior, they would be ruled as if they were women, dependent and in need of a controlling hand.[14]

When not behaving as the English wished, as in the repeal campaign and during agrarian "outrages," the Irish became savage, with all the sexual overtones implied therein, in British representations of them. Benjamin Disraeli, future prime minister of Britain, accused Daniel O'Connell, the leader of the repeal movement, of behaving disreputably, implying a sexual immorality and an unmanliness that no proper Englishman would demonstrate. His "public life and private life are equally profligate," charged Disraeli; "he has committed every crime that does not require courage." Irish protestants claimed that catholic priests urged their parishioners to fall upon their protestant neighbors with bestial fury. "From the altar, inflamed by bigotry and delighting in blood, rush out the savage populace," declared one pamphlet, "to seize upon the victim, and to consign to destruction his property, his family, his home, and his life." George Cruikshank's 1845 illustration of the *Murder of George Crawford and his grandaughter* (see Figure 9.1), recalling the Irish revolt during the Napoleonic Wars, shows Irish peasants with brutish, apelike faces running pikes through the two victims and a dog. Crawford's granddaughter has gone to his aid, pleading for them to stop, just as one rebel pierces her breast with his weapon. People like this, Britons believed, brought upon themselves the very ills they protested – poverty and famine, unemployment and landlessness, and coercive legislation from an administration firm in its resolve to bring order to an uncivilized nation. "When Ireland acts according to the principles of civilised man," announced *The Times* in 1846, "then she can be ruled by the laws of civilised man."[15] Until that time, harsh British rule would remain. British politicians, journalists, satirists, novelists, and clergy conjured up a picture of a manly Britain ruling over a feminized, effeminate Ireland.

"Niggers" all: Indian mutineers, Irish Fenians, Jamaican rebels and the fashioning of imperial manliness, 1857–73

Liberal understandings of racial differences and racial inequality as circumstantial and removable had come under attack, as we have seen, by the end of the 1840s as the voices of men like Thomas Carlyle and Charles Dickens began to make themselves heard in increasingly louder tones. Still, it was not until 1857, with the outbreak of the Indian Mutiny, that the liberal views of men like John Stuart Mill were drowned out by far more conservative assertions of the irremediable, biological nature of racial differences and inequalities. The Indian Mutiny, followed by the terror campaign of the Irish Fenians and by the revolt of black Jamaicans in 1865, led the vast majority of Britons to embrace the "scientific" racial views propagated by social Darwinism after 1860 that located racial difference in evolutionary stages and rendered racial inequalities a matter of evolutionary, biological development. Grounded in nature, most Britons believed, inequalities could not be redressed by social or political means.

The mutiny broke out in May 1857, when Indian sepoys of the Bengal army rose up against their British officers and marched to Delhi, where they proclaimed the descendant of the last Mogul ruler, Bahadur Shah, "emperor of Hindustan." From Delhi the rebellion spread across much of northern India, attracting alienated groups from all parts of society. For more than a year, hindus and muslims, merchants and landowners, princes and peasants fought against and in many cases routed local British authorities, till it seemed that the British might be ousted altogether. They were not, but it took at least fourteen months before the army that had remained loyal to Britain, made up predominantly of the "manly" warrior Sikhs, was able to re-establish control in large parts of Oudh and the Punjab, and reassert their authority and rule over the subcontinent as a whole.

The mutiny destroyed Britons' confidence in their liberal view of empire. They

Murder of George Crawford and his grandaughter.

Figure 9.1 "Murder of George Crawford and his grandaughter," George Cruikshank, 1845
Source: By permission of the British Library, 2396c4 Maxwell; *The Irish Rebellion* (1864)

understood their mission in India and elsewhere to be that of educating and Christianizing the indigenous population to the point where they could expect someday, even if that day were long off, to govern themselves. They believed they were bringing progress and improvement to people who had fallen under the sway of "oriental despots" but who, because they were born rational men and with exposure to liberal reforms, education, free trade, and Christianity, could learn the ways of self-government. Now, *The Economist* declared in a classic statement of conservative versus liberal views of empire in September 1857, Britons had to decide:

> whether in future India is to be governed *as a Colony or as a Conquest*; whether we are to rule our Asiatic subjects with strict and generous justice, wisely and beneficently, as their natural and indefeasible superiors, by virtue of our higher civilisation, our purer religion, our sterner energies ... or whether we are to regard the Hindoos and Mahomedans as our equal fellow citizens, fit to be entrusted with the functions of self-government, ripe (or to be ripened) for British institutions, likely to appreciate the blessings of our rule, and, therefore, to be gradually prepared, as our own working classes are preparing ... for a full participation in the privileges of representative assemblies, trial by jury, and all the other palladia of English liberty.[16]

The answer was clear. If previously loyal sepoys, trained in the military discipline of the British army, proved so ungrateful for the tutelage of their British masters as to betray them at the first opportunity, how could other, less developed, "natives" be expected to respond? In Oudh, especially, which the British annexed in 1856, dislodging the nawab and the local aristocracy, and bestowing property rights upon the peasantry, the British expected the peasantry to side with them against the rebels. Instead, they followed their ruler and nobles in revolt, a clear sign of their irrationality and inability to pursue their own interests. Just how possible would it be for people who demonstrated so incomplete an appreciation for their own interests that they would rise against those who sought to act for them in their own interests to rule themselves? So demonstrably irrational were the actions of the Indian people that they could not be perceived any longer to be like Britons at heart and be expected to respond to efforts to educate and civilize them. From this moment on, Britons would see their role in India as one of conquest rather than civilization, and regard Indians not as human beings potentially like themselves but as wholly and utterly different who would need British rule if order were to be established and kept. In 1858, the government abolished the East India Company, which operated in a quasi-contractual fashion under the local rulers of Indian states, and placed the subcontinent under the authority of the British crown. The mutiny led Britons to argue that Indians were not just unlike themselves, but were inhuman, cruel savages. Throughout the rebellion and long after, tales of the most horrible atrocities committed by Indian men against the British, and most especially against British women, circulated throughout India and the home country. Though these stories could not be verified and in fact were later debunked by British officials, accounts of rape, torture, mutilation, and murder of "our countrywomen" continued to circulate as truth. They electrified the British public, searing the British imagination with pictures of scalped and dismembered white women, infants cut from their mothers' wombs, children burned alive, and women crucified. In private letters home, newspapers in Bombay and London, histories of the mutiny, and in subsequent novels right up through the 1960s and 1970s, the rape of English women served as the indelible sign of Indian savagery. Colonial insurrection, rebellion against imperial rule, took on not the dimensions of a political act carried out by oppressed people seeking to overthrow foreign domination but of a sexual crime committed against an English woman, indeed against all of British womanhood.

In story after story, British women and girls were stripped of their clothes, sexually molested, and thrown to the masses for further abuse. One clergyman claimed in a letter to *The Times* that he witnessed Indians taking "48 females, most of them girls of from 10 to 14, many delicately nurtured ladies, – violated them and kept for the base purposes of the heads of the insurrection for a whole week. At the end of that time they made them strip themselves, and gave them up to the lowest of the people to abuse in broad daylight in the street of Delhi. They then commenced the work of torturing them to death, cutting off their breasts, fingers, and noses, and leaving them to die. One lady was three days dying." Reports of a massacre of British hostages at Cawnpore by a rebel leader, Nana Sahib, took on immense proportions as a myth of mass rape and torture grew up around the execution of 200 British women and children by Nana Sahib's retreating forces. The rebels threw the women's bodies into a well in order to conceal them. Subsequent official investigations found no evidence of rape or torture, but the site of the massacre, the Bibighar, became a shrine to desecrated womanhood for the British soldiers marching through. They passed stories of violated women along to their fellow soldiers, and left messages written in blood on the walls of the Bibighar that purported to be from the "Mutiny ladies" demanding that their hideous treatment at the hands of Nana Sahib be avenged. Rebels and Nana Sahib in particular took on the persona of sexually sadistic monsters in novels about the mutiny.[17] George Trevelyan's history of the mutiny, *Cawnpore*, published in 1865, attributed its outbreak to "the ambition of the soldiery. ... Chafing under restraint, they panted to indulge themselves in unbridled rapine and licence." In James Grant's *First Love and Last Love: A Tale of the Indian Mutiny*, published in 1868 after the atrocity stories had been discredited by British officials investigating them, "women were outraged again and again, ere they were slaughtered, riddled with musket balls, or gashed by bayonets; and every indignity that the singularly fiendish invention of the Oriental mind could suggest, was offered to the dying and the dead." Grant charged that the sexual proclivities of Indians, along with "religious fanaticism and Oriental cruelty," had caused the rebellion. "Had not the Nana Sahib at Cawnpore ... slain the Christian women by the hundreds and flung them into a well, because not one of them would enter his zenana?" he demanded.[18]

Certainly British women and children, like those at Cawnpore, as well as British men, died at the hands of the rebels. But they died, most of them, from shots fired in battle or from diseases they contracted during long sieges of their towns and stations, where lack of clean water, food, and medical supplies made them susceptible to cholera and dysentery. Such deaths, however, could not readily be mobilized to justify a ferocious British response to the revolt, in which British soldiers retaliated against the rebels by executing whole villages, burning civilians and soldiers alive, and blowing Indians out of cannon. The outrages committed by British soldiers against sepoys and Indian civilians were reported at the time and in later nineteenth- and twentieth-century historical accounts to have been the consequence of uncontrollable fury provoked by the rape and torture of British women and children by the sepoys. "Remember the Ladies! Remember the Babies!" they were reported as crying as they rode into battle seeking revenge from men who had degraded their women and desecrated their homes. George Lawrence's fictional character in *Maurice Dering* (1864) journeys to India to avenge the death of his fiancé. He explains that her "foul murder" incited him to previously unthinkable actions:

> Has any one forgotten the evil Spring, when there swept over this country of ours a blast from the East – fatal to many households ... chilling to many hearts ... ? Have we forgotten how, with each successive mail, the wrath and the horror grew wilder; till the sluggish Anglo-Saxon nature became, as it were, possessed by a devil, and through the length and breadth of the land ... there went up one awful cry for vengeance?

Urged by a minister to show mercy to his enemies, he refuses because they had no thought of mercy "when my innocent darling was given up to those unchained devils." "He gnashed his teeth as he spoke, and his moustache grew white and wet with foam."[19]

In accordance with a logic that saw in the status and treatment of women a measure of civilization, Indian men and men of color generally came, as a consequence of the mutiny, to be regarded as defilers of innocent British women, till the image of the rape and mutilation of white women by black men came to stand not merely for the mutiny itself but for the whole relationship of Britain to its colonial subjects. And white men, Britons, having responded with fury at the outrages committed against their women, as the new imperial narrative had it, would see their mission as one of protecting innocent, chaste white women from "black" men and saving "black" women from "black" men as well. "We who live among the records and associations of chivalry," wrote Trevelyan, "still make it our pride to regard women as goddesses. The Hindoos, ... the Mohammedans ... cannot bring themselves to look upon them as better than playthings."[20] A new model of British manliness began to emerge from the events and accounts surrounding the Indian Mutiny. No longer exclusively the Christian man of reason, as embodied by the minister urging mercy upon the hero in *Maurice Dering*, but also a man of action, passion, and romance, the post-mutiny prototype of English manliness possessed a love of justice; he was slow to anger but capable when provoked of meting out a terrible, violent retribution against his foes. A man of body more than of mind now, as the notion of "muscular Christianity" promoted by Charles Kingsley suggests, he nevertheless continued to demonstrate his capacity to reason, one of the most important elements in distinguishing this newly aggressive Briton from the "manly" Sikh warrior who had put down the mutiny. With the infusion of "scientific" arguments about racial superiority and inferiority drawn from the evolutionary theories of Charles Darwin, the story of imperialism changed from one of liberal Christian gentlemen bringing free trade, civilization, and the tools of self-government to childlike, feminized peoples of lesser development to that of an aggressive, powerful, authoritarian, racially superior British nation conquering savage, sexualized, and feminized lands, and establishing order over subhuman, animal-like "niggers" of a biologically inferior breed.

The images of dishonored white women and swift, violent retribution from manly British imperialists reverberated fiercely in the minds of Britons eight years later when Jamaican blacks rebelled at Morant Bay in October 1865 in response to high food prices, low wages, racial injustice, and the political indifference of the white-dominated legislature to their grievances. The British governor in Jamaica, Edward Eyre, believed that the rising would spread throughout the island, and ordered a severe crackdown on the rebels. His troops killed 439 blacks and people of mixed race, whipped hundreds of men and women, and burned down some 1,000 homes. Eyre ordered the arrest of George Gordon, a Jamaican of mixed race and his political enemy in the House of Assembly whom he held responsible for the revolt, had him tried and, on the strength of very flimsy evidence, had him hanged for his offense.

Led by John Stuart Mill, a number of prominent liberal thinkers joined together in the Jamaica Committee to lobby the British government to prosecute Eyre for excessive force and illegal procedures. The government felt pressured enough by public opinion against Eyre to establish a Royal Commission to investigate the uprising and Eyre's response to it. Thomas Carlyle formed a defense committee on behalf of Eyre, which included such literary lights as Charles Dickens and Charles Kingsley. Carlyle argued that rather than be prosecuted for his actions, Eyre deserved the thanks of all of Britain for having saved Jamaica from anarchy and horrors unmentionable. As for his excesses in establishing order, they amounted to little in the scheme of things. "If Eyre had shot the whole Nigger population and flung them into the sea," he opined, no harm would have been done, for Britain "never loved anarchy; nor was wont to spend its sympathy on miserable mad seditions, especially of this inhuman and half-brutish type; but always loved order, and the prompt suppression of sedition." With the memory of the Indian Mutiny still fresh, the bulk of British opinion tended to side with Carlyle rather than with Mill.[21]

Indeed, Eyre and some who testified on his behalf explicitly raised the specter of sexual violence against women that had become synonymous with colonial rebellions. His first report back to London after the rebellion told of atrocities committed by black rebels that "could only be paralleled by the atrocities of the Indian mutiny." When news of criticism from the Jamaica Committee reached him, he pointed out to the Colonial Office "that the negro is a creature of impulse and imitation, easily misled, very excitable, and a perfect fiend when under the influence of an excitement which stirs up all the evil passions of a race little removed in many respects from absolute savagery." John Tyndall, a prominent scientist, reminded the government and British public that Eyre, "one of the very finest types of English manhood," had provided safety for 7,000 British men and protected the honor of 7,000 British women from the "murder and lust of black savages." He recalled with approval the "conduct of those British officers in India who shot their wives before blowing themselves to pieces, rather than allow what they loved and honoured to fall into the hands of the Sepoys," and appealed to "the women of England" to make their voices heard in this matter. For while British men might be able to look into the face of death, "there is nothing in the soul of woman to lift her to the level of that which I dare not do more than glance at here," making clear allusion to the atrocity stories of the rape and torture of British women at the hands of Indian men. Eyre's biographer and member of the defense committee, Hamilton Hume, made the connection to the purported rape and murder of Englishwomen in India explicit. He told readers of "those fearful and bloody acts which were scarcely paralleled by the massacre at Cawnpore." Eyre himself testified that his "proudest recollection" of his actions at Morant Bay had been that he had saved the "ladies," the white women, of Jamaica.[22]

The rising at Morant Bay convinced many colonial officials, virtually all of the white population of Jamaica, and much of the British public that what Carlyle had argued in 1849 was indeed true: blacks could not govern themselves and would have to be ruled by a firm but benevolent British government. Over the protests of some of the mixed-race members, Jamaica's House of Assembly and the

Legislative Council abolished themselves and placed the country under the direct rule of the Colonial Office. Jamaica, like India, became a crown colony, governed from London.

The characterization of Irishmen, too, took on harder racial classifications in the 1860s after nationalists in the Irish Republican Brotherhood, also known as the Fenians, began to plan for a rising against Britain to establish independence for Ireland. In January 1867 a number of Fenians arrived in London and set off what was intended as a campaign of guerrilla warfare. A plan to raid Chester Castle in early February, where the British stashed supplies of arms and ammunition, was cut short by the arrival of British police, but in September Fenians succeeded in attacking a prison van in Manchester and rescuing two of their comrades, killing a police sergeant in the process. In December 1867, they blew out a wall of Clerken-well Prison, where the Fenians' chief of arms procurement was awaiting trial. This time, twelve Londoners were killed and over thirty others were wounded, many of them quite badly. These actions, as had been intended, vividly brought the Irish question and the issue of Irish grievances before the English public. But they also struck terror in the hearts of many English citizens, and helped to sear the picture of wild-eyed, bloodthirsty, savage Irish rebels on the English imagination.

In these imaginings, catholic Irish men took on the coloration and qualities of other rebels of the 1850s and 1860s. Like Indians and Africans, they were black. In fact, the facial and bodily features of Irish men, constantly depicted in *Punch's* cartoons after 1860 in simian, ape-like forms, testified to the fact that the Irish were "the missing link between the gorilla and the Negro." Irish males were not men, not by any standard of definition put forward by the British. Rather, claimed countless English, Scottish, Welsh, and protestant Irish observers in the new "scientific" racial language of social Darwinism, they constituted a subhuman species, located on the evolutionary chain somewhere between apes and Africans. By contrast, Britons represented themselves as chivalric defenders of a highly feminine, virtuous Ireland endangered by the Fenian menace. In an 1866 *Punch* cartoon entitled "The Fenian pest," an innocent, chaste "Hibernia" seeks protection against the scarcely disguised sexual violence of gorilla-like Fenians from a strong, resolute Britannia who, despite her female figure, exudes manly courage, confidence, and the threat of physical force (see Figure 9.2). A December 1867 cartoon showed an apish Irishman sitting atop a keg of gunpowder ready to blow, as a woman, with a child at her bare breast, and small children milled around (see Figure 9.3). The Fenian threat did not last long, as its terror campaigns alienated many Irish people, but the imagery used to depict Irish catholics as inhuman and incapable of self-government would prevail long into the 1880s and beyond, when new movements for land reform and home rule came to the fore.[23]

THE FENIAN-PEST.

Hibernia. "O MY DEAR SISTER, WHAT *ARE* WE TO DO WITH THESE TROUBLESOME PEOPLE?"
Britannia. "TRY ISOLATION FIRST, MY DEAR, AND THEN———"

Figure 9.2 "The Fenian-Pest," illustration in *Punch*, 3 March 1866
Source: Reproduced with permission of Punch Ltd

THE FENIAN GUY FAWKES.

Figure 9.3 "The Fenian Guy Fawkes," illustration in Punch, 28
    December 1867
Source: Reproduced with permission of Punch Ltd

Virtue's reward: the Reform Act of 1867 and the reconfiguration of empire

It was amidst this atmosphere of rebellion in Jamaica and Ireland that the campaign to enfranchise working-class males in the 1860s took place.[24] An economic downturn, widespread unemployment, and high prices provoked fears among élites that workers might resort to rioting just as unrest in the empire seemed to threaten Britain's control, a prophecy that appeared to be borne out by a massive and illegal demonstration of skilled and unskilled working people in Hyde Park in 1866. Debates over granting working men the vote took place within the context of imperial problems and were framed in the language of race and empire as well as gender.

Evangelicals and liberals had long seen working-class men and women as little different from the people of color they ruled over within the empire. Missionaries, in particular, in order to justify their activities at home, frequently described the working classes in much the same, and even stronger, language they employed to discuss the objects of their efforts abroad. In 1829, for instance, the Newcastle Town Mission reported that the poor and outcast in their area and in other British towns were "more profligate and more perverted than Hindoos." Ten years later, John Campbell observed of the poor and working-class people of Britain that "they ... present a population as blind, corrupt, and brutish, as could be furnished from any city of the heathen world – they are seared in conscience, almost divested of moral sense, and sunk into all but hopeless degradation. They are in all respects 'earthly, sensual, devilish,' without God and without hope in the world."[25]

Opponents of the working-class franchise like Robert Lowe and Earl Russell cast working people in decidedly racial terms. The "ignorance and passion" of the masses, trumpeted one pamphlet, rendered them incapable of weighing national interests carefully, and, besides, would give sexually irresponsible Irish men who married early a preponderance of votes over responsible, diligent Scottish men who married late in life after they had established themselves. Lowe asserted that granting the working-class franchise amounted to giving the "Australian savage and Hottentot of the Cape" colony the same rights as "the educated and refined Englishman." It would lead, warned Sir Thomas Bateson, to "emasculation of the aristocracy." Earl Russell insisted that the nation needed "independent, thoughtful voters" who could take on the problems of "cholera, cattle pest, the Nigger Pest – white murder by blacks – and Fenians," not working-class men who should themselves be governed according to the "natural order" of things. Class, in these debates, was defined in gendered and racial terms.

But as *The Economist* noted in 1857 in its discussion of Indian governance after the mutiny, British working men were "preparing ... for a full participation in the privileges of representative assemblies, trial by jury, and all the other palladia of English liberty." After the demise of Chartism in 1848, skilled working men concentrated their efforts on building up an image of themselves as respectable, moderate, home-loving, and, above all, independent and manly individuals. They behaved with discipline and restraint in their trade union activity, seeking to persuade employers of the rightness of their demands by adopting employers' visions of the proper patriarchal family in their demands for a sufficient wage to keep their wives and children. They turned the language of domesticity, used against them after 1832 by middle- and upper-class politicians to deny them the vote, to their own ends, embracing visions of the male bread-winner and the woman at home in order to demonstrate their compatibility with bourgeois notions of independence and citizenship. Their lives and values, they insisted, showed that they were no different from middle-class men. Like them, they deserved to vote on the affairs of the nation.

Liberals like prime minister William Gladstone and John Bright used the language of domesticity and, significantly, of empire and nation, to make the case for enfranchising working men. Gladstone introduced a reform bill to grant the vote to working men in 1866 with the reminder that they were "the fathers of families," and "our own flesh and blood." He wished to bring them "within the pale of the constitution," a reference to the area of early English settlement in Ireland which imaginatively marked off the "civilized" English from the "barbaric" Irish. Not a race apart, as conservatives would have them, working men were "one of us," as shown by their adherence to domestic and patriarchal practices. Liberals and working-class men compiled a litany of the qualities that made working men just like them. The fact that they saved money, eschewed drink, and "struggled manfully" to support their families demonstrated their virtue, and guaranteed that they would be a force for stability for the state rather than one of disruption and upheaval.

As it turned out, it was the conservative government of Benjamin Disraeli that enfranchised working men in 1867 rather than the liberal government of Gladstone. In a formulation that reflected the shift of notions of British manliness away from the liberal view of reason and education to the more conservative one of body and strength, Disraeli sought to utilize the "muscle and might" of working men to help defend Britain's imperial interests, and to deflect the energies of the working classes away from potential conflict with the state toward support of the state's policies overseas. After 1867 it was no longer possible to lump British working-class men, with some exceptions (largely the poor and immigrant population of London's East End), in with colonized subjects as unruly, barbaric, indolent, and insolent people. Disraeli's "leap in the dark" had made working-class men part of the respectable nation; divisions between them and people of color — divisions between those who were capable of citizenship and those who were fit only to be ruled – became more pronounced. As had been the case with the abolition of slavery, racial classifications and distinctions between black and white were drawn with increasing starkness.

Although he was voted out of office by a coalition of liberals and working men newly enfranchised by the Reform Act of 1867, Disraeli embarked upon a series of ventures designed to increase Britain's empire and thereby enhance its status *vis à vis* the European great powers. In 1872 he delivered a speech at the Crystal Palace in which he asked Britons to decide whether they wanted to live in a "comfortable England" or in "a great country – an Imperial country," from which they would "command the respect of the world." When he came into power again in 1874, Disraeli immediately put his plans into effect, purchasing in 1875 shares in the Suez Canal that had belonged to the bankrupt ruler of Egypt. He had done so, he informed parliament, because controlling the canal was "necessary to maintain the empire." In 1876, in a vivid display of Britain's new imperial intentions, Disraeli's government passed the Royal Titles Bill, which conferred upon Queen Victoria the title "Empress of India." This appellation signaled the culmination of a dramatic shift in Britons' understanding of empire. Where it had once connoted a relationship of white colonies of settlement, of a union between Britons and their free and loyal kin overseas, best exemplified by the colonies of Canada, Australia, and New Zealand, empire now signified possession of, and despotic rule over, peoples of color.

And with the new imperialism came a new model of masculinity, one characterized by racial superiority over "blacks," action, and physical force, and one which recognized working men as manly as much by virtue of their "sinew and muscle" as by their temperance, self-reliance, and possession of women in the home. The liberal gentleman of the 1830s and 1840s, all mind – morally and spiritually earnest, rational, and convinced of the inherent equality of all men – would not disappear entirely, but he would increasingly be overshadowed by the new man of body, a figure who would most vividly appear in the guise of the imperial pioneer and hunter.

NOTES

1 See Thomas R. Metcalf, *Ideologies of the Raj* (Cambridge, 1994).
2 Quoted in Patrick Brantlinger, *Rule of Darkness: British Literature and Imperialism, 1830–1914* (Ithaca, 1988), pp. 79–81.
3 Quoted in Metcalf, *Ideologies of the Raj*, pp. 33–4.
4 Quoted in Metcalf, *Ideologies of the Raj*, p. 34.
5 See Catherine Hall, " 'From Greenland's icy mountains … to Afric's golden sand': Ethnicity, race and nation in mid-nineteenth-century England," *Gender and History* 5(2), 1993: 212–30.

6 See Catherine Hall, "Missionary stories: Gender and ethnicity in England in the 1830s and 1840s", in Lawrence Grossberg, Cary Nelson, and Paula Treichler, eds, *Cultural Studies* (New York, 1992), pp. 240–70.

7 Quoted in Hall, "Missionary stories."

8 Quoted in Hall, "Missionary stories."

9 Quoted in Brantlinger, *Rule of Darkness*, p. 32.

10 Quoted in Howard Temperley, *White Dreams, Black Africa: The Antislavery Expedition to the Niger, 1841–1842* (New Haven, 1991), pp. 157, 162.

11 Quoted in Brantlinger, *Rule of Darkness*, p. 178.

12 See Eugene R. August, ed., *Thomas Carlyle, "The Nigger Question." John Stuart Mill, "The Negro Question"* (New York, 1971).

13 Quoted in Richard Ned Lebow, *White Britain and Black Ireland. The Influence of Stereotypes on Colonial Policy* (Philadelphia, 1976), pp. 39–40.

14 Quoted in Lebow, *White Britain and Black Ireland*, p. 57.

15 Quoted in Lebow, *White Britain and Black Ireland*, pp. 62, 63, 67.

16 Quoted in Metcalf, *Ideologies of the Raj*, p. 58.

17 Quoted in Jenny Sharpe, *Allegories of Empire: The Figure of Woman in the Colonial Text* (Minneapolis, 1993), ch. 3.

18 George Otto Trevelyan, *Cawnpore* (New Delhi, 1992; originally published 1865), p. 18; quoted in Brantlinger, *Rule of Darkness*, p. 209.

19 Quoted in Brantlinger, *Rule of Darkness*, p. 209.

20 Trevelyan, *Cawnpore*, p. 75.

21 Quoted in Catherine Hall, *White, Male and Middle Class: Explorations in Feminism and History* (London, 1992), p. 283.

22 Catherine Hall, "Imperial man: Edward Eyre in Australasia and the West Indies," in Bill Schwartz, ed., *The Expansion of England: Race, Ethnicity and Cultural History* (London, 1996), pp. 160, 162; Hall, *White, Male and Middle Class*, pp. 284, 285.

23 Quoted in Lebow, *White Britain and Black Ireland*, p. 40.

24 For the discussion of the Reform Act of 1867, I rely upon Anna Clark, "Gender, class, and the nation: Franchise reform in England, 1832–1928," in James Vernon, ed., *Re-Reading the Constitution: New Narratives in the Political History of England's Long Nineteenth Century* (Cambridge, 1996).

25 Quoted in Susan Thorne, " 'The conversion of Englishmen and the conversion of the world inseparable': Missionary imperialism and the language of class in early industrial Britain," in Frederick Cooper and Ann Laura Stoler, eds, *Tensions of Empire: Colonial Cultures in a Bourgeois World* (Berkeley, 1997), p. 249.

SOURCES

Michael Adas, *Machines as the Measure of Men: Science, Technology, and Ideologies of Western Dominance*. Ithaca, NY, 1989.

Eugene R. August, ed., *Thomas Carlyle, "The Nigger Question." John Stuart Mill, "The Negro Question"*. New York, 1971.

Patrick Brantlinger, *Rule of Darkness: British Literature and Imperialism, 1830–1914*. Ithaca, 1988.

Anna Clark, "Gender, class, and the nation: Franchise reform in England, 1832–1928," in James Vernon, ed., *Re-Reading the Constitution: New Narratives in the Political History of England's Long Nineteenth Century*. Cambridge, 1996.

L. Perry Curtis, Jr., *Apes and Angels: The Irishman in Victorian Caricature*. Washington, DC, 1971.

Catherine Hall, *White, Male and Middle Class: Explorations in Feminism and History*. London, 1992.

——, "Missionary stories: Gender and ethnicity in England in the 1830s and 1840s", in Lawrence Grossberg, Cary Nelson, and Paula Treichler, eds, *Cultural Studies*. New York, 1992.

——, " 'From Greenland's icy mountains … to Afric's golden sand': Ethnicity, race and nation in mid-nineteenth-century England," *Gender and History* 5(2), 1993: 212–30.

——, "Imperial Man: Edward Eyre in Australasia and the West Indies," in Bill Schwartz, ed., *The Expansion of England: Race, Ethnicity and Cultural History*. London, 1996.

Thomas C. Holt, *The Problem of Freedom: Race, Labor, and Politics in Jamaica and Britain, 1832–1938*. Baltimore, 1992.

Robert Kee, *The Green Flag, Volume II: The Bold Fenian Men*. London, 1972.

Richard Ned Lebow, *White Britain and Black Ireland. The Influence of Stereotypes on Colonial Policy*. Philadelphia, 1976.

Lata Mani, "Contentious traditions: The debate on SATI in colonial India," *Cultural Critique* 7, Fall 1987: 119–56.

Thomas R. Metcalf, *Ideologies of the Raj*. Cambridge, 1994.

Jenny Sharpe, *Allegories of Empire: The Figure of Woman in the Colonial Text*. Minneapolis, 1993.

Howard Temperley, *White Dreams, Black Africa: The Antislavery Expedition to the Niger, 1841–1842*. New Haven, 1991.

Susan Thorne, " 'The conversion of Englishmen and the conversion of the world inseparable': Missionary imperialism and the language of class in early industrial Britain," in Frederick Cooper and Ann Laura Stoler, eds, *Tensions of Empire: Colonial Cultures in a Bourgeois World*. Berkeley, 1997.

George Otto Trevelyan, *Cawnpore*. New Delhi, 1992 (originally published 1865).

Chapter 10

Liberalism besieged, masculinity under fire, 1873–1911

In the last quarter of the nineteenth century and the first years of the twentieth, confidence in the principles of liberalism and faith in the assumptions that underlay them came under assault from a variety of political, social, economic, and intellectual and cultural developments. In the realm of economics, what historians call the second industrial revolution began in the areas of oil, electricity, and chemicals, transforming the nature of industry and class relations, spurring another round of massive population growth, and helping to create a mass society. In 1884, agricultural laboring men received the vote, a situation that, combined with population growth, produced a flooding of the electorate with so many additional voters that politicians felt compelled to change the way they conducted their affairs and those of the country in order to tap the potential support of them. Technological developments in transportation and communications, made possible by the second industrial revolution, and a demand for the raw materials necessary to sustain it, enabled and encouraged European countries to embark on ambitious imperial ventures. International rivalries generated by the recent appearances of a powerful Germany on the continent and a dynamic America across the Atlantic reinforced European impulses to expand in Asia and Africa, and helped to instill doubt in Britons of their superiority to the rest of the world.

In cultural and intellectual life, the promulgation of Darwinist and social Darwinist theories of evolution and "racial" deterioration undercut the assumptions about human nature, of progress, reason, *laissez-faire*, and individual rights upon which liberal theory rested. Irish nationalists combined a constitutional program for home rule with an extra-legal campaign of violence against protestant landlords in the 1880s. Feminists overtly challenged the ideology of separate spheres by attacking the institution of marriage and the laws that, making them the property of men, permitted and even encouraged abuse against women. "New women" entered colleges and universities, trained for the professions, found work in newly created white-collar sectors of the economy, and disputed the "scientific" doctrines that proclaimed their "passionlessness." In 1895, the trial of Oscar Wilde

Figure 10.1 "Girl with a bicycle," photograph of *c.* 1910, anon.
Source: Reproduced with permission of the Royal Photographic Society Collection

brought homosexuality, which had been made criminal in 1885, to the attention of a broad segment of society, introducing a new element of uncertainty into ideas about masculinity that had seemed hard and fast, and provoking an intensification of anxiety about gender and sexuality.

Mass society and the "depression" of 1873–96

The first industrial revolution involved the application of steam power to manufacturing processes, raising output and productivity astronomically in already existing industries such as textiles and mining. The second industrial revolution entailed the creation of whole new products altogether, transforming the way individuals lived their lives in the space of a single generation. Rubber for tires,

Figure 10.2 "The Toast," photograph of 1912, W.B.B. Wellington
Source: Reproduced with permission of the Royal Photographic Society Collection

minerals that made possible the cost-effective development of strong and light-weight metals like steel and aluminum, petroleum products to fuel automobiles – these and countless other discoveries and innovations introduced Westerners to consumer goods that we now take for granted, and created a demand for raw materials that seemed insatiable. New modes of transportation and conveyance – bicycles, trams, trolleys, buses, refrigerator ships, automobiles, airplanes, the Panama and Suez canals, and tunnels through the Alps – enabled people and goods to move and be moved quickly from formerly distant parts of the world. New forms of communication – the telephone and telegraph, typewriters – brought individuals, groups, and nations into almost instant contact with one another, exposing formerly isolated peoples to one another and making the long-distance governance of vast non-European populations by small numbers of Britons possible in ways it had not been before. New medicines, foodstuffs, preservatives, and purification practices improved the health and longevity of the British population, vastly increasing its size despite a falling birth-rate among middle- and upper-class families and a vast outflow of migration to North America and the white colonies of settlement. The population of England, Scotland, and Wales grew from about 30 million in 1881 to 37 million in 1901 to almost 41 million in 1911, a dramatic increase by any standard (Ireland's fell from 5.1 million to 4.3 million between 1881 and 1901, as emigration following the famine took its demographic toll). Factories and firms became massive in scale and scope, employing thousands of workers who were sited together in huge agglomerations where they were distant from management but proximate to one another. Cities grew rapidly in terms of numbers and of space, producing vast stretches of urban corridors where farm and pasture lands and forests once existed. Electricity provided lighting for homes and streets, and brought recorded music into private homes by means of the gramophone, paving the way for later development of consumer items like radios, washing machines, vacuum cleaners, and other household appliances.

These developments provoked changes in virtually every area of life in Britain. Where economic and technological changes reduced the possibilities of wage-paying occupations for Irish women and drove them back into their own homes as unpaid housekeepers,[1] in other parts of Britain new white-collar positions in industry, finance, education, government, commerce, and the professions opened up, making it possible for single middle-class women to take up work without a loss of respectability. The Education Act of 1870 required that all children attend school until they turned 11 years of age; its provisions stimulated a great demand for teachers, most of whom were women. In 1861, some 80,000 women held teaching positions in England and Wales. Their numbers increased to 172,000 by 1901. Between 1861 and 1911, the number of women teachers had grown by 129 percent. Nursing jobs for women expanded by 210 percent in the same time span; while the number of shop assistants rose from 87,000 to 366,000. Between 1871 and 1901, the number of women working as clerks in commercial enterprises rose from 1,412 to 55,784; ten years later, 117,057 women held these jobs. As teachers, typists, clerks, social workers, or nurses, middle-class women might gain an independent, if meager, income, and the potential for independence of action that accompanied it. Bicycles enabled them to move around freely (see Figure 10.1); clothing was modified so that they might ride them. The emphasis on physical fitness made sport and exercise a proper undertaking for women, though not without resistance from a number of quarters. Women played golf, tennis, field hockey, and cricket: healthier and less restricted now, women stood to gain a great deal of freedom in, and from, these activities. The "new woman" of the 1880s and 1890s – educated, independent, active, and assertive – represented a dramatic departure from the model of femininity pressed upon women in the previous decades.

Among workers, broad-based industrial unions of general workers began to replace the small skilled artisan unions of mid-century. Organized according to industry – involving all transport or textile workers, for instance – rather than to skill within a craft – like engineering or weaving – these new unions could boast a membership numbering in the thousands. Moreover, they were not loath to take action on behalf of their members: where craft unions sought to demonstrate the steadiness and respectability of their workers by avoiding agitations or strike activity, the new unions embraced the strike as a weapon with which to confront industrialists on issues of wages, hours, or working conditions. In the 1880s, strikes broke out with some frequency. In 1888, the women of the London match industry went out in order to improve working conditions; in 1889, the gasworkers followed, presaging the Great London Dock Strike of the same year. In the 1890s, unionism spread among workers in non-industrial trades as well, incorporating white-collar workers in shops and offices. By 1900, some two million Britons belonged to trade unions; the numbers had increased to four million by 1914. Strikes by railway workers in 1907, by shipbuilders and coal-miners in 1908, by dock workers in 1911 and 1912, and by miners in 1912 testified both to the power and to the dissatisfactions of workers with their lot. In 1913 and 1914, miners struck again, and industrial action broke out in Dublin as well. Some of these agitations provoked violence among the workers, and the government responded with troops in order to quell it in places like South Wales. In 1913, the "Triple Alliance" of railway workers, transport workers, and miners formed, and in 1914 threatened a general strike designed to shut down the country. The outbreak of war in August 1914 prevented the action from taking place for the time being.

The political might of the new trade unions soon manifested itself. In the past, the old skilled craft unionists had tended to embrace liberalism and to vote for Liberal candidates, helping to create the so-called Lib–Lab alliance (for Liberal–Labour) that dominated working-class politics for almost thirty years after the Reform Act of 1867. In 1885, for example, 11 members of parliament called themselves Lib–Lab MPs. Of those, six had at one time worked in the mines. By the 1890s, however, the workers organized in the new unions sought a different kind of representation, one that would express their increasingly socialist outlook. They sought not merely the amelioration of working conditions and a rise in wages but looked to a more collectivized system of land and industry ownership. In 1892, workers elected James Keir Hardy, a Scottish miner, and John Burns, a leader of the London dock strike, to parliament as independents. Keir

Hardy took his seat dressed in tweeds and the cloth cap worn ubiquitously by working-class men. His appearance, in contrast to that of the other MPs, who wore formal dress, signaled that a new kind of working-class politics had arrived.

In 1893, Keir Hardy formed the Independent Labour Party, espousing an explicit socialist agenda of redistribution of income from the wealthy to the poor; free secondary and university education in addition to the already available primary education; cash payments to the unemployed, disabled, and elderly; and the nationalization and therefore public ownership of land, industry, banking and financial services, and transportation systems. The Independent Labour Party gave way first to the Labour Representation Party and then to the Labour Party in 1906; by that time, most workers had abandoned the program of the Liberal Party, and embraced the collectivist and socialist aims put forward by Keir Hardy. These demands would constitute the Labour Party's program for decades to come; the electoral strength of the Labour Party in the decade before World War I would make it necessary for the Liberal Party to concede to some of its demands in order to maintain its majority after 1905.

If new unionism and working-class politics challenged liberal principles of individualism and *laissez-faire* by seeking to tax the wealthy and redistribute income throughout society, other initiatives derived from the economic situation of the last quarter of the nineteenth century did as well. Beginning in 1873, what Europeans perceived to be a depression (it was in reality a deflation caused by an insufficient supply of gold, to which the currencies of much of the world were tied, a situation remedied by the discovery of gold fields in Kimberly, South Africa, in the 1890s) took hold of the world's capitalist economies for over two decades. Falling profits and stiff competition from Germany, France, and the United States led many British industrialists, business leaders, and politicians to question the by now orthodox commitment to free trade. Powerful voices like that of MP Joseph Chamberlain championed the creation of an imperial trading bloc – made up of Britain, the self-governing colonies of Canada, Australia, and New Zealand, and the territories held by Britain in Asia and Africa – within which trade would continue to flow unimpeded but around which tariff barriers would be erected so as to raise the price of foreign goods entering it and thereby protect British business and industry from competing industrial nations. As it turned out, the British government maintained its free trade practices throughout this period, but the full-fledged commitment to free trade that gave Britain its decisive liberal character in economic affairs no longer held sway.

The depression compelled – and the developments in technology permitted – many of the other European powers and the United States to embark upon a path of what is called "new imperialism." Believing that Britain's great prosperity derived from its holding of colonies, politicians and business interests in France, the United States, Italy, Belgium, and Germany resolved to gain their own. In the early 1880s, what has come to be called the "scramble for Africa" took place, whereby the various European powers carved out large areas of the continent they deemed to be their "spheres of influence." Faced with competition for imperial power they had not seen since the end of the eighteenth century, British statesmen and politicians responded in kind, formally annexing vast territories in Asia and Africa – Egypt, the Sudan, Afghanistan, southern Africa, Uganda, Rhodesia, Kenya, and Nigeria – and placing them under the administrative control of the crown in order to protect British "interests" there from encroachment on the part of other European countries. Britain faced competition from Europe and the United States in the geo-strategic as well as economic realms. In 1870, the German states had unified under the leadership of the kingdom of Prussia. Where once some thirty states had existed in a kind of power vacuum in central Europe, now a large and mighty German empire threatened to undo the balance of power that had been forged in the years following Napoleon's defeat in 1815. Under the leadership of Chancellor Otto von Bismarck, Germany contented itself with consolidating the gains it had made in central Europe and sought to calm the fears of the other European great powers of Russia, France, Austria–Hungary, and Britain by maintaining a low, peaceable profile in international affairs. With the accession of Wilhelm II to the throne in 1890, however, Germany undertook to establish itself as a world power comparable to Britain. Seeking to gain Germany's "place in the sun," the kaiser and his military and civilian officials embarked upon a naval race against Britain, commenced to threaten and bully their French and British rivals unmercifully, and exploited situations where the British colonial officials found themselves challenged by internal resistance and even revolt.

Beginning in the 1880s, Britain entered a new, more self-consciously imperial phase of colonial acquisition that Disraeli had foreseen was England's destiny if it was to retain its status as a pre-eminent world power. Placed on the defensive by the rise of the new industrial powers, Britons responded with an aggressive display of imperial might designed to counter any notion of economic or military weakness. Poets and writers told of untold wealth and unparalleled adventures to be had in the frontier areas of Asia and Africa; celebrations like that of Victoria's Diamond Jubilee in 1897 made manifest the power and glory of empire. Politicians, military men, and commercial adventurers extolled the virtues of imperial power for national health, seeing in empire and imperial rule the means by which Britain was to preserve its international standing. Men like Chamberlain, Lord Rosebery, Cecil Rhodes, and Lords Curzon and Milner regarded the empire as key to Britain's very survival, the training ground that would prepare it, Rosebery insisted, "for the keen race of nations."

"Race degeneration" and the maternal welfare movement[2]

Fear of German economic might and military aggression received impetus from another quarter as well. Although Britain's population had grown dramatically in the late nineteenth century, it was dwarfed by those of the United States and the continental powers, and its birth-rate had slowed considerably. Fears of population decline joined concerns about the quality of the British population, especially in light of a growing awareness of the depth and degree of poverty, as rural migrants fled to the cities to escape the agricultural depression, and of the high levels of infant mortality that existed throughout the country. For despite the improvement in real wages enjoyed by those who had regular work, poverty levels increased during the 1880s and 1890s, and urbanization made this poverty far more visible than it had been when most people lived on the land. Twenty-eight percent of York's population earned incomes insufficient to maintain a household; London's percentage was even higher. Perhaps one-third of all Britons lived below the poverty line. Moreover, infant mortality rates were on the rise. In England and Wales in the 1880s, 142 of every 1,000 infants born died within their first year of life; that figure increased to 154 during the 1890s till by 1899 it had reached 163.

The existence of so much poverty, disease, and death in the midst of such plenty demanded explanation. Physicians, scientists, politicians, churchmen, writers, and moralists believed that cities depleted the health and vigor of populations, regarding them as "the graves ... of our race," as the dean of Canterbury put it in 1887. The *Fortnightly Review* warned its readers of the effects of urban life in its description of the "town type." "The child of the townsman is bred too fine, it is too great an exaggeration of himself, excitable and painfully precocious in its childhood, neurotic, dyspeptic, pale and undersized in its adult state, if it ever reaches it." The conditions of city life, they believed, enervated formerly healthy specimens, demoralizing them and causing physical deterioration. The solution lay in gathering up the remaining "unoccupied" territories of the world and peopling them with Britons. It was through acquisition, possession, and rule of colonies overseas that Britain's health was to be maintained. "New imperialism" gained momentum from the social Darwinist theories that saw in competition with the other European powers, the United States, and Japan the means by which to create a robust society of virile men and proper, moral women. As Lord Rosebery put it in a letter to *The Times* in 1900, "an empire such as ours requires as its first condition an Imperial Race – a race vigorous and industrious and intrepid. Health of mind and body exalt a nation in the competition of the universe. The survival of the fittest is an absolute truth in the conditions of the modern world."[3]

For others, conflict offered the most effective means of strengthening the citizens of a nation. In the eyes of many who embraced Darwin's notions of the survival of the fittest and applied them to the species of human beings as well, war constituted a positive good, an arena in which men could be hardened and those who were unfit could be selected out and prevented from procreating, and thus passing on inferior or degenerate traits to a subsequent generation. Through war, the "effeminate" could be weeded out, the manly preserved. "The stimulus of a great patriotic excitement," wrote one apologist for war and empire, "the determination to endure burdens and make sacrifices, the self-abnegation which will face loss, and suffering, and even death, for the commonweal, are bracing tonics to national health, and they counteract the enervating effects of 'too much love of living,' too much ease, and luxury, and material prosperity. ... Strength is not maintained without exercise."[4]

The fears of deterioration that informed the writings of imperialists and social Darwinists were confirmed and exacerbated in the very last years of the nineteenth century, when Britain provoked a war against a small but determined group of Dutch Afrikaner farmers – called, derisively, Boers – in the Transvaal in South Africa in 1899 in order to secure its hold on the gold mines of the Rand. Confident of their success and determined to teach the Boers a lesson about the power and glory of the British empire, politicians and the public were stunned when their armies suffered a series of humiliating and embarrassing defeats in the first months of the war. By late 1900, those losses had been reversed, but the defeat of the 45,000 Afrikaner guerrilla soldiers required an additional eighteen months and 450,000 British soldiers.

In the process of recruiting those soldiers, British officials discovered that fully one-third of those who sought to enlist did not meet military standards of physical health. They were too short, suffered from heart trouble or rheumatism, had weak lungs or flat feet or bad teeth. The small-chested "New Town Type" could not stand up to the rigors of physical training and war, and even many of those who passed through the initial screening had to leave the army later when their health failed. Major General Frederick Maurice reckoned in 1903 that when both the first rejections and the subsequent drop-outs were counted, only two of every five volunteers had proved to be competent soldiers. These figures promised disaster, he warned, for "no nation was ever yet for any long time great and free when the army it put into the field no longer represented its own virility and manhood."[5] When compared to the Germans – indeed even to the Boers and the Japanese – the British "race" of men paled. Near panic about "race degeneration," "physical degeneration," and "deterioration" ensued.

The embarrassments of the British army during the Boer War and the hysteria over "race deterioration" in the following years helped to give rise to an organization designed to prepare boys for the rigors of life in a world fraught with imperial and international competition, to prepare them, even, for war. In 1908, R. Baden-Powell published *Scouting for Boys*, a handbook that described the process of training boys in the attributes and characteristics necessary to create a race of men capable of upholding Britain's place in the world. Boys, if they were to grow into the right kind of men, would have to accept and obey the orders given them by their elders or superiors; they would have to accept that violence was a part of the natural order of things and be prepared to act violently themselves, which would require them to learn to handle firearms capably; and they would have to recognize and reinforce clear rules of separate spheres for men and women. Baden-Powell's Boy Scouts were:

> *real* men in every sense of the word, and thoroughly up on scout craft, i.e., they understand living out in jungles, and they can find their way anywhere, are able to read meaning from the smallest signs and foot-tracks; they know how to look after their health when far away from any doctors, are strong and plucky, and ready to face any danger, and always keen to help each other. They are accustomed to take their lives in their hands, and to fling them down without hesitation if they can help their country by doing so.[6]

Drawn from the stereotypical images of the imperial pioneer and hunter that populated the adventure stories of writers like H. Rider Haggard, the quintessential Boy Scout countered the image of the narrow-chested, puny, flat-footed tubercular urban male that so haunted the imaginations of politicians, statesmen, military officials, scientists, and physicians. He acted in a natural world free of the contaminations of urban industrial society, according to strict rules about class and gender roles that seemed to be under assault from so many avenues in Britain. Like the white characters in Rider Haggard's *King Solomon's Mines*, *Allan Quatermain*, and *She*, he was honest, independent, and self-reliant, and among "the most generous and chivalrous of [his] race." A gentleman, he demonstrated the qualities of honor, decency, courage, physical strength, and endurance that had enabled Britain to obtain its empire in the first place. Now, if the nation was to hold on to it in the face of international rivalries and urban deterioration, it would have to build up a race of men from all classes schooled in the lessons of the frontier.

The imperial frontier, and one of its most cherished activities, hunting, provided the best means, short of actual war itself, for developing an imperial race. Baden-Powell used the example and writings of Theodore Roosevelt to promote his ideas in *Scouting for Boys*, citing Roosevelt's pioneer and hunter as "the archetype of freedom." He "possesses, in fact, few of the emasculated, milk-and-water moralities of the pseudo-philanthropist; but he does possess, to a very high degree, the stern, manly qualities that are invaluable to a nation." In hunting, the frontier man learned how to train for war. He tracked, stalked, and observed the habits of his quarry; he possessed skill in marksmanship. A man of action rather than reflection, he relied on his senses and his wits, lived off the land, endured nature's dangers, and ultimately triumphed. Free of women and of the society they inhabited, he displayed a virility that "town types" could not possibly possess, a manliness upon which the survival of Britain and the empire depended.[7]

If scouting was to train up a new breed of men ready and able to defend Britain and the empire from international rivals and indigenous threats, the Boy Scouts, like the army, needed better raw materials from which to fashion their model citizens. "Town types" might be turned into proper soldiers but they would have to be improved physically first. Major General Maurice and other military and civilian officials assigned responsibility for the deficiencies they found in the rejected recruits for the Boer War to mothers of the working classes. "Whatever the primary cause," Maurice declared, "the young man of 16 or 18 years of age is what he is because of the training through which he has passed during his infancy and childhood. ... Therefore it is to the condition, mental, moral, and physical, of the women and children that we must look if we have regard to the future of our land." The Inter-Departmental Committee on Physical Deterioration, reporting in 1904, and a number of other parliamentary committees stressed the "ignorance" and "fecklessness" of mothers as a factor in the physical decline of the population, blaming mothers for making their children sick. Maurice suggested that Britons might learn from the Germans how to raise "a virile race, either of soldiers or of citizens." The one essential ingredient, he observed, was that "the attention of the mothers of a land should be mainly devoted to the three K's – Kinder, Küche, Kirche [Children, Kitchen, Church]." Others looked to practices in Japan, which was "in no danger of race-suicide." They proposed a series of reforms that would compel mothers to learn "mothercraft" in order to improve the health and welfare of their children, and thus the health and welfare of the state.[8]

A spate of child welfare provisions followed. In 1906, an education act providing for meals for poor London schoolchildren was enacted; another in 1907 required children to undergo medical inspection. The 1907 Notification of Births Act mandated that fathers or those attending deliveries register all live births with the local authorities within thirty-six hours; midwives required training. The 1908 Children Act set up a separate system of justice for youths, made it illegal for children under fourteen to enter pubs, criminalized the "overlaying" (suffocation) of children if the adult was drunk at the time he or she went to bed, and provided punishments if a child died for lack of fireguards in the home. In keeping with the often punitive tone and substance of the infant welfare movement, much of it directed at women, the Children Act identified and penalized for the first time the neglect of children by their parents.

Contrary to liberal convictions that the individual should operate free of interference from, or compulsion by, the state, the infant welfare movement of the early twentieth century imposed on individuals – and in this case particular individuals: mothers – to address and resolve national problems of public health, domestic politics, and imperial and international conflict. The raising of children now became a national obligation on the part of women[9] rather than a moral or social duty, and if they did not perform this function adequately, the state would step in to insist that they do it better. Wholly ignoring the environmental factors working-class families faced – poverty, overcrowding, unsanitary streets, water, and sewage systems, pollution, epidemic and chronic disease – the state conferred upon women who had no control over them the responsibility, but not the resources, to improve the stock of the nation. And, operating according to a largely negative set of images of working-class women, state officials and voluntary agencies like the Charity Organisation Society turned to laws that coerced mothers into providing a certain kind and level of care, rather than legislation designed to help them by providing the necessary means. As working-class women saw it, reformers were requiring them to reallocate scarce resources from one part of the family to another. This situation demanded, given the tradition of husbands keeping a part of their pay-packet for themselves to buy tobacco and drink and giving the remainder to their wives to manage as best they could, that women themselves go without food, clothing, rest, and good health so that the new state requirements for their children could be met. And if they were not, working-class mothers faced "countless humiliations" from officious, intrusive, arrogant, and impolite middle-class district visitors: fines; jail sentences; and even loss of their children. As Anna Martin, a social worker and feminist, observed of the working-class mother at the time, the child welfare movement expected that she become "the unpaid nursemaid of the State."[10]

Middle-class men and women had accepted for some time now that the nurturance of children by their mothers constituted a significant aspect of their role and identity as women. Working-class and poor women had regarded themselves as responsible for seeing to the material survival of their family members, the key to which involved careful management of the household. Working-class and poor women certainly did not lack feeling for their children; numerous autobiographical accounts testify to the unstinting dedication of mothers in caring for their charges and of deep and intimate relationships between mothers and children. But nurturing children simply could not take priority in the vast majority of homes where insufficient resources required that women expend all their energy in keeping their children fed, clothed, and well. Their primary obligation, as they saw it throughout the nineteenth century, lay in providing material, not emotional, sustenance, and when poverty, unemployment, and lack of basic necessities kept them from doing so, they despaired, but did not see it as their fault. The outcry against "race deterioration," its assessment of blame against women, and the legislation and propaganda of the child welfare movement introduced among working-class mothers a new and profound sense of personal responsibility when their children fell ill. Without the material resources by which to improve conditions for children in the home, unable to control their births with reliable forms of birth control, lacking even the most basic amenities of plumbing, clean and running water, heat, light, and ventilation let alone able to provide nutritious and plentiful meals or proper medications, mothers nevertheless internalized the failures of capitalist, liberal society as their own, and suffered acute pangs of guilt for them.

Concerns about the "deterioration of the race" and its impact on Britain's power and place in the world, as well as pressure from a restive electorate made up of many working-class voters, finally compelled the Liberal government, which had come back into power in 1905, to abdicate long-held positions about the need of the state to stay aloof from the workings of the economy and of society, and to introduce measures that taxed the wealthy in order to provide basic (and usually inadequate) subsistence to (some of) the unemployed, the elderly, and the sick. In 1908, the chancellor of the exchequer, Herbert Henry Asquith, included a plan to provide old-age pensions in the budget. The sums prescribed were small, and limited to those who had earned a certain level of income before they turned seventy, but some one million elderly immediately benefited from them, and their provision marked an unprecedented departure from classical liberal principles. Classical liberals believed that government's proper function consisted solely in providing opportunities for the exercise of freedom and liberty; in what historians have regarded as one of the first steps on the road to creating the welfare state of the twentieth century, the government recognized that one of its major obligations was to provide some measure of material security to at least some of its citizens. In 1909, when the Welshman David Lloyd George, now chancellor of the exchequer under the prime ministership of Asquith, presented his "People's Budget" before parliament, he extended this obligation to the unemployed and the sick. He proposed to pay for these pensions and other social services designed to reduce poverty by levying a new "supertax" on the wealthy; the budget also raised death duties on the inheritance of large estates to 25 percent of their worth, placed a tax on gasoline and automobiles, and worst of all, from the perspective of élites, imposed capital gains taxes on land and minerals when they changed hands. In short, the People's Budget sought to redistribute a modest portion of the wealth of the country from the very rich to the poor.

Resistance from the Conservative Party proved to be so great that the Liberal government felt compelled to cripple the power of the Lords, where Conservatives held a majority, to scuttle legislation. By the Parliament Act of 1911 – which only passed the House of Lords after the king threatened to create hundreds of new Liberal peers, thus diluting both the Conservative majority and the prestige of nobility – Britain's ancient constitution was significantly altered. From here on, the House of Lords could only delay, rather than veto, legislation. If passed by the Commons in three successive years, the measures would become law. The Parliament Act ensured, as we shall see below, that legislation granting home rule to Ireland would be just a matter of time. Dependent upon Irish as well as Labour votes for its majority, the Liberal Party had had to promise that it would introduce a measure for home rule the very next year.

Irish politics

In Ireland, the depression that began in 1873 devastated a populace still reeling from the famine of mid-century. As prices for agricultural products dropped, so too did peasants' income, till they were no longer able to pay rent for the land they farmed. Their mostly protestant landlords took harsh steps in response to their loss of income, evicting tenants by the thousands, many of whom then became violent. In 1879, an ex-Fenian by the name of Michael Davitt formed the bitter catholic peasantry into the Land League, an organization that sought relief for farmers in the short run and the elimination of the landlord class in the long term by nationalizing the land and giving it over to the peasants. In conjunction with a newly formed Irish Party under the leadership of the aristocratic protestant Charles Parnell, whose MPs pledged themselves to obstruct the workings of parliament until that body took up the issue of home rule for Ireland, the Land League forced politicians to pay attention to the needs and desires of the Irish people.

In 1880, Gladstone introduced a measure to assist some tenants who had been evicted. The House of Commons passed the bill, but the Lords quickly turned it down. In Ireland, a new round of agrarian violence erupted, and Parnell initiated a campaign to ostracize anyone who took over a farm from which a tenant had been evicted. These boycotts – so named after its first object, Captain Boycott – proved successful in reducing the number of tenant evictions by protestant landlords who could no longer find tenants to work their land.

Gladstone's government, meanwhile, reacted to the violence with a coercion bill suspending habeas corpus and permitting police to arrest and detain Land Leaguers without cause. Parnell was arrested under its provisions on 13 October 1880 and the Land League was proscribed a week later. Faced with the choice of letting the Land League agitations cease upon the arrest of its leaders, Davitt persuaded his colleagues to turn the activities of the Land League over to women in order to keep the cause alive. Fearing "public ridicule," they balked at this "most dangerous experiment," but finding no alternative, relented. In January 1881, they asked the Ladies' Land League, led by Parnell's mother Delia, and his sisters Anna and Fanny, to take over their mass movement. In London, *The Times* gloated that "when treason is reduced to fighting behind petticoats and pinafores it is not likely to do much mischief," but Davitt countered that "no better allies than women could be found for such a task. They are, in certain emergencies, more dangerous to despotism than men. They have more courage, through having less scruples, when and where their better instincts are appealed to by a militant and just cause in a fight against a mean foe."[11] Members of the Ladies' Land League like Claire Stritch, Hannah Lynch, Harriet Byrne, Hannah Reynolds, Jenny Power, and Ellen O'Leary, to name just a smattering of the women involved, carried on the Land League's boycotts and campaigns of resistance against eviction and non-payment of rent in what came to be called the Land War; they held and addressed mass meetings throughout the country. Starting in January 1882, they began to be arrested under laws targeting prostitutes. Unlike their male counterparts, who as political prisoners were isolated from the rest of the prison population and could move about and associate with one another freely, the women, having transgressed the conventions of proper womanhood, were treated as common criminals, indeed, like prostitutes.

The arrests and imprisonment of these women compelled countless others to take their place within the Ladies' League. When in early 1882 the imprisoned male leadership instructed them to drop the no-rent initiative, the women refused, believing it impolitic to change policy mid-course. Agrarian "outrages" against protestant landlords increased, a phenomenon credited to the Ladies' Land League. Davitt congratulated the women for producing "more anarchy, more illegality, more outrages, until it began to dawn on some of the official minds that the imprisonment of the male leaders had only rendered confusion worse confounded for Dublin Castle, and made the country more ungovernable under the sway of their lady successors." Their courage, commitment, and conviction put the male leadership to shame, as an editorial in United Irishmen conceded. "We only wish the men had done [their business] as stoutly, as regularly, and as fearlessly," it lamented. "Is it easier to cow a nation of men than a handful of women? Shall it be said that, while the Ladies' Land League met persecution by extending their organisation and doubling their activity and triumphing, the National Land League to which millions of men swore allegiance melted away and vanished the moment … policemen shook their batons at it?"[12]

From prison, Charles Parnell condemned the activities of the women, not least those of his sister, Anna. Sharing the panic of government officials over the "revolutionary end and aim" the women appeared to be creating, he began to negotiate with Gladstone for his release. By the terms of the so-called "Kilmainham Treaty" – after the prison in which he was held – of 2 May 1882, Parnell pledged to bring his influence to bear to stop the agrarian "outrages" in return for the government's promise to release the Land League prisoners and substantially address the question of rents and land tenure. While presenting the treaty as a victory for the Land League, Parnell had actually given way to the government by disavowing the agitations in the Irish countryside and clandestinely offering to co-operate with Gladstone. Upon his release, he expressed to Davitt his indignation over the behavior of the women and accused them of having harmed the movement. When Davitt replied that their activities – and, by implication, not Parnell's – had brought about the end of the coercion measures and the release of prisoners, he was even more incensed, declaring that if they were not eliminated from the Land League he would retire from public life.

When, on 6 May, the lord lieutenant of Ireland, Lord Frederick Cavendish, and his undersecretary, Thomas Burke, were murdered in Phoenix Park in Dublin by catholic gunmen, Parnell despaired. The English blamed him, while Parnell attributed the assassination, at least in part, to the Ladies' Land League. He used the incident to publicly declare his disapproval of the association, and within three months brought about its dissolution. Women activists came to understand that if they were to continue to engage in political activities, they would have to do so either as subordinate to men or within their own, separate organizations.

In 1886, following four years of relative calm in parliament over the situation in Ireland, Gladstone brought forward a home rule bill, seeking to give Ireland its own legislature for consideration of most domestic Irish concerns. He had little support from his own party, and the bill failed. His efforts brought about an irreparable split in the Liberal Party that enabled the Conservatives to come to power in 1886 and stay there for the next two decades. The Liberal Unionists – so named for their desire to keep Ireland in union with Britain – joined with the Conservatives in the election of 1886 to realize a victory over the Liberal and Irish parties. For the next twenty years, Irish politics effectively disappeared from the national political scene as a sometimes belligerently imperialist Conservative Party dominated parliament.

In Ireland, the dream of independence continued to exercise the hearts and minds of thousands and thousands of people. In the absence of any viable political opportunity in Westminster, and in the aftermath of a split in the Irish Party caused by Parnell being named as a co-respondent in the divorce trial of his lover, Kitty O'Shea, nationalism took on a more exclusively cultural form in the "Gaelic Renaissance" of 1880 to 1910. Perhaps not surprisingly, given the prominent – and for many Irish men, the humiliating – part played by women in the Land War, and the continued representation of catholic Irish men as apes in much of the British press, a great deal of the nationalist work centered on building up an image of masculinity of which Irish men could be proud. In 1884, the Gaelic Athletic Association (GAA)[13] formed to promote and regulate the ancient games of hurling and Gaelic football. Under its auspices, the violent and often riotous mêlées that took place in these sports were transformed into orderly demonstrations of virtuous Irish manliness. Hurling and Gaelic football became arenas within which to articulate Irishmen's sense of themselves and of their British oppressors.

At a time when large numbers of Welsh, Scots, Australians, New Zealanders,

Indians, and South Africans began to embrace the quintessentially English sports of cricket, rugby, and soccer as a way to demonstrate their integral place within the British empire, the catholic Irish self-consciously eschewed these games for their own "native" sports in order to assert their independence of British influences. Moreover, hurling's connections with warfare enabled Irish men to display themselves as modern warriors in defiance of an imperial overlord. A good many members of the Irish Republican Brotherhood (IRB), successor organization to the Fenians, belonged to the GAA, and GAA members carried the heavy wooden clubs called hurleys at the funeral of Charles Parnell in 1891.

Irish manhood as depicted through Gaelic sports countered the various portrayals of the Irish as apelike, drunken, uncivilized barbarians, malnourished and emaciated famine victims, or effeminate and naïve children in need of guidance from a paternal England. The muscular, athletic body of the hurler or footballer, the fearlessness required to participate in the often dangerous games – these attributes dramatically set Irish men apart from British men (as well as Irish boys and Irish women), who were shown as feminized or neutered, unmanly. Those Irish catholic males who had not joined in the regimen of Gaelic games could not claim authenticity as Irish or as men, insisted GAA founder Michael Cusack in the *Celtic Times*. The "fine, strapping men" of the GAA, Cusack reported, outshone the men of Kilkenny, "pale, emaciated figures, seemingly engaged in criticizing the dress and motions of everybody moving past them. ... Another crowd of persons, who probably call themselves men, was slothfully reclining with their faces toward the sun." The GAA *Annual* spoke of "the instinctive dread of the 'Anglo-Saxon' for manly vigour," while Archbishop Croke, a patron of the GAA, contrasted the "youthful athletes ... bereft of shoes and coat, and thus prepared to play" of catholic Ireland to the "degenerate dandies ... arrayed in light attire ... and racket in hand" that characterized the élite Anglo-Irish. Cusack described true Irish men as muscular and virile beings before whom an effete "daddy-long-legs" Briton or Anglo-Irishman would have no chance in winning the ladies. In presenting the British oppressors as unmanly, emasculated degenerates and themselves as muscular, virile, and virtuous, Irish men turned on their heads the British representations of the manly imperial power dominating the effeminized colonial subject.

Questioning marriage

We have seen how liberal assumptions and liberal principles came under attack from a variety of social, economic, and political forces. Starting in the 1880s, marriage, one of liberalism's central institutions, without which it could not effectively exist in its classical form, sustained a wide-ranging assault from a vocal segment of British society.[14] Domestic ideology, upon which liberalism was based, imbued marriage and motherhood with an element of the divine. The integrity of family life and the guardianship of all the comforts and benefits to be accrued therefrom rested with the wife and mother who presided over them. Marriage and motherhood were the crowning achievements of a woman's life, her "natural destiny" and "best earthly happiness," as one women put it in 1914. Reverence and awe surrounded her position and function. She was worshipped and exalted in literature; poets conferred upon her praise of the highest order. The "angel in the house" enjoyed a degree of respect and adoration second to none.

Victorians and Edwardians viewed marriage as "the equal yoking together of the man and the woman for the performance of high and sacred duties." Marriage was the sphere in which the relations between men and women were said to be inspired by love, purity, and altruism, in marked contrast to the institution of prostitution, where greed, base sensuality, and corruption characterized male and female interaction. The deliberate refusal of a woman to marry constituted a clear sign of her intentions to defy conventional expectations of the female role. But those women who sought marriage and yet "got left on the shelf," as the saying went, realized some improvement in their situation. For most of the nineteenth century, they would have been regarded, and would have regarded themselves, as failures. By the 1890s, with the increase in respectable occupations available to women, judgment would not have been quite so harsh, and perhaps not so readily internalized.

The traditional, patriarchal marriage, characterized by inequality between spouses and the notion of the "natural" subordination of the wife, remained the accepted norm throughout the Victorian and Edwardian eras. Ignorance about sex, unreliable methods of contraception, and the ever present dangers of childbirth often meant that the intimate aspects of marriage for women could be quite unpleasant. But at least partly as a result of such reforms as the Married Women's Property Acts and the Matrimonial Causes Act of 1857, the spread of contraceptive information among the middle classes after 1876, and the feminist attack on marriage as a trade, matrimony slowly took on a new meaning, one that emphasized companionship and partnership. This trend continued with the establishment of the Royal Commission on Divorce, whose recommendations for equalization of grounds for divorce became law in 1923.

Marriage and family life produced untold happiness for vast numbers of people in Britain. But starting in the 1880s, many of the women involved in the various women's rights movements seeking to obtain property rights, education and employment opportunities, the repeal of the Contagious Diseases Acts, to raise the age of consent for girls, and win the vote embarked upon a campaign to expose the inequalities and iniquities of marriage as constituted by coverture. For them, marriage epitomized and helped to perpetuate the notion of the meek, submissive, powerless woman. It appeared to be "incompatible with freedom & with an independent career," wrote Elizabeth Garrett, one of the pioneer physicians in England, on the eve of her own marriage in 1870.

By the late 1880s, because employment and educational opportunities for women had begun to increase markedly, spinsterhood was no longer regarded as a woman's failure but could be embraced out of choice as a positive, beneficial experience. The *Englishwoman's Review* noted in 1889, "whatever may be said by narrow-minded biologists, who apparently cannot regard a woman except as a female animal, we maintain that facts reveal to us the existence of a certain number of women who, in their estimation, at least, are happier and better as spinsters than wives." The "new woman" novels about independent, free-thinking, intelligent women that surfaced in the 1890s pointedly attacked marriage in their pages, espousing a decidedly feminist point of view, and even began treating the formerly forbidden topic of sexuality.

Although at no time in the nineteenth century do we find any notion of women's sexuality that is independent of men's, variations in ideas about sexuality did arise. Social purity campaigns, the idea of the passionless woman, and repression dominated the culture until the 1880s or so, by which time the repressive ways of the Victorians probably stimulated new thinking. Starting in the late nineteenth century, in part in consequence of Josephine Butler's campaign to repeal the Contagious Diseases Acts, a whole spate of writings about sex and sexuality appeared. People like Edward Carpenter, Henry Havelock Ellis, and the "new woman" authors arose to challenge the advocates of sexual ignorance and innocence, of passionless women, commencing a contest for the hearts and minds of society between social purity and greater liberalization that lasted until the outbreak of the Great War in 1914.

By the twentieth century, sex theorists like Ellis had begun to recognize an autonomous female sexuality, though they continued to insist that it was harder to arouse than that of the male. Moreover, it remained dependent upon male initiative. "The female responds to the stimulation of the male at the right moment just as the tree responds to the stimulation of the warmest days in spring," wrote Ellis, maintaining that while the boy spontaneously develops into a man, the girl "must be kissed into a woman."

The notion of passionless women and the interdependence of constructions of male and female sexuality rendered Victorians incapable of conceiving of female sexual activity that did not involve a male partner. Male homosexuality was acknowledged and condemned in the nineteenth century; the passage of the Criminal Law Amendment Act of 1885 made any private or public sexual activity between men against the law. In 1889 and 1890, the Cleveland Street scandal erupted and was quickly suppressed when it was discovered that aristocratic men, among them royal insiders and even the heir apparent to the throne, Prince Albert Victor, were buying the sexual services of boys. In 1895, the prosecution of Oscar

Wilde under the Criminal Law Amendment Act trumpeted the existence of homosexuality among men throughout the nation, raising questions about how one might truly recognize manliness, what role the British public schools played in fashioning masculinity and promoting homosexuality, and introducing a shift in the meaning of the word "effeminate." Where up until this time effeminacy had connoted the characteristics of men who spent too much time in the company of women, who were captivated by women and in thrall to their sensualizing effects, now effeminacy referred to men who engaged in sexual activity with other men, to homosexuals.[15] A new awareness of homosexuality among men compelled a more rigid definition of masculinity if "normal" men were to be separated out from "deviant" ones.

Lesbianism was not only ignored in the nineteenth century, it was actively denied, despite the fact that romantic friendships of great intensity flourished between women. Victorians tolerated and even encouraged these passionate friendships between women, confident that they could only be innocent, pure relationships that were wholly compatible with heterosexual marriage. They did not entertain the possibility that these might contain a sexual component, for the dominant beliefs defined women as without passion.

The early reforms achieved by feminists, especially those that expanded employment and education opportunities, spurred a slight alteration in the perception of passionate friends. The fact that women could now claim an existence independent of men seems to have inspired a new apprehension. As early as 1880, Eliza Lynn Linton, a well-known anti-feminist journalist, hinted in her novel, *The Rebel of the Family*, that the "Lady President of the West Hill Society for Women's Rights," Mrs Bell Blount, engaged in deviant behavior with her followers. Blount, separated from her husband, lived with Miss Connie Taylor, whom she called her "little wife." Taylor, in turn, referred to Blount as her "husband." When Bell brought the heroine, Perdita, into the women's movement, she did so by "suddenly taking her in her arms and kissing her with strange warmth." Later, having left town, she wrote to Perdita every day letters of great "warmth of her expressions of affection," which "made Perdita's cheeks burn, she scarcely knew why; but certainly with more pain than pleasure. ... Half-attracted and half-repelled – fascinated by the woman's mental power and revolted by something too vague to name yet too real to ignore." The inference to lesbianism is meant to denigrate feminists as unsexed; indeed, all of Lynn Linton's feminist targets, whom she called "wild women," always seemed to know too much about sex. Lynn Linton's dark intimations of sexual deviance were not representative of late nineteenth-century observers, but they foreshadowed society's response in the twentieth century, when, following World War I, the existence of large numbers of single women with jobs seems to have excited the popular imagination with anxieties about widespread "perversion."

The heroines of "new woman" novelists like Sarah Grand and Mona Caird rejected at least some aspects of the feminine role defined by Victorians and found themselves in situations that demonstrated that marriage was not the haven depicted in conventional popular literature. Sarah Grand, accepting the ideal of monogamous relationships within legal marriage, focused on the institution of marriage in order to expose its hypocrisy. Her characters spoke candidly and without guile about venereal disease, prostitution, and adultery, rejecting the stereotype of feminine delicacy. Grand's Ideala, for example, read Huxley's *Elemental Physiology* in order to learn about how the human body functioned. She wished to strengthen the institution of marriage by shattering the barriers between husbands and wives, not to destroy it. Other novelists treated the theme of female sexuality more radically than did Grand; Mona Caird's Hadria, in *Daughters of Danaus*, for example, displayed an awareness about the role of sexuality in women's lives to a far greater extent than Ideala.

Freedom for women, insisted Caird, was impossible "without the marriage-relation, as at present understood, being called in question." The demand for a modified marriage, whether or not intended by all those women who claimed freedom, was inherent in the feminist message, she claimed. "The spirit of liberty among women is increasing rapidly," she argued, "and as soon as an approach to economic independence gives them the power to refuse, without harsh penalty, the terms which men have hitherto been able to dictate to them, in and out of marriage, we shall have some just right to call ourselves a free people." By the twentieth century, feminist attacks on marriage had become commonplace.

Femininst critics did not object to marriage in the abstract. Most of them believed that a good marriage offered opportunities that could not be found elsewhere. They condemned marriage in its present, corrupt state, arguing that the private sphere, where women's purity and special moral nature supposedly prevailed, had in fact been invaded and conquered by the destructive values and behavior of the public sphere, presided over by men. Society's understandings of male sexuality created tensions within the ideology of separate spheres, rendering it inherently contradictory and hypocritical.

In their writings about marriage, feminists borrowed terms and concepts utilized in discussions about the political economy of nineteenth-century Britain. Their critiques incorporated notions of "contract," "production," "labor," and "class," terms most appropriate for the public sphere of men and industrial commerce. Feminists analyzed the terms of the marriage contract, the meaning of the contract for the parties involved, the relative strength of each party in determining it, and the conditions of marriage for women as determined by the contract. The adoption of a commercial idiom to speak about the institution most exalted by Victorians helped to demonstrate that the private sphere of women – the realm where generosity, compassion, kindness and decency were to prevail –

had been tainted by the intrusion of the public, male sphere, symbolized for Britons by greed, competition, exploitation, and lust. By using this idiom, feminists sought to show that the notion of a clear separation between public and private was a sham, and to demonstrate instead the public nature of all of domestic life, even the most intimate aspects of the marital bond. Feminists attacked male sexuality and asserted their differences from men in the areas of morals and values in hopes of eliminating the notion of separate spheres and extending the qualities associated with women to society at large.

Challenging the prevalent ideas about marriage as "connubial bliss," feminists posited that marriage resembled nothing more closely than a commercial contract, in which women exchanged themselves – their legal rights, their property, their bodies, and the fruits of their labor – for a wage paid in the form of material subsistence. Barred by law and custom from entering trades and professions by which they could support themselves, and restricted in the possession of property, women had only one means of livelihood, that of marriage. Those who controlled production, declared Cicely Hamilton in her 1909 *Marriage as a Trade*, demanded of woman:

> that she should enkindle and satisfy the desire of the male, who would thereupon admit her to such share of the property he possessed or earned as should seem good to him. In other words, she exchanged, by the ordinary process of barter, possession of her person for the means of subsistence.

This state of affairs, Hamilton concluded, "justifies us in regarding marriage as essentially (from the woman's point of view) a commercial or trade undertaking." Sanctification of marriage by the church, custom, and public opinion obscured the motives of women who sought marriage; feminists insisted that the underpinning of marriage was material. Woman "frequently obtains a husband only in order to support life," Hamilton claimed. "The housekeeping trade is the only one open to us – so we enter the housekeeping trade in order to live. That is not always the same as entering the housekeeping trade in order to love."

Marriage, finally, was only a legal form of prostitution, feminists and even avowedly anti-feminists argued. "A woman who has sold herself, even for a ring and a new home," advised Lyndall, Olive Schreiner's heroine in *The Story of an African Farm*, "need hold her skirt aside for no creature in the street. They both earn their bread in one way." Eliza Lynn Linton, the anti-feminist journalist who railed against "new women" in a series of articles about "the wild women," spoke out against marriage in its present form in 1888, noting that "in the street it goes by an ugly name; but society and the Church call it marriage."

Having only one profession open to her, and limited in the possibility of making the best deal for herself, the respectable woman found herself a seller in a buyer's market, feminists argued. The laws of supply and demand favored the buyer in the determination of the terms of the contract. Although, in affixing his seal to the contract, a man pledged to a woman, "with this ring, I thee wed, with my body, I thee worship, and with all my worldly goods I thee endow," the terms of marriage, critics pointed out, bore inequitably upon the respective parties to it. Under English law, wives became the property of their husbands, ceding to them their rights to own property and to earn money (until the passage of the Married Women's Property Acts of 1870 and 1882); apart from a limited custody over infants, mothers had no rights to their children; husbands could sue their wives for restitution of conjugal rights and have them imprisoned if they refused sexual intercourse; they might rape their wives with impunity under the law; and they were free to indulge in extramarital sex without fear of a divorce action against them. Such a breach on the part of women constituted grounds for invalidating the contract. Feminists argued that this one-sidedness made marriage for women akin to "a state of slavery." Within it, Caird noted acidly, "father and mother are to share pleasantly between them the rights and duties of parenthood – the father having the rights, the mother the duties."

Asserting their rights to equality in marriage, feminists demanded for women the possibility of bargaining freely and fairly with men. This necessitated economic independence for women – the ability to support themselves before marriage without loss of status or respectability, making marriage an option rather than an imperative; and the right to retain property and earning they brought to and accumulated during marriage. Feminists demanded a single standard of divorce, but most sought divorce reform that would raise the level of men's moral standards rather than one that would make divorce easier to obtain. Divorce reform, custody rights to children, and an end to laws that made wife-beating and rape legal – these were fundamental demands for women who would ameliorate the condition of slavery within marriage. Equal rights in marriage would help raise the institution to a level approaching that touted by Victorian ideologists; at least it would be a step toward a "thought-out rational system of sex relationships," rather than "a lineal descendant of barbarian usages, cruel and absurd," as Caird put it. "Is it conceivable," she asked, "that when there are, in good sooth, really two to the marriage bargain, one of the parties to it will consent to fetter herself by bonds which the other repudiates?"

The marriage contract, buttressed by the laws of Britain, gave husbands complete possession of their wives' bodies. Feminists charged that the rights of husbands to force sexual intercourse and compulsory childbearing on their wives established a condition of "sex-slavery," as *Common Cause*, the official newspaper of the National Union of Women's Suffrage Societies described it in 1910. For many, this issue stood at the center of the feminist movement. "Foremost of all the wrongs from which women suffer," declared Elizabeth Wolstenholme Elmy in

1888, "and in itself creative of many of them, is the inequality and injustice of their position in the marriage relation, and the legal denial to wives of that personal freedom, which is the most sacred right of humanity." Laws that taught men to regard women as their property, she asserted, permitted and encouraged "outrages upon women, especially upon wives." Marion Leslie wrote to the *Women's Penny Paper* in 1890 that "so long as in the eyes of the law a woman is the property of her husband, and can be lawfully chastised by him, men will be brutal and overbearing to women, despite the most energetically conducted palliative schemes."

Couched in rather vague terms, the issue that so inflamed the passions of feminists was marital rape. A husband's right to sexual intercourse with his wife was absolute, superseding even the right of a woman to protect herself and/or her unborn children from disease. In the ruling handed down in *Regina v. Clarence* in 1888, the judge established the precedent that a husband could not be found guilty of raping his wife even if she had refused intercourse because he had venereal disease. Elmy denounced "this infamy in the name of the wife, the mother, the child, the race, and the higher humanity to which we aspire." She wrote to her friend Harriet McIlquham in 1897 that "the making criminal in a husband the communication of foul disease to his wife" and the overturning of *Regina v. Clarence* were "two of the first things at which we shall have to work when once we win the Suffrage, and they will carry us very far indeed."

While Victorian theorists praised the moral, spiritual qualities of women, feminists emphasized that patriarchal society valued women only for their capacity to satisfy male sexual needs and to reproduce the race. The male design for women, Caird contended, no matter how well camouflaged and sanctified by marriage, remained:

> that a woman's main duty and privilege was to bear children without limit; that death and suffering were not to be considered for a moment, in the performance of this duty; that for this end she had been created, and for this end ... she must live and die.

Hamilton proclaimed that "women have been trained to be unintelligent breeding-machines until they have become unintelligent breeding-machines." So pervasively had the private sphere of women been taken over by the values of the public sphere of men that the terms "woman" and "breeding-machine" had become indistinguishable, she lamented. Constraints on a woman's ability to secure a livelihood outside marriage, a legal system that gave husbands absolute control over their wives' bodies, and an ideology that insisted upon the primacy of the sexual functions of women engendered a situation in which motherhood reflected not "the mighty creative power which more than any other human faculty seems to bring womanhood nearer the Divine," but compulsory, forced labor. Hamilton argued that childbearing was "an involuntary consequence of a compulsory trade." Children "are born of women who are not free," Caird declared, "not free even to refuse to bear them."

The feminist critique of marriage necessarily involved a critique of masculinity. Male sexuality, exemplified in microcosm by the institution of marriage, was, women like Josephine Butler, Elizabeth Wolstenholme Elmy, and Frances Swiney believed, destructive both to women and ultimately to the whole of humanity. "One of the most revolting spectacles still extant in our 'civilization,'" lamented Elmy in 1896, was "that of a husband wearing out (i.e., literally killing) his wife with child-births … with sheer licentiousness." Swiney decried the fact that "one fortnight after confinement some men will insist on resuming sexual relations with their wives." Such practices led her to conclude that "men have sought in woman only a body. They have possessed that body. They have made it the refuse-heap of sexual pathology."

The experiences of women in marriage, where, in the words of Elmy, they were subject to "the excess of sexual proclivity and indulgence general on the part of man," led feminists to demand the right to control their bodies and their fertility. Yet artificial means of birth control were anathema to feminists, who believed that they would simply allow men easier and more frequent access to their wives by eliminating the fear of pregnancy. When Charles Bradlaugh and Annie Besant were prosecuted in 1877 for disseminating information about contraception, feminists remained conspicuously silent. In fact, when called upon to testify for the defendants, Millicent Fawcett refused and warned that "if we were called as witnesses, we could effectively damage your case." Feminists opposed contraception because they feared it would "give men greater sexual license." Contraceptive knowledge did not become an explicit feminist demand until after the turn of the century, and even then it only rarely found its way into print until after the First World War. Feminists certainly favored "voluntary moth-erhood" – the right to abstain from sexual intercourse. For some, in fact, the right to refuse intercourse stood at the core of their movement. Lady Florence Dixie announced in the *Woman's Herald* in 1891 that the feminist "Plan of campaign" for women prominently included "rights over their own person and the control of the birth of children." Elmy insisted that "the functions of wifehood and motherhood must remain solely and entirely within the wife's own option." But abstinence from sexual intercourse was possible only if men agreed to it, something feminists doubted the willingness of most husbands to do. Their critique of masculinity instilled in them the conviction that only a massive transformation in the laws, customs, mores, and traditions of Britain could produce a society in which women could exercise the same freedom and liberty accorded to men. That transforma-tion, they insisted, required that women arm themselves with the vote.

NOTES

1 See Joanna Bourke, *Husbandry to Housewifery: Women, Economic Change, and Housework in Ireland, 1890–1914* (Oxford, 1993).
2 The classic account of this phenomenon will be found in Anna Davin, "Imperialism and motherhood," in Frederick Cooper and Ann Laura Stoler, eds, *Tensions of Empire: Colonial Cultures in a Bourgeois World* (Berkeley, 1997).
3 Quoted in Richard A. Soloway, *Demography and Degeneration: Eugenics and the Declining Birth Rate in Twentieth-Century Britain* (Chapel Hill, NC, 1990), p. 39; and Bernard Porter, *The Lion's Share: A Short History of British Imperialism, 1850–1983* (London, 1975), p. 130.
4 Quoted in Porter, *The Lion's Share*, p. 129.
5 Quoted in Davin, "Imperialism and motherhood," pp. 93–4.
6 Quoted in John M. MacKenzie, "The imperial pioneer and hunter and the British masculine stereotype in late Victorian and Edwardian times," in J.A. Mangan and James Walvin, eds, *Manliness and Morality: Middle-Class Masculinity in Britain and America, 1800–1940* (New York, 1987), p. 177.
7 See MacKenzie, "The imperial pioneer," pp, 177, 178.
8 Quoted in Davin, "Imperialism and motherhood," p. 94.
9 This account is based on Ellen Ross, *Love and Toil: Motherhood in Outcast London, 1870–1918* (New York, 1993).
10 Quoted in Ross, *Love and Toil*, p. 197.
11 Quoted in Margaret Ward, *Unmanageable Revolutionaries: Women and Irish Nationalism* (London, 1995), p. 13.
12 Quoted in Ward, *Unmanageable Revolutionaries*, pp. 28–9, 30.
13 This discussion draws from Patrick F. McDevitt, "Muscular Catholicism: Nationalism, masculinity and Gaelic team sports, 1884–1916," *Gender and History* 9(2), 1997: 262–84.
14 This discussion derives from Susan Kingsley Kent, *Sex and Suffrage in Britain, 1860–1914* (Princeton, 1987), ch. 3.
15 See Ed Cohen, *Talk on the Wilde Side: Toward a Genealogy of a Discourse on Male Sexualities* (New York, 1993), p. 136; and Angela V. John and Claire Eustance, eds, *The Men's Share? Masculinities, Male Support and Women's Suffrage in Britain, 1890–1920* (London, 1997), p. 7.

SOURCES

Gregory Anderson, ed., *The White-Blouse Revolution: Female Office Workers since 1870*. Manchester, 1988.

Joanna Bourke, *Husbandry to Housewifery: Women, Economic Change, and Housework in Ireland, 1890–1914*. Oxford, 1993.

Ed Cohen, *Talk on the Wilde Side: Toward a Genealogy of a Discourse on Male Sexualities*. New York, 1993.

Anna Davin, "Imperialism and motherhood," in Frederick Cooper and Ann Laura Stoler, eds, *Tensions of Empire: Colonial Cultures in a Bourgeois World*. Berkeley, 1997.

Richard Dellamora, *Masculine Desire: The Sexual Politics of Victorian Aestheticism*. Chapel Hill, 1990.

R.F. Foster, *Paddy and Mr. Punch: Connections in Irish and English History*. London, 1993.

Jose Harris, *Private Lives, Public Spirit: Britain, 1870–1914*. London, 1993.

Lee Holcombe, *Victorian Ladies at Work: Middle-Class Working Women in England and Wales, 1850–1914*. Devon, 1973.

Angela V. John and Claire Eustance, eds, *The Men's Share? Masculinities, Male Support and Women's Suffrage in Britain, 1890–1920*. London, 1997.

Susan Kingsley Kent, *Sex and Suffrage in Britain, 1860–1914*. Princeton, 1987.

Jane Lewis, *Women in England, 1870–1950: Sexual Divisions and Social Change*. Bloomington, IN, 1984.

Anne McClintock, *Imperial Leather: Race, Gender and Sexuality in the Colonial Contest*. New York, 1995.

Kathleen E. McCrone, *Playing the Game: Sport and the Physical Emancipation of English Women, 1870–1914*. Lexington, KY, 1988.

Patrick F. McDevitt, "Muscular Catholicism: Nationalism, masculinity and Gaelic team sports, 1884–1916," *Gender and History* 9(2), 1997: 262–84.

John M. MacKenzie, "The imperial pioneer and hunter and the British masculine stereotype in late Victorian and Edwardian times," in J.A. Mangan and James Walvin, eds, *Manliness and Morality: Middle-Class Masculinity in Britain and America, 1800–1940*. New York, 1987.

Henry Pelling, *Modern Britain, 1885–1955*. New York, 1966.

Bernard Porter, *The Lion's Share: A Short History of British Imperialism, 1850–1983*. London, 1975.

Ellen Ross, *Love and Toil: Motherhood in Outcast London, 1870–1918*. New York, 1993.

Richard A. Soloway, *Demography and Degeneration: Eugenics and the Declining Birth Rate in Twentieth-Century Britain*. Chapel Hill, NC, 1990.

Margaret Ward, *Unmanageable Revolutionaries: Women and Irish Nationalism*. London, 1995.

Part IV

The twentieth century

Crises of conflict, crises of gender

GENERAL INTRODUCTION

The twentieth century witnessed a remarkable increase in and intensity of global conflicts. The Great War, the great depression, the Second World War, the cold war and the nuclear arms race, and nationalist struggles to throw off European colonization in Asia, Africa, the Middle East, and the Caribbean produced crises throughout the world. As we have seen so frequently in the past, contemporaries often turned to languages of gender and sexuality to articulate anxieties and fears for which they could find no other adequate expression. The Great War, for instance, found its most pervasive and vivid representations in metaphors of sex and gender, as tales of German atrocities committed against Belgian women circulated throughout the country and provided the justification for Britain's war effort. In the postwar period, sexual conflict and polarization between the sexes provided one of the few adequate means by which the political, economic, and social upheaval occasioned by the Great War could be represented.

The broken world to which belligerents returned at the end of 1918 offered little solace to societies devastated by four years of unprecedented loss and destruction. Across Europe, soldiers and civilians, men and women, élites and commoners, victors and vanquished alike, faced disorder in every aspect of their lives. The upheavals produced by the First World War provoked responses designed to recreate the social, political, and economic order that had prevailed prior to August of 1914. In recasting bourgeois Europe along corporatist economic and political lines, conservative forces sought to re-establish stability and to reassert their status in a world that looked and felt dramatically different from that of the prewar period. In cultural terms, too, attempts to return to what was perceived to be a quieter, happier, more ordered time, were prodigious. Nowhere is this more evident than in the realm of gender identity and relations between men and women. Political and economic restructuring found their counterpart – indeed, their necessary corollary – in the reconstruction of gender after the Great War.

Conservative and reactionary images of masculinity and femininity emerged as British society sought in the establishment of harmonious marital relationships a resolution to the anxieties and political turmoil caused by the Great War. Britons sought a return to the "traditional" order of the prewar world, an order based on natural biological categories of which imagined sexual differences were a familiar and readily available expression.

Violence, war, and conflict could only be avoided, it appeared to British society after 1918, by redrawing separate spheres for men and women, not now necessarily marked as public and private by laws and institutional practices that had barred women from public life in the past. A psychologized version of separate spheres, one consequence of depicting war in the imagery of sexual violence, and of postwar sexological and psychoanalytic discourses that represented sexual relations in the imagery of war, proved to be just as effective in limiting women's scope and agency as barriers between public and private spheres had been in the past.

The rhetoric of separate spheres proved dangerously effective when war came again in 1939. The Second World War obliterated the distinctions between men and women, warrior and wife, but the government had to resort to decidedly illiberal measures in order to mobilize men and women for total war, so powerful had the domestic ideology been in persuading women that their place was in the home. Just as men were conscripted into the armed forces, so too were women conscripted into various forms of war work. As in the Great War, women undertook jobs previously performed by men, but unlike the First World War, when peace came, they did not leave their jobs and return home in anything like the same numbers they had earlier. Instead, working wives and mothers became a recognized and permanent element of the labor force.

The enormous sacrifices made by the British public during the Second World War, along with a largely mythic belief that unity had been forged in the fighting of it, produced a consensus that social justice must prevail after the war. Commitment to a full employment economy and the creation of the welfare state followed, which, in paying out benefits, utilized the now outmoded family model of the male bread-winner and the stay-at-home mother. Full employment and a postwar boom in the economy in the 1950s produced a sense of affluence throughout the country, though large pockets of poverty and substandard conditions persisted, giving rise in some intellectual quarters to dissatisfaction with society. Immigration from "new commonwealth" countries that had recently won their freedom introduced new sources of anxiety for white Britons, much of which was articulated through images of sexual excess and miscegenation.

Discontent with social and economic conditions, repressive moral legislation, racial and gender inequalities, and the exercise of power by established politicians reached serious proportions in the 1960s and early 1970s, especially among youth. Student protests, sexual revolution, black power demonstrations, gay rights initiatives, and the women's liberation movement – all taking place within a context of international decline, rising unemployment, and a stagnating economy – helped to create in the minds of many Britons the conviction that the "permissive" society had wreaked havoc with traditional British values and had produced a society of chaos and anarchy. Margaret Thatcher's promise to return Britain to the values of the Victorian period resonated with a majority of voters in 1979, and ushered in a regime committed to *laissez-faire*, capitalism, law and order, élitism, "traditional" morality, and a notion of the family as an exclusively heterosexual institution in which fathers worked outside the home to support the women and children who remained within it. But the needs of the economic system and the success of two waves of feminism in transforming the expectations and assumptions about femininity ensured that a return to the practices of the nineteenth century would not be possible.

Chapter 11

Crises of masculinity
Sex and war, 1908–18

The challenges to liberalism and to the gender order that upheld it became increasingly pronounced in the years after 1908. Labour disputes became harder to settle and violence frequently accompanied workers' efforts to obtain wages with which they could support their families. The Parliament Act of 1911 ensured that the House of Lords could not block forever the attempts by Liberals to gain home rule for Ireland. When it became clear in 1912 that home rule would indeed prevail, northern Irish protestants armed themselves to oppose the British government. They received support and encouragement from Conservative politicians and members of the military high command in a series of measures that came terribly close to treason. Above all, a provocative mass movement in support of women's suffrage vigorously challenged the ideology of separate spheres and the understandings of masculinity and femininity and of male and female sexuality that underpinned liberal practice.

By the end of July 1914, striking workers, Irish rebels, Tory die-hards, and militant suffragists had brought liberal England to its knees. Virtually every principle and assumption of classical liberal thought had been called into question. Free trade, *laissez-faire*, constitutionalism and the rule of law, and a restricted male franchise – all came under fire from various groups ranging from union officials, Conservative and Unionist politicians, Irish protestants and Irish catholics, and feminists from every quarter of the kingdom. The domestic ideology of separate spheres for men and women, and the notions of masculinity and femininity and of male and female sexuality that informed it, had been vigorously, publicly, and spectacularly contested, and masculinity discredited. When the war broke out in August 1914, it came as a relief to Britons, who saw in it the opportunity to re-establish the social, economic, political, imperial, and gender orders of Britain. The civil war, the class war, and the sex war of the spring and summer of 1914, as contemporaries regarded them, would be subsumed within, and extinguished by, the far more seemly war of European nations. What Britons could not know, in the first weeks before trench lines were established and a vicious war of attrition set in, was that the war would change every aspect of their lives, and forever.

Resurrecting a "manly" Ireland

Irish politics returned to Westminster when the Liberal Party gained power in 1905. In 1912, acting on their bargain with the Irish Party to introduce home rule in return for the party's support for the 1911 Parliament Act, the Liberals enacted a bill that would create an Irish parliament in Dublin through which legislation affecting local Irish concerns could be created. Although rejected by the Lords, the act, under the new constitutional terms of the Parliament Act of 1911, could not be delayed beyond 1914; home rule would come to Ireland, it was clear. Immediately, the seven northern provinces of Ulster announced their intention to oppose home rule by all means, and under the leadership of Sir Edward Carson – and with the explicit support of Conservative leader Andrew Bonar Law – built up a mass movement of resistance. In 1913, Ulstermen began to arm themselves and formed the Ulster Volunteer Force, promising to defend union with the United Kingdom through violence if necessary. In April they obtained 24,000 guns from Germany.

The south of Ireland responded on 25 November 1913 with the establishment of the Irish Volunteers at a meeting in Dublin. Because the home rule provisions did not include votes for Irish women as well as Irish men in the proposed Irish parliament, Irish feminists insisted upon their inclusion. They received little support for their demands. For the meeting, reported the *National Student* some days later, "addressed itself to the manhood of Ireland." Operating behind the scenes as much as possible, the Irish Republican Brotherhood formed a significant core of the Irish Volunteers, and used the specter of the armed protestant north to persuade the bulk of Irish people that independence would come not from parliamentary maneuvering but from armed conflict. The IRB welcomed the provocation from the north, for through armed resistance, they declared, the Irish Volunteers would make an "honest and manly stand." Through membership in the Volunteers, Irish males could "realise themselves as citizens and as men," and all those who were "manly, liberty loving and patriotic" would follow their example and join themselves. In this scenario, in which Irish men were to find and assert their masculinity through armed conflict against both the protestant Irish and the British, it was difficult, within the parameters of separate sphere ideology, to find a place for women. The Volunteer manifesto noted that "there will also be work for women to do," but it did not go any further to define that work or the rights that women would gain within an independent Ireland.[1]

In 1914, nationalist women joined together to form the Irishwomen's Council (Cumann na mBan), a kind of auxiliary organization aimed at supporting the men's armed struggle. Women themselves were not, except in the "last extremity," to partake in the men's battle; they were not even expected to discuss the politics of it. Rather, as Agnes O'Farrelly described their roles in the language of domesticity, they would "advance the cause of Irish liberty" by assisting in arming the men:

> Each rifle we put in their hands will represent to us a bolt fastened behind the door of some Irish home to keep out the hostile stranger. Each cartridge will be a watchdog to fight for the sanctity of the hearth.

The Irishwomen's Franchise League, led by Hannah Sheehy Skeffington, though it opposed violence in the getting of independence, protested against the exclusion of women from the activities of the Irish Volunteers and the deference of the Cumann na mBan to its all-male policies.[2]

In March of 1914, as home rule for Ireland was just about to be passed into law, the government ordered troops in Ireland to march north to cut off an anticipated rising by the Ulster Volunteers. In what became known as the Mutiny at the Curragh, a significant number of army officers resigned so as to avoid carrying out their orders. They did so at the secret urging of Bonar Law and of Sir Henry Wilson, chief of military operations at the War Office. This near treasonous act took place at a time when the situation in Europe was approaching crisis, and it may have helped to persuade the German General Staff that Britain could be ignored as they went about making plans to conquer Europe.

By the end of July 1914, Ireland — and England, too, if the actions of Carson, Bonar Law, and the highest echelons of the military command are taken into account — teetered on the precipice of civil war. The Great War came just in time to prevent it, dousing the flames of insurrection with a bracing blast of cold water. Tens of thousands of Irishmen from north and south volunteered their services in support of Britain's fight, and many thousands gave their lives in the effort. But a good number of catholic Irish refused to enlist, arguing that Britain's war had nothing to do with Ireland. On the contrary, members of the Irish Republican Brotherhood insisted to their compatriots, Britain's war against Germany offered the Irish an opportunity that they must not let pass.

Under the leadership of Patrick Pearse and James Connolly, and with the support of the Cumann na mBan, Irish republicans rebelled against the British in what is known as the Easter Rising of 1916. Roger Casement, a former British diplomat, had arranged with German officials to land arms and ammunition in support of the Irish rebels, but the ship carrying the weapons had been caught by the British navy and was scuttled by its captain; Casement, on board a German submarine trying to put him off at Tralee Bay, was captured. The rising, without sufficient arms for its participants, and, because of communications difficulties, short the five to ten thousand men expected to respond to the call to arms, sputtered out after a week, but not before the rebels captured a number of significant positions in Dublin. The Irish Citizen Army, headed by Michael Mallin and the Countess Constance Markiewicz, for example, took St Stephen's Green, and then retreated under heavy fire to the College of Surgeons, where they held out for six days, with little food or fire power. Heavy fighting took place throughout the city, with casualties amounting to 450 dead and 2,500 wounded, the vast majority of them civilians. The republican cause suffered mightily in the eyes of most Irish catholics, who declaimed against the violence and the great losses of life.

But Pearse and Connolly had never expected to defeat the British army. Their goals had been more modest: to ignite, by means of a blood sacrifice on the part of Irish manhood, nationalist feeling throughout the country; to redeem through an assertion of heroic manliness the old hag that was Ireland, in the imagery of William Butler Yeats's *Cathleen ni Houlihan* (1902), and turn her back into a beautiful young queen by shedding their blood for her. "If any one would give me help he must give himself," the old woman tells her would-be rescuers in Yeats's play, "he must give me all." Pearse's own writings had continued the themes of degradation and redemption through a blood sacrifice of its men on behalf of a feminized Ireland. He had raged against the anglicanization of Irish children by the British educational system, casting his charges in the language of sexual violence. The British, he insisted, "have planned and established an education system which more wickedly does violence to the elementary human rights of Irish children than would an edict for the general castration of Irish males. ... It has made of some Irishmen not slaves merely, but very eunuchs, with the indifference and cruelty of eunuchs; kinless beings, who serve for pay a master that they neither love nor hate." Until Irish men asserted their manliness, the enslavement of the country to England would continue. Manliness would have to be instilled in them through the lessons of Ireland's past, through the sagas of the noble and heroic Cuchulain, for example, who had defended Ireland against its numerous enemies in ancient times and had met his death in her defense. "What Ireland wants beyond all other modern countries," Pearse declared:

> is a new birth of the heroic spirit. ... A new education system in Ireland has to do more than restore a national culture. It has to restore manhood to a race that has been deprived of it. Along with its inspiration it must, therefore, bring a certain hardening. It must lead Ireland back to her sagas.

For Pearse, the Easter Rising would constitute a call to the men of Ireland to gird their loins, throw off their English shackles, and make their hag-like Ireland young and beautiful again by giving her their lives. Just as Cuchulain's death had been avenged by those who followed him, so too would the rebels' martyrdom spur revenge against the English. "We die that the Irish nation may live," declared one of Pearse's lieutenants the night before he was executed by the British for his part in the rebellion. "Our blood will rebaptise and reinvigorate the land."[3]

It did no such thing, at least not on account of its own shedding. Severe English reprisals against the rebels, however, followed by legislation conscripting Irish men into the British army in 1918, did serve to kindle a deep-seated and broad-based revolutionary spirit among the majority of the catholic Irish where it had not existed before. Beginning in 1917, Sinn Fein, the political arm of the revolutionary forces, began to defeat the constitutionally oriented Irish Party in a series of local elections. In December 1918, it won a large number, though not a majority, of votes in the national election. The Sinn Fein MPs refused to take their seats at Westminster and instead, in January 1919, established themselves as the parliament for an Irish Republic, setting off a guerrilla war for independence from Britain that would last for the next three years.

The suffrage campaign: "votes for women, chastity for men"[4]

In 1905, with the advent of militancy arising out of the Women's Social and Political Union (WSPU), the whole of the feminist movement centered around suffrage as the means by which women could free themselves from servile bondage to men. As a symbol of civic and political personality, the vote would be an effective agent in eliminating the notion of women as "the Sex." As an instrument of power, feminists believed – as did their adversaries – it would transform the elevating "influence" of women into a tool with which to create a greater and truer morality among men by eliminating the distinctions between public and private spheres. They meant to use it to build a sexual culture in Britain that would reflect the needs, desires, and interests of women.

With the arrival of the WSPU, under the leadership of Emmeline and Christabel Pankhurst, the suffrage campaign took on new life and meaning. The militant tactics of the WSPU electrified the country and galvanized the whole of the suffrage movement in England, Scotland, Ireland, and Wales. From 1897, when all suffrage societies were federated in the National Union of Women Suffrage Societies (NUWSS), to 1903, when the WSPU formed, the NUWSS encompassed only sixteen societies. By 1909, fifty-four additional societies had come into being and joined the NUWSS. In 1911, 305 societies made up the constitutional group; that number swelled to 400 by 1913.

In marked contrast to the strategies pursued by the NUWSS, the WSPU followed a policy of spectacular protests. "Deeds not Words" was its motto. Militancy began in Manchester in October 1905 when Christabel Pankhurst and

Annie Kenney demanded of Sir Edward Grey his stand on women's suffrage. They refused to yield the floor when he did not respond. Their defiance resulted in their being bodily – and brutally, by some accounts – thrown out of the Free Trade Hall by Liberal stewards. Outside, wishing to commit an assault, Pankhurst spat at a policeman and ended up in jail. Their treatment at the hands of men spurred many women to action.

Until the summer of 1909 militant action was nonviolent; suffragists heckled cabinet ministers and obstructed political meetings, and they marched on parliament to meet with MPs who refused to see them. When the police learned to anticipate and try to cut short militant deputations to parliament, the suffragettes responded with surprises and clever disguises to circumvent them. "Now one would appear as a messenger boy," Ray Strachey, a prominent member of the NUWSS, recounted:

> now another as a waitress. … They sprang out of organ lofts, they peered through roof windows, and leapt out of innocent-looking furniture vans; they materialised on station platforms, they harangued the terrace of the House from the river, and wherever they were least expected there they were.

Men often responded to nonviolent militant tactics with fury. An unprecedented display of brutality occurred on 18 November 1910, a day ever after referred to in the annals of suffrage history as "Black Friday." Three hundred suffragists marching on Parliament Square were confronted by uniformed and plain-clothed police, whose order was to prevent the women from reaching the Houses of Parliament. For six hours, the women suffered "violent and indecent treatment" at the hands of police and male bystanders, as one account described the scene. Ada Wright was "knocked down a dozen times in succession." Police "struck the women with fists and knees, knocked them down, some even kicked them, then dragged them up, carried them a few paces and flung them into the crowd of sightseers." Victims and bystanders testified to "deliberate acts of cruelty, such as twisting and wrenching of arms, wrists, and thumbs; gripping the throat and forcing back the head; pinching the arms; striking the face with fists, sticks, helmets; throwing women down and kicking them; rubbing a woman's face against the railings; pinching the breasts; squeezing the ribs." Cecilia Haig died in December 1911 from injuries sustained that day. The incidents in 1912 at Llanystmdwy, in Wales, where suffragists heckled David Lloyd George, rivaled the ferocity of Black Friday. According to Sylvia Pankhurst, "men and women were beaten, kicked and stripped almost naked. The hair of women was torn out in handfuls."

Emmeline and Christabel Pankhurst may well have welcomed, if they did not court, these displays of sexual violence against women, for they served as powerful recruiting agents for the suffrage cause. Militants and nonmilitants alike expressed appreciation that the "brute" sexuality in men had finally been exposed. Lucy Re-Bartlett, an ardent enthusiast of militancy, stated that only the militants were doing anything to eradicate from civilization the "brute consciousness" and "sexual excess" of men. Their activities had "brought to the surface the 'brute' in many men," thereby removing "the fetters of sentimentality and illusion from many thousands of women," she claimed.

In the summer of 1909, militants took up stone-throwing. In a symbolic protest against the politicians who refused to meet their demands, they broke countless government windows. Stone-throwing had a more pragmatic effect as well – it cut short the struggles with the police and reduced the amount of suffering suffragists experienced before being arrested. That same summer, militant suffragists began to stage a hunger strike in prison. They demanded that their sentences be reduced to reflect more accurately the severity of their crimes – heckling, demonstrating, and stone-throwing – and that the courts regard them as political prisoners rather than common criminals. Instead, the authorities responded with forced feeding, whereby a tube was inserted through the prisoner's nostril down into the stomach, and liquid nourishment poured down it. The violence of forced feeding led to a great outcry against the government's actions from sympathizers and opponents of women's suffrage alike. Like the displays of male brutality during suffrage demonstrations, it aided the suffrage societies in their recruitment efforts.

The WSPU succeeded in focusing enormous publicity on the suffrage issue, but the parliamentary response to women's demands for the vote remained cool. Suffragists enjoyed a great deal of support in parliament, but H.H. Asquith, the prime minister, refused to back a women's suffrage measure. After the election of 1910, however, it appeared that a women's suffrage bill might pass. A Conciliation Committee, composed of members from all parties, formed to draft a bill that would enjoy the support of all shades of political opinion. In order to give the Conciliation Bill a chance, the WSPU called a truce in militancy. The bill passed its second reading in July 1910, but before it could go further, Asquith, with the complicity of Lloyd George, torpedoed the bill.

The militants immediately abandoned their truce. On 18 November 1910, suffragettes marched from Caxton Hall to parliament, where they were attacked and sexually molested by police and male bystanders in the above-mentioned incident known as "Black Friday." The subsequent public outrage helped revive the Conciliation Bill in 1911, upon which militants again called a truce in their activities. When the government appeared to throw over the bill for a second time by introducing a measure for manhood suffrage without an amendment including women, the WSPU erupted in acts of deliberate law-breaking. On 1 March, Emmeline Pankhurst and two other women broke the windows of the prime minister's residence at 10 Downing Street, while, in a simultaneous attack, over

200 other women shattered windows all over London. Police arrested 217 women. Mrs Pankhurst was arrested and charged with inciting to riot. Court officials also issued a warrant for Christabel Pankhurst's arrest, but she evaded their grasp by fleeing to Paris. Mrs Pankhurst received a sentence of nine months in the criminal division and immediately embarked on a hunger strike. She became so ill that officials released her from prison shortly thereafter.

In January 1913, Asquith's government introduced its manhood suffrage bill, having earlier promised suffragists that it would be open to amendment. When it reached the floor of the House of Commons, the government announced that it would not permit an amendment for women's suffrage. Crying betrayal, the WSPU embarked upon another campaign of destruction. Christabel Pankhurst designed a strategy that included cutting telegraph wires, pouring acid into postal boxes to destroy letters, slashing pictures in public art galleries, arson, and even the bombing of churches. In February 1913, someone attempted to burn down Lloyd George's country house. On 31 May 1913, Derby Day, the militant suffragists gained their first true martyr to the cause. In the midst of the race, Emily Wilding Davison jumped from the spectators' box, threw herself in front of the king's horse, and was trampled to death. It is impossible to know how far the militants might have gone in their efforts to achieve votes for women had not the Great War intervened to bring their activities to a sudden and decisive halt.

Such militant behavior on the part of respectable women shocked society, seemed to confirm that the degeneracy of the race was not restricted to the working classes and the poor, and provoked numerous attempts at explanation. Sir Almroth Wright, a physician, believed that the "severe sexual restrictions" faced by surplus women in Britain produced certain "physiological conditions" that led women to act militantly. Denied husbands, "sexually embittered" and "incomplete," these women, he explained in a letter to *The Times* in 1912, suffered from "mental disorder" caused by "physiological emergencies" within their reproductive systems. In 1913, Wright published *The Unexpurgated Case against Woman Suffrage*, in which he argued that the questions of women's suffrage and of women's proper sphere turned on the issue as to "what imprint woman's sexual system leaves upon her physical frame, character, and intellect." Marshaling his authority as a physiologist, he insisted that "the sexual products influence every tissue of the body," establishing "intellectual immoralities and limitations" in women as "secondary sexual characteristics," like beards and deep voices in men. Women's character defects, "as irremediable as 'racial characters,'" Wright claimed, delineated their proper sphere and settled once and for all any nonsense as to women's suffrage.

Politicians drew upon all the "scientific" and "biological" stereotypes in their refusal to admit women to the franchise. Governed by their reproductive systems, as doctors and scientists insisted, women were thought to be too emotional, too unstable, too lacking in intellectual capacity to participate in the running of government. F.E. Smith announced his opposition to women's suffrage in the House of Commons by quoting H.G. Wells on women's disabilities. "The trend of evolutionary forces through long centuries of human development," he read:

> has been on the whole towards differentiation. An adult white woman differs far more from a white man than a negress or pigmy woman from her equivalent male. The education, the mental disposition of a white or Asiatic woman reeks of sex; her modesty, her decorum, is not to ignore sex but to refine and put a point to it; her costume is clamorous with the distinctive elements of her form.

Austen Chamberlain, in the debate on the second reading of the Conciliation Bill in 1910, argued that nature had distinguished between men and women, stating "it is on that ground that I am an opponent of woman suffrage. In my opinion the sex of a woman is a disqualification in fact, and we had better continue to so regard it in law."

Christabel Pankhurst argued in 1913 that the ideology of separate spheres and its justification for the subjection of women only camouflaged the "doctrine that woman is sex and beyond that nothing." In a series of articles published first in the WSPU's *Suffragette* and later compiled in a book entitled *The Great Scourge* (a reference to venereal disease), she offered a scathing attack on the interdependent cultural constructions of masculinity and femininity and of male and female sexuality. The doctrine of "woman as sex," she claimed, might be expressed in the belief that "women are mothers, and beyond that nothing," but what men who said that really meant was "that women are created primarily for the sex gratification of men, and secondarily, for the bearing of children if he happens to want them." Men opposed women's suffrage because they held women to be "a sub-human species useful in so far as female, but not otherwise." They valued women "only because of their sex functions, which functions [they] also believe are to be used at the orders and in the service of men."

The vote, as the NUWSS's *Common Cause* argued, would raise women from "the stultifying servitude of sex." It would bring about their descent from the pedestal of "the angel in the house"; in short, it would confer upon them a humanity, a reality as human beings. The anti-suffragists feared that votes for women would constitute a revolutionary transformation of the relations between the sexes, a transformation that would permeate every aspect of society, including that of sexual relations. Frederic Harrison acknowledged the radical nature of the suffrage campaign when, writing in 1909, he observed, "it cuts down to the roots of our family life." Greater manhood suffrage, he argued, did not pose the peril to the state that votes for women entailed; it concerned only politics. Harrison cautioned that female suffrage would "disintegrate families" and "plant anarchy in the Home." " 'Votes for Women' cannot be separated from the entire consensus of the domestic, social, and spiritual existence of Woman as a sex distinct from Man," he warned. "It affects life on a thousand sides."

The ideology of women's private sphere rested on definitions of female sexuality. It is not surprising, then, that women who challenged the ideology of separate spheres addressed the central premise of the ideology – the question of women's, and men's, sexual identity. Feminists charged that in presenting women as "the Sex," the ideology did not protect them and enshrine their virtue but permitted the abuse of women by men. As "the Sex," women had not been elevated to a pedestal as the moral guardians of hearth and home but had been dragged through the mire either as prostitutes or as "respectable" receptacles for male sexuality. Feminists sought to eliminate the stereotypes of women – both the idealized and the feared – that rendered them inhuman and, through the weapon of the vote, to create a society that was consistent with their needs, interests, and self-defined reality. "Votes for Women, Chastity for Men," Christabel Pankhurst's summation of the demands of feminist women, reflected the deeply-felt conviction that the regimes of male sexuality and female subordination called into being by separate sphere ideology had to be transformed. The suffrage movement, she insisted, constituted "a revolt against the evil system under which women are regarded as sub-human and as the sex slaves of men."

From sex war to real war[5]

The outbreak of war in August 1914 brought to a halt the activities of both militant and constitutional suffragists in their efforts to gain votes for women. By that time, the suffrage campaign had attained the size and status of a mass movement, commanding the time, energies, and resources of thousands of men and women, and riveting the attention of the British public. In early 1918, in what it defined as a gesture of recognition for women's contribution to the war effort, parliament granted the vote to women over the age of thirty. This measure, while welcome to feminists as a symbol of the fall of the sex barrier, failed to enfranchise some three million out of eleven million adult women. When war ended, feminists continued to agitate for votes for women on the same terms as they had been granted to men, but organized feminism, despite the fact that a considerable portion of the potential female electorate remained disenfranchised, never regained its prewar status as a mass movement. By the end of the 1920s, feminism as a distinct political and social movement had become insignificant. The experiences of the Great War – articulated and represented in specific languages of gender and sexuality – forged dramatically different ideas about gender and sexual identity for many men and women than those prevailing in the late Victorian and Edwardian eras, and these languages and the identities they spawned provide the context within which interwar feminism operated and by which it was constrained. Feminists' under-standings of masculinity and femininity – of gender and sexual identity – became transformed during the war and in the postwar period until they were virtually indistinguishable from those of anti-feminists.

The outbreak of war in August 1914 was experienced by thousands of men as an ecstatic, liberating moment, a release from the stifling domesticity and conflicts of industrial bourgeois society. The war offered an opportunity to escape from a society in which wealth, class status, and domestic ideology limited one's range of activities and experiences, one in which the conflicts laid out in the last chapter could be left behind. Escape from it meant escape to the world of men, to the domain of the masculine, the army or navy, to the world of discipline, obedience, action; an effacing of the partisan conflicts, of the feminine.

H.G. Wells gave expression to the idea of an effeminate prewar England through his character Mr Britling in 1916. "How we had wasted Ireland!" Britling despaired, bewailing the state of things in the summer of 1914. "The rich values that lay in Ireland, the gallantry and gifts, the possible friendliness, all these things were being left to the Ulster politicians and the Tory women to poison and spoil, just as we had left India to the traditions of the chattering army women and the repressive instincts of our mandarins. We were too lazy, we were too negligent. We passed our indolent days leaving everything to somebody else." But with war imminent, Britling exults in the manliness that will prevail. Setting out to visit his mistress, Mrs Harrowdean, he loses himself in the Essex countryside. "There was little room in the heart of Mr Britling that night for any love but the love of England. He loved England now as a nation of men. There could be no easy victory. Good for us with our too easy natures that there could be no easy victory." For Wells, women, and the silly, unimportant things they symbolized, were upstaged by the serious activities of war. In this representation, war promised to destroy prewar effeminacy by delivering men from the domain of domesticity and the concerns of women, to remasculinize them by asserting "more commanding interests" such as troop movements and battles.

Politicians, writers, and critics such as Edmund Gosse, Selwyn Image, and Rupert Brooke viewed the war as an antidote to the diseased and decadent state of Edwardian society, characterized, in part, by a militant feminist movement that challenged and contested traditional roles and behaviors for men and women – as a means to substitute, in effect, a "real" war for "sex war." "We have awakened from an opium-dream of comfort, of ease, of that miserable poltroonery of 'the sheltered life,'" wrote Gosse, in terms usually applied to the lives of privileged women.

Our wish for indulgence of every sort, our laxity of manners, our wretched sensitiveness to personal inconvenience, these are suddenly lifted before us in their true guise as the spectres of national decay; and we have risen from the lethargy of our dilettantism to lay them, before it is too late, by the flashing of the unsheathed sword.

He and others believed that England had brought the war upon itself by offering the Germans a soft and tempting target. Unwilling, or unable, to suppress striking laborers, Irish nationalists, or militant suffragists, England looked ripe for conquest.

The sudden and dramatic prospect of a newly masculinized English manhood had its counterpart in the reassertion of women's traditional roles, which included a large measure of passivity, despite feverish attempts on the part of countless women to feel useful to the war effort by knitting enough socks and mufflers to outfit half the British Expeditionary Force. As Carolyne Playne described it, "the great era of knitting set in; men should fight but women should knit." Vera Brittain turned, on 6 August 1914, to "the only work it seems possible as yet for women to do – the making of garments for the soldiers." "All day long I knitted away," she recorded the next day, as if she and her compatriots could repair the damage to the social fabric that war might bring.

The reassertion of traditional norms of masculinity and femininity, and of separate spheres for men and women, found expression in the efforts to legitimate and justify the war itself. Much of the official propaganda presented the war as a fight for, and on behalf of, Belgium, which was often depicted in the guise of womanhood. "Little Belgium" evoked images of an innocent woman in need of protection from a paternal male. Such chivalric imagery became charged by, and infused with, sexual implications as accounts of the invasion of Belgium and rumors of German atrocities reached England and seared the collective British memory. Tales of destruction, rape, and murder on the part of German soldiers circulated throughout the country, casting Belgium in the role of a violated maiden left to die by cruel, inhuman invaders.

Much of the atrocity propaganda that circulated throughout Britain focused on outrages committed against women. Stories of women with their breasts cut off appeared regularly in both the respectable and the mass daily press and gained wide acceptance. In May 1915, the government issued the Bryce Report, the findings of a commission charged with investigating stories of German atrocities in Belgium. For the cost of a daily newspaper, Britons could purchase the "summary of evidence" and an appendix of selected case histories. The report gave lurid descriptions of hideous atrocities. One Belgian refugee reported the case of a family in which the mother and father were shot by the Germans, and "a daughter of 22, having been outraged, died because of the violence she had received." Another related the account of two women he met on the road to Hayne. "I know them both," he attested:

One told me that the Germans had raped her in her house at Hayne near Soumagne and the other told me the same. The women were both together when they were raped. They were raped by a great many Germans.

A Belgian told of his neighbor, Mrs. D., whose daughter was "driven ... up into the loft" by two Germans soldiers, who then raped her. "She was 8 1/2 months gone in pregnancy. ... The child was born the following day."

A Belgian soldier watched Germans:

> going into the houses in the Place and bringing out the women and girls. About 20 were brought out. ... Each of them was held by the arms. They tried to get away. There were made to lie on tables which had been brought into the square. About 15 of them were then violated. Each of them was violated by about 12 soldiers. While this was going on about 70 Germans were standing round the women including five officers (young). ... The ravishing went on for about 1 1/2 hours.

A refugee from Pepinster stated that he saw:

> the Germans seize a baby out of the arms of the farmer's wife. ... The two privates held the baby and the officer took out his sword and cut the baby's head off. The head fell on the floor and the soldiers kicked the body of the child into a corner and kicked the head after it. ... After the baby had been killed we saw the officer say something to the farmer's wife and saw her push him away. After five or six minutes the two soldiers seized the woman and put her on the ground. She resisted them and they then pulled all her clothes off her until she was quite naked. The officer then violated her while one soldier held her by the shoulders and the other by the arms. After the officer each soldier in turn violated her, the other soldier and the officer holding her down. ... After the woman had been violated by the three the officer cut off the woman's breasts.

A litany of atrocities committed against women and children, and civilian men by German soldiers continued for some 238 pages.

This kind of imagery linked sex and war in the conscious and unconscious minds of Britons, creating a lasting theme for subsequent descriptions and understandings of the Great War. The images of violence and cruelty were images, primarily, of acts against women, so that the rape and sexual mutilation of women served as one of the major means by which the war was imagined and represented by contemporaries. Demanding, on a conscious level, revenge from the Germans for such acts, these attempts also appealed to the desire to defend the sexual property in women at the level of the unconscious.

Recruiting efforts drew explicitly upon the images of the rape and sexual mutilation of women to increase the ranks of the army and navy. In February 1915, *The
Official Book of the German Atrocities*, preparatory to describing incidents such as those
recounted above, made a plea for more men. "It is the duty of every single
Englishman who reads these records," it intoned:

> and who is fit to take his place in the King's Army, to fight with all the resolu-
> tion and courage he may, that the stain, of which the following pages are only
> a slight record, may be wiped out, and the blood of innocent women and chil-
> dren avenged.

A poster addressed "To the Women Of Britain" reminded them, "You have read
what the Germans have done in Belgium. Have you thought what they would do if
they invaded this Country? Do you realise that the safety of your home and children depends on our getting more men *NOW*?" "Mothers!" were exhorted to give
up their husbands and sons if they wanted to avoid the fate of Belgian women.
"Have you forgotten the Belgian Atrocities? Do you realise what will be the lot of
you and your children if the Germans successfully invade England?"

While the imagery of sexual violation of women served as a means of recruitment and justification for the war, it may well have acted, if only unconsciously, to
reinforce the promises of sexual punishment, reward, and release for enlisting that
bombarded the British public. Philip Gibbs, a war correspondent, maintained that
some soldiers were sent to the front "by the taunt of a girl," while Sir George
Young recounts that his chauffeur was threatened by his "lady love" with rejection
if he did not enlist, despite the fact that this young man's parents had forbade him
to. "What will your best girl say if you're not in khaki?" sneered one recruiting
poster; another in the same vein, but addressed to "The Young Women of London,"
asked them, "Is your 'Best Boy' wearing Khaki? If not don't *YOU THINK* he should
be? If he does not think that you and your country are worth fighting for – do you
think he is *WORTHY* of you?"

Promises of sexual reward for enlisting appeared frequently. In one song that
carried unmistakable undertones of prostitution, long the acknowledged avenue
by which British men were first initiated in sexual activity, and by means of which
they were expected to find relief from pent-up sexual tension, women urged men
to "take the King's shilling" – to enlist – with the following:

> On Sunday I walk out with a soldier,
> On Monday I'm taken by a tar,
> On Tuesday I'm out
> With a baby Boy Scout,
> On Wednesday with a Hussar.

On Thursday I gang oot with a Kiltie,
On Friday the captain of the crew,
But on Saturday I'm willing, if only you'll take a shilling,
To make a man of any one of you.

The representation of the war as unleashed heterosexuality included women in its purview as well. The sexologist Magnus Hirschfeld, in a statement figuring the war as a form of sexual release, asserted that:

> the great experience of the outbreak of the war, the tremendous emotional excitement that it brought, exercised a stimulating effect upon the women of every land and appears to have raised their need of love considerably … woman reacted to the war with an increase of her libido.

Winifred Holtby testified to such an experience, recounting that when the war started, "the first thing it made me do was to fall in love." Lady Randolph Churchill wondered aloud about this phenomenon, asking in 1916, "Why is it that men who have served their country and us for years in difficult, dangerous, and disagreeable occupations never interested us until we saw them in khaki? Such is the magic of the trappings of war!" As reports of "khaki fever" and dire predictions about "war babies" spread through the land, women bore the brunt of the anxiety that the war produced in the population. "When quite ordinary men donned khaki," scolded *The Times History of the War* in August 1915, "they became in the eyes of a number of foolish young women objects to be pestered with attention that very few of them desired."

The sexual imagery utilized to represent the war reflected developments in the prosecution and fortunes of the war and the extent to which the home front was involved. During the first phase, lasting from August 1914 into 1915, the war was often depicted as a remasculinization of English culture, perceived to have become degenerate, effeminate in the years before the war. This kind of representation relied upon a corresponding imagery of women as refeminized, especially in the aftermath of a widespread feminist movement that had challenged the dominant cultural norms of masculinity and femininity. Thus, an assertion of, and emphasis on, traditional notions of separate spheres for men and women characterized the first year of the war. It was accompanied by the notion of war as unleashed sexual desire, as gruesome tales of German atrocities committed against Belgian women spread through the land. These representations of the sexual imperatives of war were put forward within a framework of traditional gender and sexual relations, and did not seriously threaten the bourgeois domestic ideology of separate spheres based upon belief in a single model of sexuality for men and in the dual nature of female sexuality. Images of sexual release, of loosening the sexual restraints between men and women in the depictions of khaki fever and stories of war babies, while containing hints of middle-class women adopting male sexual values and ignoring traditional standards of reticence and chastity, were nevertheless heavily weighted by class, and could thus adequately represent a war that was still thought about and presented in traditional terms. But by mid-1915 or so, as those on the home front began to understand that their's was not a traditional war, this kind of sexual representation began to change too.

By 1915, the need of the nation for more soldiers and women to work in the positions vacated by men overrode any objections to women's work. As men went off to war, women joined the workforce in unprecedented numbers, taking jobs as munitions workers, agricultural laborers, tram conductors, ambulance drivers, frontline nurses, and, finally, after the disasters of 1916, auxiliary soldiers. The exigencies of the war after mid-1915 dramatically upset the perceived gender system of the Victorian and Edwardian periods. Mary Somerville exclaimed in the *Women's Liberal Review*, "Oh! This War! How it is tearing down walls and barriers, and battering in fast shut doors." Nina Boyle could rejoice that "woman's place, by universal consensus of opinion, is no longer the Home. It is the battlefield, the farm, the factory, the shop." For many women, the opportunity to contribute to national life, to work and to be well paid, was a rewarding and exhilarating experience. Irene Rathbone, who worked in a YMCA canteen, confided to her diary that "for years I have not been so completely free and happy." In 1918, Harriet Stanton Blatch was struck by "the increased joyfulness of women. They were happy in their work, happy in the thought of rendering service, so happy that the poignancy of individual loss was carried more easily."

The dismantling of barriers between men's and women's work and the evident joy women experienced in their new roles fostered a blurring of distinctions that had helped to form traditional versions of gender identity. Mrs Alec-Tweedie rejoiced in the fact that by the events of the war, "women have become soldiers." Moreover, she predicted, it might not be long before:

> we may have to have women fighters too. ... For ... the war has literally metamorphosed everything and everybody. To-day every man is a soldier, and every woman is a man. Well, no – not quite; but speaking roughly, war has turned the world upside down; and the upshot of the topsy-turveydom is that the world has discovered women, and women have discovered themselves.

She argued for the formation of a Woman's Battalion, foreseeing the day when:

> rather than let the Old Country go under, the women of the Empire would be willing, aye more than willing, to take a place in the firing line. ... Give them the chance of the trenches ... and they would step in right royally and loyally

again. ... Women have done more for their country than handle a rifle, and
thousands of us are ready to do that, too.

As Blatch observed, "the British woman had found herself and her muscles.
England was a world of women – women in uniforms." This was a far cry from
knitting socks and rolling bandages or providing relief for Belgian refugees; the
language of traditional femininity, of separate spheres for women and men, could
not adequately articulate the experiences and requirements of a war that failed to
respect the boundaries between home and front, between civilian and soldier.
Winifred Holtby realized that "so far as modern war is concerned, the old division
of interest between combatant and non-combatant decreases, and the qualifications of the combatant lose their dominatingly masculine traits. ... War ceases to
be a masculine occupation."

Many saw in this development a promising future for men and women. For
many others, however, the notion of women doing men's work created enormous
anxiety. Women in uniform were seen disapprovingly to be "aping" men. One
woman wrote to *The Morning Post* in July 1916, describing four women dressed in
khaki:

> they had either cropped their hair or managed so to hide it under their khaki
> felt hats that at first sight the younger women looked exactly like men. ... I
> noticed that these women assumed mannish attitudes, stood with legs apart
> while they smote their riding whips, and looked like self-conscious and not
> very attractive boys. ... I do not know the corps to which these ladies belong,
> but if they cannot become nurses or ward maids in hospitals, let them put on
> sunbonnets and print frocks and go and make hay or pick fruit or make jam,
> or do the thousand and one things that women can do to help.

A perception of blurred gender identities appeared at the front as well as at
home. Non-commissioned officers in charge of supplying or transporting troops,
for instance, might regard their work in maternal terms, as in the case of the
sergeant-major in Ford Madox Ford's *Parade's End*, whose "motherly heart ...
yearned ... over his two thousand nine hundred and thirty-four nurslings," and
who wished even "to extend the motherliness of his functions" to officers.
Collecting the wounded, battle-hardened men carried them "tenderly, soothing
[them] with the gentleness of women." The altered lyrics of a sentimental song
about Old England gave explicit recognition that traditional gender identity had
broken down under the extremes of war:

> Oh, they've called them up from Weschurch,
> And they've called them up from Wen,

And they'll call up all the women,
When they've fucked up all the men.

The war made many men anxious about their masculinity: Captain McKechnie, in *Parade's End*, agonized, "Why isn't one a beastly girl and privileged to shriek?" The unprecedented opportunities made available to women by the Great War – their increased visibility in public life, their release from the private world of domesticity, their greater mobility – contrasted sharply with the conditions imposed on men at the front, where they were immobilized and rendered passive in a subterranean world of trenches. Instead of becoming heroes as they had hoped as they marched gaily off to war, they felt emasculated by the horrors they faced and their incapacity to do anything to alter their situation. The terrors of the war and the expectations of manliness on the part of the front-soldier combined to produce in large numbers of men a condition that came to be known as "shell shock." These cases of shell shock were in fact cases of male hysteria, in which, given the prescriptions of masculinity that saw in fear a sign of unmanliness, men could articulate their terrors only through a language of the body, as women had done for decades. Robert Graves, testifying on behalf of Siegfried Sassoon who had been brought up on charges for desertion, and whose defense rested upon the claim that he had experienced shell shock, was himself in such a bad "state of nerves" that "I burst into tears three times during my statement."

The association of sex and war carried potentially explosive implications for society when it became clear that this war would require the participation of all segments of the population; anxiety about the war frequently took shape as anxiety about sex, or was articulated in sexual terms. The charges of khaki fever and war babies that predominated in 1914 had contained a kind of patronizing and even good-hearted tone; as the war effort worsened attacks on women's sexuality increased in virulence. Making no distinction between prostitutes infected with venereal diseases on the one hand, and young girls or women infected with khaki fever on the other, Arthur Conan Doyle wrote to *The Times* in February 1917 of "vile women ... who prey upon and poison our soldiers ... these harpies carry off the lonely soldiers to their rooms ... and finally inoculate them ... with one of those diseases." A December 1917 letter to *The Times* referred to women as "sexual freelances" who "stalked through the land, vampires upon the nation's health, distributing and perpetuating among our young manhood diseases which institute a national calamity." In July 1918, Imperial War Conference attendees heard tales of infected women "lying in wait for clean young men who came to give their lives for their country." The government, for its part, introduced regulation 40d of the Defence of the Realm Act in March 1918, at the height of worries about the German advance, declaring that "no woman suffering from venereal disease shall have sexual intercourse with any member of His Majesty's Forces, or solicit or invite any member to have sexual intercourse with her." Clearly, in the minds of many Britons, sex presented as great a threat to the survival and existence of England as did Germany; the two were, indeed, conflated in the minds of many. Mrs Alec-Tweedie made this connection abundantly clear when she warned that "every woman who lets herself 'go' is as bad as a German spy, and a traitor, not only to her sex, but to her country."

Women who labored in the munitions factories and served in the auxiliary forces excited adverse comment; many implied that their earnings came from working an "extra shift," by which they meant prostitution. Siegfried Sassoon's Sherston told of his Aunt Evelyn complaining of "the disgracefully immoral way most of the young women were behaving while doing war work." Before they even reached France, members of the Women's Auxiliary Army Corps (WAAC) were accused of loose living and of corrupting the morals of "our poor lads."

By focusing on sex as one of the major issues of the war, contemporaries hit upon a means by which they could imagine, represent, and even narrate – that is, make sense of – the war, which defied traditional terms and habits of thought. As women began to take up jobs previously held exclusively by men, and even to serve as auxiliaries in the armed forces, sexual representation utilizing traditional heterosexual terms and images was no longer adequate to the task of giving meaning to a war so completely out of line with all precedent. Visions of sexuality in which women had become fully as unrestrained as men began to predominate. Such images threatened traditional gender and sexual arrangements. Moreover, warnings about prostitution and venereal disease were joined now by charges of sexual perversions and of homosexuality, raising the specter of behaviors that dramatically challenged the system of separate spheres and heterosexuality itself in imagery consonant with concerns about the blurring of gender lines.

Male homosexuality, perceived as men behaving like women, appeared to contemporaries to pose a great danger to the war effort. If the war provided the manly alternative to the prewar threat of effeminacy, then the logical conclusion might easily be drawn, as it was by many, that defeats on the battlefield could be attributed to sexual "laxity," or homosexuality among the men charged with prose-cuting the war. In 1915, Lord Alfred Douglas wrote in *The Antidote* that "it is just as important to civilization that Literary England should be cleansed of sex-mongers and pedlars of the perverse, as that Flanders should be cleared of Germans." In May 1916, the *English Review* reported on "the moral and spiritual invasion of Britain by German urnings [homosexuals] for the purpose of undermining the patriotism, the stamina, the intellect, and the moral [sic] of British Navy and Army men, and of our prominent public leaders." MP Noel Pemberton Billing claimed in the House of Commons in February 1918 that the German secret service had the names of 47,000 "English perverts," whom they were blackmailing in order to further their war aims. A few days later, Pemberton Billing's charges appeared in a popular newspaper, *The Referee*, as statements of fact.

Heterosexuality was challenged in other, more pragmatic terms as well – the facts of demography. Women's wartime gains could not avoid associations with dismemberment and death, which had created the need for women's participation in the war in the first place. Women's gains could be perceived as being entirely at the expense of men, and of men's lives. Blatch reported of war-working women:

> peace will mean an insufficient number of breadwinners to go around and ... a maimed man may have low earning power. The women I met were not dejected at the prospect; they showed, on the contrary, a spirit not far removed from elation in finding new opportunities of service.

Mabel Daggett enthused:

> every time a man drops dead in the trenches, a woman steps permanently into the niche he used to hold in industry, in commerce, in the professions, in world affairs ... the ultimate programme toward which the modern Woman Movement to-day is moving is no less than Paradise Regained! It may even, I think, have been worth this war to be there.

Men at the front often felt alienated and estranged from those left behind in comparative safety at home, which was exacerbated by the apparent pleasure with which those at home were prosecuting the war. War correspondent Philip Gibbs reported that many soldiers returned from leave:

> "fuming," holding the frightful suspicion ... that at home people liked the war and were not anxious to end it, and did not care a jot for the sufferings of the soldiers. ... Everybody was having a good time. Munition-workers were earning wonderful wages and spending them on gramophones, pianos, furs, and the 'pictures.' Everybody was gadding about in a state of joyous exultation. The painted flapper was making herself sick with the sweets of life after office hours in government employ, where she did little work for a lot of pocket-money. The society girl was dancing bare-legged for "war charities," pushing into bazaars for the "poor, dear wounded," getting her pictures into the papers as a "notable war-worker," married for the third time in three years. ... Millions of girls were in some kind of fancy dress with buttons and shoulder-straps, breeches and puttees, and they seemed to be making a game of the war and enjoying it thoroughly.

People at home "don't care a fuck what 'appens to 'us'ns," exclaimed Madeley in Manning's *Her Privates We*. "When this bloody war's over," chimed in his mate, Glazier, "you'll go back to England an' fin' nought but a lot o' conchies [conscientious objectors] and bloody prostitutes."

The hostility and anger directed toward the home – symbolized and epitomized by women – by the front-soldiery could be intense. Soldiers fantasized about inflicting pain and even death on civilians at home, who they regarded as totally out of touch with what those at the front had to face. In "Blighters," Siegfried Sassoon amuses himself in a music hall with thoughts of:

> a Tank com[ing] down the stalls,
> Lurching to rag-time tunes, or 'Home, sweet Home'.

In "Yellow-Pressmen," victorious soldiers parading through London turn their weapons on the civilians lining the streets; the author later grabs hand grenades:

> And with my trusty bombers turned and went
> To clear those Junkers out of Parliament.

This hostility was probably intensified by the identification of men with characteristics regarded as feminine in a war that seemed to be effacing distinctions between men and women. Fearing their own feminization, men turned those fears outward, and expressed hostility toward women. D.H. Lawrence's wartime poem "Eloi, Eloi, Lama Sabacthani?" conveys his sense of being preyed upon by women:

> Why do the women follow us, satisfied,
> Feed on our wounds like bread, receive our blood
> Like glittering seed upon them for fulfilment?

These impressions, in light of the dramatic gains in employment and freedom women achieved precisely because of the war, coalesced into a perception that the persistent horrors of the war were, somehow, women's fault. Robert Graves believed that his longevity at the front was a consequence of his maintaining his virginity, of abstaining from contact with women, clearly linking women with death. This association appears too in the appellations soldiers gave to German howitzer shells – "grandma" and "aunty"; women usually figured as beneficent and maternal have become deadly. In *Parade's End*, a private by the name of O Nine Morgan refused leave to return home to deal with his wife's infidelity with a prize-fighter on the grounds that the boxer would kill him, was killed instead by a mortar. "This was what done it, I should say," announced his sergeant-major, holding up a piece of heavy metal. "No, I don't believe that did it," replied Tietjens, who had made the decision to keep O Nine Morgan at the front. "Something bigger. ... Say a prize-fighter's fist ..." "Oh, I take your meaning, sir," the sergeant-major said. "O Nine Morgan's wife, sir." The cause of death has been displaced from a mortar shell on to a woman.

From the home front, the war appeared, at least after 1916, as a massive, mind-less destruction committed by machine-like men. The picture of masculinity conjured up by such imagery was often that of "mechanical dolls who grin and kill and grin," "a grimacing phantom," "a creature at once ridiculous and disgusting," as R.H. Tawney described it resentfully in October 1916 while recuperating from wounds received on the Somme in July. He castigated the newspapers for "inventing a kind of conventional soldier" who revels in the "excitement" of war and finds " 'sport' in killing other men," and hunts "Germans out of dug-outs as a terrier hunts rats."

> We are depicted as merry assassins, rejoicing in the opportunity of a 'scrap' in which we know that more than three-quarters of our friends will be maimed or killed, careless of our own lives, exulting in the duty of turning human beings into lumps of disfigured clay.

Moreover, the imagery of sexual assault raised by the Belgian atrocities continued to inform representations of the war. Valentine Wallop, in Ford's *Parade's End*, believed that "all manly men were lust-filled devils, desiring nothing better than to stride over battlefields, stabbing the wounded with long daggers in frenzies of sadism." Such representations of masculinity bore little resemblance to the way men at the front perceived themselves. On the contrary, soldiers understood their manliness not in terms of aggression but in terms of the psychological and physical wounds they had suffered. But the power of these bloodthirsty images was lasting, and would have significant impact on the way women at home understood the nature of masculinity, femininity, and the relations between the sexes.

In the second phase of war, then, from about mid-1915 on, the representation of war as unleashed sexual desire gave way to visions of sexual disorder, a blurring of gender lines as women went off to factories and front to do war work and men found themselves immobilized in trenches. Toward the end of the war, sexual disorder came to be depicted as sexual conflict and polarization between the sexes, or sex war, as men perceived women to be emasculating them, and began, at least rhetorically, to strike back. The use of sexual metaphor – specifically, the images of sexual disorder and then sex war – to give meaning to the experiences of the Great War after 1915, and the notions of masculinity and femininity created thereby, would have a distinct bearing on issues seemingly unrelated to the war.

Suffrage proved to be one such issue. In 1918, parliament granted the vote to women over the age of thirty. Contemporary observers in the suffrage and anti-suffrage camps attributed the government's willingness to enfranchise women to its appreciation of the work women performed during the war. Millicent Fawcett noted in 1925 that "there was not a paper in Great Britain that by 1916–17 was not ringing with praise of the courage and devotion of British women in carrying out war work of various kinds, and on its highly effective character from the national point of view." Minister of Munitions Edwin Montagu proclaimed to the House of Commons in August 1916, "it is not too much to say that our Armies have been saved and victory assured by the women in the munition factories where they helped to produce aeroplanes, howitzer bombs, shrapnel bullets, shells, machine tools, mines, and have taken part in shipbuilding." Winston Churchill, for his part, declared that "without the work of women it would have been impossible to win the war." Herbert Asquith, an inveterate foe of women's suffrage, announced his conversion to the enfranchisement of women on precisely these grounds. "I think that some years ago I ventured to use the expression, 'Let the women work out their own salvation,' " he recalled in March of 1917.

> Well, Sir, they have worked it out during this War. How could we have carried on the War without them? Short of actually bearing arms in the field, there is hardly a service which has contributed, or is contributing, to the maintenance of our cause in which women have not been at least as active and as efficient as men, and wherever we turn we see them doing … work which three years ago would have been regarded as falling exclusively within the province of men.

While contemporaries emphasized women's war service, they did so within a framework of past and current understandings about sex, war, and sex war that colored their proceedings and heightened the urgency of reaching a satisfactory conclusion. MPs and suffragists worked out their compromise over women's suffrage on the basis of three widely held assumptions: that a sex war had, prior to August of 1914, been raging throughout the land; that it had been subsumed in the larger international conflagration; and that failure to resolve the suffrage issue would result in its flaring up again. Several MPs hinted that the militancy of the prewar years might very well resurface after the war if women were not enfranchised; this contingency persuaded many former antisuffragists in parliament to reverse their position. Lord Hugh Cecil reminded the Commons of:

> the strong feeling which animates a certain number of women in order to obtain the franchise. That is a very important consideration. I believe it to be a very serious matter that any important body of opinion should be discontented and dissatisfied, and it always ought to weigh heavily on Parliament in

extending the franchise that there is a body of citizens who very much wish to have it and who wish it so keenly that it produces a disordering and disturbing effect on them ... it seems to me that to give women suffrage ... is to adopt a conservative measure which is likely to allay discontent, to promote justice, and to maintain the efficiency of representative institutions in Parliament.

Walter Long cautioned his fellow MPs that "a renewal of those bitter controversies over which we have wasted so much time in the past" must be avoided, and urged antisuffragists "to think twice and thrice before they commit themselves to this policy of destruction. I implore them to join with the Government in a policy of construction and progress" by voting for women's suffrage. Long never changed his conviction against women's suffrage; he voted for it precisely to avoid the "bitter controversies" of the past.

Fear of renewal of the sex war so characteristic of the prewar period, but raised now to intolerable levels, also helped to determine the terms under which women would be admitted to the franchise. While the Representation of the People Act gave men the vote on the basis of residence of premises, a grant of universal manhood suffrage, it restricted the women's vote to those who were householders or the wives of householders, and who had attained the age of thirty. The age requirement ensured that women would not enjoy a majority over men, whose numbers had been greatly reduced in the slaughter of war. Moreover, it ensured that those eligible to vote were likely to be wives and mothers; those excluded were largely single, working-class women who had made so significant a contribution to the war effort, who might seek to continue their work after the war and even to sacrifice marriage and motherhood to do so.

In consenting to the age qualification, suffragists abandoned their long-held principle of sex equality: votes for women on the same lines as it was or should be granted to men. While welcome to feminists as a symbol of the fall of the sex barrier, the provisions of the Reform Act fell far short of what feminists had been demanding for almost sixty years. The terms of the discourses about suffrage, infused with representations of war, sex, and sex war, helped to circumscribe feminists' abilities to achieve the goals of their long struggle. As we shall see in the next chapter, fears of sex war continued unabated, and were exacerbated by popular accounts of, and scientific explanations for, the behavior of men returning home from the war.

NOTES

1 Quoted in Margaret Ward, *Unmanageable Revolutionaries: Women and Irish Nationalism* (London, 1995), pp. 90, 91.

2 Ward, *Unmanageable Revolutionaries*, p. 93.

3 See Declan Kiberd, *Inventing Ireland: The Literature of the Modern Nation* (Cambridge, MA, 1995), ch. 11; and Sean Farrell Moran, *Patrick Pearse and the Politics of Redemption: The Mind of the Easter Rising, 1916* (Washington, DC, 1994), especially ch. 6.

4 This section draws from Susan Kingsley Kent, *Sex and Suffrage in Britain, 1860–1914* (Princeton, 1987), ch. 7.

5 This discussion relies upon Susan Kingsley Kent, *Making Peace: The Reconstruction of Gender in Interwar Britain* (Princeton, 1993), chs. 1, 2, 3.

SOURCES

George Dangerfield, *The Strange Death of Liberal England, 1910–1914*. New York, 1961.

Paul Fussell, *The Great War and Modern Memory*. New York, 1975.

Sandra Gilbert, "Soldier's heart: Literary men, literary women, and the Great War," *Signs* 8(3), 1983: 422–50.

Nicoletta F. Gullace, "White feathers and wounded men: Female patriotism and the memory of the Great War," *Journal of British Studies* 36, April 1997: 178–206.

Samuel Hynes, *A War Imagined: The First World War and English Culture*. New York, 1991.

Susan Kingsley Kent, *Sex and Suffrage in Britain, 1860–1914*. Princeton, 1987.

——, *Making Peace: The Reconstruction of Gender in Inter War Britain*. Princeton, 1993.

Declan Kiberd, *Inventing Ireland: The Literature of the Modern Nation*. Cambridge, MA, 1995.

Eric J. Leed, *No Man's Land: Combat and Identity in World War I*. Cambridge, 1979.

Sean Farrell Moran, *Patrick Pearse and the Politics of Redemption: The Mind of the Easter Rising, 1916*. Washington, DC, 1994.

Elaine Showalter, *The Female Malady: Women, Madness, and English Culture, 1830–1980*. New York, 1985.

Alan J. Ward, *The Easter Rising: Revolution and Irish Nationalism*. Wheeling, IL, 1980.

Margaret Ward, *Unmanageable Revolutionaries: Women and Irish Nationalism*. London, 1995.

Chapter 12

Searching for peace
The reconstruction of gender, 1919–39

The perceived blurring of gender lines occasioned by the upheaval of war and the social and economic disorder that followed led many in Britain to see in a re-establishment of sexual difference the means to recreate a semblance of order. Some Britons sought to return to the "traditional" order of the prewar world, an order based on natural biological categories of which sexual differences were a familiar and readily available expression. Other segments of society responded to the disorders created by war not so much by sharpening sexual differences between men and women as by modifying what constituted "manliness." In both instances, the mobilization of gender and sexuality in the efforts to recast postwar society had a decisive effect on the way many men and women felt they must present themselves as they went about their everyday lives. For working-class men and women, going about their everyday lives proved extraordinarily difficult as years of depression set in and unemployment skyrocketed. Without work, men faced severe challenges to their identities as men; working-class women sought ways to ameliorate the threats to masculinity posed by unemployment, often at great physical cost to themselves.

Boyish women and unmanly men[1]

Something like the blurring of gender lines that took place during the war continued in the 1920s, as young women of virtually every class – called "flappers," "boyettes," "Modern Women," or "Modern Girls" by society – dressed in boyish fashions, cut their hair short, smoked cigarettes, drove cars, and generally pursued an active, adventurous lifestyle. Their counterparts, the "bright young things," men who had been too young to go to war in the years 1914–18, offered themselves as effeminate contrasts, till it appeared, in the popular press at least, that young men and women had simply switched roles, characteristics, and styles with one another. Boyish women and effeminate men dominated the fashion pages of newspapers and magazines, and were satirized regularly in the pages of *Punch*. They represented the carefree, youth-oriented, pleasure-seeking, even hedonistic nature of the postwar generation sick and tired of a devastating war to which they had been unable to make a contribution; for others they constituted proof that society still had to be put right and a traditional gender order restored if things were ever to return to "normal" in the postwar period.

The boyish young woman wore simple, plain-cut, tailored clothing that was best shown off on a lithe, slim, athletic figure with small breasts and narrow hips. She dressed in suits; sported a short haircut, wearing it bobbed, shingled, or Eton-cropped like her élite brothers; she smoked, demonstrated great confidence in herself by her masculine posture and movements, and might boast of a sexual freedom not possible for her prewar sisters. She donned short skirts, drove fast cars, flew airplanes, played golf and tennis with abandon; by her youthful antics, boyish figure, and frantic social pace, she asserted a refusal of maturity and motherhood that elicited adverse comment, especially in the aftermath of a war that had killed half a million men.

Her foil, "the modern young man," excited a great deal of negative comment, most of it alluding to his effeminacy and impotence. As early as 1921, the *Daily Mail* worried that "Healthy young girls are more boyish than boys." In a 1925 front-page story about the disappearance of manliness, the *Daily Express* denounced "The modern girl's brother." In contrast to her – portrayed as strong, healthy, self-confident, and independent – he was described as listless, bored, and dandyish, all "dolled up like a girl and an exquisite without masculinity." *Punch* carried a cartoon in 1928 (see Figure 12.1) that depicted a "helpless clinging masculine type" sitting before his assertive, bold fiancé: he with his hands held gracefully in his lap and his legs crossed at the knee, gazing up at her with fawning eyes and sweet expression; she standing above him with her legs astride, hands on hips, and an authoritative manner.

Sometimes the androgyny of the "boyettes" produced consequences they did not perhaps intend, as when some of the homosexual "bright young things" found themselves attracted to boyish women. Cyril Connolly, for instance, succumbed to the "very lovely and boyish" appearance of Horatia Fisher in 1927; in 1929, Jean Bakewell's "short boy's hair" and "lovely boy's body" captivated him. Evelyn Waugh married a boyish woman, Evelyn Gardner, described as "a ravishing boy, a page." Friends distinguished between the two by referring to "He-Evelyn" and "She-Evelyn." But these were young women dressing in the style and conducting themselves in the manner of young men, not women seeking to pass as them. They were "boyish," not "mannish." The boyish look suggested an androgyny or ambiguity of gender roles, but women were careful not to transgress the dictates of fashion that might land them in the category of the "perverted." They did not generally wear trousers, for instance, and did add accessories like earrings and

"BUT HE'S NOT EVEN AMUSING. WHAT ON EARTH DOES YOUR SISTER WANT TO MARRY HIM FOR?"
"OH, WELL, I SUPPOSE HE'S THAT HELPLESS CLINGING MASCULINE TYPE THAT WOULD APPEAL TO A GIRL LIKE JOAN."

Figure 12.1 Illustration in *Punch*, 15 February 1928
Source: Reproduced with permission of Punch Ltd

make-up so that they would not be mistakenly identified as men. Boyishness was the dominant fashion of the time for young women, permitting a freedom of expression and of activity that proved exhilarating to many, many young women.

Until 1928, that is, when publicity surrounding the obscenity trial against Radclyffe Hall's *The Well of Loneliness* made it impossible for heterosexual women to partake any longer of fashions that might suggest "mannishness," a code-word since the 1890s for "perversion." *The Well of Loneliness* told the story of a tortured, confused, good-hearted, and morally upright lesbian heroine, Stephen Gordon, who finds love during the war with an ambulance driver named Mary, and acceptance of their relationship within a community of lesbians living in Paris after the war. The fact that Stephen is a sympathetic character, presented by Hall as a victim of society's ignorance and cruelty rather than a "pervert," caused a suit to be brought against the novel on the grounds of obscenity.

Radclyffe Hall, like many other lesbian artists and writers, dressed in the "boyish" manner of the 1920s. Attired in suits, smoking conspicuously, ostentatiously sporting monocles, they were regarded throughout the 1920s as stylish women of fashion. Indeed, just two days before *The Well* was banned, the *Newcastle*

Daily Journal and North Star carried a feature on Hall that described her as "a most arresting personality."

> She may frequently be seen at West End Theatres dressed in what is, save for a tight skirt, a gentleman's evening dress suit, with white waistcoat complete. She wears her Titian hair in a close Eton crop, and looks the strong silent woman to the life. With her notably fine forehead and beautiful hands, her whole aura is high-brow modernism.

The banning of the novel and the trial established an immediate and highly visible link between masculine clothing and lesbianism, and helped to usher in the "new feminine look" that dominated fashion for the next decade. *Eve*, a women's magazine, announced in August 1928 that "it looks as if everyone will dress ... with just an added touch of femininity. The masculine woman is as dead as the dodo in the streets of fashion." The *Sunday Times* celebrated the shift from a fashion that made it almost impossible to discern whether one was looking at "men or girls" to a much more traditional, comfortable one. It cheered on the "generation which is going back to long hair, judging by many pretty young schoolgirls one sees, and may make modesty and shyness, feminine frills, and the shade instead of the blaze of limelight, the fashion." Boyish or masculine dress served now to announce the "mannishness" of those attired in it to society at large; for a significant sexual subculture of lesbians it became the sartorial emblem of their identities. Many lesbians who had formerly "passed" as heterosexual women of high fashion, women such as Una Troubridge or Vita Sackville-West as well as Radclyffe Hall, could no longer do so. Those women who did not wish to be taken for lesbians, heterosexual and homosexual women alike, had to adorn themselves in the "feminine" fashions of the 1920s and 1930s in order to conform to societal expectations of gender and norms of sexuality, whose lines were becoming drawn with increasing rigidity. As we shall see below, the return of the soldier to a Britain in which women played a much larger role in politics and the economy than ever before was seen to pose a serious threat to the social order of the kingdom, one that was met by efforts articulated in languages of sexuality and gender.

Social peace, sexual peace[2]

The violence and upheaval of the Great War seemed to continue even after hostilities between Britain and Germany ceased in November 1918, finding new outlets for expression in the empire and at home. Many ex-soldiers, for instance, jumped at the chance to re-enlist during the Irish war for independence, joining units of the dreaded "Black and Tans" whose atrocities against Irish rebels and civilians alike earned them a reputation for unprecedented brutality. The bloody-mindedness of

British soldiers manifested itself in Amritsar, in the Punjab, where a purported attack on a white woman by Indians (shades of the Indian mutiny) called forth a reprisal by troops headed by General Dyer in April 1919. Enclosed within a garden bounded on three sides by walls, peaceful Indian demonstrators were listening to a political oration when Dyer ordered his troops to fire on them. For six minutes they did so, killing and maiming and inducing panic among the crowd, which had no means of escape. When the firing ceased 379 people were dead, and 1,500 were wounded. The Amritsar massacre shamed hundreds of thousands of Britains, who recoiled from the murderous ramifications of holding empire, and it served to galvanize a mass nationalist movement within India under the leadership of Mohandas Gandhi. But for many thousands of other Britons, Dyer's orders had forestalled a second Indian mutiny. He lost his commission, but the House of Lords voted him a commendation for his action, and readers of the *Morning Post* responded to an appeal on his behalf by pledging £25,000.

The hostility and anger directed toward the home – symbolized and epitomized by women – by front-soldiers seemingly got played out after the war. Cicely Hamilton described the postwar era as "an ugly epoch," when "the passion of enmity, fanned through four years, was not extinguished by the mere act of signing an armistice; it took time to burn itself out, and so long as it burned we had need to hate, and our hatred, deprived of an outward object, turned inward. ... The war mood seemed to have become a habit with us; instead of hating by nation we hated by party and by class." Though she didn't mention hatred by sex, in keeping with an almost total postwar feminist silence on sex war, she did relate an incident that occurred in 1919. "I remember asking a conductor to stop his bus for me in the Fulham Road; as he made no movement, I thought he had not heard and pulled the cord myself – whereupon the man turned and struck me." Front-soldiers returned home in a violent frame of mind. Philip Gibbs wrote in 1920 of the veterans:

> all was not right with the spirit of the men who came back. Something was wrong. They put on civilian clothes again, looked to their mothers and wives very much like the young men who had gone to business in the peaceful days before August of '14. But they had not come back the same men. Something had altered in them. They were subject to queer moods, queer tempers, fits of profound depression alternating with a restless desire for pleasure. Many of them were easily moved to passion when they lost control of themselves. Many were bitter in their speech, violent in opinion, frightening.

In January 1919, returning soldiers rioted all over England; in June 1919, soldiers waiting to be demobilized attacked the Epsom police station, and killed the station sergeant; in July, ex-servicemen rioting in protest against having been excluded from the ceremonies that marked "Peace Day" in Luton destroyed the town hall, resulting in 100 casualties. Irene Rathbone's fictional protagonist, Joan, who went to work in a War Pensions Committee office after the war ended, observed that:

> to refuse a man his claim was a detestable task, and was often to provoke his fury. ... All the men seemed to be nervy, and some definitely unhinged. Doubtless they would settle down in time, but their release from the military machine was not, at the moment, beneficial to them.

The Vote reported in May 1919 that "certain disquieting features marked the demonstration of the Discharged Soldiers and Sailors last Monday afternoon." It especially noted, with deep concern, "the animus ... displayed against the women conductors on the omnibuses as they passed the procession," and the attempt by "a party of demonstrators" to drag "a young woman off a service car in which she was driving an officer who, by the way, did nothing to assist her." In 1920, an article in *Time and Tide* entitled "Child assault" lamented the fact that as a result of the Great War "many people have become ... mentally and morally unstable, and that in consequence crimes of a certain class are to-day alarmingly common over the entire country. Among these crimes is that of child outrage."

Accounts of sexual attacks upon women filled the columns of newspapers. Gibbs reported that "the daily newspapers for many months have been filled with the record of dreadful crimes, of violence and passion. Most of them have been done by soldiers or ex-soldiers." He was struck by the:

> brutality of passion, a murderous instinct, which have been manifested again and again in ... riots and street rows and solitary crimes. These last are the worst because they are not inspired by a sense of injustice, however false, or any mob passion, but by homicidal mania and secret lust. The murders of young women, the outrages upon little girls, the violent robberies that have happened since the demobilizing of the armies have appalled decent-minded people.

The Vote, explaining "Why carriages reserved for women are needed," reported that:

> a young soldier, described in court as a desperate and dangerous man, was charged with assaulting a girl, aged 16, a domestic servant, in a railway carriage ... he sprang at her and caught her by the throat ... the accused said ... he would have "done her in."

The version of masculinity fashioned by these media stories of criminal acts and sexual assaults recalled and played upon the images of rapacious and lustful soldiers circulating during the war; they informed interwar fears of postwar disorder and the solutions that would be put forward to allay them.

Gibbs blamed the war for producing these violent acts against women. "Our armies," he explained:

> established an intensive culture of brutality. They were schools of slaughter. It was the duty of officers … to inspire blood-lust in the brains of gentle boys who instinctively disliked butcher's work. By an ingenious system of psychology [officers] played upon their nature, calling out the primitive barbarism which has been overlaid by civilized restraints, liberating the brute which has been long chained up by law and the social code of gentle life, but lurks always in the secret lairs of the human heart. It is difficult when the brute has been unchained, for the purpose of killing Germans, to get it into the collar again with a cry of 'Down, dog, down.' … Or men, living in holes in the earth like ape-men, were taught the ancient code of the jungle law. … The code of the ape-man is bad for some temperaments. It is apt to become a habit of mind. It may surge up when there are no Germans present, but some old woman behind an open till, or some policeman … or in a street riot where fellow-citizens are for the time being "the enemy."[3]

Gibbs blamed "the seeds of insanity in the brains of men" on the "abnormal life of war" and on women who gave them venereal disease. In this version, the war and women become confused. "Sexually [the men] were starved," he argued.

> For months they lived out of the sight and presence of women. But they came back into villages or towns where they were tempted by any poor slut who winked at them and infected them with illness. Men went to hospital with venereal disease in appalling numbers. Boys were ruined and poisoned for life.

Whatever the explanation, contemporaries could readily believe, on the basis of immediate past experience, that aggression, destructiveness, and violence were inherent characteristics of masculinity, and that social peace and order would depend upon minimizing the provocations of men to anger. One of the solutions to disorder following a war that had been represented in sexual imagery and sexual metaphor would itself be depicted in sexual terms. Sexual conflict provided one of the few adequate means by which the political, economic, and social upheaval occasioned by the Great War could ultimately be represented. The intro-duction and popularization of Freudian theory in the early 1920s offered both language and explanation for what had gripped the nations between 1914 and 1918. By the time of Freud's popularization in Britain, the English could readily accept the notion that impulses towards sex and aggression were intertwined with one another; indeed, many Britons held a view of the war as a release from long suppressed libidinal energies. Sexologists H.C. Fischer and E.X. Dubois articulated this view in *Sexual Life During the World War*. "The subconscious motives of war," they argued:

> include the sexual factor. There is a close connection between war and all that is comprised in the concept of eroticism, though it is not claimed that eroticism has a direct, deliberative causative effect ... war, no matter with what ostensible object it is waged, is to some extent similar to the contest normally fought during the mating season by the males of certain species of animals for the possession of the female.

"The lust for killing goes parallel with sexual lust," they wrote, "for love and death – creation and destruction – are psychologically inseparable allies." "Sexual lust and blood lust are compelling primeval instincts," they continued:

> and it is hardly possible to conceive that whole nations throw themselves into an orgy of murder and indescribable horror without some such psychological urge. Economic interest, greed, even so-called idealism, are inadequate, in themselves, as an explanation of such a cataclysm as the Great War.

The intimate cultural associations of sex and war made it possible for sexologists to theorize and present to the public the notion that sexual relations between men and women resembled war. Fischer and Dubois declared that:

> woman is the enemy of man, whom she constantly combats by every means at her disposal. ... This war between the sexes is intensified by international war. Woman then makes every effort to exploit the situation into which such an event places her to score over the opposition sex. The great upheaval involved in war is used by her as a sort of springboard. That is the explanation of the enormous progress of feminine emancipation during the last war.

This development would have a significant impact upon the thinking of those involved in theorizing about the relations between men and women, particularly physicians, psychiatrists and sexologists, and feminists, many of whom embraced the conservative images of femininity and masculinity that arose as British society sought in the establishment of harmonious marital relationships a resolution to the anxieties and political turmoil caused by the Great War. Many Britons, including feminists, looked to create peace and order in the public sphere of social, economic and political relations by imposing peace and order on the private sphere of sexual relations.

The inscription of large societal anxieties and conflicts on to marital relationships operated on at least two levels. On the one hand, gender, sexuality and the relationship between the sexes served as metaphors through which issues of power might be resolved by referring to notions of sexual difference. On the other hand, sexuality and war were understood by the culture – consciously or unconsciously – to be inextricably intertwined. Thus, the resolution of conflict through mutual, pleasurable sexual experiences within marriage was regarded by many sexologists and sex reformers as a means of reducing the threat of war by removing the sexual repressions and tensions that, they sometimes implied, helped to bring it about. War, claimed Fischer and Dubois, "constituted a respite from rigid moral laws that were contrary to fundamental human nature." It provided "an outlet for latent erotic needs" driven underground by society's imposition of "many sexual constraints," against which "the caveman within" civilized men revolted. "The primitive combative and sexual instincts are undoubtedly there, and have led the world into many irreparable disasters," they argued.

> These instincts can neither be completely repressed, nor eliminated. But they must be given another outlet than war. Judicious and progressive sexual reform, tending to liberate the world from the false morality that ultimately leads to the degradation of war, would be an obvious first step in this direction.

The discourses on sexuality that predominated in the postwar years appropriated the language and imagery of war as psychoanalysts, sexologists and sex reformers sought in the study of sexuality the solutions to the maintenance and salvation of civilization itself. As Havelock Ellis, the most influential sexologist in interwar Britain, wrote in *The Psychology of Sex*, his popular textbook, sex "is not merely the channel along which the race is maintained and built up, it is the foundation on which all dreams of the future world must be erected." For Ellis, as for all "scientists of sex" in the 1920s and 1930s, sexual activity was firmly located within marriage, and its chief and central aim, after the carnage wrought by the Great War, was procreation. (G.K. Chesterton, as quoted by Dora Russell, wrote that "sex without gestation and parturition is like blowing the trumpets and waving the flags without doing any of the fighting.") A more insistent ideology of motherhood demanded that women leave their wartime jobs, give up their independence, and return to home and family, where their primary occupation – their obligation, in fact – would be the bearing and rearing of children.

If the sexual disorder of war was to be followed by peace, the metaphor required sexual peace, a model of marital accord achieved through mutual sexual enjoyment. Discourses about female sexuality that before the war had emphasized women's lack of sexual impulse, and even distaste for sexual intercourse, underwent modification to accommodate the political, social, and economic requirements of the postwar period. The new accent on motherhood was accompanied by a growing emphasis on the importance of sexual activity, sexual pleasure, sexual compatibility between husband and wife.

As marriage and marital sex bore the brunt of restoring social harmony in postwar Britain, sex manuals – how-to guides to conjugal fulfillment – became bestsellers. Marie Stopes's *Married Love*, published in 1918, sold more than 2,000 copies in the first two weeks, and 400,000 by 1923. Theodore Van de Velde's *Ideal Marriage, Its Physiology and Technique* (1926) went through forty-three printings. Such books as Isabel Emslie Hutton's *The Sex Technique in Marriage* (1932), Helena Wright's *The Sex Factor in Marriage*, and Van de Velde's *Sex Hostility in Marriage* (1931) attest to the broadly perceived need to establish sexual peace through sexual pleasure. Domestic harmony, and thus social peace, appeared to Britons to depend upon the establishment of a managed and controlled sexuality whereby warriors could be rendered peacelike and wherein women could find, acknowledge, and express their sexuality within a framework of "scientific" approbation.

Manly men, womanly women[4]

Feminism appeared to contemporaries to threaten the social peace created by domestic harmony. In 1918, women over the age of thirty received the vote, ostensibly in return for their efforts on behalf of the war effort. Some six million out of eleven million adult women were enfranchised, the age restriction serving to ensure that women would not enjoy a majority over men, whose numbers had been dramatically reduced by the war. The vote was followed by the Eligibility of Women Act of 1918, which permitted women to stand for parliament. The same year, the bastardy laws of 1872 were amended, thus increasing from five to ten shillings a week the amount a father could be made to pay to support an illegitimate child. In 1919, the passage of the Sex Disqualification Removal Act gave women access to all branches of the legal profession. By 1925, despite the ferocious opposition of entrenched bureaucrats, the civil service admitted women to its competitive examinations, though it refused to pay female civil servants the salaries given to men holding the same position, an inequity that feminists would battle against for years in their equal-pay campaign of the 1930s. The Matrimonial Causes Act of 1923, a direct outcome of intense feminist lobbying, eliminated the double standard of divorce. The dissemination of contraceptive information at maternity centers and mothers' clinics, pioneered by birth control advocate Marie Stopes and then established as policy by the Labour government in 1930 after a long battle among feminists themselves, and between men and women within the

Labour Party, had an immediate impact on family size. In 1913, England and Wales had seen 1,102,500 births. That number dropped to 900,130 births in 1923; 777,520 births in 1926; and to 761,963 births in 1931. The average size of the British family fell from 5.5 in the last quarter of the nineteenth century to 2.2 between 1925 and 1929. In 1928, women finally obtained the franchise on the same terms as it was granted to men.

These were impressive victories by any measure. In addition to other welfare benefits implemented during the war to compensate families for the loss of income as men went off to war, some never to return and others to return too disabled to hold a job – to which, however, married women had no independent right – they improved the lives of many women to a large extent. Certainly these legislative reforms, along with the gains women had made in employment and wages during the war, contributed to an impression that the war had been a boon to women, that it had enhanced their position in the workplace and in political life, and that it had done so at the expense of men.

As early as 1916, in fact, the *Factory Times* urged that "we must get the women back into the home as soon as possible. That they ever left is one of the evil results of the war." Removing women from their wartime jobs so as to eliminate competition with men for work was regarded as one way to assure, as Ray Strachey put it, "that everything could be as it had been before." Where once women had received accolades of the highest order for their service to the country during wartime, by 1918 they were being vilified and excoriated for their efforts. Irene Clephane, writing in 1935, believed that press attitudes towards women workers began to change between 1918 and 1919. "From being the saviours of the nation," she wrote:

> women in employment were degraded in the public press to the position of ruthless selfseekers depriving men and their dependents of a livelihood. The woman who had no one to support her, the woman who herself had dependents, the woman who had no necessity, save that of the urge to personal independence and integrity, to earn: all of them became, in many people's minds, objects of opprobrium.

Philip Gibbs returned from the front and charged that ex-soldiers couldn't find jobs because "the girls were clinging to their jobs, would not let go of the pocket-money which they had spent on frocks." E. Austin Hinton, in a letter to the *Saturday Review* in December 1918, attempted to trivialize and invalidate women's war efforts, insisting that the woman who took up "what she calls 'war work'" did so "for the sake of a love or flirtation and associated giddiness, which the freer and more licensed life has made it possible to indulge." A correspondent for the *Leeds Mercury* wrote in April of 1919 of his "unfeigned pleasure" that women bus conductors and underground drivers would no longer be holding their positions. "Their record of duty well done," he complained, "is seriously blemished by their habitual and aggressive incivility, and a callous disregard for the welfare of passengers. Their shrewish behavior will remain one of the unpleasant memories of the war's vicissitudes." Given the actual nature of the war's vicissitudes, this is quite a profound statement of hostility. As W. Keith pointed out in the *Daily News* in March 1921, in an article titled "Dislike of women," "the attitude of the public towards women is more full of contempt and bitterness than has been the case since the suffragette outbreaks." The pressures on women to leave their jobs and return to the domestic sphere were intense – and often successful. By 1921, fewer women were "gainfully employed," according to the census of that year, than in 1911.

But this is only one part of the story. Women did leave their wartime jobs as munitions factories shut down for lack of orders. And, beginning in 1921, the traditional employers of women, the great textile factories of Lancashire, began to feel the serious effects of recession, laying off both male and female workers in large numbers, as did other old industries in the north of England like shipbuilding and coal-mining. Women put out of work by the end of the war and by the beginnings of economic depression refused, as they would not have in the past, to seek employment as domestic servants, an expression of self-regard that certainly helped to drive up their unemployment rates. But in the south of England, new industries providing household consumer goods by means of large-scale assembly line production began to appear, and they relied upon women to make up the bulk of their semi-skilled workforce. The electrical appliances and the ready-made goods that enabled middle-class women to provide even greater levels of domestic comfort in the interwar years were supplied by wage-earning women. New work opportunities for women in offices as typists, bookkeepers, or cleaning staff, and in shops as assistants and cashiers cropped up, as Britain's economy underwent restructuring from heavy industry in the north to light consumer and service industries in the south.

During this period, women in the Labour Party increased their numbers and their influence. A number of women became MPs for Labour – Susan Lawrence, Ellen Wilkinson, and Margaret Bondfield, to name only those who became cabinet ministers – and many, many more served their communities on local governing boards and authorities. To be sure, they faced strongly anti-feminist attitudes within the party, and struggled, usually in vain, to gain acceptance for their demands, but their energies and their activities on behalf of poor and working women helped to improve their lives considerably. More importantly, their visions of how women should be able to live helped to give shape to the provisions and the expectations of the welfare state established in Britain after the Second World War.

With their enfranchisement in 1918, women joined local branches of the party to a far greater degree than did men. In 1923, 120,000 women belonged to the women's sections of the Labour Party; they increased their numbers to as many as 300,000 between 1927 and 1939, comprising at least half of the membership of the party as a whole. In some areas, like Cardiff, they made up as much as three-quarters of the membership. They made their voices heard, urging policies such as the dissemination of contraceptives or family allowances upon their male colleagues. They demanded equal pay for men and women, and, because in only a few jobs could it be claimed that women and men did the same work, comparable pay for women who did work of the same value as men. They strove to endow home- and housework with the dignity of paid labor, and the majority of them believed that married women had the right to work just like their unmarried sisters. In holding this opinion, Labour women departed from the powerful cultural norm that mothers should not work. Indeed, throughout the interwar period, the vast majority of wives, and especially mothers, did not work outside the home. The bread-winning husband and his stay-at-home wife continued to characterize working-class ideals of masculinity and femininity, however difficult they were to achieve.

The efforts to eliminate women from their wartime jobs constituted only one aspect of a larger wave of anti-feminism that inundated Britain in the interwar years. If propaganda and government policy did not always succeed in their aims, they contributed to an ideological backlash against the victories women had secured during and after the war. With the popularization of Freudian theory in the 1920s, separate sphere ideology became psychologized. Whereas Freud had first posited a psychological bisexuality in males and females, and asserted that masculinity and femininity and sexuality were cultural phenomena that required explanation, British psychiatrists and sexologists put forward theories of sexuality and sexual difference that stemmed from biology. Femininity, argued Ernest Jones, "develops progressively from the promptings of an instinctual constitution." While undermining the belief in the passionlessness of the female – a development that had considerable appeal for many women – Freud's British followers thus gave credence to the belief that biological factors determined the differences between masculinity and femininity and male and female sexuality. "Anatomy is destiny," Freud declared in 1924 in "The dissolution of the Oedipus complex," in contradiction to his earlier beliefs. In "Some psychical consequences of the anatomical distinction between the sexes," published in 1925, Freud argued that the personality development of the female centered upon her discovery in early childhood that she lacked a penis; penis envy created in the female child a lifelong dissatisfaction with her identity as a woman. Her discomfiture could only be overcome through the substitution of the penis with a child.

Happiness and health for women, in other words, depended upon motherhood. What *The Encyclopedia of Sexual Knowledge* (1934), under the general editorship of Norman Haire, a prominent British sex reformer, called "the physiological need of childbirth" in women, stemmed from "the obvious fact" that "her organism is essentially fitted for maternity." "The organic need of children, which is latent in every woman, is so imperious that prolonged enforced sterility drives her body to revolt, and this revolt may manifest itself in a number of disorders and growths." This physiological need for children, argued the physicians and sexologists who contributed to the huge tome, was matched by a psychological one to fill the "void in a woman's life." Lacking the activities and opportunities of her husband, and:

> the care of children being the occupation most suited to her temperament, she will seek an outlet for her energy in that direction. Thus, in order to preserve her physiological and psychological equilibrium, a woman, to what-ever social stratum she may belong, needs children.

Those women who refused motherhood, who continued in their work or study, or who sought equality between men and women, brought down upon their heads the wrath of many psychiatrists and sexologists, who found in their presumptions a sexual pathology. "After all is said and done," declared Van de Velde, "the biolog-ical difference between masculine and feminine cannot be explained away; neither can the physical and mental contrasts between man and woman proceeding from this." Characterized by its capacity for emotion, the feminine psyche, he declared, rendered women incapable of objectivity, of weighing the sides of an argument or of distinguishing the right and wrong of things. "Just as her body is fashioned for maternity, so the mental quality dominating all others in the woman is mother-hood." Permanent equality in marriage, Van de Velde asserted, was abnormal because "sexuality is always present in man and woman, and upper and lower place is inseparably allied with it." Hostility in marriage, which was now construed as in part responsible for the disorders of contemporary life, resulted from women who sought to dominate their husbands or who struggled with them for power, he cautioned. Even Havelock Ellis, an advocate of women's rights in the prewar period, could write that the idea that women might have "the same education as men, the same occupations as men, even the same sports" constituted "the source of all that was unbalanced ... in the old women's movement."

Diagnoses of a "female castration complex" or of frigidity were applied to women who ventured out of their assigned domestic, sexual sphere. Using termino-logy and imagery evocative of war, sexologist Walter Gallichan wrote in *The Poison of Prudery*, "these degenerate women are a menace to civilisation. They provoke sex misunderstanding and antagonism; they wreck conjugal happiness." He blamed frigid women for producing spinsters, attributing to women what was, in fact, a consequence of the great losses of life on the battlefield. "Many daughters of cold mothers die spinsters. They imbibe the maternal prejudices and ideas at the school age or earlier, and they grow up with a smouldering antipathy towards men."

The description of feminists as abnormal, sexually maladjusted women who hated men and the equating of feminism with sex war were not, of course, new, but the context in which such charges were levelled was entirely different now. The first postwar census revealed that England and Wales contained 1,920,000 more women than men. During the nineteenth century, the disparity of females to males had remained steady at about 1,068 to 1,000. In 1921, it rose to 1,096 to 1,000 amongst the whole population; for three particular age cohorts, the imbalance was shocking. Among those aged twenty to twenty-four, 1,176 women existed for every 1,000 men; for ages twenty-five to twenty-nine, the number of women climbed to 1,209 for every 1,000 men; and at thirty to thirty-four years, the disparity was 1,186 to 1,000. The existence of large numbers of unmarried and unmarriable women produced a great deal of anxiety. The diatribes directed at them reflected society's longing to return to the familiar, "traditional" ways of life before August 1914, a nostalgic projection that failed to recall the way life "really" was in Edwardian times. Denied husbands, many of them, by the destruction of the Great War, single women were visible reminders of the war that had only recently ended. Feminism soon became linked in the public mind not merely with sex war, a somewhat familiar concept, but with armed conflict, death, and destruction. Arabella Kenealy, a lecturer at the Royal College of Physicians in Dublin, argued in 1920 in a book pointedly titled *Feminism and Sex-Extinction*, that:

> men and women are naturally dependent upon one another in every human relation; a dispensation which engenders reciprocal trust, affection and comradeship. Feminist doctrine and practice menace these most excellent previsions and provisions of Nature by thrusting personal rivalries, economic competition and general conflict of interests between the sexes.

She urged women to recognize the inevitability of sex differences and to give up their wartime jobs to men, explaining that men would use violence against them if they refused to vacate their positions. After the horrific events of the Great War, the specter of conflict between men and women could hardly be tolerated; postwar society sought above all to re-establish a sense of peace and security in an unfamiliar and very insecure world. The insistence upon gender peace – a relationship of complementarity between men and women in which women did not compete with men in the public arena, and thereby provoke men to anger, the world of separate spheres – appears to have been a fundamental step in that direction.

In these constructions, and those of feminists who also saw in sex the salvation of civilization and world peace, the metaphors of war had come home: the return of the soldier had placed Britain, or at least the women of Britain, under military occupation. Where once they had conceived masculinity and femininity to be the products of laws, attitudes, and institutions that encouraged an unfettered and aggressive male sexuality and a passive, even non-existent, female sexuality, many feminists now took up a variation of the "drive-discharge" model that relied upon the notion of biological drives to explain male behavior. The social bases of masculinity and femininity gave way to a biologically determined, innate male and female sexuality, which in turn suggested that women must act differently in order to protect themselves and society from the aggression unleashed by war. The rhetoric of separate spheres had become infected with the rhetoric of war. In classic anti-feminist terms, these feminists gave voice to the cultural belief that the war had demonstrated the need for recreating barriers between men and women, for the recognition of sexual difference, if society were to return to a condition of normalcy, defined in biological or natural terms. But because many of the legal barriers barring women from public life were being dismantled, the institutional practices enforcing separate spheres came to be replaced by psychological ones. The power of psychologized separate spheres, the extent of the psychic and linguistic internalization of military occupation by the women of Britain, insured that all the parliamentary reforms in the world would be of little avail to those seeking equality with men.

For millions of laboring men and women, the newly justified gender ideals of bread-winning male and stay-at-home wife could not easily be realized. The years of depression that began in Britain as early as 1921, when one million Britons were out of work – that number rising to 2.5 million by 1935 – severely challenged one of the most fundamental of criteria for masculinity, that of bread-winner status. Men who prided themselves on their independence and on their ability to keep their family found themselves out of work, sometimes for years at a stretch. Women had to make do on dramatically reduced pay-packets or the unemployment assistance that came to be called, derisively, "the dole," going without food themselves in order that their husbands and children might eat, and introducing economies that they withheld from their husbands' knowledge for fear that his diminished sense of manliness might be further eroded. Families broke apart over the implementation of the draconian and humiliating "means test," through which eligibility for assistance was established. By 1935, unemployment for millions of people appeared to be the normal state of things in many parts of Britain.

Work conferred a status on working-class men that no other attribute could replace. Certain jobs created a higher manly standing than others, as least for some men, even at the height of unemployment, when most men took any job they could find.[5] Colliers, for example, Clifford Steele recounted, "were apt to look on lesser laborious tasks as being a bit cissyish. They were he-men when they went down the pit," a categorization, he believed, that "is what got lads down the pit." When he himself began to work and to bring home a wage to help his family, "I was the big he-man. I had to be catered for. ... I got a bit of prestige then." No wonder that when unemployment struck many of the coal fields, men would travel for miles over mountainous terrain to find other jobs. One South Wales collier, Kenneth Maher, recalled that these "desperate men" got up at 3:00 a.m., walked for three hours to make it to the pit by 6:00 a.m., worked an eight-hour shift, and walked back another three hours to get home. Conditions of work became abominable, and the treatment meted out to many men by the bosses constituted an acute threat to their sense of manliness. Many struck back. Maher witnessed one collier who had been insulted by the behavior of a pit under-manager. "I have a woman in the house who thinks of me as a husband and a man, three children who look up to me and think they see a man, their father," the collier yelled. "But I can't be a man to put up with this." He took hold of the under-manager's tie and pulled him against the window separating the two men, breaking his nose and cutting off his air supply. Four men had to pull the collier away. He was fired, Maher remembers, "but he could hold his head up. He didn't grovel to them."

Men took on work that endangered their health and their lives, "desperate to get a job," as Charles Graham recalled. His stepfather lost his sight working on a building site where he shoveled caustic lime all day, "the dust blowing into his eyes and it does peel your eyes." Men who could not find work after they had been laid off struggled mightily to maintain a sense of dignity, but many fought a losing battle. "A lot of people did go to the billiard halls and the public libraries," Graham stated, "but a terrible lot of them just sat in their chairs and were afraid to go out. I've seen chaps with their nails curled right over through lack of use. Men became just like cabbages."

Emotional depression, especially among older skilled working men who could not find work, became pronounced. Bitter, humiliated, feeling hopeless, useless, and impotent, these men lost their self-respect and self-confidence. One such skilled artisan was described by an observer as being:

ashamed of his lapse from higher standards, but the shame only depresses him more. He wanders about with no end in view, more and more alone, chewing the cud of all the insults, and slighting remarks he may have addressed to him, a ghost among living men, inhabiting a no-man's-land, without hope, without purpose, without human contact.

Many men in this situation "broke down" as they faced a future of permanent unemployment, lost "spirit" or "heart," as they put it.

Younger men, some of whom had never been employed, showed different signs of strain, according to officials investigating the effects of joblessness on the population. "For many," one group reported, "self-confidence is shattered and this, in itself, becomes a barrier to further employment. Personal worth tends to be assessed at a lower level and, in contrast to the ambitions and day-dreams of their earlier days, they go forward to maturing manhood with more limited ideas as to the worth of their contribution to life and work."[6] Some became violent as a consequence of unemployment, others took on an attitude of fatalism, apathy, or carelessness. For all men out of work, malnutrition drained their physiques, leaving them weakened, more fragile, even delicate in appearance. As Charles Graham put it, "after three or four years of unemployment some men were quite incapable of work, even if it was offered to them."

Physicians and public-health officials reported that men who had been unemployed for long periods of time produced symptoms of "nerves" and "psycho-neurotic" illnesses – what during the war had been called "shell shock," which, as we have seen, came about very frequently when men could not articulate the terrors they felt for fear of being considered "unmanly." Dr Haliday of Glasgow estimated that a third of the unemployed men he saw suffered from illnesses for which there was no organic basis; among those who had been without work for more than six months, the number of men who had "gone to pieces" rose to 42 percent. Suicide rates among unemployed men rose. In 1932, according to the Home Office, two out-of-work men killed themselves every day. In the years from 1921 to 1931, the numbers of suicides among men under 25 years of age rose by 60 percent.

In some instances, investigators found that the severe economic conditions had reduced women to unusual levels of apathy as well, describing some places where "women had lost all pride in personal appearance and appearance in the home." But, for the most part, wives of the unemployed and under-employed strove valiantly to protect their men from the degradations and humiliations of having lost their bread-winner status, having become "unmanned." Women went without food, "literally starving themselves in order to feed and clothe the children reasonably well," health investigators discovered; in a third of the families these officials looked in on the wife was ill. Undernourished, exhausted, and driven to distraction by anxiety, many of these women could not withstand the trials of childbirth: maternal mortality rates in the distressed areas of Britain were far higher than those in the south, for instance.[7] Others secretly pawned items that could be spared for the week in order to keep food on the table or Sunday shoes on their children, a ritual long practiced by poorer working-class women in the nineteenth and early twentieth centuries, but now one undertaken by those of the more respectable ranks as well. Clifford Steele described how he:

> was sent to the pawnshop once and I hadn't to let my father know. He'd have gone mad if he'd have thought. But what he didn't realise was how my mother was having to budget. He wasn't aware of a lot of things that we had to do, my mother and myself, to keep the cart on the wheels.

Gladys Gibson, an employee of the Unemployment Assistance Board (UAB) in London, recounted the tale of one woman whose husband had spent his "dole" allotment before bringing it home to her. Instead of castigating him for it, at least in front of the UAB, she protested to Gibson for holding up the next payment until the family had literally run out of food. "You've shamed him long enough, haven't you?" she demanded. "How'd you like to see your old man shamed in front of his mates?" George Orwell reported that the wives of unemployed men in the north of England had to work much harder than ever before, trying to manage their households on less money, but that they would not think of asking their husbands to pitch in. He declared:

> Practically never in a working-class home, will you see the man doing a stroke of the housework. Unemployment has not changed this convention, which on the face of it seems a little unfair. The man is idle from morning to night but the woman is as busy as ever. ... Yet so far as my experience goes the women do not protest. I believe that they, as well as the men, feel that a man would lose his manhood if, merely because he was out of work, he developed into a 'Mary Ann' [shorthand for a homosexual].[8]

But in another sector of society, among the middle classes, as we shall see in the next section, domestic life had its appeal: as an alternative means to stemming the violence and conflict of the wartime and postwar years to those we saw above, many middle-class men adopted a style of manliness that centered not on the public world of politics but on the private world of the home.

The modified male

Earlier ideals of the virile male, like that of the frontier pioneer and hunter, and current ones exemplified by the Black and Tans or by General Dyer, it appeared now to many, had led Britain into the bloody disasters of the war. A number of women who had seen action overseas during the First World War were convinced that the emphases on sexual difference current in the late 1920s and 1930s would not serve to prevent domestic and international conflict, but might actually help to bring them about, with disastrous consequences for feminism, democracy, and liberty generally. Winifred Holtby offered the words of the British fascist Oswald Mosley as a warning to those who valorized maternity and domesticity for women. "The part of women in our future organization will be important, but different from that of men," Mosley had written. "*We want men who are men and women who are women.*" In a review of a book by James Drennan about Mosley, Labour MP Ellen Wilkinson noted the author's approval of Mosley's emphasis on traditional masculinity as he summoned "the manhood of Britain to a disciplined and peaceful revolution" that would replace the effeminate world of politics with decisive, physical action. Drennan crowed:

> With his wrestling, boxing and fencing [Mosley] has walked in the tradition of the Regency Buck in a time when people have gotten into the habit of expecting younger politicians to have horn-rimmed spectacles and soft white hands and spend their holidays at Geneva.

But this kind of gendered imagery, "this fencing-master idea of politics," Wilkinson insisted, "is playing the devil with modern Europe."[9] Such a model of masculinity had to be disavowed if Britain was to avoid the catastrophe of another war.

At the élite schools, where boys had been training to enter the war once they came of age, there was a pronounced reaction against any kind of activities or behavior that could be associated with militarism. At Oxford and Cambridge, undergraduates fluctuated in their feelings between disgust at the war's great brutality and guilt over not having served in it. George Orwell confessed that "you felt yourself a little less than a man, because you had missed it," but the postwar generation's ideals of masculinity would never correspond to those of the society that had gone off so lightly to war in 1914. Instead, the "bright young things" of the 1920s, as the aesthetes around Evelyn Waugh and other writers were called, glorified not action but art, not bravery but beauty. They eschewed maturity and responsibility in favor of frivolity and carelessness. This new male figure made his differences with the old model of British manliness quite clear when, in February 1933, members of the Oxford Union moved that "this House will in no circumstances fight for its King and country."

At the more popular level, boys' literature took on different colorations from its prewar renditions.[10] Where before the war aristocratic values and norms of masculinity had prevailed, and men's character in the popular adventure stories derived in great part from their thinking and acting independently of the mores of mass society, now conformity to community norms of behavior characterized a proper manliness. Stories directed at working-class youth, especially, often taking place in a school setting, played up the role of teachers and parents in educating and training boys in the right way to comport themselves. Teachers quite often appeared as heroes in these stories, as was the case of Septimus Green in a series of tales called *The Big Stiff*. Instead of beating or humiliating his charges, as would have been the case in Victorian and Edwardian school stories, Green engaged the interest of his students and taught them by example. The authority of father figures and the needs of the community received great emphasis in these tales, testimony to the uneasiness felt by the culture about the place of working-class men in a society wracked by unemployment.

Adventure stories continued to exert the greatest pull on youthful male readers in the interwar period, but they tended to be set within Britain rather than outside of it and were concerned with the development of sporting prowess, and, often, business success, something that would never have appeared in the prewar genre. In "Peter sticks it," for instance, the protagonist, the son of a shipping tycoon, does poorly in school because he spends too much time perfecting his athletic skills. His father's displeasure leads him, in a fit of anger, to seek a job as a sailor; unbeknownst to Peter, his father has arranged a berth for him on board one of his own ships. When it appears that the ship will have to return to England with an empty hold, Peter mobilizes his athletic skills to ensure that the trip will be profitable. He challenges an arms dealer to a game of golf. If he wins, he can take a load of cargo at the price he names; if he loses, the dealer gets his asking price. Peter takes the match and gets the cargo at the lower price, thus maximizing the profits earned by his father's company. By the time the adventure ends, Peter's father has acknowledged the usefulness of Peter's athletic talents, and Peter has returned to school to gain the necessary academic skills to go to work for the family business. In this story, Peter achieves manhood through a process that combines his own competence and his father's guidance. Education and success in individual sports, not trial by ordeal in a showdown against a wild beast or a tribe of fierce Afghan fighters, proves to be the route to manliness in the years after the war.

In fact, sentiment about Britain's possession of empire seemed to be undergoing a sea change in the years following the Great War. The loss of Ireland in 1922 began a process of demoralization on the part of Britons, even the most imperialist among them, that culminated in independence for India in 1947, an act that in turn foreshadowed decolonization in the rest of Asia and in Africa and the West Indies as well. Those who recorded the decline in imperial spirit for good or ill blamed it on a feminization of empire, on the women whose failure to understand the needs of imperial rule and whose small and petty concerns had undermined the firm hand with which British men had held sway over subject peoples. As E.M. Forster, no devotee of imperial rule himself, had Ronny Heaslop, the city magistrate, retort in *A Passage to India* (1924), when his mother, Mrs Moore, reported that another main character, Adela Quested, objected to the way the British treated Indians, "oh, how like a woman to worry over a side-issue!" Mrs Moore, taken aback, replies, "a side-issue, a side-issue? ... How can it be that?" "We're not out here for the purpose of behaving pleasantly," Ronny exclaims, furious. "We're out here to do justice and keep the peace. ... India isn't a drawing room. ... I am out here to work, mind, to hold this wretched country by force." Alternatively, women's disapproval of sexual relations between white men and black women, it was hinted, had weakened a bond between ruler and ruled through which subject peoples had been rendered loyal to their masters. "Nothing like a bit of black to cement race relations, was there?" went a crude, but telling comment.[11] Forster put it somewhat differently when he had Mr Fielding, a teacher who loved Indian culture and sympathized with Indian aspirations for independence, ruminate on his relationships with various groups.

> He had discovered that it is possible to keep in with Indians and Englishmen, but that he who would also keep in with Englishwomen must drop the Indians. The two wouldn't combine. Useless to blame either party, useless to blame them for blaming one another. It was just so, and one had to choose.

An imperial ideology of gender that had sanctified British womanhood in the nineteenth century and justified imperial rule on the basis of the need to protect British women from native men, turned by the interwar period to one in which women were castigated or held responsible for Britons losing their hold on formerly docile subjects. Even when the agency of native peoples themselves was recognized as a factor in creating resistance to British rule, the phenomenon was depicted in a gendered language. Winston Churchill, for instance, expressed his disgust at the "nauseating and humiliating spectacle" of a deeply feminized Gandhi – a proponent of *satyagraha*, by which one resisted oppression and force "by suffering in one's own person," a perfect example of the self-abnegation expected of women – "this one-time Inner Temple lawyer, now turned seditious fakir, striding half-naked up the steps of the Viceroy's palace ... to negotiate and parley on equal terms with the representative of the King-Emperor."[12]

Amongst the middle classes, a kind of domestication of British life and of British masculinity took place in the 1920s and 1930s.[13] The widely read detective literature of the 1920s and 1930s, for example, offered up heroes who departed dramatically from their prewar predecessors, though adventure heroes did not disappear entirely, as the continued popularity of such figures as "Sapper" and "Bulldog Drummond" attest. Dorothy Sayers's Peter Wimsey, Agatha Christie's Hercule Poirot, Dorothy Allingham's Albert Campion – these were protagonists who eschewed violence and even action, and who in some instances resembled the broken, empty men who returned home from the war. They were prim, even prissy, men, whose talents lay in the use of their sharp wits rather than their bodies. They behaved in ways that mocked conventional masculinity, giggling and mincing their way through situations, all the while accumulating small details and matters of fact that would enable them to solve the most impenetrable of crimes. They dressed with exquisite attention to their personal appearance, bringing a delicacy and foppishness to their demeanor that recalled the effeminacy of eighteenth- and early nineteenth-century "dandies." They lacked the traditional manly qualities of physical courage and endurance: Wimsey suffered from shell shock, which occasionally reduced him to cowering in terror; Poirot, according to his rather ineffectual assistant, Captain Hastings, was a man for whom "a speck of dust would have caused him more pain than a bullet wound." Christie's whodunits, in particular, took place in decidedly domestic venues: such mysteries as *The Body in the Library* and *The Peril at End House* offered homely settings in which the puzzles of what one literary critic has called "the literature of convalescence"[14] – through which the reader could transform the acute anxieties of postwar society into the small, unimportant, yet pleasurable activities of private home life – could be worked out.

Fear of a renewal of war, especially after 1933, when Adolph Hitler came to power in Germany, gripped the nation, and the prewar stance of aggressive imperialism hardly seemed calculated to stave it off. Instead, a far more inward-looking, private, quiet, "little" Englandism seemed to many to be the more correct national stance. As Joseph Priestly put it in his 1935 *English Journey*, "it is little England I love. And I considered how much I disliked Big Englanders, whom I saw as red-faced, loud-voiced fellows, wanting to go and boss everybody about all over the world." This version of national identity in turn required a more inward-looking, private, quiet, little man as the standard bearer of peace. In 1938, the figure of Neville Chamberlain, impeccably tailored, with his bowler hat and umbrella, returning from Munich with "peace in our time," seemed to exemplify those qualities of masculinity that would help keep Britain out of war. But the men in uniform with whom he negotiated – men whose dress asserted aggression and militarism – would in the end decide the issue.

NOTES

1 This section relies upon Laura Doan, "Passing fashions: Reading female masculinities in the 1920s," *Feminist Studies* 24(3), Fall 1998: 663–700.
2 This discussion draws upon Susan Kingsley Kent, *Making Peace: The Reconstruction of Gender in Interwar Britain* (Princeton, 1993), ch. 5.
3 Philip Gibbs, *Now It Can Be Told* (1920), pp. 551–2.
4 See Susan Kingsley Kent, *Making Peace*, ch. 5.
5 This section is drawn from the oral histories conducted by Nigel Gray in *The Worst of Times: An Oral History of the Great Depression in Britain* (Totowa, NJ, 1985).
6 Quoted in John Stevenson and Chris Cook, *Britain in the Depression: Society and Politics, 1929–1939* (London, 1994), p. 101.
7 Stevenson and Cook, *Britain in the Depression*, p. 98.
8 George Orwell, *The Road to Wigan Pier* (New York, 1958), p. 81.
9 Quoted in Kent, *Making Peace*, p. 142.
10 For this section, see Kelly Boyd, "Knowing your place: The tensions of manliness in boys' story papers, 1918–1939," in Michael Roper and John Tosh, eds, *Manful Assertions: Masculinities in Britain since 1800* (London, 1991).
11 Quoted in James Morris, *Farewell the Trumpets: An Imperial Retreat* (London, 1978), p. 401.
12 Quoted in Morris, *Farewell the Trumpets*, p. 293.

13 This discussion relies upon Alison Light's wonderful *Forever England: Femininity, Literature and Conservatism Between the Wars* (London, 1991).
14 Alison Light, *Forever England*, p. 69.

SOURCES

Sally Alexander, "Becoming a woman in London in the 1920s and 1930s," in David Feldman and Gareth Stedman Jones, eds, *Metropolis: London*. London, 1989.

Ronald Blythe, *The Age of Illusion: Some Glimpses of Britain Between the Wars, 1919–1940*. Oxford, 1983.

Kelly Boyd, "Knowing your place: The tensions of manliness in boys' story papers, 1918–1939," in Michael Roper and John Tosh, eds, *Manful Assertions: Masculinities in Britain since 1800*. London, 1991.

Laura Doan, "Passing fashions: Reading female masculinities in the 1920s," *Feminist Studies* 24(3), Fall 1998: 663–700.

E.M. Forster, *A Passage to India*. London, 1924.

Philip Gibbs, *Now It Can Be Told*. 1920.

Miriam Glucksmann, *Women Assemble: Women Workers and the New Industries in Inter-War Britain*. London, 1990.

Robert Graves and Alan Hodge, *The Long Weekend: A Social History of Great Britain, 1918–1939*. New York, 1963.

Nigel Gray, *The Worst of Times: An Oral History of the Great Depression in Britain*. Totowa, NJ, 1985.

Samuel Hynes, *A War Imagined: The First World War and English Culture*. New York, 1991.

Susan Kingsley Kent, *Making Peace: The Reconstruction of Gender in Interwar Britain*. Princeton, NJ, 1993.

Alison Light, *Forever England: Femininity, Literature and Conservatism Between the Wars*. London, 1991.

James Morris, *Farewell the Trumpets: An Imperial Retreat*. London, 1978.

George Orwell, *The Road to Wigan Pier*. New York, 1958.

Raphael Samuel, ed., *Patriotism: The Making and Unmaking of British National Identity. Volume I: History and Politics*. London, 1989.

Harold L. Smith, "British Feminism in the 1920s," in Harold L. Smith, ed., *British Feminism in the Twentieth Century*. Aldershot, 1990.

John Stevenson and Chris Cook, *Britain in the Depression: Society and Politics, 1929–1939*. London, 1994.

Pat Thane, "The women of the British Labour Party and feminism, 1906–1945," in Harold L. Smith, ed., *British Feminism in the Twentieth Century*. Aldershot, 1990.

——, "Visions of gender in the making of the British Welfare State: The case of women in the British Labour Party and social policy, 1906–1945," in Gisela Bock and Pat Thane, eds, *Maternity and Gender Policies: Women and the Rise of the European Welfare States, 1880s-1950s*. London, 1991.

Chapter 13

War, welfare, and postwar "consensus," 1939–63

War again

The outbreak of the Second World War had been expected for a number of years, and was dreaded and feared by all those who could recall or had heard tale of the horrors and dislocations of the First World War. The men who went off to fight the Germans the second time around had none of the expectations of glory, honor, or comradeship that marked their Great War predecessors. They enlisted or were conscripted fully aware of the privations and difficulties that awaited them. They knew, unlike the men of 1914, what life and death in war entailed. Because they entered the war with a far more realistic understanding of its brutalities and their places within it, they did not suffer from the massive threat to their manliness that First World War soldiers experienced.

People at home knew what was coming as well. Advances in industry and technology meant that civilian populations would not escape the arena of war. But the rhetoric of separate spheres and the broad-based appeal to women to return to their homes and families in the years following the Great War had proved to be so effective that when war came again in September 1939, the ability of Britain to wage war and to defend its people was compromised. Industries producing items now considered "luxuries" – textiles, shoes, clothing, and the like – cut their workforce dramatically as their markets dried up under the threat of war, but their female labor force was not absorbed into industries now considered "essential" to the war effort, largely because employers did not feel it proper to employ women in "men's jobs." Women who sought to help defend the country after the retreat at Dunkirk in May 1940 made invasion by the German army seem likely were turned away from the volunteer forces that made up the Home Guard. Women who enlisted in the Land Army found that their services were not wanted, so that even as late as December of 1941 fewer women worked on the land than had in 1918.

The government had to face the fact that ideas about women's proper sphere had proved so entrenched that it would be difficult to persuade sufficient numbers of women to move into critical wartime industries to replace called-up men and even harder to get employers to hire them. By early 1941, under siege from constant bombardment during the blitz, and facing a critical labor shortage, the British government found it necessary to impose on women, aged nineteen to forty, compulsory registration at employment exchanges so that the Ministry of Labour might know who was available and where for employment in the "essential" industries. At the same time, by declaring the Essential Work Order, it forced factory owners to employ and to keep women in these jobs. By this order, workers were not free to leave work in the essential industries without gaining permission of the Ministry of Labour, though the officials involved generally allowed women to leave if they could demonstrate that their absence from home caused hardship for others.

Having stressed women's domestic duties for almost two decades now, government officials found that they could not simply run roughshod over those women who had taken them seriously and argued that their responsibilities at home precluded them from working for wages, and yet the need for women's labor in both industry and the armed forces was severe. The Ministry of Labour turned to some of the women sitting in parliament for advice. Edith Summerskill, a Labour MP, and Irene Ward, a Conservative MP, headed the Women's Consultative Committee, made up of representatives of trade union women and the women's voluntary organizations that had sprung up upon the outbreak of war. The committee insisted that all single women without dependents at home should be ordered to work wherever the need was greatest, and endorsed the National Service Number 2 Act of December 1941, which conscripted single women aged twenty to thirty into service for the state. On the question of conscripting wives and mothers for work there was a great deal of reluctance. Some of the committee members opposed it on the grounds that it would impose a double burden of housework and waged work on women. Others drew upon the notions of women's proper sphere to resist conscription for married women and mothers. In the end, the committee recommended that no mothers of children under the age of fourteen be ordered to work; they also created an exemption category for housewives, whereby recruiting officials might determine that a woman's household obligations – even a woman looking after a household with only one other adult present, with domestic help available to her – were great enough to exempt her from work that required her to travel from home. She might be compelled to work locally if the recruiting officer determined that her domestic duties enabled her to do so. As the labor shortage worsened over the next year, the government expanded its conscription powers to direct exempt women into part-time work on behalf of the war effort.

Resistance to the conscription of women came from a variety of sources. Some simply did not wish to leave home. Working-class women hesitated to take on what would amount to a second job. "It's all right for them young ladies with butlers and chauffeurs who don't have to worry their sweet little heads about keeping home," explained one woman from Coventry, but women without suffi-cient income to hire domestic help faced enormous burdens. Others warned that conscripting women to work would destroy homes and marriages as men lost the services women provided them on a day-to-day basis. "Men coming home on leave will find that they can only see their wives for an hour or two a day," noted an air raid warden. "Men in reserved occupations will come back to cold untidy houses with no meal ready." One woman declared that she'd be happy to do part-time work, but that full-time work was out of the question because her husband disap-proved. "We would get war in our homes if we took it," she lamented. A Scottish MP feared for the morality of Scottish women and for the survival of Scotland as thousands of young women deemed "mobile" by the Ministry of Labour were moved south to work in munitions factories. "The Scots as a nation will be wiped out if denuded of their womenfolk," he protested.[1]

But many women did want to help the war effort; some 155,000 volunteered for the auxiliary forces – the Auxiliary Territorial Service (ATS), the Women's Auxiliary Air Force (WAAF), the Women's Royal Naval Service (WRNS), and the Women's Land Army (WLA) – in 1941, before conscription was introduced. Most of these women hailed from middle-class families, where their income was not necessary for family survival and where the conventions of femininity chafed. "I wasn't very happy at home," recalled Joan Welch, "because my father had such a strict regime." She would have found no less strict a regime in the WRNS, however, which imple-mented military discipline over its charges. Despite efforts to keep meticulous order, the WRNS, along with all the other women's auxiliary services, were subject to scurrilous attack. As was the case in the First World War, rumors of promiscuity and sexual immorality followed women who enlisted. "Up with the lark and to bed with a Wren," one witty saying slurred the WRNS; another described the Women's Land Army as workers with their "backs to the land."[2]

The combination of volunteer recruitment and conscription utterly trans-formed the composition of the workforce and the nature of the work women did during the Second World War. Most single working-class women worked before they married in the interwar years but suspended their employment upon marriage; only 16 percent of working women were married in 1931. In 1943, 43 percent of working women were married. These figures represented only full-time wage-earning women. If volunteers and part-time workers had been counted as well, they would have shown that a whopping 80 percent of married women were working to aid the war effort. Ninety percent of the single women of Britain offered their labor as well.

As in the First World War, women took on work in industries formerly consid-ered "male." Where they had worked in textile and consumer goods manufacturing in the 1920s and 1930s, now they took up jobs in chemicals, munitions, transport, utilities, shipbuilding, commerce, government, agriculture, civil defense, and the armed forces. Many joined unions for the first time, and involved themselves in trade union activities and politics, though their participation frequently provoked adverse comment from male leaders. Especially after 1943, women workers began to use strikes to increase their pay or to make pay scales among women more uniform, despite the fact that strikes in wartime were illegal and unions refused to support them. In a Rolls-Royce airplane engine plant outside Glasgow, women struck against policies that paid less experienced men more than they made for the same kinds of work. They succeeded in getting positions graded and the pay scales attached to those grades made consistent, but they did not gain equal pay for men and women. Despite the tireless efforts of feminists and women MPs, unequal wages for women and men continued to be the norm in every industry except transport.

The war disrupted women's lives in numerous and profound ways. Marriage rates rose in 1940 as couples raced to wed before the men shipped out, but then plummeted. The long absence of husbands put great strain on marriages. Divorce rates skyrocketed, more than doubling in the years between 1938 and 1945, and increasing thereafter. In those marriages that remained intact throughout the war years, loneliness and boredom prevailed. One woman related her "very long and agonized war story" as she waited five years for her husband to return home.

> Now can you imagine that? I had a few mild and meaningless flirtations and they were just as meaningless as they had been at school. I wasn't interested. I was aware of needing sex, but I wasn't prepared to have sex without love … it's hard to explain to you what it was like emotionally that you kept faith for five years and it was perfectly normal. You waited for your bloke to come home. … The deadly boredom of it. The War wasn't heroic, it was just a bloody bore.[3]

Sexual harassment and violent assaults against women seem to have increased during the war, as more and more women were relocated away from their families to work for the war effort. Women serving as conductors on trams late at night, traveling on trains with servicemen, or working in isolated areas as members of the Land Army or munitions workers found themselves subject to unwanted sexual advances from men who sometimes would not take no for an answer. The blackout, women pointed out, provided countless opportunities for these kinds of encounters.

For many single women, the war offered freedoms they had not known before. Away from home and the supervision of their parents for the first time, they had money in their pockets, companions to spend time with, and places to go in their off hours. They visited pubs, attended dances, and socialized with servicemen, whose attentions could be fun and flattering. Although overall birth rates dropped during the war years, the rate of children born out of marriage rose to twice its level in the prewar years. This increase reflects not so much an increase in premarital sexual activity during the war as a decrease in the number of marriages that followed the birth of a child. In the prewar years, perhaps one-third of all mothers conceived children before they married, but they married shortly thereafter. The dislocations and upheavals of wartime made subsequent marriages far less feasible, thus driving up the illegitimacy rates.

The Second World War obliterated the lines between civilians and soldiers, home and front, women and men. In the first three years of the war, more civilians died than did soldiers. The German air attacks on England began in 1940, as first the port towns of Plymouth, Portsmouth, and Hull, and then London fell prey to endless hours of bombardment. Over the course of a few months in 1940 and 1941, Hull was bombed seventy times during the night and 101 times during daylight hours; some of the air raids went on from 9:00 p.m. to 4:00 a.m. Beginning in September 1940, Londoners underwent fifty-eight straight nights of bombardment. Casualties were high and damage severe. Of the 93,000 homes existing in Hull, only 6,000 of them did not suffer any damage. In central London and in the East End, where the bombing was the heaviest, nine of every ten houses were damaged. Across Britain as a whole, two of every seven houses were destroyed, as well as two out of every ten schools.

Bombed out of their homes during the blitz, Britons suffered enormously. Fully one-fourth of Plymouth's population was homeless by April 1941; in London, 177,000 people slept in the underground railway stations on a nightly basis. 12,000 were still living there in 1945. Streets were blown apart and rendered impassable; transportation systems broke down; people lacked gas, water, and electricity; fires raged. Thousands and thousands of people died, and some 40 percent of all British children were evacuated from the cities to the countryside. Those who survived were faced with carrying on "normal" activity in the midst of devastation. Trying to keep house and even body clean when running water could not be readily obtained involved strenuous effort. Foodstuffs and essential commodities had to be rationed and luxury items done away with altogether. Women walked miles and then stood in line for hours trying to obtain a bit of soap or the weekly quota of sugar due them. Charged with the responsibility of keeping their homes and families together without the proper means of doing so, women of all classes in the bombed-out cities of Britain performed heroically, but they did so at a cost. They experienced greater fatigue, strain, despair, and depression than did the men in these areas or the women in rural or less vulnerable parts of the country; mothers whose children had been evacuated suffered extreme bouts of guilt over abandoning them, compounding their sense of loss.

In a bitter irony, the blitz helped women MPs achieve one major step toward equality of women with men. The Personal Injuries Act of 1939, requiring the government to compensate people injured during bombing raids, paid men seven shillings more a week than it did women. Vera Douie of the Six Point Group pointed out that "there is nothing chivalrous about bombs; they do not discriminate between men and women," and women in and out of parliament protested strongly against the presumption that women's lives were somehow worth less than men's. The government conceded the argument after months of debate in 1943, and agreed to pay out compensation equally. For the 63,000 civilian women (48 percent of the total number of civilians) who suffered wounds and injuries during the war, over 25,000 of whom later died of them, this victory produced meaningful concrete results for themselves or their families.[4]

The Beveridge report and the postwar welfare state

Historians looking back upon the Second World War have identified it as a time when an unusual degree of unity and consensus amongst the various classes of Britain was attained. In fact, class and other divisions that had grown so acutely during the years of depression proved to be just as intransigent during the war, and in order to get and keep Britons fighting on behalf of their nation, government officials had to promise that the nation for which they were sacrificing everything would, in the future, be one worth fighting for. These were not, moreover, promises that could be made in a vague or unformed way, not to a population that had experienced terrible privations after the Great War under a government that would do little or nothing to remedy them. Social injustice and poverty would have to be directly and visibly addressed by the sitting government if the efforts of the nation's people were to be counted on in this war.

Accordingly, the government of Winston Churchill introduced a number of emergency welfare programs designed to sustain the population. It distributed milk and orange juice to babies and children. It rationed food fairly across social class, a policy that proved limiting to the better off segments of the population, but actually resulted in an improved diet for most people. Churchill also appointed a commission to prepare a blueprint for social reform after the war ended. Headed by William Beveridge, a Liberal, the commission issued its report in late 1942. Its recommendations quickly established in the public mind the most basic of expectations for the development of welfare provisions in the postwar period; within two weeks of its appearance, nine of every ten Britons believed that its proposals should be implemented. The Labour Party immediately embraced its principles while Churchill and some of his fellow Conservatives expressed reservations about the costs it would entail and the extent to which it might distract attention away from the effort of fighting the war. Labour Party leaders capitalized on their lukewarm response when elections were held upon war's end in 1945. The electorate, though grateful to Churchill for having led them to victory, decisively voted the Conservatives out of office and a Labour government under Clement Atlee came to power. The upper classes knew that dramatic change was in store for them, and that life as they had known it before the war would never be the same. Novelist Elizabeth Bowen, using a pronounced language of the feminine to denigrate them, decried the advent of "all these little middle-class Labour wets with their Old London School of Economics ties and their women. Scratch any of these cuties and you find the governess."[5]

In formulating what he called "a scheme of social insurance against interruption and destruction of earning power and for special expenditure arising at birth, marriage or death,"[6] Beveridge articulated a number of basic assertions about the nature of the welfare state that themselves turned on assumptions about the gendered nature of home and work. His plan established some fundamental ground rules. First, social services like health care, unemployment insurance, pensions, and the like were to be paid for through a combination of contributions from employers, employees, and the state. Second, these contributions and the benefits they would pay out would be set at a standard rate across classes, and not be limited to the poor. Third, all citizens could expect a minimal level of subsistence from the state, derived from a combination of full employment, social-security payments, family allowances, and the provision of free or inexpensive health care through a national health service. This all added up to a view of the welfare state as the guarantor of support in the event of lost wages.

This vision of the welfare state, given the predominant thinking about who should work and who should not work, shaped the way in which contributions were made and benefits paid out. Beveridge broke down the population of Britain into six categories, the largest of which consisted of employed persons. This designation encompassed both men and women working for wages, with the explicit, and very large, exception of married women. The 1.4 million married women working in 1942 who would not be covered by the insurance scheme, Beveridge told the National Council of Women, constituted an "anomaly." They wouldn't normally work, he said; they were housewives before they were wage earners. Moreover, if they became sick or unemployed, they had husbands to look after them. And most importantly, "she has the liability to have pregnancy, and ought to have it; that is what she is in a sense there for," he declared. Married women shouldn't work, for they had another job to do. "In the next thirty years," he stated, "housewives as mothers will have vital work to do in ensuring the adequate continuance of the British race and of British ideals in the world."

A number of feminists protested against his "reactionary measure in regard to married women," as Conservative MP Mavis Tate put it, but their denouncement fell on deaf ears. When the National Insurance Act passed in 1946, it enshrined the notion of Beveridge and others that the family unit within the Welfare State consisted of a team of husbands and wives carrying out very different duties. Wives bore and raised children, and men worked to support them. Thus, benefits paid to the family in situations of unemployment were paid to, and on the basis of the income of, the husband and father. The married woman's benefit, as befitting someone dependent upon her husband for material existence, was subsumed into his. Women who interrupted their waged work upon marriage and later sought to re-enter the workforce found it difficult to retain their insurance rights, and when they did, they received a smaller benefit than did men. Under the provisions of the National Insurance Act, the bread-winner ideal enjoyed official sanction: unemployed, ill, or disabled men received benefits from the state to make up their lost wages; unemployed, ill, or disabled married women received (fewer) benefits from the state only when the provider of first resort – their husbands – were unable to support them.

Beveridge's recommendations for family allowances, or payments made to families in support of children, did not become implemented in law. He had favored subsistence support for children, that is, a payment sufficiently large to maintain them. Feminists like Eleanor Rathbone and Eva Hubback had settled for this plan, though it compromised their intentions to promote family allowances in order to then gain equal pay for men and women. Working-class men and women had long argued against equal pay on the grounds that men required a higher wage because they had to support their families on it. Family allowances, or the "endowment of motherhood," as feminists termed it, would pay women for the work they did in the home as mothers and housewives and therefore nullify the argument that men had to bring home more money than women, bring home a "family wage." Trade union officials opposed family allowances on the ground that it would undermine masculine identity and the role of men in the family. As H.L. Bullock of the National Union of General and Municipal Workers argued in February 1941, "Family Allowances will tend to dig at the roots of a virile Trade Unionism."

Trade union opposition to family allowances was overcome, but only because the government, when it came time to actually put Beveridge's plan in place, paid out family allowances at a minuscule rate. They could not, in themselves, possibly affect the wage rates paid to men, and were not regarded as a substitute for men's wages. Initially, family allowances were to be paid to men, but an indignant outcry from every segment and every class of the population caused civil servants to reconsider and to make the payments to women. In this form, as a means of relieving only the worst levels of poverty among children and not of providing an independent income to women, family allowances came into being, and helped to uphold the notion of bread-winning men and dependent women.

The implementation of the Beveridge Report, along with additional provisions for secondary and university education and for housing, dramatically transformed the ideology underpinning the British social polity. The notion that citizenship now entailed social as well as civil and political rights became part of Britons' understandings about their place within the nation. Certainly class and/or gender divisions and inequalities did not disappear, but ordinary men and women and their children now had the means of obtaining the necessities of life without inordinate struggle on a daily basis. And the state guaranteed their minimal subsistence. In the process, it helped to recreate and fortify earlier beliefs about the bread-winning male and the stay-at-home wife and mother that had been undercut by the great depression and the Second World War.

Postwar realities: working women

The welfare state's assumptions about male bread-winning and dependent wives did not jive with reality after the war ended, and this inconsistency provoked sometimes intense efforts to correct the situation. For when war ended, women did not leave their jobs *en masse* in 1945 as they had after 1918. To be sure, many of them were forced to give up jobs in high-paying, "male" occupations in engineering, manufacturing, or office work. But the increase in the number of functions undertaken by local and national government during the war required a huge bureaucracy, and these positions did not diminish appreciably after the war ended. Conscription of men into the armed forces lasted until 1950, followed by the introduction of a national service requirement of two years for boys leaving school. This helped to keep demand for workers fairly high. The implementation of health and welfare provisions and new educational policies necessitated an increase of nurses and teachers. Professional positions in law and medicine, while relatively small compared to those for men, had grown during the war as well, and this time around, women were able to maintain their presence in these occupations. Moreover, the Labour government had pledged itself to a policy of full employment. After the Great War, a downturn in the economy had produced vast numbers of layoffs in a number of industries, ultimately leading to depression and massive unemployment. The government, following conventional thinking, would do nothing to relieve workers' plight. This time around, informed by Keynesian doctrines of pump-priming and deficit spending, the government maintained controls over employment, production, and consumption, thus providing work for men – and women – who would otherwise be without.

Governmental officials did expect, in accordance with the conventional thinking about women as wives and mothers, that women would leave work upon marriage or upon return of their husbands from the armed forces. Women who had had to move far from their homes to take up employment in essential industries were expected to give it up and go home. And women with small children, especially, were not expected to work now that the war was over. Indeed, the government reduced by half the subsidies it had paid to nurseries so that women with children might work, forcing local governments to shut them down. The members of the Women's Advisory Committee of the Trades Union Congress shared the views of government officials. They insisted that married women should not have to work if they did not wish to, and that women with young children should not work at all.

These official views did not reflect those of the population at large, however. Many married women did not want to leave their wartime jobs, despite the fact that it entailed upon them the double burden of caring for the home as well. Some two-thirds of the women in engineering jobs in 1945 wished to stay on after the war ended, though their numbers were decreased when their jobs were given to returning soldiers. But because employment could be found in a number of other industries like food processing or the manufacture of synthetic fibers, the percentage of married women earning wages remained as high after the war as it had been during it. In 1951, 22 percent of married women worked outside of the home, compared to 10 percent in 1931. Far many more older women worked in 1951 than before the war, when half of all women workers were under the age of twenty-five. Now, women under twenty-five comprised only one-third of the female workforce, and the remaining two-thirds spread themselves fairly equally over the age cohorts of thirties, forties, and fifties. In 1950, 40 percent of the female workforce was married; six years later in 1956, the number had risen to 50 percent. Employment for married women had become a significant social fact, in large part because labor shortages in a number of areas prevailed in the postwar years. The government both acknowledged and facilitated the trend by eliminating the marriage bar in teaching and civil service positions.

The increase in numbers of married women workers provoked broad-based discussion about the effects it would have on children and on the birth-rate as a whole. Concerns about the birth-rate had long exercised public officials; with increased use of contraceptives across the social spectrum helping to lower the birth-rate to the levels of the hard-bitten 1930s, government agencies placed great stress on family life with an eye toward encouraging women to bear more children. Indeed, the welfare state as envisaged by William Beveridge, himself an eager imperialist, had been designed to "ensur[e] the adequate continuance of the British Race and of the British Ideal in the world," and family allowances gained acceptance from as many quarters as it did because it was sold as an inducement to more childbearing. Stimulated by many diverse concerns, not least of them a fear about what effects separation from their mothers might have had on children evacuated during the war, a pro-natalist discourse emerged in the 1940s, urging women to recognize and act upon their maternal functions – to have babies – and counseling them on the dangers of going out to work and leaving young children in the care of others.

In 1949, a royal commission set up in 1945 to find ways to encourage parent-hood reported its findings. In terms not dissimilar to those we saw being used in the interwar period, the commission blamed feminism for having contributed to the decline of the birth-rate. By promoting the interests of working mothers and by contesting the paternal authority of men within the family, feminists had intro-duced friction between husbands and wives, thus reducing the birth-rate and threatening the stability of the family. But where attacks on women ignoring their proper maternal functions in the late nineteenth and early twentieth centuries had focused on the "racial," eugenic consequences of their actions, those of the postwar period emphasized the effects women's working outside the home would have on the mental health and emotional development of their children. Among the many women who still suffered pangs of guilt over having sent their children out of the cities during the blitz, the pro-natalist arguments obtained a powerful purchase.

The writings of child psychologists D. W. Winnicott and John Bowlby informed the thinking of welfare officials, jurists, physicians, criminologists, social workers, and policy makers in the late 1940s and 1950s. Though the data presumably drawn from the wartime experiences of evacuated children did not support his asser-tions, Bowlby concluded firmly "that prolonged separation in the early years is sometimes the principal cause of the development of delinquent character can in fact hardly be doubted." His *Maternal Care and Mental Health* (1951) and *Child Care and the Growth of Love* (1953), and Winnicott's *The Child and the Family* (1957) helped create a climate of opinion in which the "normal" social and psychological development of children depended virtually entirely upon mothers being constantly present in their lives. The small child "needs her as an ever-present companion," Bowlby declared. "This usually continues until about his third birthday." Women with young children who worked risked producing juvenile delinquents or children who suffered irreparable damage to their psyches. The directives aimed at women could be extreme, as in the case of one child psycholo-gist who suggested that the delinquent behavior of a group of children could be laid at the feet of their mothers' absence while they walked to school and back. Bowlby's 1958 pamphlet, *Can I Leave My Baby?*, while conceding that mothers might leave their children for brief periods of time in the care of grandmothers or fathers, or neighbors in the event of emergencies, underscored in the popular imagination the notion that mothers must supply continuous care and nurturance to their children. "This exacting job is scamped at one's peril," he cautioned. The mother "is going to be his anchor – whether she likes it or not – and separations from her are going to give rise to problems." Fathers of young children are curi-ously absent from the scene in the writings of the child psychologists. They serve as bread-winners, certainly, reinforcing the separate sphere ideology of men as producers, women as childbearers and -rearers, but their presence in the emotional lives of their children is slight.[7]

The pressures upon married women to remain at home and focus all of their attention on their children, while pervasive and powerful, encountered counter-pressures that directed them outward to the world of work and public life. A postwar boom in consumer goods, in particular, spurred women into work so that they might earn the money with which to purchase the products that would render their homes comfortable and nurturing. Refrigerators, washing machines, vacuum cleaners, gas and electric stoves, irons, water heaters – these commodities, though not available to all families in the 1950s, nevertheless helped to transform the standards of cleanliness and housekeeping to which women should aspire (and in the case of middle- and upper-class families, without the labor of domestic servants now, who refused to re-enter a profession they had escaped during the war and found so demeaning). Without the help of husbands to maintain a household in spotless conditions, women had to earn an income to buy the products that would enable them to meet new standards of domesticity. Thus the very ideology that urged them to remain at home acted to send them out in order to adhere to it. Bread-winning women, though unacknowledged in official pronouncements or the popular press, comprised a central element of the success of the postwar economy.

Moreover, even those women who eagerly turned to marriage and domesticity after the war did so with changed expectations of married life. Contraceptives made it possible for them to plan their births, so that childbearing and -rearing might take up only one short period of their lives. The desire to experience the larger world around them, to socialize more with friends and neighbors, to make contributions to society at large, to do more significant work than cleaning house – all of these played a role in motivating married women to work outside the home, which, as we have seen, they did in increasing numbers even after the war ended. The incompatibilities between pro-natalist and family discourses on the one hand and the forces impelling women outside of a restricted sphere of home and children on the other helped give rise to tensions and contradictions within the ideologies of gender that informed the beliefs and activities of the generations to follow in the 1960s and 1970s.

In the shorter run, the contradictions provoked debate about the extent, or even the reality, of "maternal deprivation" for children whose mothers worked. A 27-year-old housewife named Margaret Thatcher wrote in 1954 that the working mother:

> still sees a good deal of the children. The time she spends away from them is a time which the average housewife spends in doing the housework and shopping, not in being with the children assiduously. From my own experience I feel there is much to be said for being away from the family for part of the day. When looking after them without a break, it is sometimes difficult not to

get a little impatient. ... Whereas, having been out, every moment spent with them is a pleasure to anticipate. ... Later on there will not be that awful gap which many women find in their lives when their children go away to school.

Thatcher's article reflected one element of a larger concern about women's roles, responsibilities, and position in the workforce, concerns that for the most part were articulated in terms of the "problem" women posed for society.[8] Like Thatcher, sociologists Alva Myrdal and Viola Klein suggested in *Women's Two Roles* (1956) that women could have both a career and motherhood. Their text, regarded as a characteristically feminist work of the 1950s, argued that women could establish their careers shortly after marriage, take time out from them to have children, and resume working after their children reached school age. Like most feminist thinking of the decade, it tacitly accepted the broader societal emphases on family life, marriage, and maternity for women; its potential subversion rested on the assumption that the requirements of the state and of the economy for women's respective contributions to them created both the need and the justification for women working, for their "having it all," both career and family. Myrdal and Klein did not claim, nor had Margaret Thatcher, that women's rights formed the basis for women carrying out "two roles." And at no time did any participant in the debate over the "problem" of women put forth the notion that husbands and fathers might help resolve the problem by taking on one of the roles themselves. Not until the late 1960s would a new generation of feminists raise questions about women's personal rights and liberation from societal expectations, and, in consequence, open up possibilities for changes in men's lives and identities as well.

Angry young men ... and women

The welfare state came into existence on the basis of a wartime consensus that the world for which thousands were fighting and dying would have to be rendered more fair and more just. The implementation of its policies perpetuated a belief in that consensus and contributed to the belief that a classless society could be established. Throughout the 1950s, an ideology of "affluence" based on the postwar economic boom circulated throughout the country, giving voice to the notion that class differences and distinctions were on the wane, that poverty had been eliminated, and that anyone, regardless of the origins of their birth, could aspire to and attain the economic, educational, sartorial, and cultural attributes that signaled success. The Conservative Party rode to power on the back of this widespread set of assumptions, buoyed by the votes of women tired of years of rationing during and immediately following the war, and maintained itself in office from 1951 to 1964 on the basis of its claims that while this society might not yet be realized, it was only a matter of time until it materialized. But class distinctions, divisions, and conflicts did indeed exist, despite the very real improvements in employment rates and wages. Inequalities in income continued. The discrepancy between an ideology that promised social equality and a reality of substandard housing, overcrowding, and dead-end jobs for a large percentage of Britons produced an angry response from an articulate literary element who castigated establishment culture and despaired of the conventional thinking that class conflict was a thing of the past.

Epitomized by John Osborne's *Look Back in Anger* (1956), rage over the state of things domestic and international found expression through gender. As early as 1947, Cyril Connolly had lamented Britain's loss of power and its subsidiary relationship to the United States by comparing the "confident, affable and aggressive" Americans to the dispirited British. "Most of us are not men or women," he despaired, "but members of a vast, seedy, overworked, over-legislated, neuter class." Unmanly men, unwomanly women – these were not specimens of some sort of potentially creative androgyny but bloodless, demoralized, lifeless people, who in the 1950s contributed to the making of a stiflingly conventional society. The "dark grey undead" men attired in suits of standardized cut, color, and cloth epitomized the society touted as unified and virtually without class. Osborne's play, written in a better economic context but a worsened international climate of British decline, recreated the sense of demoralization through his characters, Jimmy Porter and his wife Alison, and through the setting in which all of the action takes place, a drab one-room flat in the Midlands without sink or bathroom.[9]

Jimmy hails somewhat vaguely from a lower middle-class family, but espouses what he imagines are working-class virtues. Alison is a member of the upper classes. Though educated at university through the largess of the new welfare reforms, Jimmy despises the upper-class values that élite education and his wife represent. Caught in a kind of no-man's-land of class and individual identity, he rages against a society that has trapped him in an existence of dissatisfaction and disillusionment. He does so through a series of confrontations with his wife and subsequent mistress, Helena, and by means of misogynist exhortations against the perfidy of women. Class hatreds and crises of masculine identity become articulated through gender conflict. "Have you ever noticed how noisy women are?" he demands of his friend Cliff. "The way they kick the floor about simply walking over it. Or have you watched them sitting at their dressing tables, dropping their weapons and banging down their bits of boxes and brushes and lipsticks." Contemptuous of their inferior concerns ("bits of boxes and brushes and lipsticks"), Jimmy nevertheless concedes to women a power to intrude upon, to disrupt, even to do harm (with their "weapons") to the vulnerable psyches of men.

The fact that Britain had begun its slow, inexorable slide toward powerlessness and decline in world affairs gives Jimmy's anger over the hypocrisy and complacency of the "affluent society" a sharper edge. He disdains the world in which principled stands and great acts of heroism seemingly are no longer possible. He associates the decline of Britain and the degeneration of its culture with femininity, linking the potential of nuclear annihilation with the power of women to render men impotent, psychically dead. "I suppose people of our generation aren't able to die for good causes any longer," he tells Cliff:

> There aren't any good brave causes left. If the big bang does come and we all get killed off, it won't be in aid of the old-fashioned, grand design. It'll just be for the Brave New-nothing-very-much-thank-you. About as pointless and inglorious as stepping in front of a bus. No, there's nothing left for it, me boy, but to let yourself be butchered by the women.

Jimmy's desperate search for an unambiguous and meaningful class status and for an individual sense of subjectivity succeed only through the metaphorical destruction of Alison, the representative of upper-class superiority and the threat to his masculine identity.[10]

The inconsistencies contained within the ideology of affluence fueled the anger and resentment of everyday people as well as of cultural élites. Carolyn Steedman recalls, in an extraordinary account of her life and that of her mother, *Landscape for a Good Woman*, the time in 1951 when a health visitor told her mother, "this house isn't fit for a baby," reducing her mother to tears and searing Steedman's soul with "my secret and shameful defiance" against her own vulnerability to the injuries of class. "I will do everything and anything until the end of my days to stop anyone ever talking to me like that woman talked to my mother," she promises:

> I read a woman's book, meet such a woman at a party (a woman now, like me) and think quite deliberately as we talk: we are divided: a hundred years ago I'd have been cleaning your shoes. I know this and you don't.

Her class consciousness, she says, she learned at her mother's elbow as she watched her time and again being excluded and being made to feel excluded from the world of opportunity, emotional security, and material possession represented by the middle-class health visitor.

Steedman's 1950s childhood was informed by the complaints, resentments, desires, and longings of her mother, whose 1930s childhood experiences instilled in her the understanding that life was no more than a series of unfairnesses and helped to create in the adult mother what Steedman calls a politics of envy, a politics that found its expression in voting Conservative. Steedman's very identity – in both an individual subjective and a class sense – derives from her own sense of exclusion from the experiences of middle-class women who felt wanted by their parents, particularly their mothers. What she calls "structures of deprivation" –

poverty, material want – produced "structures of feeling" for working-class girls that middle-class girls could not experience or understand. For Steedman:

> mothers were those who told you how hard it was to have you, how long they were in labour with you ("twenty hours with you," my mother frequently reminded me) and who told you to accept the impossible contradiction of being both desired and a burden; and not to complain.

She and her sister suffered the painful realization that they were a nuisance, that they were not wanted by their mother, that they were responsible for her life having turned out so unfairly. "I don't think the baggage will ever lighten for me or my sister," she confides:

> We were born, and had no choice in the matter; but we were burdens, expensive, never grateful enough. There was nothing we could do to pay back the debt of our existence. "Never have children dear," she said; "they ruin your life."

Steedman grew up during the period of the 1950s when real wages rose and a vast array of consumer goods became available. Her mother's inabilities to purchase the new items as early as her neighbors did, the blame for which she laid at the feet of the children's father, produced in her a powerful desire for the things she could not have and acute envy for those who had them. Steedman recalls that when things like vacuum cleaners and televisions did arrive in the homes of her neighbors, they appeared as gifts for children. "The fridge in the house of the children we played with over the road was given to the youngest as a birthday present." She and her sister, like most kids, received clothes and shoes for their birthday and Christmas, "but the record player also came into the house in this way, as my eleventh birthday present. I wasn't allowed to take it with me when I left, though: it really wasn't mine at all."

Steedman ultimately came to recognize that the poverty in which she was taught to believe she lived, and was responsible for simply by existing, was not real but "a belief" carried over from the stories her mother told of the 1930s and the economies they practiced in the 1950s to save money. Steedman's father, even when he did not live with them, paid the rent and all the bills, provided pocket money for her and her sister, and turned over a good amount of housekeeping money to her mother each week. When she died, Steedman's mother had amassed savings of £40,000, a very large sum. But for Steedman, the poverty seemed real.

> We believed we were badly off because we children were expensive items, and all those arrangements had been made for us. "If it wasn't for you two,"

my mother told us, "I could be off somewhere else." ... The house was full of her terrible tiredness and her terrible resentment; and I knew it was all my fault.

The anger, dissatisfaction, and discontent felt by her mother – the politics of longing provoked by the ideology of affluence – did not reproduce itself in Steedman, in part because she was a recipient, unlike her mother, of material benefits given her by the state. She and her sister had access to medicine and food that her mother did not, and Steedman believes that these "structures of provision," we might call them, gave to her a sense of importance that her mother did not enjoy as a child.

> I think I would be a very different person now if orange juice and milk and dinners at school hadn't told me, in a covert way, that I had a right to exist, was worth something. My inheritance from those years is the belief (maintained always with some difficulty) that I do have a right to the earth. ... Being a child when the state was practically engaged in making children healthy and literate was a support against my own circumstances.

The welfare state policies of material provision gave to Steedman a "sense of self," in marked contrast to the scenarios created by John Osborne and the other "angry men" authors, who found in it a source of confusion and threats to their identity.

"Would you let your daughter marry a negro?": black Britons

World War II initiated a long-term process during which Britain became transformed from a largely homogeneous white society in 1939 into a multiracial, multicultural one by the 1960s. As a result of the influx of black colonial workers to alleviate the labor shortage occasioned by the war, the presence of black American soldiers between 1942 and 1945, and immigration from the colonies and commonwealth countries of Great Britain after 1948, the "whiteness" of the British nation could no longer be taken for granted. This profound change in the racial and ethnic composition of the country caused anxiety in many quarters, and gave rise to calls for, and ultimately legislation, placing restrictions on the immigration of people of color into the kingdom. Anxiety on the part of white Britons found expression through languages of race steeped in the gendered and sexualized imagery that had informed Britain's dealings with its imperial subjects in the past.

Labor shortages during the war compelled the government to recruit workers from the colonies to work in a number of industries and in the armed forces. Twelve-hundred British Hondurans, for instance, were brought to Scotland to log forests for timber; 1,000 West Indians worked in the munitions factories in Merseyside and Lancashire. Most Britons had never laid eyes on a person of color before the war; now they met them more frequently, though at first they did not know quite who they were dealing with. Lilian Barker, a West Indian worker, recounted the time a group of people evacuated from London saw her on the street, and yelled out, "Nazi! Nazi!" at her, thinking that all Germans were black.[11]

When the war started, a color bar restricted recruitment into the armed forces, and the senior officers sought to maintain it, arguing that "commissions should be reserved for British subjects of British parents of *pure European descent*." They sought to register blacks living in Britain but not to call them up for training, especially not in the navy or air force. The color bar was suspended in October 1939 for as long as "the present emergency" lasted, but little really changed. Significant numbers of West Indians, Asians, and Africans did serve in the Allied armed forces, some 10,000 West Indians in the air force alone, but commissions in the armed forces were reserved for whites. Black troops were less disciplined than white troops, British officials believed. White troops would not respond to black superior officers, they argued. "British troops do not take kindly to being commanded by coloured officers and further ... the presence of coloured officers in a unit in peacetime is apt to be a source of embarrassment," the War Office told the Colonial Office in December 1944. Because they lacked the "social" traditions of the mess, black officers would not mix well with white officers, another War Office opinion had it. They would not be able to deal with "family and personal problems" that might arise among their troops; and finally, and perhaps most unsettling for military officials, there might be "incidents" in the married quarters. The unspecified nature of these "incidents" could not mask the fears on the part of the War Office that the sexuality of blacks, long a trope of racial thinking, could not be contained. Only one black man, Arundel Moody, obtained a commission in the army, and the color bar remained part of army and navy recruitment until 1948.[12]

The imminent arrival of American troops moved government officials to request that the black men among them not be stationed in Britain, or that their numbers be limited. The Americans refused this request; when black American troops arrived in Britain in 1942, segregated from their white comrades, British officials went along with American policies. In August 1942, district commanders in Britain received copies of "notes on relations with coloured troops" instructing them to advise their charges that they should not fraternize with black American troops or comment negatively upon the treatment meted out to black Americans by their white counterparts. Most of all, the instructions warned, fearing that British women and black American troops might engage in sexual relations with one another – which, indeed, they did – white women should not be permitted to socialize with black men. Fears of miscegenation seemed to permeate many layers of society. The Duke of Marlborough appealed to Winston Churchill, his cousin, to do something to halt sexual activity between black troops and white Englishwomen. The Duke of Buccleuch complained about the relationships between the local women and the British Honduran loggers working his estate in Scotland. And the government made it illegal for British women to marry black American soldiers, despite the fact that thousands of them married white GIs.[13]

In 1947, after an exhausted and powerless Britain had ceded their independence, India and Pakistan joined with the white commonwealth countries of Britain, Canada, Australia, and New Zealand to form a "new commonwealth." Soon thereafter Burma and Ceylon gained independence, and Ceylon, though not Burma, joined the commonwealth as well. Nationalist movements in Africa, the Middle East, and the West Indies gained strength and momentum from the example of India, and Britain fought a series of colonial wars in order to hold on to its colonies throughout the 1950s and early 1960s. It failed. From 1956, when it was humiliated in a military showdown with Gamal Abdul Nasser of Egypt over control of the Suez Canal – an incident that made it abundantly clear that the once most powerful nation in the world could no longer sustain its great power status – Britain began to climb down from its imperial heights and one by one granted most of its colonies their freedom and autonomy.

In the ten years between 1948 and 1958 a large number of migrants from the so-called "new commonwealth" countries of Asia and from the Caribbean entered Britain. They came for jobs, education, for greater prosperity than they enjoyed at home, for a chance "to get the money to build a decent life," as one West Indian woman put it. Another responded to pleas from Queen Elizabeth II to "come over and work to build up the Mother Country. Of course, that was the way Britain was seen in those days, and a lot of us really did believe that the streets were paved with gold." Once in Britain, however, having left behind spouses, parents, children, brothers and sisters, and friends, they found that all was not as they had been led to believe. One West Indian woman trained as a nurse found that hospitals "wouldn't have me. Someone had told me that they would take me on as an auxiliary nurse and that later on I could train. But when I got to the hospital, the woman there offered me a cleaning job." Many other well-trained immigrants could find only the most menial of jobs, as employers hesitated to employ them in skilled positions. Co-workers disparaged or shunned them, and their unions failed to protect their interests in the workplace. The first generation of commonwealth immigrants found life in Britain alienating, hostile, and difficult.[14]

In the 1940s, no more than 1,000 people of color entered the country each year. By the mid-1950s, that figure had risen to 20,000 each year. In 1961, the year before Britain placed restrictions on the numbers of immigrants who might legally enter the country, 100,000 black people immigrated. In 1951, the numbers of blacks in Britain totaled perhaps 74,500. By 1959, it had grown to 336,000, and reached

500,000 by 1962. These figures set off alarm bells among politicians and government officials, who saw in the flow of black migrants a threat to the identity and social stability of Great Britain. Despite the fact that Britain needed workers to keep the small postwar boom going in the 1950s, and despite the fact that the sluggish birth-rate had created fears about population decline, migrants of color from Britain's former and current colonies did not receive a warm welcome even from official sources. As the Royal Commission on Population put it in its report in 1949:

> immigration on a large scale into a fully established society like ours could only be welcomed without reserve if the immigrants were of good human stock and were not prevented by their religion or race from intermarrying with the host population and becoming merged with it.[15]

As this statement and many other pronouncements, official and unofficial, infer, Britons seemed obsessed by fears of black sexuality and miscegenation. Winston Churchill opposed immigration from commonwealth countries and colonies because "we would have a magpie society: that would never do." White English people thought it wouldn't be a good idea for there to be black milkmen delivering milk to their doorsteps; white cab drivers protested against the entry of West Indians to their ranks because driving a taxi was an "intimate business." But the references to blacks approaching one's home or whites contained within a small enclosed space with black drivers should alert us to their meaning. Anthropologist Geoffrey Gorer identified in 1955 the "shyness" of English people in their dealings with people who were not like them, people who might "corrupt or contaminate one, either by undermining one's moral principles and leading oneself or one's family into disapproved-of indulgences ... or by undermining one's social position ... through association with people 'who don't know how to behave.'" Sociologist Judith Henderson asserted in 1960 that "Africans and West Indians do manifest an exuberance and lack of restraint which is the very reverse of English reserve and self control," while an official of the Conservative Party declared in 1963 that "most of them have vile habits. If only they behaved like us it would be all right." Sociologist Sheila Patterson's sociological study of West Indian immigrants to Brixton in the 1950s, entitled *Dark Strangers*, delineated the traits, as whites saw them, that differentiated black Britons from white Britons. "Primitiveness, savagery, violence, sexuality, general lack of control, sloth, irresponsibility – all these are part of the image." These descriptions and terms could have been lifted right out of any eighteenth- or nineteenth-century tract on the nature of Britain's subject peoples.[16]

Sympathetic efforts to understand racial differences and antagonisms nevertheless reinforced through repetition the imagery of blacks as savage and sexualized. In 1955, a psychologist sought to explain "Negrophobia" as a manifestation of sexual repression on the part of white people. "There is a good deal of evidence to show that in modern Western civilization erotic or sexual impulses are subject to a great deal of repression and renunciation," he wrote.

> In so far as the Negro is popularly identified with the "savage" and thought to live a life which is relatively free from the conventions and restrictions associated with "civilization," he is often believed to be free from sexual restraints. As a result it is suggested that the Negro comes to represent in the mind of the white man or woman that aspect of his own unconscious with which he is in a state of conflict. Hostility which the individual directs towards the part of himself that wants to break away from the sexual restraints is projected onto the Negro, who is accused of doing all the things that the white person himself would like to do, but dare not.[17]

White women who involved themselves in relationships with black men provoked heated responses, even from race relations "experts" who sought to dispel stereotypes about black male sexuality in the 1950s. They described these women as gender and cultural "outlaws," branding them as "unstable," "deviant," and even "sociopathic." One such writer regarded them as having "failed to find a satisfying role in English society" and as women for whom the ordinary constraints of family and society did not operate. Like white homosexual men who "came around the cafes and the public houses of the coloured quarter looking for coloured 'friends,' " these women were quite literally "beyond the pale" of conventional norms and values, and outcast from white society as a result. "It is noticeable," this sociologist argued in 1955, "that many of the whites who are interested to make contact with coloured people are themselves neurotic or otherwise not representative of the white population." Ideas like this, even among individuals seeking to ameliorate race relations in postwar Britain, made it possible for the oft-asked question, "would you let your daughter marry a Negro?" to resonate with such force for white Britons of all classes and religious and political persuasions.[18]

As we have seen in the incidents surrounding the Indian Mutiny and the Amritsar Massacre, violence against people of color by white Britons was often depicted as a product of black men transgressing the boundaries that set them apart from white women. In August 1958, whites in Nottingham rioted after "a Jamaican" began a conversation with a white woman in a pub. Between 1,500 and 4,000 whites took to the streets and burned and looted. A month later, a four-day riot in Notting Hill in West London broke out in protest of blacks settling there. George Rogers, the Labour MP for the area in which Notting Hill was located, justified the attacks by whites on blacks by calling upon familiar sexualized racial stereotypes.

> The government must introduce legislation quickly to end the tremendous influx of coloured people from the Commonwealth ... overcrowding has fostered vice, drugs, prostitution and the use of knives. For years the white people have been tolerant. Now their tempers are up.

These riots gave the issue of immigration a national prominence it had not enjoyed before, giving rise to televised debates, editorials in the press, sermons from the pulpits, and opinion polls seeking to gauge the thinking of Britons. A Gallup poll taken just after the rioting revealed that 27 percent of those polled blamed whites for the rioting, 9 percent blamed blacks, and a large percentage, 35 percent, blamed both whites and blacks for whites having taken up violence against black people. Seventy-one percent opposed mixed marriages. Eighty percent of the poll's respondents favored controlling immigration of people of color. In July 1962, the Conservative government obliged them, passing into law the Commonwealth Immigration Bill, which restricted the immigration of people of color, though not whites, from the commonwealth countries and the colonies of Great Britain. The act marked the first phase of the process through which people of color in Britain would be scapegoated for all the postwar problems the nation faced.[19]

NOTES

1　Quoted in Gail Braybon and Penny Summerfield, *Out of the Cage: Women's Experiences in Two World Wars* (London, 1987), pp. 161–2.
2　Braybon and Summerfield, *Out of the Cage*, pp. 163, 165.
3　Quoted in Alan Sinfield, *Literature, Politics and Culture in Postwar Britain* (Berkeley, 1989), p. 8.
4　Quoted in Braybon and Summerfield, *Out of the Cage*, p. 182.
5　Quoted in Sinfield, *Postwar Britain*, p. 18.
6　Discussion of the Beveridge report is drawn from Susan Pedersen, *Family, Dependence, and the Origins of the Welfare State: Britain and France, 1914–1945* (Cambridge, 1993), pp. 336–56.
7　Quoted in Denise Riley, *War in the Nursery: Theories of the Child and Mother* (London, 1983), pp, 100, 101.
8　Quoted in Martin Pugh, *Women and the Women's Movement in Britain, 1914–1959* (London, 1992), p. 297.
9　Quoted in Robert Hewison, *In Anger: British Culture in the Cold War, 1945–1960* (New York, 1981), p. 14. See Frank Mort and Peter Thompson, "Retailing, commercial culture and masculinity in 1950s Britain: The case of Montague Burton, the 'Tailor of Taste,'" *History Workshop Journal* 38, 1994: 106–27.
10　See Michelene Wandor, *Look Back in Gender: Sexuality and the Family in Post-War British Drama* (London, 1987), ch. 2.
11　Bill Schwarz, "Black metropolis, white England," in Mica Nava and Alan O'Shea, eds, *Modern Times: Reflections on a Century of English Modernity* (London, 1996), p. 196.

12 Schwarz, "Black metropolis, white England," p. 196.
13 Zig Layton-Henry, *The Politics of Immigration* (Oxford, 1992), pp. 25, 26.
14 See Beverley Bryan, Stella Dadzie, and Suzanne Scafe, *The Heart of the Race: Black Women's Lives in Britain* (London, 1985), pp. 22–7.
15 Quoted in Chris Waters, " 'Dark strangers' in our midst: Discourses of race and nation in Britain, 1947–1963," *Journal of British Studies* 36(2), April 1997: 207–38.
16 Quoted in Layton-Henry, *Politics of Immigration*, p. 31; Schwarz, "Black metropolis, white England," p. 196; Waters, " 'Dark Strangers,' " pp. 207–38.
17 Waters, " 'Dark Strangers,' " pp. 207–38.
18 Waters, " 'Dark Strangers,' " pp. 207–38; Schwarz, "Black metropolis, white England," p. 198.
19 Layton-Henry, *Politics of Immigration*, pp. 39, 40.

SOURCES

Gail Braybon and Penny Summerfield, *Out of the Cage: Women's Experiences in Two World Wars*. London, 1987.

Barbara Caine, *English Feminism, 1780–1980*. Oxford, 1997.

Phil Goodman, " 'Patriotic femininity': Women's morals and men's morale during the Second World War," *Gender and History* 10(2), August 1998: 278–93.

Robert Hewison, *In Anger: British Culture in the Cold War, 1945–1960*. New York, 1981.

Zig Layton-Henry, *The Politics of Immigration*. Oxford, 1992.

Jane Lewis, "Myrdal, Klein, *Women's Two Roles* and postwar feminism, 1945–1960," in Harold L. Smith, ed., *British Feminism in the Twentieth Century*. Aldershot, 1990.

Frank Mort and Peter Thompson, "Retailing, commercial culture and masculinity in 1950s Britain: The case of Montague Burton, the 'Tailor of Taste,' " *History Workshop Journal* 38, 1994: 106–27.

Neil Nehring, *Flowers in the Dustbin: Culture, Anarchy, and Postwar England*. Ann Arbor, 1993.

Susan Pedersen, *Family, Dependence, and the Origins of the Welfare State: Britain and France, 1914–1945*. Cambridge, 1993.

Martin Pugh, *Women and the Women's Movement in Britain, 1914–1959*. London, 1992.

Denise Riley, *War in the Nursery: Theories of the Child and Mother*. London, 1983.

Bill Schwarz, "Black metropolis, white England," in Mica Nava and Alan O'Shea, eds, *Modern Times: Reflections on a Century of English Modernity*. London, 1996.

Alan Sinfield, *Literature, Politics and Culture in Postwar Britain*. Berkeley, 1989.

Harold L. Smith, ed., *War and Social Change: British Society in the Second World War*. Manchester, 1986.

Carolyn Kay Steedman, *Landscape for a Good Woman: A Story of Two Lives*. New Brunswick, NJ, 1987.

Penny Summerfield and Nicole Crockett, " 'You weren't taught that with the welding': Lessons in sexuality in the Second World War," *Women's History Review* 1(3), 1992: 435–54.

Michelene Wandor, *Look Back in Gender: Sexuality and the Family in Post-War British Drama*. London, 1987.

Chris Waters, "'Dark strangers' in our midst: Discourses of race and nation in Britain, 1947–1963," *Journal of British Studies* 36(2), April 1997: 207–38.

Chapter 14

The end of consensus

"Permissiveness" and Mrs Thatcher's reaction, 1963–90

The 1960s marked the beginning of the breakdown in what had appeared to most Britons to be a postwar consensus about the appropriate nature of government and society. Forged in the heat and tragedy of the Second World War, the belief in a common future of full employment, social justice, and a minimum level of welfare for all people informed the politics of both the Labour and Conservative Parties, and served as the ideal to which their respective governments aspired while in office. As we have seen, the postwar consensus was a myth that concealed the reality for many, many people: inequalities abounded and gave rise to protest in the late 1950s. In the 1960s, when unemployment began its dramatic climb and Britain's economic situation turned sour, a series of popular and political counter-cultural movements appeared, which produced throughout mainstream society a profound sense of "moral panic," as one critic has termed it, over what many people regarded as a "permissive" culture out of control.

Notions of "permissiveness" contained at least two strands of thought against which conservatives railed: in one manifestation, permissiveness connoted the sexual revolution, gay rights, and feminism; in another, it referred to a purported breakdown in respect for law and order, a situation attributed to immigrants to Britain and their children, and articulated through a language of race. The advent of "Thatcherism," an economic, political, and cultural movement calling for a return to "Victorian" values, in 1979 in reaction to the "moral panics" of the late 1960s and 1970s marked a decisive end to the postwar consensus. Thatcher's call for a renewal of nineteenth-century economic, political, and even imperial philosophies and her championing of moral, social, and gender norms of an earlier time found great favor among a large segment of the population in a period when Britain's international status and economic conditions had fallen into steep decline.

Sexual revolution, gay rights, feminism, and "the enemy within"

The relative affluence of the 1950s and its apparent continuation in the years 1963 to 1968 among many sectors of the population spawned the creation of a dynamic and, to many, disturbing youth culture. Centered first around the mod fashions and the pop and rock offerings of the Beatles and the Rolling Stones, and later gravitating toward punk groups like the Sex Pistols, youth culture marked a definitive shift of both cultural authority and resistance to mainstream society away from élite writers to a mass movement of working- and middle-class young men and women. Aware of the great pockets of poverty existing within their society of affluence, and subject themselves to the dead-end jobs that offered no means of escape from a lifetime of drudgery, working- and lower-middle-class youth, followed by huge numbers of their middle-class age cohort, gave vent to their frustrations and dissatisfactions with their parents' way of life by mocking their values and traditions and celebrating their own nonconformity with them. Mod fashions, rock music, experimentation with drugs, and the flouting of sexual conventions epitomized the generational revolt against postwar society, producing anxiety and unease among significant segments of the population.

In contrast to the mod and pop cultures, which presented an androgynous, "unisex," even feminine face to the world and were far more accessible to young women, the style and lyrics of rock groups struck observers with their sexual aggressiveness and their hostility toward women. In the songs of the Stones, for example, class antagonism frequently found expression through misogynous diatribes against wealthy women by working-class men. "Playing with fire" and "19th nervous breakdown," among others, scorned their upper-class female protagonists for their preoccupation with material possessions and their empty, superficial lives. In their live performances, the Rolling Stones sought to present themselves as sexually charged, violent, destructive, dangerous malcontents who were capable of almost any outrage. Mick Jagger, according to a contemporary rock critic, "trampled the weak, execrated the old, poured out a psychotic flood of abuse against women."

Freer attitudes about sex and sexuality, though not necessarily freer practices, accompanied the flowering of youth culture in the 1960s. The so-called "sexual revolution" derived from the convergence of a number of developments. First, the consumer market for sex-related commodities burgeoned in the postwar period, as affluence and a youth-age-skewed demographic upturn increased the commercial possibilities of selling sex. Advertising firms seized upon sex to sell any number and manner of products, taking their cue from the sexually explicit lyrics and erotic posturings of rock stars that so captivated youth audiences. Hugh Hefner's *Playboy* magazine capitalized on the commodification of sex with extraordinary success. London's Playboy Club opened its doors in 1966, followed by a spate of less respectable, sometimes pornographic establishments that catered to a seemingly insatiable male demand for sexual pleasure. A kind of hedonistic lifestyle emerged in the "swinging" sixties, within which "wife swapping" and other unconventional sexual practices might take place. Censorship laws regulating the content of publications and the theater were overturned in 1959, 1964, and 1968. Savvy media types and entrepreneurs exploited the new freedom surrounding sex to improve their bottom lines, and in the process extended the scope of the "sexual revolution."

Second, the material consequences of sex for both men and women changed remarkably. The availability of the "pill," a reliable contraceptive, and of legal abortion after 1967, made it possible for women to engage in sexual intercourse with a much reduced fear of pregnancy. Venereal diseases like syphilis and gonorrhea could be readily treated by antibiotics. These material improvements could help to open up whole new possibilities of physical pleasure for women, who were more free to explore and experience sexual opportunities than previous generations of women had been. But they also made it possible for men to put a great deal of pressure on women to engage with them sexually; absent the constraints of unwanted pregnancy, women were far more susceptible to accusations of prudery and other forms of verbal coercion. As Celia Haddon put it in her 1983 *The Limits of Sex*, "in some ways, the sexual revolution had freed me from guilt and anxiety; in other ways it had enslaved me anew, with different fetters."[1] As we shall see below, the negative implications of the sexual revolution for women helped to provoke a new wave of feminism in the early 1970s.

Despite what appeared to contemporaries to be a dramatic change in sexual practices, actual sexual behavior remained pretty consistent with that of earlier decades. Attitudes and styles had altered, to be sure, but little in the way of real substantive behavioral change can be detected. Young people engaged in sexual relations at a younger age now, but improved diet and health consequent upon the provision of welfare benefits lowered the age of sexual maturation; physiological rather than moral shifts may well account for earlier sexual activity. In the late 1960s, a *Sunday Times* poll found that over one-quarter of the men and almost two-thirds of the women surveyed had been virgins at the time they married. Men and women might live with one another for a considerable period of time before marriage, but the rate of marriage did not fall; in fact it went up. Divorce rates rose with a liberalization of the divorce laws in 1969, but serial monogamy in the form of second and third marriages continued to be the trend among the vast majority of men and women.

The sexual revolution may well have appeared so threatening to many traditional and conservative people because it was closely tied in with other countercultural movements that challenged the political, social, and gender orders of Britain. Anti-war protests, student demonstrations and sit-ins, racial equality and black power groups, gay rights organizations, and a powerful women's liberation movement appeared right on the heels of the "sexual revolution," presenting mainstream society with a multi-pronged assault on its values and institutions. The civil rights quest of catholics in Northern Ireland gave way to violence on the part of both catholics and protestants, which spilled over to the rest of the United Kingdom in the form of domestic terrorism. Union demands for higher wages and industrial unrest resulting in violence appeared endemic. The amalgamation of all these developments produced in the minds of a good portion of the population by 1970 the sense that a general breakdown in morality had occurred during the 1960s, that "enemies within" were undermining the nation, and that something had to be done to make Britain right again.

The appearance of a gay rights movement to reform the laws against homosexuality proved unsettling to many people, gay and straight alike. In 1957, the Wolfenden Committee on Homosexual Offenses and Prostitution had recommended that sexual activity between consenting males in the privacy of the home should not be illegal. The report did not produce legislation for another decade, when the passage of the Sexual Offences Act of 1967 decriminalized sexual activity between men over the age of twenty-one "in private" in England and Wales, though not in Scotland or Northern Ireland. (The act did not pertain to women, as lesbianism had not been recognized in the earlier prohibitions against same-sex behavior and laws against it did not therefore exist.) Over the course of the next decade, attitudes about homosexuality and towards homosexuals tended to become increasingly tolerant, so that by 1970 or so, gay men and lesbians felt sufficiently safe to abandon their closeted existences and venture out to form a distinct community with a visible subculture and lifestyle. Driven by the same market forces that generated much of the "sexual revolution," gay pubs, clubs, and discos sprang up. Among some gay men, the new freedom produced a great deal of promiscuity and hedonism; for most others and for lesbians generally, it offered an opportunity to live their lives honestly, comfortably, and openly. Eschewing conventional gender prescriptions for a society based on individual family units presided over by heterosexual couples of husband and wife conforming to current standards of masculinity and femininity, gays and lesbians offered alternative models for intimate relationships and community ties. These included families headed by same-sex couples or groups of gay men and lesbians acting communally to raise and care for children.

While the Sexual Offences Act of 1967 marked a liberalization of the law, it maintained significant exceptions that limited its reach and operated to increase discrimination against homosexual men. It did not apply to the armed services or merchant marine, for example. It strengthened the powers of the police to crack down on activity that might be construed as sexual in "public" places like gay bars, or even in private homes where more than two men might be engaged in sexual activity. Northern Ireland and Scotland did not fall under its provisions. And where the age of consent for heterosexuals was set at sixteen years, that for homosexuals was raised to twenty-one years, making behavior that was perfectly legal for heterosexual couples criminal for homosexual couples if they had not reached the age of consent. Gay rights activists in England, Scotland, and Northern Ireland sought change in order to make homosexuals equal with heterosexuals under the law. The Campaign for Homosexual Equality, the Scottish Minorities Group, and the Union for Sexual Freedom in Ireland pooled their energies and resources in 1974 to demand passage of a bill that would lower the age of consent to sixteen; give "equal freedom with heterosexuals to express affection in public"; extend rights to homosexuals in the armed forces; and apply the law to Scotland and Northern Ireland.

Members of the Gay Liberation Front (GLF) wanted to go beyond legal equality to eliminate attitudes and practices that oppressed homosexuals, and to instill pride and honor in those who identified themselves as gay or lesbian. "The long-term goal," declared GLF's manifesto, "is to rid society of the gender role system which is at the root of our oppression." In the early 1970s, their efforts appeared to be successful in some quarters of society. The *Manchester Guardian* published an article in 1971 expressing appreciation for what gay rights seemed to promise and for gay liberation's shattering of hateful stereotypes of gay men in particular. "The young homosexuals," the article noted:

> by their very acceptance of the normality of homosexuality, challenge the status quo. … And they are beautiful to see. It is lovely to be with men and women who are not ashamed to express their affections openly, in the normal heterosexual ways, the hand in hand, the arm in arm, the occasional cuddle, the quick kiss. Suddenly, watching them, the whole evil, squalid image of homosexuality crumbles – are these bright young faces corrupters of children, lavatory solicitators, the something nasty in all our woodsheds?

Later that year, Vera Brittain applauded the Gay Liberation Front in *The Times* for providing "an alternative to sexual shame." And in 1977, Maureen Colquhoun, Labour MP for Northampton North, announced that she was "gay and proud of it" in response to efforts on the part of the local branch of her party to remove her as a candidate for the next election. Local party members claimed that her record was unsatisfactory, but Colquhoun suspected that her sexuality was at issue. She fought against her de-selection as a candidate, insisting that "I am not 'Britain's Lesbian MP.' I am the working Member of Parliament for Northampton North and I am carrying on with my job. My sexuality is of no more relevance to that work than is the sexuality of heterosexual MPs – something people do not continually question." The *Daily Mirror* supported her right to remain as party candidate despite her sexual identity, deriding the Labour Party as a whole for its hypocrisy in attempting to get rid of her on the basis of her work in parliament. Colquhoun's battle proved successful; she stood as Labour's candidate in the next election, only to lose her seat in the landslide victory of the Conservatives in 1979.[2]

Just as the gay liberation movement went beyond a mere reform of the laws to transform the culture that imposed upon them uncomfortable heterosexual norms as the basis for their relationships and their behavior, so too did women's liberation, arising in 1968 with demands for women's freedom from roles, portrayals, and expectations that limited, diminished, and oppressed them. The sexual revolution of the 1960s had placed a premium on men's pleasures and the fulfillment of their sexual desires at the expense of women, whose highly sexualized images appeared in magazines like *Playboy* and *Penthouse*, on billboards and posters, and on page three of the *Sun*. Women's liberation activists protested loudly and vividly against such depictions of women as sexual objects. One of their first actions took place in 1970 at the Miss World beauty contest in London, when a group of women interrupted the pageant by leaping on stage and blowing whistles, hooting, mooing like cattle, and brandishing signs that read "Miss-conception," "Miss-treated," "Miss-placed," and "Miss-judged." They lobbed stink bombs, flour bombs, and smoke bombs at the contestants, the judges, and at Bob Hope, the master of ceremonies. Their actions resembled those of the militant suffragists of the first decade of the twentieth century, and earned them the same result – arrest. They created a spectacle that succeeded in garnering for the movement enormous publicity.[3]

Some seventy women's liberation groups existed in London alone by 1969, spreading quickly to other cities in Scotland, Wales, and the Republic of Ireland. In 1970, the first Women's Liberation Conference convened in Oxford, the idea for which originated with socialist women affiliated with the new left History Workshop. Publications like *Shrew*, *Red Rag*, and *Spare Rib* appeared, analyzing women's oppression, recounting earlier feminist efforts, spreading the feminist message, and making claims for women's personal, sexual, and familial freedom.

The Equal Pay Acts of 1970 and 1975 and the Sex Discrimination Act of 1975 made it possible for women to gain equal treatment with men in education, training, and wage-earning. But "second wave" feminists looked for more than equality with men before the law; they sought changes in the law, the social and economic system, and the culture that would "liberate" them from current conceptions of femininity that, they argued, locked them into stifling, unfulfilling, slavish positions, and often made them vulnerable to sexual predations from men. Unlike contemporary liberal feminists and those of the nineteenth and early twentieth century, feminists seeking liberation believed that the very system in which they lived required abolition or complete overhaul.

Feminists differed in their designation of just what system it was that oppressed them. Socialist feminists, hailing from "new left" organizations like the International Marxist Group, identified capitalism as the source of conditions that rendered them inferior to men. Like Marx, explained Hilary Rose, who "was able to go behind the appearance of freedom in the labour market in which buyers and sellers freely bought and sold, to reveal the systemic relations of domination and subordination which are located within the capitalist mode of production itself," socialist, or materialist, feminists must "go behind – above all in personal life – the appearance of love and the naturalness of a woman's place and a woman's work, to reveal the equally systemic relationships of the sex-gender world." [4] The family, in particular, socialist feminists argued, in which the understandings and assumptions and the labor force necessary to keep capitalism working were reproduced, required complete transformation. For socialist feminists, adherence to Marxist doctrine and to socialist groups remained a significant aspect of their politics, the goal of which was to eliminate the unjust class system produced by capitalism and reproduced by the family. The achievement of feminist aims would follow upon its extinction. At the same time, their insistence that women's work, experiences, and functions in a capitalist society could not simply be subsumed into those of men forced traditional socialists to enlarge their understandings and expand their analyses of capitalism.

Radical feminists, by contrast, saw in domination by men, in patriarchy and not in the economic system, the root of their oppression. They insisted that if women were to be liberated, they would have to arrive at a "consciousness" of their oppression. As Dale Spender put it:

> a patriarchal society depends in large measure on the experience and values of males being perceived as the *only* valid frame of reference for society, and ... it is therefore in patriarchal interest to prevent women from sharing, estab-lishing and asserting their equally real, valid and *different* frame of reference, which is the outcome of different experience. [5]

Having gained through "consciousness-raising" sessions at which they explored their personal lives in depth an understanding of how patriarchy operated in the most insidious ways to make women complicit in their own subservience to men, they would ultimately have to remove themselves from sexual and social relation-ships with men, radical feminists asserted. Separatism, as they saw it, provided the only avenue to liberation. As Amanda Sebestyn described radical feminists later:

> we wanted to leave men no matter what, we started squatting so we could live with other women, we acquired of necessity new "male" skills of plumbing, electricity, carpentry and car maintenance, setting up our own discos and

then forming bands to dance to. We cut our hair very short and stopped wearing "women's" clothes, we stopped smiling and being "nice."[6]

Despite their differences, which would become increasingly evident and acrimonious in the mid- and late-1970s, feminists of virtually every stripe agreed that women's sexual freedom, their capacity to choose the kind of intimate or social grouping in which they would live, and determining for themselves the kind of work they would do, were vital to their liberation. They could readily come together to support reforms that contributed to that end: access to free and legal contraception and abortion; equal pay; health, educational, and social services; increased penalties for rape and domestic violence; nursery and day care for children; and provisions that enabled women to be legally and financially independent like divorce law reform and wages for housework. They made clear from the start that they intended their varieties of feminism to create entirely different roles, expectations, identities, and material realities for women than those currently operative. Their focus on personal and family issues, and on social and cultural practices – like the clubs, bookstores, magazines, and literature of the "sexual revolution" that gratuitously portrayed women as the proper objects of male sexual desire and violence – gave their movement a broad comprehensiveness that touched the lives of subsequent generations of women – and men – to come.

Women of color in Britain found themselves in a kind of political no-man's-land in the late 1960s and early 1970s. Disconcerted by their treatment at the hands of the male-dominated black power movement, yet finding women's liberation and feminism entirely irrelevant and blind to their needs and desires, women of color began, under the stimulus of the demands made by women in the revolutionary struggles in Zimbabwe, Angola, and Eritrea, to form their own organizations to gain liberation for themselves. Iyamide Hazeley graphically laid out the grievances black women felt within black power organizations in a poem called "Political union." "You call me 'Sister' Brother," she observed, "yet I know/ that it is simply a psychological lever to prise apart/my legs./ 'Sister, make coffee for the movement,/Sister, make babies for the struggle'/You rape my consciousness with your body/my body with reason,/and assuage your unconscious guilt by oral politicking/make believing/ 'Sister, Sister.'"[7]

When they looked toward white feminist groups, black women saw a political programme that addressed few of their concerns. "We felt they had different priorities to us," remarked one women instrumental in forming the Brixton Black Women's Group in 1973.

At that time, for example, abortion was the number one issue, and groups like Wages for Housework were making a lot of noise, too. These were hardly burning issues for us – in fact they seemed like middle-class preoccupations.

To begin with, abortion wasn't something we had any problems getting as Black women – it was the very reverse for us! And as for wages for housework, we were more interested in getting properly paid for the work we were doing outside the home as nightcleaners and in campaigning for more childcare facilities for Black women workers.[8]

In order to deal with a dual oppression arising from racism and sexism, a number of women formed other local Black Women's Groups throughout London and in cities like Leicester, Manchester, Liverpool, Sheffield, and Nottingham. Coalitions of women of color such as the Organization of Women of Asian and African Descent (OWAAD) enabled a broader national movement to emerge within which issues of racism and sexism that concerned women of color could be addressed and a national dialogue established.

As Hazel Carby noted in a hard-hitting article, the structures of racism meant that black women experienced different kinds of subjection than white women. What white women regarded as an oppressive institution – the family – black women often found to be a place from which to resist political and cultural forms of racism. White radical feminists might espouse separatism from men; black women relied on "progressive" men in their struggles for equality and justice. "Our situation as Black people necessitates that we have solidarity around the fact of race, which white women of course do not need to have with white men, unless it is their negative solidarity as racial oppressors." White feminists, Carby argued, had not recognized their role in continuing imperialist and colonialist regimes around the world, or, indeed, in acting as oppressors of black people at home, and if they did, they refused to acknowledge their complicity for fear "that this will be at the expense of concentrating upon being oppressed."[9] Carby's critique of white women's feminism raised profoundly uncomfortable issues for many women, and it ultimately served to open up feminism as a whole to the existence of diversity in women's lives that compelled the development of far more sophisticated understandings of gender through post-structuralist analyses than either socialist or radical feminism had been able to provide.

The sexual revolution, gay liberation, and feminism profoundly challenged conventional norms of masculinity and femininity and of male and female sexuality. Together, within the context of rising unemployment, union intransigence, and economic downturn, they provoked in a good portion of the popular mind a conviction that standards of behavior and propriety were under grave assault, that "permissiveness" was producing "moral collapse" in Britain. Conservatives and traditionalists decried the apparent loss of a British "way of life," attributing it first to an "enemy within" in the guise of the younger generation, but increasingly seeing the threat to earlier values deriving from the presence of "alien," "outsider" immigrants. Distress over the "permissive" nature of society often found voice as a lament about a breakdown in "law and order," so that popular anxieties about morality became collapsed into fears about crime and delinquency. And in Britain, by the early 1970s, crime and delinquency signified "blacks."

In the 1940s, 1950s, and 1960s, debates about immigration centered on criminal behavior on the part of blacks in Britain; they focused on what police and civil authorities believed was a disproportionate participation in criminal activities that were sexual in nature, and which usually involved white women. Newspapers, and in 1954, the Home Secretary, reported on the existence of a large class of black men living off the earnings of white prostitutes, pimping for them in numbers far in excess of their proportion to the population as a whole. In 1958, Tory MP Sir Cyril Osborne declared that "the tendency of those crimes to occur among coloured people is a hundred times more per person, than among white people in the London area."[10] Fears of sexuality and of miscegenation dominated discussions of the roles played by immigrants and their children in the life of the nation.

By the late 1960s, these fears combined with anxieties about safety to produce a slightly different racial discourse. In 1968, Enoch Powell, Conservative MP for Ulster, had declared the settlement of blacks in Britain to be a threat to the nation's very existence. In his so-called "River of blood" speech, he foresaw, "like the Roman, … 'the River Tiber foaming with much blood,'" if immigration was not banned outright and the "re-emigration" of West Indians, Pakistanis, and Indians back to their countries of origin not put into effect. He framed his images of violence around a story about an elderly white woman under siege from blacks who had "invaded" her neighborhood. "Eight years ago in a respectable street in Wolverhampton," he recounted, "a house was sold to a negro. Now only one white (a woman old-age pensioner) lives there." Powell suggests an image of "negroes" breeding like rabbits till they have overwhelmed the white population. "With growing fear, she saw one house after another taken over. The quiet street became a place of noise and confusion. Regretfully, her white tenants moved out."Without their protection, Powell intimates, the pensioner finds herself at the mercy of her new neighbors:

> The day after the last [white tenant] left, she was awakened at 7:00 a.m. by two negroes who wanted to use her phone to contact their employer. When she refused, as she would have refused any stranger at such an hour, she was abused and feared she would have been attacked but for the chain on her door.

This tale utilizes elements from the 1950s that emphasized the encroachment upon whites' private spaces by black people and the intimations of miscegenation and hypersexuality among blacks, and mixes them in with new fears about violence and personal safety. Isolated, alone, and unwilling to let rooms in her house out to immigrants, the white woman "is becoming afraid to go out. Windows are broken. She finds excreta pushed through her letterbox. When she goes to the shops, she is followed by children, charming, wide-grinning piccaninnies. They cannot speak English, but one word they know. 'Racialist,' they chant." In this account, in which the nation is represented by an elderly, frail white woman vulnerable to the sexual and physical threats of black men, Powell means to convey the ominous message that if blacks in Britain are given the same freedoms from discrimination that white Britons enjoy, then those very freedoms and the British "way of life" they represent will be destroyed in a traumatic blood-letting.[11]

By the 1970s, concerns about the presence of blacks in Britain had shifted on to a slightly different ground, and what had once been the racist rantings of a fringe politician became core beliefs held by many a Briton. Crime in the forms of robbery, "mugging," and urban riots came to the fore in discourses about black settlement, race relations, and social disorder. One critic claimed that "in Britain, 'mugging' is, indeed, a form of self-employment … that is disproportionately practised by unemployed West Indians." Black people, black men in particular, came to stand in for illegality, a decidedly "unBritish" trait, conservatives told themselves, despite the facts that government reports showed that "immigrant crime rates were, if anything, a little lower than those for the indigenous population," and union militancy, Ulster politics, and soccer "hooliganism" had been producing a great deal of violence among white Britons for years. Commissioner of the Metropolitan Police Sir Kenneth Newman declared that "in the Jamaicans, you have a people who are constitutionally disorderly. … It's simply in their make up, they're constitutionally disposed to be anti-authority."[12] They represented for many conservatives the forces responsible for Britain's decline, for the social instability brought on by unemployment and recession. "The nation has been and is still being, eroded and hollowed out from within by implantation of unassimilated and unassimilable populations … alien wedges in the heartland of the state," asserted Powell in 1976. By this time, his message of racial intolerance and of black people as the source of danger to British society had been embraced by a majority of Britons and would soon help to produce the electoral victory of the Conservative Party, with Margaret Thatcher at its head. As Alfred Sherman, a prominent right-wing theorist, put it in September 1979 on the eve of Thatcher's election as prime minister, articulating the affiliation of "permissiveness" with all of the countercultural and political movements we have been discussing:

> the imposition of mass immigration from backward alien cultures is just one symptom of this self-destructive urge reflected in the assault on patriotism, the family – both as a conjugal and economic unit – the Christian religion in public life and schools, traditional morality, in matters of sex, honesty, public display, and respect for the law – in short, all that is English and wholesome.[13]

Thatcherism and the return to Victorian values

Margaret Thatcher sought to undo the system created by the welfare state and social democracy, and to return Britain to an economic, political, and social regime characteristic of the Victorian period. She abhorred what she saw as the socialism of the 1950s, 1960s, and 1970s, seeking to replace it with an economy in which market forces of supply and demand, private ownership of industries, and *laissez-faire* prevailed. Politics, she declared, would no longer be a matter of "consensus" but of "conviction," promising an injection of firm authority and decisive action into a situation that, largely due to union intransigence over wages and industrial militancy, appeared to most to be one of "ungovernability." Britain would be returned to a position of world prominence, the "Iron Lady" asserted, pitting British nationalism against the collective aspirations of the European Community, taking a hard line against the Soviet Union, and sending troops to the far-off Falkland Islands to protect some 1,800 inhabitants of British descent from the Argentine government, which had invaded the islands and claimed them as its own. All of this would be accomplished, she promised, through a renewal of traditional values of morality, discipline, and restraint; an economic and social system based on unencumbered capitalism, élitism and social deference, and family life strengthened by a return to separate spheres for men and women; and a new "nationalist" spirit that incorporated Powellite racial thinking under its rubric.[14]

Thatcherite analysis of the country's grave crisis drew upon ideas formulated in 1971 by John Gummer, a man who would become a prominent Tory frontbencher after 1979. He compared Britain's current state of affairs to that of the nineteenth century, concluding that the combination of economic freedom and sexual repression characteristic of the latter period had been turned upside down, to the detriment of the economy and society. He stated:

> The twentieth century has increasingly reversed that position ... restricted and cosseted us economically while leaving us more and more free to do as we like in bed. Today we are much more preoccupied with a man's economic effect on others. ... We protect the individual from every possible material harm which may come to him ... and restrict his freedom of material decision ... [yet] we increasingly deny, at least in theory, that private sin makes for public danger. Whereas the Victorians believed that the State had to be restrictive in the field of private moral actions or society would suffer, we believe that a man's private life is his own and the State need take no account of it.

Welfare state capitalism, Gummer lamented, had produced a society so lacking in moral direction that "the traditional moral standards of western Christian civilisa-

tion are not merely found difficult or merely ignored – they are actively challenged."[15]

For Margaret Thatcher, informed by Gummer's arguments, restoring Britain to
greatness required first an ideological battle under which all other struggles were
subsumed. She maintained the need to resolve the political and moral problems
facing the country before the economic ones could be tackled. "Serious as the
economic challenge is, the political and moral challenge is just as grave, and
perhaps more so," she told the Conservative Party in 1975, "because economic
problems never start with economics. They have much deeper roots in human
nature, and roots in politics, and they do not finish at economics. ... These are the
two great challenges of our time – the moral and political challenge, and the
economic challenge. They have to be faced together and we have to master them
both." The moral problems stemmed from the permissiveness of the 1960s, she
maintained. "We are reaping what was sown in the sixties," she insisted in 1982.
"The fashionable theories and permissive claptrap set the scene for a society in
which the old virtues of discipline and self-restraint were denigrated."[16] The
breakdown of law and order, sexual freedom, gay rights, women's liberation – all
the excesses of 1960s permissiveness would have to be eliminated, and virtue
restored before the difficulties of the economy could be addressed. But those
problems, too, she declared, could be redressed by a simple return to the days of
the Victorians, when the principles of entrepreneurial capitalism and domesticity
ruled society.

Thatcher resolved to deal with the "political" problem by introducing what one
critic has called "authoritarian populism," a regime characterized by the exercise of
the disciplinary powers of the state against what were regarded as disruptive
elements in society who had no respect for law and order.[17] At a time when the
number of unemployed had reached two million, widespread concerns about law
and order – shorthand in the parlance of many Britons for the existence of Indians,
Asians, West Indians, and Pakistanis among them, whose "alien" cultures had come
to be represented as being synonymous with violence and crime in Britain –
enabled Thatcher's government to expand the power of the police, of the law, and
of agencies of surveillance to control and suppress activities and behaviors it
deemed dangerous to the state, activities and behaviors construed as "alien,"
"unBritish," committed by "outsiders." One such tool, the use of mass "stop and
search" powers against black men and women in Brixton by the police in April
1981 provoked a major riot there four days later. The June debate over a new
Nationality Bill demonstrated just how readily white Britons displaced on to racial
"others" the consequences of economic problems that seemed to have no solution.
MP Ivor Stanbrook declared:

we are in the grip of forces which, because of the large influx of immigrants into Britain, we now seem unable to control. Racial violence is occurring with increasing frequency. The British people are sick at heart about it all.

In July 1981, riots involving young people of all races and ethnicities broke out in a number of cities across the nation, prompting the *Financial Times* to declare an "Outbreak of an alien disease" in its headline, attributing to the presence of immigrants and their children protests produced by poverty, unemployment, and heavy-handed police measures.[18]

Economic difficulties and dislocations continued throughout 1981 and into 1982, creating much dissatisfaction in the country with the Conservative Party, which, it appeared in early 1982, was in danger of losing its majority in the upcoming 1983 election. Thatcher's popularity plummeted in the fall of 1981, while that of the newly created alliance between the Social Democratic and Liberal Parties soared. In March of 1982, the government of Argentina, acting on its claim that the Malvinas islands – what the British claimed as the Falklands, containing 1,800 people of British "stock" and 600,000 sheep – belonged to Argentina, invaded them, throwing Britons at home into a frenzy of jingoistic, neo-imperialist patriotism; prompting the British government to declare war; and, with victory secured in June 1982, re-establishing the popularity of Mrs Thatcher and the Conservative Party at record levels.

"Great Britain is great again," exulted Thatcher in the fall of 1982, collapsing victory over the unions and over nationalization of industry into that over the Argentines. "We have ceased to be a nation in retreat. We have instead a new-found confidence – born in the economic battles at home and tested and found true 8,000 miles away." As one perceptive critic noted of the enthusiasm surrounding the sending of the fleet to retake the Falklands from the "Argies," "if the Falkland Islanders were British citizens with black or brown skins, spoke with strange accents or worshipped different Gods it is doubtful whether the Royal Navy and Marines would today be fighting for their liberation." Indeed, he pointed out, "most Britons today identify more easily with those of the same stock 8000 miles away … than they do with West Indian or Asian immigrants living next door."[19]

The victory over the Argentines gave white Britons something to feel good about; it seemed to mark an end to the humiliation they experienced with the loss of Britain's colonies and its pre-eminent position in the world. A new mood of decisiveness and strength, which Thatcher identified as the aspects of her ruling style that made her so popular with Britons at a time when economic conditions had only gotten worse, not better, seems to have reflected a nostalgia for imperialism, evidenced in the spate of films and media projects concerning the British in India. In what Salman Rushdie termed a "raj revivalism," films like *Gandhi* and *A Passage to India*, and the television productions of *The Far Pavilions* and *The Jewel in the Crown* made their appearance and found welcoming, enthusiastic audiences. Britain seemed, once again, a manly nation in control of its destiny, one that is "not prepared to be pushed around." Its imperial incursion overseas had made it possible for Britons to "rediscover ... ourselves" and to "recover ... our self-respect. Britain found herself again in the South Atlantic and will not look back from the victory she has won." The great irony, of course, was that a woman, Margaret Thatcher, was responsible for this change in fortunes, a paradox we can comprehend only when we realize that gender – the knowledge we as a culture think we have about sexual difference, a phenomenon we believe to be grounded in nature[20] – has virtually nothing to do with sex.

Thatcher's moral agenda entailed the recreation of an ideology of separate spheres, in which bourgeois men displayed their talents in the freewheeling arena of industry and commerce, and bourgeois women presided over the home as guardians of the nation's morality. Drawing upon essentialized notions of gender familiar to nineteenth-century moralists and medical men, Thatcherites posited a womanhood whose inherent qualities of purity, innocence, and nurturance complemented – and controlled – the aggressive, sexual, destructive instincts of men. In practical terms, as envisaged by the American sociologist, George Gilder, to whose writings British moralists like Mary Whitehouse referred in their campaign for "moral rearmament," "a married man ... is spurred by the claims of family to channel his otherwise disruptive male aggressions into his performance as a provider for wife and children." Roger Scruton, a British philosopher, argued in "The case against feminism" in 1983 that it is the obligation of women to "quieten what is most vagrant" in men, namely the "unbridled ambition of the phallus."[21] Feminists, in the minds of these thinkers, threatened the peaceful ordering of families and societies by injecting their individualistic, egalitarian demands and their assertions of sexual freedom, thus disrupting the harmony that sexual difference and gender complementarity established.

Although, as we have seen in the previous chapter, Margaret Thatcher had championed in the 1950s the right of women to work outside the home on the grounds that it made them better mothers to their children, her rise within the ranks of the party and her elevation to the prime ministership "owed nothing to feminism." Instead, Thatcher, it was said, was the "best man" to head the Conservative government. Thatcher's policies and her statements seemed to contain something of the same sort of contradiction that her life story indicated. On the one hand, Thatcherism espoused the return home of women who worked outside it. Patrick Jenkin, a cabinet minister in Thatcher's first government, insisted in 1979, "if the Good Lord had intended us to have equal rights to go out to work, He wouldn't have created men and women." In 1990, Thatcher told a BBC interviewer that nurseries for the children of working mothers undercut the welfare of children; her government slashed financial support for them. Thatcher's policies hampered women who depended upon obtaining state-sponsored child care so that they could go out to work to help support their families. On the other hand, at the Pankhurst lecture in 1990, she lauded the contributions women had made and were making to public life, helped by "legislation and tax reforms to stamp out discrimination." These were women, she made it clear later in the lecture, who had the resources to hire "reliable help" to care for their children, "what my mother would have called 'a treasure': someone who brought not only her work but her affections to the family."[22]

For Thatcher and her supporters, the Victorian model of the two-parent family in which the husband and father went out to work in order to support the wife and mother at home served as the ideal to which all should aspire. Strong families provided the bedrock stability of a secure society. "Marriage and the family are two of the most important institutions on which society is based," Thatcher asserted. "Particularly at this time of rapid social change and accompanying stresses marriage has never been more important in preserving a stable and responsible society."[23] Education secretary Kenneth Baker introduced legislation that would require schools to teach students about sex only within the context of "commitment, love and family life." The welfare state and educational opportunities for women, Thatcherites held, had weakened family ties by releasing them from a number of familial obligations and encouraging them to pursue opportunities outside of childbearing and -rearing. The resurgence of market force-based capitalism and the return of women to their proper sphere would restore society to the moral level it had enjoyed before "permissiveness" had undermined it. As one obstetrician declared in support of the efforts to reinscribe the Victorian system of separate spheres, "it is a fact that there is a biological drive to reproduce. Women who deny this drive, or in whom it is frustrated, show disturbances in other ways."[24] No nineteenth-century physician could have said it better.

Accordingly, efforts to change the abortion law flourished in the new climate of Thatcherism. The Abortion Reform Act of 1967 had made it legal for women to obtain abortions within twenty-eight weeks of their pregnancies, provided that a doctor certified that carrying the pregnancy to term would endanger the mental or physical health of the mother, the welfare of her other children, or result in abnormalities of the fetus. In 1975, 1977, and 1979, private members' bills were introduced into parliament, seeking to restrict access to abortion, to limit the number of weeks within which it could take place, and to make it easier for nurses and doctors to refuse to perform them on the grounds of conscientious objection. These bills failed, as did the attempt of the health secretary in 1981 to bypass parliament altogether by implementing an administrative change that would limit the meaning of a woman's "health" to a strictly physical definition.

Again in 1988, a bill that would outlaw abortion after eight weeks of pregnancy was introduced in parliament, but it too failed when a large campaign made up of feminists, trade union delegates, Labour MPs, medical professionals, and the general public as a whole mobilized against it and defeated it. Public support for abortion proved far too strong – encompassing some 79 percent of the population – to overturn the 1967 act.

Efforts toward moral rejuvenation by means of anti-gay measures proved far easier to implement. The relative tolerance of homosexuality exhibited by society in the 1960s eroded in the 1970s and 1980s, as a backlash against "permissiveness" intensified. In 1981, the Criminal Law Revision Committee, upon which gay rights activists had pinned their hopes for an equalization of the age of consent for homosexuals to that of heterosexuals, recommended against such an action, arguing that it would be "wholly unacceptable to public opinion." Instead, it offered a compromise age of eighteen years. Tory MP Nicholas Winterton articulated the feelings of many in opposing even this reduction in the age of consent. "It's appalling that such a proposal is even being considered," he railed. "I will not tolerate recommendations that encourage youngsters to indulge in unnatural relationships." The Police Federation denounced the committee's recommendations, declaring that its members had "surrender[ed] to the pressure groups who try and persuade society that homosexual conduct is perfectly normal." It saw the 1967 Sexual Offences Act as liberalization enough, and condemned any further extension of reform. The government made known its opposition to further reform of the 1967 act by refusing to repeal the section of the law that excluded men in the armed forces from its provisions, and by taking up a private prosecution brought by Mary Whitehouse against a theater production for "procuring an act of gross indecency between two males." The play, *The Romans in Britain*, at the National Theatre depicted a scene in which the actors simulated anal intercourse. Before the case was thrown out by three judges at the Old Bailey, the government had spent £20,000 of the public's money.[25]

Police raided private parties where gay men gathered, allegedly in violation of the provision of the 1967 act that made sex between more than two men a "public" activity. Arrests and prosecutions for homosexual "solicitation" rose dramatically: in 1977, 488 men were convicted of this offense; in 1980, 1,208 convictions were obtained, an increase of 247 percent in three years. In February 1984, two men were arrested and fined £100 for kissing in Oxford Street, their actions constituting "insulting behaviour likely to cause a breach of the peace." Similar arrests followed in subsequent months. Police harassed gay bars on the grounds that they violated licensing laws. Customs and Excise officials raided gay bookshops in London and in Scotland, seizing books by authors like Rita Mae Brown and Truman Capote. When some Labour MPs sought to bring evidence of the violation of civil rights that these incidents suggested before the public, they were excoriated by their Conservative colleagues. Reviving and revising a political slogan of 1964 when Tory MP Peter Griffiths defeated the Labour opposition candidate with the cry, "if you want a Nigger for a neighbour vote Labour," a platform speaker at the 1985 Conservative party conference urged her listeners, "if you want a queer for a neighbour, vote Labour."[26] When the magnitude of the AIDS epidemic came to the attention of the British public in 1985, the anti-gay atmosphere of the past several years ensured that governmental response to it would be limited and ineffective in helping to slow its spread.

Press coverage of the AIDS crisis grew increasingly hysterical. In 1986, the media trumpeted the reaction of one Conservative leader of the South Staffordshire council to a film meant to educate viewers about AIDS and its transmission. "Those bunch of queers that legalise filth in homosexuality have a lot to answer for, and I hope they are proud of what they have done," he seethed. "As a cure I would put 90 per cent of queers in the ruddy gas chamber." When the Chief Constable of Manchester, James Anderton, announced that AIDS was "a self-inflicted scourge," and that gays, prostitutes, and promiscuous people generally were "swirling about in a human cesspit of their own making," the *Sun* cheered his remarks. "Their defiling act of love is not only unnatural. In today's Aids-hit world it is LETHAL. ... What Britain needs is more men like James Anderton – and fewer gay terrorists holding the decent members of society to ransom." The *Standard* weighed in with its kudos to Anderton for "articulating a deep-rooted feeling in Britain," while the *Sunday Mirror* headlined its edition, "WHEN BEING GAY SHOULD BE A CRIME."[27]

The AIDS panic, the irresponsibility of the press, and the unsatisfactory response of the government produced a climate in which homophobia reached new heights. A 1986 Social Attitudes Survey poll found that some 70 percent of Britons felt that homosexual relationships were mostly or almost always wrong. In December 1987, following a speech by Thatcher in October in which she told the Conservative party conference that "children who need to be taught to respect traditional values are being taught that they have an inalienable right to be gay," a Tory MP introduced an amendment to a Local Government Bill that made it illegal for any local authority to "promote homosexuality or publish material for the promotion of homosexuality; ... promote the teaching in any maintained school of the acceptability of homosexuality as a pretended family relationship by the publication of such material or otherwise."[28] The amendment, which came to be called Clause 28, also banned local councils from providing "financial or other assistance" to anyone involved in the activities proscribed. Despite protests from the Labour party, from individual Labour politicians like Ken Livingstone, from prominent actors like Ian McKellen, from representatives of the worlds of art and literature, and from a newly united and galvanized mass gay constituency, Clause 28 passed the House of Commons in March of 1988 to become Section 28 of the Local Government Bill, passed into law in May 1988. "Moral rearmament" had produced a major victory in Thatcher's battle to restore "Victorian values" to Britain.

The mobilization of gendered and sexualized rhetoric to somehow deal with or disguise the problems faced by Britain in the world of the 1980s proved insufficient to save Margaret Thatcher when she ran up against an issue that could not be camouflaged by an appeal to morality. In the global economy of the late twentieth century, British fortunes would literally depend on the nation's willingness to join with the countries of the continent in a European union. Thatcher's unwillingness to entertain seriously the integration of Britain into Europe produced within her own party the idea that perhaps she was not, after all, the "best man" to lead the Conservatives. In 1990, she lost her position as head of the party, and thus as prime minister, to John Major, a man of far less "conviction" and "iron" than his predecessor. Thatcherism, having prevailed over British society and politics for over a decade, gradually lost its hold on the electorate, allowing for an easing of moralistic gendered, sexualized, and racialized prescriptions of an authentic "Britishness," and making way for a moderate, centrist style of rule under the Labour party's Tony Blair in 1996. Labour MPs counted among themselves, as did Blair's cabinet, a number of women, publicly identified gay men, and men and women of color in prominent positions. Sheer numbers suggest that the British electorate had grown intolerant of moral crusades against men and women identified as "enemies within" the state. When, in the autumn of 1998 some Labour MPs were "outed" and others threatened with exposure as homosexuals, the *Sun*, a popular tabloid, found that the vast majority of its readers, some 79 percent, did not care if an MP or cabinet minister was gay or not. The "moral panics" of the 1970s and 1980s seemed to have come to an end.

NOTES

1 Quoted in Jeffrey Weeks, *Sexuality and Its Discontents: Meanings, Myths and Modern Sexualities* (London, 1985), p. 18.

2 Stephen Jeffrey-Poulter, *Peers, Queers and Commons: The Struggle for Gay Law Reform from 1950 to the Present* (London, 1991), pp. 102, 103, 136, 137.

3 See Barbara Caine, *English Feminism, 1780–1980* (Oxford, 1997), Afterword.

4 Hilary Rose, "Women's work: Women's knowledge," in Juliet Mitchell and Ann Oakley, eds, *What is Feminism? A Re-examination* (New York, 1986), p. 161.

5 Dale Spender, *Women of Ideas (and What Men have Done to Them)* (London, 1982), pp. 4–5.

6 Quoted in Caine, *English Feminism*, p. 266.

7 Beverley Bryan, Stella Dadzie, and Suzanne Scafe, *The Heart of the Race: Black Women's Lives in Britain* (London, 1985), p. 147.

8 Bryan, Dadzie, and Scafe, *The Heart of the Race*, pp. 149–50.

9 Hazel Carby, "White woman listen! Black feminism and the boundaries of sisterhood," in Centre for Contemporary Cultural Studies, *The Empire Strikes Back: Race and Racism in 70s Britain* (London, 1982), pp. 213, 221.

10 Quoted in Paul Gilroy, *"There Ain't No Black in the Union Jack": The Cultural Politics of Race and Nation* (Chicago, 1991), p. 81.
11 J. Enoch Powell, *Freedom and Reality* (London, 1969), pp. 287–8.
12 Powell, *Freedom and Reality*, p. 72.
13 Quoted in Gilroy, *"Ain't No Black"*, p. 43; John Solomos, Bob Findlay, Simon Jones and Paul Gilroy, "The organic crisis of British capitalism and race: The experience of the seventies," in Centre for Contemporary Cultural Studies, *The Empire Strikes Back: Race and Racism in 70s Britain* (London, 1982), p. 27.
14 For one of the best critiques of Thatcherism, see Stuart Hall, *The Hard Road to Renewal: Thatcherism and the Crisis of the Left* (London, 1988).
15 Quoted in David T. Evans, *Sexual Citizenship: The Material Construction of Sexualities* (London, 1993), p. 73.
16 Quoted in Jeffrey Weeks, *Sexuality and Its Discontents*, p. 18.
17 See Hall, *The Hard Road to Renewal*, chs. 8, 9.
18 Solomos, Findlay, Jones, and Gilroy, "The organic crisis of British capitalism and race," pp. 29, 31.
19 Quoted in Gilroy, *"Ain't No Black"*, pp. 51, 52.
20 See Joan W. Scott, *Gender and the Politics of History* (New York, 1988), Introduction.
21 Quoted in Weeks, *Sexuality and Its Discontents*, p. 42.
22 Quoted in Evans, *Sexual Citizenship*, pp. 243, 244.
23 Evans, *Sexual Citizenship*, p. 240.
24 Evans, *Sexual Citizenship*, p. 251.
25 Jeffrey-Poulter, *Peers, Queers and Commons*, pp. 159, 160.
26 Jeffrey-Poulter, *Peers, Queers and Commons*, p. 201.
27 Jeffrey-Poulter, *Peers, Queers and Commons*, pp. 193, 196–7.
28 Jeffrey-Poulter, *Peers, Queers and Commons*, pp. 218–19.

SOURCES

Beverley Bryan, Stella Dadzie, and Suzanne Scafe, *The Heart of the Race: Black Women's Lives in Britain*. London, 1985.

Barbara Caine, *English Feminism, 1780–1980*. Oxford, 1997.

Hazel Carby, "White woman listen! Black feminism and the boundaries of sisterhood," in Centre for Contemporary Cultural Studies, *The Empire Strikes Back: Race and Racism in 70s Britain*. London, 1982.

David T. Evans, *Sexual Citizenship: The Material Construction of Sexualities*. London, 1993.

John R. Gillis, *For Better, For Worse: British Marriages, 1600 to the Present*. New York, 1985.

Paul Gilroy, *"There Ain't No Black in the Union Jack": The Cultural Politics of Race and Nation*. Chicago, 1991.

Stuart Hall, *The Hard Road to Renewal: Thatcherism and the Crisis of the Left*. London, 1988.

Stephen Jeffrey-Poulter, *Peers, Queers and Commons: The Struggle for Gay Law Reform from 1950 to the Present*. London, 1991.

Peter Jenkins, *Mrs. Thatcher's Revolution*. London, 1987.

Angela McRobbie, *Feminism and Youth Culture: From "Jackie" to "Just Seventeen"*. Boston, 1991.

Elizabeth Meehan, "British feminism from the 1960s to the 1980s," in Harold L. Smith, ed., *British Feminism in the Twentieth Century*. Aldershot, 1990.

Tom Nairn, *The Break-up of Britain: Crisis and Neo-Nationalism*. London, 1977.

Neil Nehring, *Flowers in the Dustbin: Culture, Anarchy, and Postwar England*. Ann Arbor, 1993.

J. Enoch Powell, *Freedom and Reality*. London, 1969.

David Reynolds, *Britannia Overruled: British Policy and World Power in the Twentieth Century*. London, 1991.

Hilary Rose, "Women's work: Women's knowledge," in Juliet Mitchell and Ann Oakley, eds, *What is Feminism? A Re-examination*. New York, 1986.

Edward W. Said, "Introduction," in Rudyard Kipling, *Kim*. London, 1987.

Alan Sinfield, *Literature, Politics, and Culture in Postwar Britain*. Berkeley, 1989.

Alan Sked, *Britain's Decline: Problems and Perspectives*. Oxford, 1987.

John Solomos, Bob Findlay, Simon Jones, and Paul Gilroy, "The organic crisis of British capitalism and race: The experience of the seventies," in Centre for Contemporary Cultural Studies, *The Empire Strikes Back: Race and Racism in 70s Britain*. London, 1982.

Dale Spender, *Women of Ideas (and What Men have Done to Them)*. London, 1982.

Jeffrey Weeks, *Sexuality and Its Discontents: Meanings, Myths and Modern Sexualities*. London, 1985.

Index

Page references in italics indicate illustrations.